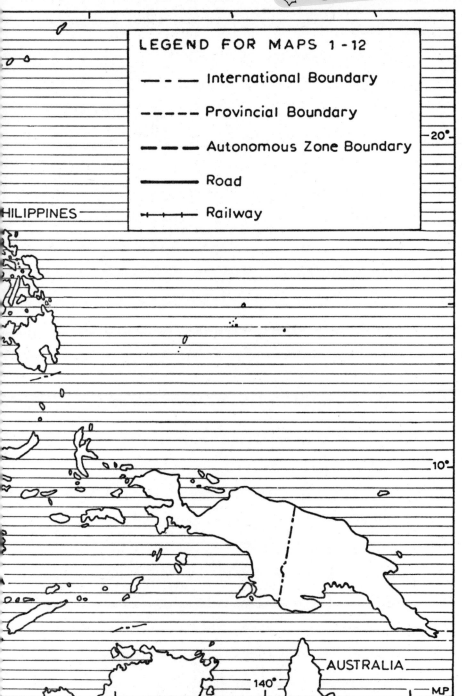

LEGEND FOR MAPS 1-12

— · — International Boundary

— — — — Provincial Boundary

— — — Autonomous Zone Boundary

——— Road

—+—+— Railway

HILIPPINES

—20°

—10°

AUSTRALIA

140°

MP

AN INTRODUCTION TO

Southeast
Asian
Politics

AN INTRODUCTION TO

Southeast Asian Politics

J.R.E. Waddell

Department of Political Studies
University of Papua and New Guinea

John Wiley & Sons Australasia Pty Ltd

Sydney   *New York*   *London*   *Toronto*

ISBN and National Library of Australia Card Number:
Paper: 0 471 91301-4
Cloth: 0 471 91300-6

Library of Congress Catalog Card Number: 73-174900

Registered at the General Post Office, Sydney, for transmission
through the post as a book.

Printed at The Griffin Press, Adelaide, South Australia

To JEAN
JANET, PETER AND DAVID
and in memory of PETER.

Acknowledgements

My biggest debt is to all those authors who have written about Southeast Asia before me and from whose works I have drawn most of my basic information. Many of these are mentioned in the text and in the bibliography but some are not and to these latter I offer my apologies.

My next debt is to those who were my mentors at the School of Oriental and African Studies in London in 1966-67, namely Doctors Bastin, Cowan, Smith, Tinker and Vatikiotis.

I must also thank the University of Papua and New Guinea for giving me a research grant which enabled me to make a tour of Southeast Asia in 1969-70. On this tour I was given help, advice and information by a great number of people who must remain anonymous on this occasion but whom I nevertheless should like to thank wholeheartedly.

I am most grateful to Marlous Ploeg, of the Geography Department of the University of Papua and New Guinea, for drawing the maps which appear both in the text and as end-papers.

Finally I should like to record my thanks for their secretarial assistance to Ellen Jones, Heather Anderson, Rennie Macnab and, as always, my wife Janet.

J.R.E. WADDELL

Boroko
November, 1971

Contents

MAPS

PART I

Southeast Asia

CHAPTER ONE

The Common Factors

Introduction

Philosophers warn us of the dangers of reification: of thinking that because a thing has a name it must exist as a material object. Words like "Southeast Asia" and "unicorn" enable us to discuss topics about which we would not otherwise be able to hold a conversation, but we should be wary of attributing any more solidity to these concepts than the facts will allow.

Though used frequently nowadays, the term "Southeast Asia" is of fairly recent origin. D. G. E. Hall reminds us that it only came into general use during the Second World War to "describe the territories of the eastern Asiatic mainland forming the Indo-Chinese peninsula and the immense archipelago which includes Indonesia and the Philippines".[1] "Southeast Asia", then, is a convenient shorthand expression which saves us the trouble of having to enumerate the various countries which make up this arbitrarily delineated area.

Obafemi Awolowo once said: "Nigeria is not a nation. It is a mere political expression. There are no Nigerians in the same sense that there are English, Welsh or French."[2] In the same way, but much more so, Southeast Asia is a mere political expression and there are no Southeast Asians. Not only are there no Southeast Asians but there are many people living in, say, Indonesia, Burma and the Philippines who would not think of themselves, first and foremost or even *at all*, as Indonesians, Burmese or Filipinos.

If it has been difficult to build up the idea of nationhood within these countries, it is not surprising that it has been even more difficult to build up co-operation between them. Symbolic of this state of affairs is the fact that the Southeast Asia Treaty Organization (SEATO) contains only two Southeast Asian countries, namely Thailand and the Philippines, out of a total of eight signatories.

Southeast Asia is neither homogeneous nor unified, yet beneath all the differences there are certain underlying features and experiences which its inhabitants may be said to share. It is to these that we now turn.

Geography

Homo Modjokertensis, whose bones were found in Java not so long ago, could have walked on dry land from the modern Saigon through Thailand, Malaya and Indonesia and up to the northern tip of the Philippines. Only to visit West Irian and the islands, including the Moluccas off its western tip, would he have required a boat. Geographically then, in the not-so-distant Pleistocene period, Southeast Asia had a certain unity.

Race

Scholars are not yet agreed as to how exactly the area became populated. One can say, however, that succeeding migratory movements have left a division between highlanders and plainsmen everywhere in Southeast Asia. As the newcomers came down from their heartlands in Tibet or China, they either absorbed the original inhabitants into their own culture, or forced them to take to the hills where many of their descendants still remain. Having taken the best agricultural land, the invaders were able to build up a settled and prosperous life, while their predecessors were compelled to take up a nomadic existence based on the slash-and-burn type of agriculture, which was the only one suited to the forested highlands. Today there is still a feud between the highlanders and the men of the plains. The highlanders are despised by their more affluent and civilised usurpers who still call them by pejorative names, most of which mean "slave" or "savage". In this category are to be found the Igorot of the Philippines, the Dusun of Sabah, the Kha of Laos and the Moi of Vietnam. In Cambodia, too, it is only recently that an effort has been made to replace the word *phnong*, meaning "savage", by Khmer Loeu to describe the inhabitants of the northeastern highlands.

Mainland Southeast Asia presents a patchwork of ethnic and linguistic groups whose boundaries in many cases have very little in common with those imposed by the colonial powers in the nineteenth and early twentieth centuries. This particular incongruence plays a notable part in nearly all the political disorders which beset the region today. In Burma and Laos the battle is still between highlander and plainsman. In Thailand there is trouble in the north and north-west where the Meo and Yao hill-tribes live. In Cambodia and South Vietnam it is the Khmer Loeu and the *Montagnards* whose natural dislike of the lowlander has been harnessed to such good effect by the NLF.

In the long run the highlanders are probably doomed. Their culture will eventually be swallowed up by that of the majority ethnic group in the country of which they are deemed to be a part. But as long as

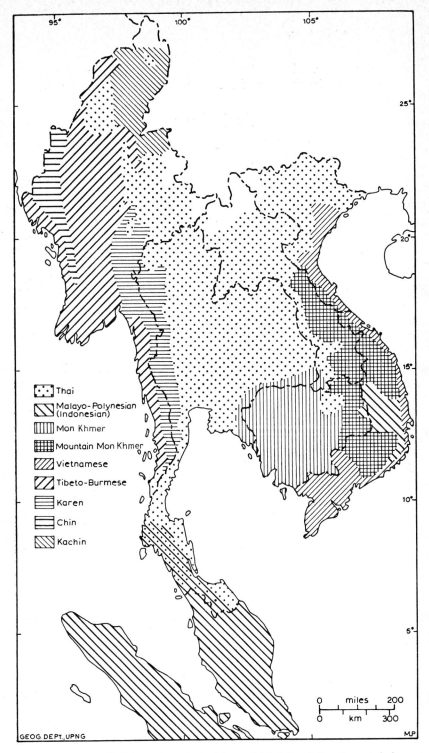

Legend:

- Thai
- Malayo-Polynesian (Indonesian)
- Mon Khmer
- Mountain Mon Khmer
- Vietnamese
- Tibeto-Burmese
- Karen
- Chin
- Kachin

GEOG. DEPT., UPNG

M.P.

Map 2. Rough Ethno-linguistic Map of Mainland Southeast Asia

the highland-lowland dichotomy continues it will remain a potential
source of great friction; ripe for exploitation by the unscrupulous.

Agriculture

In every country except Singapore the majority of the population of
Southeast Asia is engaged in agriculture. The percentage varies from
about fifty per cent in Malaya (where there is extensive tin-mining)
and the Philippines to about eighty per cent in Thailand, Cambodia,
South Vietnam and East Malaysia. Rice is probably the most significant
product within the framework of agriculture, and there is hardly anywhere in the area where the production and consumption of rice is not
of prime importance. The importance of rice is not confined to its
economic role. The *Economist* in its issue of October 19 1968 reported
that the President of the Philippines believed "that the political credit
accruing to him in the towns now enjoying the benefits of higher yields
will enable him to become the first Philippine president to be re-
elected". In fact Mr Marcos *was* elected for a second term and there is
no doubt that "miracle rice" played an important part in winning him
votes.

In spite of its famous rice research institute at Los Banos, the Philippines still has one of the lowest yields per acre in the region and one
can no doubt attribute such a state of affairs to, amongst other things,
the farmer's proverbial dislike of change. Conservative though the
farmers may be in their habits and attitudes, it would be a great mistake
to think of the average Southeast Asian country's economy and labour
force in terms that were too static. Not only are increasing numbers of
farmers using new methods, but the growth of industry is slowly drawing away the manpower from the fields. In Thailand, for instance,
J. C. Caldwell[3] notes that though "its percentage of farmers certainly
places it amongst the agrarian, less developed nations, . . . the signs of
change can be read in the occupational statistics, for, while 82% of
employed males over 60 years of age are farmers, only 72% of those in
the 20-24 age range are engaged in this activity".

Such changes will bring the farmers increasingly into what we may
call the macro-political scene. Edward Shils speaks of the "silence of the
country-side in matters of day-to-day political concern"; the silence is
now being broken. Higher productivity will either bring the farmer
greater prosperity or a greater awareness of his landlord's increased
wealth; in either case there will be a political by-product. Industrialisation will bring the countryman into the city, as in Thailand, where he
may well find employment opportunities lacking, and where he may
eventually become part of the "urban mob" which has been used to
such dramatic effect in cities like Djakarta.

The two main categories into which it is customary to divide the
agriculturists of the region are "shifting" and "sedentary". The shifting

cultivator clears part of the forest by fire or axe, grows one crop and then moves on. Such a process, though sometimes regarded as primitive —chiefly because the men who practise it are generally the highlanders of whom we have already spoken—may, in fact, if properly done, be the best way of using the otherwise very poor soil.

The best-known sedentary cultivators are those who cultivate "wet" rice in flooded *sawahs*—to use the Indonesian term. Wet rice cultivation has provided the base for some of the greatest achievements of Southeast Asian civilisation. From it arose the great engineering feats, such as the rice-terraces of Java and northern Luzon, as well as the empires centred on, for example, Madjapahit and Angkor, where a combination of wet-rice farming land and a large static population provided the wealth and surplus labour necessary for the construction of monumental buildings and the production of arts and artefacts of all descriptions. Remarkable feats were also done in the administrative field: *sawah* farming depends on water-control, and the vast system of canals and irrigation channels centred on a capital city like Angkor must have required considerable organisational expertise for its planning and upkeep. There is still controversy as to whether this expertise was an of the Javanese terraces, like to point out that none of their words for indigenous product of Southeast Asia or an import. Indonesians, proud rice, at the various stages of its life-cycle—*padi, beras* and *nasi*—have Sanskrit origins. There is indeed much evidence to suggest that Indonesia, in particular, had a strong and advanced indigenous culture before Hindu influences penetrated the area.

Religion

To those who know that the vast majority of Burmese (85%), Indonesians (90%) and Filipinos (90%) are respectively Buddhists, Moslems and Christians, it may seem fanciful to suggest that religion can be any kind of a common bond in the region. We are here, however, concerned with religion at the personal rather than the official level. At this lower level we can detect, quite near the surface, the animistic beliefs common to primitive agrarian communities from Eire to West Irian. Farmers in these circumstances feel powerless in the face of the forces of nature and seek to exercise some control over them, not by using more scientific methods, but by using propitiatory rites and magic.

J. S. Carroll,[4] writing of magic and religion in the rural Philippines, tells how fear and insecurity drive hill groups to try to "protect themselves from unseen and capricious forces which may suddenly wreak destruction upon individuals, family and crops. Large areas of life are regulated by priests or mediums who specialise in communion with the unseen world." It is also the case that organised religion has made little impact on the dweller in the Filipino village, or *barrio*. Carroll quotes a survey published in 1966 which suggested that though the great majority of the sixty-one families of a *barrio* in the province of Ilocos in northern Luzon were Roman Catholics, no regular services were held, and such as were, tended to be family—rather than church—centred. The investigators reported the existence of a common spirit-world background. Amulets and talismans were widely used: "probably every resident carries a charm to ward off witches. Animals wear charms too." Mass, apparently, is not said in this *barrio* and the majority of the inhabitants never attend Mass anywhere.

Observations such as these help to explain both the triumph and the failure of Christianity in the Philippines. The fact that Christianity came to the Philippines as early as the sixteenth century and in the form of Roman Catholicism rather than, say, Lutheranism, meant two things: first, the new religion came wrapped in the—to us—somewhat crude ideas about medicine and science of the man in the sixteenth century Spanish, or rather Mexican, street; second, the new religion brought with it a host of saints and supernatural interceding powers who could easily be fitted into the local pantheon. Landa Jocano speaks of Roman Catholicism as being "an enlargement rather than a modification of the traditional belief system". Jocano goes on to say that Christian saints are often:

> thought to possess powers similar to those of the most powerful environmental spirits, the *engkantu,* and like them may be the source of material welfare for those who know how to deal with them. And as the *baylan* with the spirits, so the priest knows the secret of dealing with the saints: if both fail and the problem is one of illness, the patient may be taken to a modern doctor without any sense of incongruity. The priest and the *baylan* are similar in their use of mysterious ritual; and the *baylan* cheerfully imitates the priest's Latin and makes use of religious objects taken from the Church, admitting that these latter contain more powerful magic than his own. Conflict between priest and *baylan* is minimised by the fact that the priest does not live in the *barrio* and these matters are seldom brought to his attention.[4]

Christianity is not the only religion which has undergone this process. Both Islam and Hinduism have "enlarged" rather than "modified" pre-existing beliefs in, for example, Malaya. The Malay peasant reaping the *padi* is obliged to cut the ears in a special way in order not to frighten the *semangat* or soul of the *padi.* Although this is not in accordance with the teachings of Islam, the "modern Malay still retains this belief and where centuries ago his ancestor would utter the magic words at the rituals associated with reaping in the Malay language, the Muslim Malay of today would incorporate also verses from the Koran".[5]

Earlier in Malaya, as in Indonesia, when Hindu influences were strong, the local *pawang,* or magician, used Sanskrit in much the same way as the *baylan* uses Latin. In this connection Wan A. Hamid mentions the *puja pantai,* or beach worship, which is held annually in Kelantan "to mark the beginning or opening of the fishing season after the north-east monsoon. The ceremony is to invoke the help of the guardian spirits of the sea so that the fishermen may be protected from evil and that they may have big catches during the following season."[5] A somewhat similar ceremony, with strong Hindu and animistic overtones, takes place every year in Moslem Indonesia. At the opening of the season for collecting edible birds' nests in mid-Java, the collectors have first to propitiate Njaji Loro Kidul, the Goddess of the South Sea —as well they may, for the nests are only to be found on narrow ledges high above the pounding surf of the Indian Ocean.

In Thailand, as D. A. Wilson[6] and S. Piker[7] among others, have observed, magico-religious beliefs play a significant part in social and political life. Like the Malays, Javanese and Filipinos, the Thais believe in the spirit-world. Spirits inhabit, or watch over, all the basic things of life such as wood and water and rice. These and the spirits of the influential dead are not only to be propitiated but *used* in order to further a man's own material and spiritual ends.

Like their counterparts in Ilocos, many villagers wear amulets to protect themselves from accident and evil. There is also a demand for amulets in Indo-China. These charms, known as *bua,* have been in use there for centuries and the Khmers in particular have acquired a reputation for making effective ones. It is interesting to note that the Jesuit missionaries in Tonkin had much the same experience as did their coreligionists in the Philippines in the early days of Spanish colonisation. In both countries baptism came to be regarded as a sovereign specific for bodily as well as spiritual ailments—not that these two categories of illness were ever very sharply distinguished from each other. This led, not only to the enhanced popularity of the new faith, but also, in Tonkin, to a sharp demand for holy water to be put in small bottles and worn as *buas.* An even more powerful form of *bua* is the *bua gong,* an amulet which will render the wearer immune from bullets. This kind of charm is found all over Southeast Asia. Tattooing has served the same purpose in Burma; in colonial days the police were especially vigilant when an outbreak of tattooing was reported among any section of the populace. The most famous occasion on which magic amulets were used in recent Burmese history was at the start of Saya San's rebellion in 1930. As well as making use of amulets and tattoos Saya San felt the need to consult the astrologers before he had himself ritually proclaimed *minlaung,* or official pretender to the throne.[8] The astrologers decided the precise moment—11.33 p.m. on October 28— at which it would be most propitious to stage the ceremony. At another, even more solemn, moment in Burma's history, the astrologers were again consulted, with the result that Burma achieved her independence at the otherwise inconvenient hour of 4.20 a.m., on January 4, 1948— the most auspicious time and day available.

We have seen from these examples how primitive beliefs can enter the field of macro-politics. Absurd as such things may seem to the sophisticated, it would be a mistake to underestimate their influence. In an area where it is strongly believed that there is powerful magic in the repetitive incantation of incomprehensible words, it is not surprising to find this technique being applied to politics. It has been cynically suggested that in many countries of the region it is enough merely to announce a Five-Year Plan; no action need follow so powerful and unintelligible an incantation. Good examples of the effect of numerology and magic on politics may be found in Indonesia. It is well known, for instance, that Indonesia's Eight-Year Plan, published on August 13, 1960, was deliberately produced in seventeen volumes divided into eight parts with 1,945 subsections in order to symbolise the date of the proclamation of independence on August 17, 1945. It is also said that the Hotel Indonesia in Djakarta, which was being built at about the same time, was going to have seventeen storeys for the same reason. President Sukarno was a great believer in government by slogan and invented a large number of acronyms like "Usdek" and "Manipol" which came to have a meaning and a force of their own, quite divorced from the actual words and ideas for which they stood. One of Sukarno's last confections was the "Pantja Azimat Revolusi" or "Five Charms of the Revolution": meaning "Nasakom", "Pantja Sila", "Manipol", "Trisakti" and "Berdikari". The word *azimat* or *djimat* means an amulet or magic formula, and was no doubt meant to be taken fairly literally.

Kingship

With the exception of the Philippines, every country of Southeast Asia has felt at some time the influence of Hindu concepts of kingship, and although these have in due course been overtaken by more democratic ideas, they still play an important part in the shaping of men's attitudes towards the government, and indeed the monarch, where one exists.

The Hindu concept of kingship took various forms, but at its heart was a belief in the near-divinity of the monarch, who was sometimes called *deva-raj* or god-king and acted as a kind of surrogate-god in his earthly kingdom. The kingdom itself was administratively and even, in the capital city, physically arranged so as to reflect the pattern of the Cosmos. Associated with the idea of divine kingship was the concept of the holy mountain, whose archetype was Mount Meru, the abode of Brahman and Vishnu. When the Cao-Dai sect in what was then Cochin-China was looking for a suitable place for the headquarters of its new religion—an eclectic mixture of many other religions—they chose Tay-Ninh. In the words of Norman Lewis

> the siting of the Cao-Daist Rome at Tay-Ninh was by no means accidental. A few miles from the town a single symmetrical moun-

tain humps up suddenly from the plain, rising from what must be practically sea-level to 3,000 feet. As there is not another hillock for fifty miles in any direction to break the flat and featureless monotony of Cochin-China, this darkly-forested plum-pudding silhouette is quite remarkable. In a part of the world where every religion has its sacred mountain, such an eminence is obviously irresistible.[9]

The holy mountain is also often thought to be the centre of the earth. In Bali, for instance, the great volcano Gunung Agung is given the appellation *pusat dunia* or "navel of the world", and shrines for it and its sister mountain, Batur, are to be found in many Balinese houses. A similar belief was current in ancient Greece where at the heart of the famous oracle at Delphi was a stone called the *omphalos* or navel. The oracle itself was placed on a spur of Mount Parnassus, whose twin peaks were sacred to Apollo and Dionysus.

These two beliefs—in the divinity of the king and in the holiness of the mountain—came together in the design of the holy capital city. The king, representing the gods, lived in a palace raised above the other buildings; there were often four main gates to the city corresponding to the four cardinal points of the compass; the king had four principal wives and there were four chief ministers to look after the north, south, east and west of the realm. To depart from this pattern was to court disaster, and it was widely believed by the Burmese that King Thibaw was defeated by the British precisely because he had, amongst other things, omitted to furnish himself with the requisite number of principal wives.

If the king lost favour with the gods and was vanquished by a rival, the capital was often moved to another place, and the original site abandoned to the jungle and wild beasts. Such a fate overtook Pagan in central Burma at the end of the thirteenth century after King Narathihapate fled from the invading Tartars. So, too, today it is not unusual for a newly-independent country to change the name of the existing ex-colonial capital and then to set about founding a new capital city on a site unassociated with the previous colonial rulers.

Colonialism

Except for Thailand, every country in Southeast Asia has had direct experience of colonial rule. The intensity of the experience varied, not only from country to country but from area to area within a country. Thus, in what was formerly Indo-China, Cochin-China was much more directly under French rule than Laos or Cambodia. Similarly, in the Dutch East Indies the main Dutch effort for the best part of three hundred years was in Java; the other islands escaped much more lightly. Thailand avoided being colonised but only, like the Russian in the fable, by dint of throwing one or two territorial babies to the wolves.

Thailand also, under the guidance of far-sighted monarchs and aided by a battery of advisers shrewdly selected from every major Power, carried out programmes of modernisation to such good effect that the colonial powers on her borders, namely Britain and France, were content to respect her neutrality and leave her as a kind of buffer-zone between their respective colonies.

Motives for colonial expansion, or "forward policies" as they were sometimes called, were many and varied, but most home governments were, in general, opposed to the acquisition of new territories and responsibilities, if their policy objectives could be achieved in some other, less expensive way. Thus Thailand, by allowing the European powers to share in the exploitation of her natural resources, to have access to her markets and to help to reorganise her administration, managed to escape the fate of her neighbours. Of all the countries of the region Thailand alone was able to enjoy the benefits of gradual modernisation without experiencing the traumatic fracturing of the traditional social structure and cultural framework which accompanied this process in the colonial territories. So today, as in the days of her two greatest kings—Mongkut and Chulalongkorn—Thailand is able to accept foreign advice, investment and aid without feeling that her pride is being affronted or her sovereignty impaired.

This is not the place to discuss the rights and wrongs of colonialism —we are much too close to the events to make dispassionate judgements—but two points need to be made. First, in most areas foreign rule was of very short duration: one man's lifetime—a mere episode in the long and eventful histories of these countries. Second, and this is a more subjective judgement, it may well prove that the most lasting effect of colonialism was psychological rather than material. Having discredited the traditional leaders of Southeast Asian society, the foreigners then added insult to injury by treating their successors, many of whom had received Western education, with that kindly condescension that so often marks the behaviour of the white man towards the black, or brown. Readers of the letters of Kartini[10] and Sjahrir[11]—not to mention the novels and writings of Indian and African authors—will know that it was this aspect of colonialism, rather than the economic exploitation, which rankled most at the time, and now survives to embitter post-colonial relations.

The Gap

Another feature which "new" states are said, by Edward Shils,[12] to have in common is the "gap in the social structure": the gap, in other words, between the rich and the poor, the city and the country, the educated and the ignorant. It is true that in nearly every country in the region there is one "primate" city which dwarfs all others in size and importance; and is both the seat of government and the focus of modernisation. It is true that politics, as its Greek derivation suggests, is largely "the business of the city". It is also true that the intellectuals—in this context the high school or university graduates or those with professional qualifications—tend to gravitate towards the capital and stay there, thus cutting themselves off from the mass of the people. There is also no doubt that income is very unequally distributed. Yet, in spite of all these things, the "gap" is not, and never has been, unbridged, and one should not give it undue weight. Even under the most despotic regime in the past the ruler ultimately relied on the passive co-operation of the populace to provide him with food, labour and warriors. This co-operation depended largely on the fact that both parties shared a common culture and both accepted that each had non-competing parts to play in life. In addition there were always middlemen whose role was both to interpret the ruler to the people and, at the same time, to protect the latter as best they could against undue harshness in the imposition of taxation or compulsory service. Nowadays the role of interpreter has been taken over by the local party boss, the teacher or—as in the Philippines—by the *barrio* captain, who is said to be the villagers' main source of information about the doings of the great.

Attitudes to Authority

To this list of ingredients which go to make up some kind of common background for the peoples of Southeast Asia, may be added one more item in the form of a somewhat tentative generalisation about the common man's attitude to authority.

The vast majority of the people of the region share a way of life in which they are constantly at the mercy of Nature. They try to control this seemingly capricious force by appeasing or, where appropriate, enlisting the aid of the good and evil spirits who surround them. As far as the world of Nature is concerned we can thus detect a certain polarity: on the one hand a resigned fatalism, and on the other a belief that a person can, given the correct formula or medium, control his fate to a certain extent. This attitude, it is suggested, is carried over into the area of politics. It produces on the one hand the resigned acceptance of government, as exemplified by the Burmese classification of it as one of the "five great evils",[13] and on the other the belief, current in the Philippines, that the government's actions like those of Nature, can be modified by the intercession of a suitable intermediary. On the whole, though, the peasant's "orientation towards government" is more one of "fatalism and resignation"[14] than anything else, and this helps to explain why the "revolution of rising expectations" is more likely to be led by the intellectuals than the peasants. For although the latter are generally considerably worse off materially, they have been conditioned over the years to expect very little tangible benefit from their remote rulers.

We should not, however, think of peasants as being long-suffering and docile. The Dutch used to refer to the Javanese as "the gentlest nation on earth" and even in recent publications they have been described as "gentle syncretists"; yet the history of the independence struggle in the late 1940s, not to mention the anti-Communist blood baths of 1965 and 1966, tells a different tale. These extremes of behaviour can also be observed in Burma where, although for much of the time the pacifist Buddhist ethic prevails, there are also outbursts of violence and assassination.

In the past the peasant has remained relatively docile mainly because he has not been socially mobilised and because there has been a satisfactory balance between the size of the population and the quantity of land available for cultivation. In both these respects there have been dramatic changes in recent years. The population has increased so quickly in some areas that the balance between land and people has been upset. While over the last fifty years or so the growth and diffusion of primary education, nationalism, political parties, propaganda, national language programmes, rural development, five-year plans, local self-government, communications and all the rest of the apparatus of modern government, have gone far to mobilise the peasant socially and to bridge the gulf between the governors and the governed. There has been, in other words, an erosion of autocracy. The politicians have shown that they need the support of the peasants and are ready to bargain for it rather than to demand it. If the politicians fail to make good their pledges to the peasants another kind of "gap" is likely to appear: a credibility gap between promise and performance which will lead inevitably to a breakdown of confidence in the democratic process. This is the gap which the Communists exploit so well. It arises out of the obvious and basic conflict of interest between landlord and tiller. If the landowners, who by and large control the political process, wish to survive politically they must carry out land reforms which will undermine their own financial base. In the Philippines and South Vietnam incentives have been given to landowners to switch their investments from land to industry. If the switch can be achieved there is a possibility that the increased employment opportunities created by industrialisation will restore the balance between land and tiller. If no effective action is taken and the peasants are denied legitimate channels of representation one can only look forward to an increase in anomic interest articulation.[15]

References

1. D. G. E. HALL, A History of South-East Asia, Macmillan, London, 1966. 2nd Edition, p. 3.
2. R. EMERSON, From Empire to Nation, Harvard University Press, Boston, 1960, p. 129.

3. J. C. CALDWELL, in T. H. Silcock (Ed.), *Thailand*, Australian National University Press, Canberra, in association with Duke University Press, Durham, North Carolina, 1967, p. 50.
4. J. S. CARROLL, "Magic and Religion" in *Solidarity*, April 1968, 3, No. 4.
5. WAN A. HAMID, "Religion and Culture of the Modern Malay", in Wang Gung-Wu (Ed.), *Malaysia*, Pall Mall Press, London, 1964, p. 182.
6. D. A. WILSON, *Politics in Thailand*, Cornell University Press, Ithaca, N.Y., 1962.
7. S. PIKER, "The Relationship of Belief Systems to Behaviour in Rural Thai Society", *Asian Survey*, May 1968.
8. R. L. SOLOMON, "Saya San and the Burmese Rebellion", *Modern Asian Studies*, July 1969, 3, Part 2.
9. N. LEWIS, *A Dragon Apparent*, Jonathan Cape, London, 1951, pp. 41-42.
10. RADEN ADJENG KARTINI, *Letters of a Javanese Princess*, W. W. Norton, New York, 1964.
11. SOETAN SJAHRIR, *Out of Exile*, Greenwood Press, New York, 1969.
12. E. SHILS, *Political Development in the New States*, Mouton & Co., The Hague, 1966, p. 30.
13. H. TINKER, *Ballot Box and Bayonet*, Oxford University Press, London, 1964, p. 4.
14. S. VERBA, "Comparative Political Culture", in L. W. Pye and S. Verba (Eds), *Political Culture and Political Development*, Princeton University Press, New Jersey, 1965, p. 522.
15. G. ALMOND and J. S. COLEMAN (Eds), *The Politics of Developing Areas*, Princeton University Press, New Jersey, 1960. See Introductory chapter.

CHAPTER TWO

Mainland and Maritime

Having examined some of the properties which the peoples of Southeast Asia have in common we now consider one respect in which their countries may be divided into two categories, corresponding to the two main types of society in pre-colonial times: mainland and maritime. These differed not only in economic and political organisation but in their attitude to the world outside, and some of these differences still survive in spite of the impact of colonialism, modernisation, the Japanese occupation and independence.

Mainland Societies

Mainland societies were centred on the great rivers of mainland Southeast Asia: the Irrawaddy, the Salween, the Mekong, the Menam Chao Phraya and the Red and Black Rivers. They were based on wet rice cultivation in well-watered areas which were able to produce the surplus necessary to support the monarch, the court, the bureaucracy, the temples, the artists and the public works. Rice was the key to their prosperity and some of the most impressive products of these societies were their irrigation systems, of which a striking example may be found in the Mekong delta. The construction, maintenance and regulation of such vast and intricate networks must have required a high degree of efficient, centralised bureaucratic control. These societies also produced some of the most famous monuments in Southeast Asia: such as the temples of Angkor and Pagan and the palaces of the Siamese kings.

On the edges of these societies lived the hill-men mentioned earlier: the Laos, the Shans, the Thais, the Meos and many others who with their shifting cultivation and nomadic life had little opportunity to produce permanent memorials in art, architecture or literature.

Maritime Societies

Maritime societies, by which we mean those which grew up in the Malay peninsula and the Indonesian and Philippine archipelagoes, were based on sea-trade and piracy. The exception was Java which produced a rice-based society which combined both "mainland" and "maritime" elements.

The difference in outlook between mainland and maritime has been well described by H. Tinker[1]: "Whereas the sacred imperial city was static and introverted, cherishing its protocol from age to age, the market city was outward looking, assimilating beliefs and techniques from the culturally dominant East or West: pioneering for example the spread of Islam." It was in the market cities of Malacca (Malaya), Acheh (Sumatra), Brunei (Borneo) and Sri Vijaya (Sumatra, near the modern Palembang) that the men of all nations met and exchanged goods and information. Empires such as Sri Vijaya were not empires in the territorial sense but were based on command of the seas; on the ability both to keep the sea-lanes open and to levy tolls and duties on ships and merchandise passing through the ports and straits under their control.

In those days—before the Dutch and the Portuguese tried to restrict and monopolise trade in the area—men of all nations, from Europe, India, Arabia and China would meet in the ports, stay in the quarters of the town assigned to them, pay dues to the local potentate and live more or less peacefully under their own laws and customs. They constituted in essence the first "plural societies".

Summary

There were two main modes of life in "traditional" Southeast Asian society: the one static, built on wet rice cultivation and a big population, producing great art and architecture at tremendous cost; the other dynamic, sea-based and venturesome, making contact with the outside world and depending for its life on trade. To these two ways of life were matched two ways of looking at the world: the one a self-centred, "navel-of-the-world" view; the other a more cosmopolitan view which recognised the existence of other nations and interests and sought to come to terms with them either by diplomacy or war.

Examples of these two outlooks may still be found in modern Southeast Asia. The Union of Burma, for instance, which is the spiritual inheritor of the introverted sacred cities of Pagan and Mandalay, still tends to withdraw from the world and live—in the classic Malay phrase —like "a frog under a coconut shell'. Until recently Burma spurned all foreign aid, expelled Chinese, Europeans and American businessmen with fine impartiality and tried to live the life of the pure neutralist. In the twentieth century this is unfortunately no longer possible and the Burmese regime has recently removed some of the barriers between it and the outside world.

Indonesia, as befits the heir to both types of empire, shows two faces to the world: sometimes brooding, dwelling on past glories and shouting "to hell with your aid"; sometimes outward looking, seeking alliances and foreign investment.

Reference

1. H. TINKER, *Reorientations*, Pall Mall Press, London, 1965, p. 39.

CHAPTER THREE

The World of the Southeast Asian Village

Introduction

So far we have talked of "traditional" society on the macro-political scale. If the steamship, the aeroplane and political upheavals have largely destroyed this world there is another—the world of the villager —which has changed very little over the centuries.

Villages, the basic units of Southeast Asia, vary a good deal in size and composition. Some are based on kinship, others on occupation. Here, you find a village consisting of one or two "extended" families; there, a village whose members share a common trade or calling such as weaving or carving or ceremonial dancing or boat-making.

In general, in times gone by, the village was a self-contained self-governing unit. Until the twentieth century there was no central political organisation strong enough to make much of a dent on the autonomy of the village; "the law of the sovereign" it was said "gives way before the custom of the village". The village was not so much ruled as led, by a man or a group of men generally chosen from the older generation and well qualified to see that tasks were fairly allotted and grievances and disputes properly dealt with according to custom. These were not the only authorities in the village: there were also those who fulfilled the functions of priest, magician and schoolmaster. Sometimes one of these leaders also acted as the agent of the central authority—whether chief, sultan or king. In this dual role he acted both as protector of the village and as tax-collector and conscriber of labour for public works.

The colonial powers tended to assume that all villages had a headman who was the sole ultimate authority in the community—which was seldom the case, as we have seen. The result was that when they appointed a man as the official "head" of the village and gave him powers which were not his by local custom, there was generally a quick reversion to the *status quo ante* as soon as the touring district officer had departed. In many cases the man put forward by the village was in fact a puppet front-man manipulated by the local *élite*.

The Structure of the Village

So much has been said by Asian politicians and writers on the subject of building a new Asian polity on the basis of the village and with "village democracy" and "mutual help" as its inspiration that it is as well to examine the internal structure of the village more closely.

Where a village is composed of an extended family one can clearly speak of a sense of community and one can expect to find a *gotong rojong* (Indonesian for "mutual help") approach to the solution of problems and the carrying out of tasks such as housebuilding which may be beyond the powers of the individual. There are, however, many villages with a looser structure. In Java, for instance, the village or *desa* is very often a territorial unit whose inhabitants may not be bound by kinship or any other tie, save that of being the tenants of a common landlord. There will, of course, be families in the *desa*, but there may be no particular ties between them.

In Thailand where the prevailing culture, whose main ingredient is Hinayana Buddhism, lays stress on the individual's responsibility for his own fate, the family circle is small and village organisation less clear-cut. "The institutions defining a village are quite likely *not* to be concerned with the corporate entity of the village itself."[1] In a particular area a temple and a government school may each "define the village by their clientele". Co-operative effort certainly exists—for instance at harvest time: but Wilson suggests that this is based more on "personal reciprocity of the individual members of fairly stable groups and is not "conceived as duty to community, village or other corporate body". Moreover, says Wilson, the villages appear to have no legal status and own no community property.

In Burma traditional society was pyramidal: broad-based upon the peasant cultivator and tapering upwards through the village and circle headmen, the *myothugyis* and the *myosans* (eaters of provinces) to the king at the apex. All land, except that reclaimed by an individual from the jungle, belonged to the king and was cultivated on a leasehold basis. Certain areas adjacent to the villages were common land and were used for the collection of firewood, the grazing of animals and the disposal of waste matter. The pagoda was the focus of village life and the pagoda school provided education for all.

The authority of the "headman" in this system varied from place to place and was not necessarily territorial but based on clan or occupation so that one might find people living next to each other but owing allegiance to different "headmen".

The British broke this system up and treated each convenient cluster of dwellings as a village (generally for tax purposes) and appointed official salaried headmen. The new system had all the faults to which we have already alluded but worked well enough so long as there was a framework of law and order in which it could operate. This framework broke under the stresses of the Second World War and the civil war which followed it. It has not yet been restored. Meanwhile the villagers tend to exhibit local and personal loyalties rather than allegiance to a distant central authority.

The Philippine village or *barrio* is different again. Here, in spite of about forty years of instruction in democracy under American rule, the social structure is virtually the same as it has been for the last two or three hundred years. The rural Filipino is typically a farmer working on a share-cropping basis by which he has to give at least a third (sometimes as much as half) of his produce to the landlord. He is perennially short of cash. Such a system seems to produce two kinds of loyalty. On the one hand a debtor-creditor bond between tenant and landlord which at best produces a rather paternalistic feudal relationship in which the peasant's only saleable asset is his vote: on the other, a lateral relationship stretching out in a network of kinship with a well-developed scheme of mutual aid (*bayanihan*). But here again as in Thailand and Indonesia loyalty is not so much to the *barrio*—the institution—as to the person.

In Vietnam one moves into the Chinese world. The classic thrust in Vietnamese history has been the Nam Tien or "Drive to the South". Vietnam's heartland was in Tonkin, now the heartland of North Vietnam. The sinicised Vietnamese, soaked in the tradition, language and culture of China, pushed southwards through Annam and into Cochin-China throughout the period from about 1400 to 1900. They founded villages as they went and brought with them all the customs, beliefs and organisational and agricultural techniques which they had largely learned from the Chinese. Prominent among their spiritual imports was Confucianism—not so much a supernatural religion as a way of life in which respect for one's ancestors, elders and the bureaucratic hierarchy were important features.

The village in this system was more highly organised than in say Laos or Cambodia. It was run by a "council of notables" whose members supervised different areas of communal life, such as education, religious observances, taxation, sanitation and so on. The civil service, which began so to speak "above" the village, was a career service open to the talents and there was a certain bond between the village and the bureaucracy in that great honour accrued to the former if one of its sons managed to pass the arduous entrance and promotion examinations of the Mandarinate. But in general the Emperor's writ stopped at the gates of the village and it was not until the arrival of the Communists that this barrier was finally breached.

Village Democracy

Various attempts have been made by Asian and African statesmen to build a new, specifically Asian or African democracy or to formulate a distinct brand of African or Asian socialism. One thinks of Nyerere's Arusha Declaration and his vision of a classless Tanzania with no need for political parties—or only one: the distinction is important but frequently blurred—where decisions are arrived at after amicable discussion and without the necessity of a final counting of heads. Likewise Sukarno, formerly President of Indonesia, used to inveigh against fifty-one per cent democracy. "You all know" he once said, "that I have never liked the system of half plus one is always right. . . . Let us cling to our own characteristics, let us cling to the only right standpoint for Guided Democracy, namely no voting. . . . Wherever possible the decision should be reached through *musjawarah* and *mufakat.*"

In this speech to the *gotong rojong* Parliament Sukarno was alluding to methods traditionally used in the village to arrive at communal decisions (*mufakat*) after a period of deliberation (*musjawarah*) during which people were free to put forward their views. In this process no formal voting took place, and the final decision represented what Quakers call "the sense of the meeting".

Sukarno appeared to think or hope that the methods of village politics might be successfully used on the national scale. Events proved him wrong. *Musjawarah* and *mufakat* may work well enough in a near-homogeneous community but they cannot stand the stress of differences on fundamental (say religious) matters. At the village level those who continually disagree with the community are generally obliged to leave. An artificial consensus is thus preserved at no great cost: after all, the man can generally find somewhere else to live. At the national level this is of course impossible; "leaving the village" becomes secession or civil war, such as broke out at the end of the 1950s in Indonesia. We might add that there seems no hope for *mufakat* between Moslems and the Communists in Java for many years to come.

One solution to this problem is that tried by both Sukarno and Nyerere, namely to try to create homogeneity either by inventing a "political religion" of such an eclectic nature that everyone can be a subscriber; or by creating a national party which everyone will join because any other party is by definition "un-Tanzanian". Sukarno's attempts at unification failed: it remains to be seen whether Nyerere will be any more fortunate.

May it not be the case in any event that many discussions on this subject are based on the presupposition that there is a clear dichotomy between Mass and *Élite*? And is this presupposition well-founded? Is it in fact true that the village lives in isolation from the mainstream of economic and social change? Is it not rather the case that the village has for many years become more and more involved in the modernisation process and that Sukarno's invocation of a "pure type" of Arcadian village was more a conscious piece of political myth-making than a reference to reality?

Three final points, then, may be made on the subject of the structure of the Southeast Asian village.

First, the democracy of the village may be something of a myth. As long ago as 1927 the Dutch sociologist Schrieke was commissioned by the colonial government to enquire into the "Causes and Effects of Communism on the West Coast of Sumatra" following a Communist inspired uprising there in 1926. Schrieke noted that the rule of *adat*, or customary law, was already disintegrating and that this disintegration was already far enough advanced in 1907 to have attracted the attention of the local Assistant Resident. The changes affected the village's basic asset—land. "This customary law, which is binding on everyone" wrote the administrator "is far from being honoured or maintained nowadays. Family land and *negeri* land, too, is sold even in cases not permitted by *adat*."[2] This breakdown of tradition was no sudden affair but a steady progressive transformation of a subsistence economy into a monetary one. In the process village democracy was eroded. "The position of the headmen, the genealogical *primi inter pares*, displays a tendency to develop in the direction of a more feudal type of authority . . . they cease to be the guardians of family property and become instead the disposers of family land."[3]

Then there is the unity of the village. On this point we have already voiced our doubt as to whether there exists in all places loyalty to the *village* as such rather than loyalty to kin, clan or religious community.

Finally, the process by which the village institutions were originally eroded—namely their involvement in the cash economy—cannot be reversed. It seems, therefore, that the only course open to a Southeast Asian government is to allow this process to continue but to guide it where possible into consciously-chosen channels. Unfortunately for those who dream of using the village as a building block, no one has yet shown how economic planning can be effectively carried out without strong central control, which means not so much that everything must be done on a grandiose scale but rather that the government's tentacles must stretch out widely and effectively into the countryside.

References

1. D. A. WILSON, *Politics in Thailand*, Cornell University Press, Ithaca, N. Y., 1962, pp. 47-48.
2. B. SCHRIEKE, *Indonesian Sociological Studies*, Van Hoeve, The Hague, 1955, Part I, p. 108.
3. *Ibid.*, p. 110.

PART II

Government and Politics in Southeast Asia

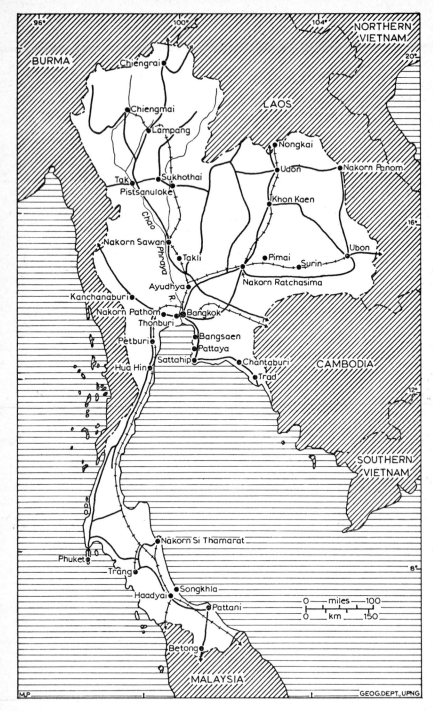

Map 3. Thailand

CHAPTER FOUR

Thailand

Historical Background

It has been said that Thailand owed her freedom from colonisation to her ability to change with the times and present such an orderly and progressive and liberal front to Britain and France that the latter were content to leave her alone, although within somewhat shrunken borders.

If it is true then that Thailand owes its independence to its ability to adapt its internal affairs to foreign pressures, King Mongkut (Rama IV) must take most of the credit for inventing this effective political style.

Mongkut (1804-1868) came to the throne in 1851. He was then forty-seven years of age and had already spent much time travelling about Siam; living in monasteries and acquiring much religious, scientific and political knowledge. In 1845 he studied English and adopted it as his second language. He had it taught to his children and it became the diplomatic language of the country.

In the monastery of Wat Samorai he met Bishop Pallegoix and studied Latin, mathematics and astronomy. A keen student of religion, he learned about Christianity but was not attracted to it; instead he resolved to refine the Buddhism of his own country and strip it of some of its more animistic and polytheistic accretions. In this he anticipated by about fifty years the early work of the Young Men's Buddhist Association in Burma. But, most importantly, Mongkut learned something of the political movements in Europe and the United States. Malcolm Smith says "There can be little doubt that the democratic forms of government practised then by France, the United States and England played an important part in shaping his policy for his Country".[1]

By the time Mongkut died in 1868 the first roads had been built (travel in Thailand was, and still is, mainly by water); books were being printed in both Siamese and English, the royal children were being exposed to a European education and scientific ideas were beginning to replace superstition. Most significant, perhaps, of all, there were said to be as many as eighty-four Europeans in the service of the Crown by 1868.

Radical changes had been made in economic policy. Trade and Consular treaties, fixing tariff rates and allowing extra-territorial rights to their citizens residing in Siam, were made with the United States of America and most of the European countries. The export of rice was encouraged—this again in contrast to Burma where it was strictly forbidden.

All this amounted to a revolution in outlook, but certainly no social revolution. The foreign advisers may have made the governmental services more efficient but there was no diminution of the power of the crown. "From all his subjects" writes Malcolm Smith "he demanded unquestioning obedience." One concession however he did make. Whereas in former times when the king went on his progresses through the kingdom the people had been expected to hide from his presence, they were now allowed to come out of their houses and to "kneel down and have a fair sight of the king who loves to see their faces".[2]

Mongkut nevertheless had set in motion the irreversible process of modernisation. His great successor Chulalongkorn, who reigned from 1868 to 1910, gave it greater momentum. With the wisdom of hindsight, students of politics can look back at his administrative reforms of 1892 and see in them the seeds of the events of 1932 after which Thailand became a constitutional monarchy. One doubts however whether anyone thought these reforms particularly democratic at the time. In effect Chulalongkorn set about "colonising" his own country. He realised that the one thing that counted in this new world was efficient government: a framework of law and order within which trade could be allowed freely to expand. In this sense he acted as a colonial governor. Instead of the "eaters of provinces" system whereby provincial rulers were virtually independent and living off the taxes raised in the province, Chulalongkorn instituted a colonial-type administrative framework on British-Burmese lines; with taxation being paid direct to the centre and with himself in the position of Governor or Viceroy (but with far greater powers). Under him was the usual hierarchy of provinces, districts, villages and hamlets—all but the last being administered by centrally appointed officials. These officials had some independence but their freedom was curbed by the appointment of parallel hierarchies of specialists, headed by Ministers who guarded their functional preserves as jealously as they had their territories previously.

As long as the king was at the apex of this bureaucracy his power was strengthened, not diminished, by these reforms; but the possibility now existed that the bureaucracy might one day sever its royal connections and become a force in its own right. It did not do so under Chulalongkorn's successor Wachirawud (1910-1925), who was a firm believer in the divine authority of kings. Wachirawud, however, died young and his place was taken by his brother Prachadipok, a man who was not cast in the same authoritarian mould. By now the bureaucracy and the army had expanded and new non-royal faces—the products of an expanded educational system—were to be seen among the middle ranks of the civil service and the armed forces. Increasing functional specialisation made the ministries both more independent and more difficult to control or co-ordinate. To counter the growing independence of the bureaucracy, whose chiefs met in the Council of Ministers, the King created the Supreme State Council to advise him and to restore the balance of expertise. There were now assembled the three main groups from which the ruling "circles" and "cliques" of Thai politics have since been drawn: the bureaucrats, both civil and military, and the King's men.

There was no effective or exclusive "cause" of the 1932 *coup* which created a constitutional monarchy: it was more the culmination of a long process begun in 1892 or even before; but one important factor was the world-wide depression which followed the Wall Street stock market crash in 1929. The drastic falling away in demand bore particularly heavily on countries such as those of Southeast Asia whose prosperity depended to such a disproportionate extent on the export of one or two primary products. As the effects of the slump began to show themselves the "new men" in the Army and the bureaucracy now realised that not only was their path to the highest ranks blocked by the numerous members of a very extensive royal family, but that if economies were to be made they would be the first to suffer.

On June 24, 1932 a group of soldiers and civilians, known to posterity as the "Promoters", staged a quiet and bloodless *coup*. Forty senior officials, including one of the King's half-brothers, were arrested and a new provisional constitution and government were imposed on, and accepted by the King. The new permanent constitution was not produced until December 10, 1932 by which time the dust had settled and a certain amount of bargaining and compromise had taken place; for the Promoters or first "ruling circle" were not an entirely homogeneous group, but rather an alliance between cliques of senior and junior civilians and soldiers; many of whom had studied abroad in France or Germany and whose main common interest was in the acquisition of more power for themselves and less for the King and the royal family. The result of the adjustments made between June and December was that the King was given more powers than had originally been intended, and that the state socialism which Nai Pridi, the young civilian ideologist of the circle, had advocated was quietly shelved. Nevertheless Thailand now had a constitutional monarchy and a legislative assembly.

Since 1932 various combinations of cliques of soldiers and civilians have seized and held office. A study of the names of the office holders in governments since 1932 will reveal how small the circle is from which these men have been drawn: the same names occur again and again as this or that clique gains the upper hand. Lest one should think that the struggle is between the "civilians" and the "military" as is the case in so many other countries, F. W. Rigg[3] makes it quite clear that every "ruling circle" has in fact contained both military and civilian cliques. It is true that the military have tended to dominate the scene of late, but they have always had to co-operate with the civilians. In the 1968 cabinet, for instance, two of the key men—Foreign Secretary Thanat Khoman and the Minister of National Development Pote Sarasin—were both civilians; it was indeed said that Thanom Kitti-kachorn the present Prime Minister (1971) wished Sarasin to succeed him.

The passing of the years has thinned the ranks of the Promoters but some are still powerful. New men have arrived but still through the traditional channels of the bureaucracy, the Armed Forces and the Police (who are now heavily armed, being equipped with machine guns, tanks and aircraft). This thread of continuity is well illustrated by the career of Thanom Kittikachorn. Not only was Thanom Prime Minister before, in 1957, but he was previously deputy commander of the Army under Marshal Sarit who, apart from having headed the government from October 20, 1958 to his death in 1963, had in turn been a deputy Minister of Defence in 1952 in the cabinet of Phibun, one of the chief Promoters.

Constitution-making

Since the announcement of the original provisional constitution in June 1932, eight constitutions have been proclaimed. David A. Wilson says "evanescence has been the most notable quality of the constitutions of Thailand and as a result it is almost impossible to take these documents very seriously". This may be so, yet every new régime has felt the need to produce one. Two explanations occur to one. It may be a ritual, meaningful or otherwise, or it could be a symptom of a desire to legitimise the new régime and to indicate to the outside world and to the home audience that power, however unorthodoxly seized, is not going to be wielded irresponsibly. Having said this, one should hasten to add that the provisions of a constitution are usually an accurate reflection of the ideology and political power-base of the current *coup* leader; one for example has restored some of the powers and privileges of the King or the princes; another those of Parliament; while a third has sought to concentrate power in the hands of the Prime Minister.

Let us compare, by way of illustration, the main provisions of the last constitution, promulgated on June 20, 1968, with those of its predecessor, the so-called "interim" constitution which was enacted in 1959.

The 1959 constitution was a short and simple document whose main provisions could be summarised as follows:

1. Thailand is a Kingdom.
2. The King shall enact laws by and with the advice and consent of the National Assembly.
3. A Constituent Assembly, appointed by the King and consisting of 240 members has the function of drafting a constitution and shall concurrently act as the National Assembly vested with legislative power.
4. The Courts of Law exercise the judicial power in the name of the King.
5. The Council of Ministers exercises the executive power.
6. The King appoints a Prime Minister and an appropriate number of Ministers forming the Council of Ministers for the national administration.
7. The Prime Minister and Ministers shall be excluded from membership of the Assembly.

The outstanding feature of this constitution was its provision for an almost total concentration of power in the hands of the Prime Minister, "nominated" by the King. There was, it is true, a nominal "separation of powers" between the Executive and the Legislature (see Item 7) but since the former appointed the latter, the "separation" was in name only and the Assembly served only to apply a rubber stamp to the decisions of the Executive.

For nine years the Thais waited for a new constitution and there was much speculation among the few to whom it mattered as to what form it would take. Interest focused mainly on the possible future composition and role of the Legislature, which was felt to be the one variable factor.

From 1932 to 1958 there had been two main types of Legislature: bi-cameral, with an elected lower house and an appointed upper house (or one elected by special procedures) and uni-cameral with some members appointed and the rest elected. The second type, which was in operation from 1932 to 1946 and again from 1951 to 1958, was said to be the brain-child of Nai Pridi: the ideologist of the 1932 *coup* whose schemes for land nationalisation and the like had so shocked his contemporaries that he was labelled a "Bolshevist" and removed—but only for a short time—from the political scene. If one looks again at his proposals one can see how misleading is the application of terms like "left", "right", "democrat" and "fascist" to Thai politics. Nationalisation of the land, the conversion of the independent farmer into a state employee, the very notion that "all Thais want to work for the Government"—these ideas belong just as much to traditional paternalistic bureaucracy as to modern Socialism. Equally paternalistic was the idea of "tutelary democracy" embodied in the proposal for a half-elected, half-appointed Assembly. The proposal allowed for an increase in the number of elected members by providing that the latter should replace appointed members in a particular province, when over half the eligible voters in that province had completed four years of primary education: it was further laid down that the Assembly would be fully elected after ten years, whether or not the electorate had reached the desired standard of literacy. In point of fact, at no time in Thailand's constitutional history has its legislature been fully elected. It is true that between 1946 and 1951 the lower house was fully elected but the 1946 constitution, drafted by Pridi, provided for an indirectly elected Senate with a life of six years. This provision ensured that Pridi's supporters, who packed the Upper House, would have a grip on the Legislature for some time to come. In the event, when the Legislature—and in particular Khuang Apaiwong's Democratic Party within it—became a nuisance, Phibun dismissed it. From then—1951—until 1958 Thailand went back to the 1932-type semi-elected, semi-appointed single chamber. There was the same provision for an increase in the elected membership which meant that by 1958 there was a 186 to 97 majority of elected members. All these democratic gains were wiped out on October 20, 1958 when Marshal Sarit dissolved the Assembly, declared martial law and subsequently produced the so-called "interim" constitution which was to last for the next nine years.

In a sense then, if we look only at its composition and method of election, the 1958 single chamber with its sizable majority of elected members, represented the high-water mark of Thai democracy. However, in 1968 those who hoped that the new constitution would restore the Legislature even to its position nine years before were sadly disappointed. The new constitution indeed was not very different from its highly illiberal predecessor.

The Constitution of 1968

The 1968 Constitution gave with one hand and took away with the other. On paper the position of the legislature was improved by the provision for all the members of the lower house, the House of Representatives, to be elected. On the other hand the legislature was made bi-cameral and the upper house, the Senate, made entirely appointive. Furthermore, it was laid down that the number of the Senators should be three-fourths of the total number of the Representatives. This provision had two main effects: it ensured that on important occasions when the two houses were required to sit in joint session as the National Assembly it would be extraordinarily unlikely that the government's opponents could ever muster the two-thirds majority that was necessary for certain purposes; second, it meant that the government, having nominated the Senators, only needed to have a quarter of the Representatives on its side in order to have a built-in majority in the National Assembly.

The executive power was placed squarely with the Cabinet. Members of the Cabinet could not also be members of either House. The Cabinet was required to submit its programme to the National Assembly but the latter was not allowed to pass a vote of confidence or no confidence in the Government. Although all bills had to receive the assent of the National Assembly before they became law, the Cabinet in fact ruled by decree: under Section 153 "The King has the power to issue Royal Decrees not contrary to law"; this was of course quite apart from the powers the Cabinet may have had in times of war or emergency.

There was provision for the National Assembly on the motion of at least a fifth of its membership to initiate a general debate at the end of which a "resolution of confidence or non-confidence could be passed "in the Ministers of State either individually or collectively". This was probably unlikely to happen but there was another way in which the legislature could exercise a modicum of control on the executive and this was by means of the interpellation. Section 126 stated that: "every member has the right to interpellate a Minister of State on all matters within the scope of his authority. The Minister of State, however, may refuse to reply if he considers that the matter should not yet be made public for reasons of public safety or of vital interests of the State." The Minister was further protected on these occasions by reason of the provision, which did not allow a resolution to be passed on the subject under debate.

All in all this was not remarkable for its liberality, but the Thais are conservative by nature and not eager for change just for the sake of change. In any case the mere fact that elections were held eased the tension built up by a decade of authoritarian rule and there were signs that the government was anxious to present as democratic an appearance as possible to the outside world, by paying much more attention to the National Assembly and in particular the House of Representatives than was strictly required under the constitution.

Government and Administration

At the apex of the governmental structure is the King, but Thailand is a constitutional monarchy and the King in the words of the Constitution "exercises the executive power through the Cabinet". The Cabinet is indeed the most powerful institution in the country. The Thais have applied the theory of the separation of powers to such good effect that the executive and the legislative scarcely need impinge on each other at all. The Cabinet is certainly required "to declare its policies to the National Assembly" but the latter is forbidden to "pass a vote of confidence or non-confidence" on the Cabinet's programme.

The effective head of the executive is the Prime Minister who has an Office of the Prime Minister to assist him. The Office contains, among others, two Deputy Prime Ministers, one of whom in 1970 was a prince of the royal blood and the other the Minister of the Interior.

In the Cabinet with the Prime Minister are the Ministers—not less than fifteen and not more than thirty—and Deputy Ministers who control the twelve Ministries. It should be noted that the Directors-General who are the executive heads of the Ministries are also appointed by the Prime Minister.

Fred W. Riggs once coined the phrase "bureaucratic polity" to describe the Thai political system. The phrase is expressive and goes far to explain the special role which the Ministries of State play in the political process.

The stated aim, says Riggs, of the promoters of the 1932 "revolution" was to transfer power from the King to the people. The people were to be represented by the Assembly and the Assembly was to control the executive in the best Westminster fashion. In the event however "it proved impossible for the assembly to control the cabinet. The cabinet, instead, gained control over the assembly. It was able to do so because the cabinet had an effective constituency, the bureaucracy (military and civil), whereas the assembly lacked any effective constituency (electorate and political parties). The resultant system of government . . . I have termed a 'bureaucratic polity'."[5]

The bureaucracy is the arena in which the political struggle takes place but those who are successful in the struggle acquire more than mere influence and prestige: they get many rich material rewards. Senior bureaucrats are regularly offered seats on the boards of private companies where their influence with the government may prove invaluable.

This, to a Westerner, unusual and undesirable connection between government and big business becomes much more understandable when it is realised that the Ministries are themselves engaged in business on their own account in no small way. For example, Riggs tells us that in 1957 the Ministries of Industry, the Interior, Agriculture and Finance ran respectively 47, 30, 18 and 10 government enterprises: yet another demonstration of how closely interlocked and interdependent are the centres of political and economic power.

For the purposes of local government Thailand is divided into twelve *changwat* or provinces each with a Governor at its head. The *changwat* is subdivided into *amphoe* or districts of which there are over five hundred, each headed by a *nai amphoe*. Below the *amphoe* are the *tambon** or communes, each with its *kamnan* or commune chief. Finally, we have the *muban* which is a *ban* or village which is represented on the *tambon* council. The head of the *muban* is known as a *puyaiban*.

The *changwat* governor and the *nai amphoe* are both career civil servants appointed by the Minister of the Interior and directly responsible to him. The *kamnan* and *puyaiban* are not civil servants but are under the control and supervision of the *nai amphoe* and governor and

---

* There were 4,893 tambons in 1966.[6]

are paid an honorarium while in office. The *puyaiban* is directly elected by the *muban,* and the *kamnan* is elected from among their own ranks by the *puyaibans* whose *muban* form the *tambon.* There are no regular elections for the office of *kamnan* or *puyaiban* and these officials remain in office until they retire voluntarily or commit some offence.

The governor is by no means the undisputed chief of the province. He is supposed to exercise a general oversight over the provincial representatives of the other "line" Ministries but in practice the latter consider themselves directly responsible only to their own Ministers and Directors-General in Bangkok. The general tendency throughout the Thai bureaucracy is for each Minister to build his own autonomous empire; co-ordination at any level of government—not only in the pro-vinces—is thus extremely difficult to achieve, particularly as there is a great deal of overlap in function between the various departments of state.

As in Cambodia there has been a move to decentralise authority somewhat. The *changwats* have been given some powers to collect their own revenue locally, a step which could make them marginally less dependent upon the Minister who normally controls the purse strings. The difficulty of course is to collect *any* extra revenue locally. The *changwat* has also been provided with a council of elected members but it has few powers and can in any case be over-ridden by the Governor or dissolved by the Minister of the Interior.

A greater degree of independence is exercised by the municipalities, of which there are three kinds. In descending order of importance and autonomy these are the *nakorn*—cities with populations of more than 50,000; the *muang*—towns with at least 10,000 inhabitants; and the *tambon* municipality—which does not have a rigid specification as regards population. There is also provision for the establishment of transitional bodies at the *tambon* and sub-*muang* level for the purpose of giving people some political education against the day when their particular community becomes eligible to become a proper *muang* or *tambon* municipality.

The main complaints about the administrative system are that it is over-centralised, impersonal, out of touch with the grass roots and corrupt. The charge of corruption is a familiar one in Southeast Asia and probably not difficult to substantiate. That the local administration is out of touch with the people is evidenced by Kamol Janlekha's findings in his survey of life in the *tambon* of Saraphi in north-eastern Thailand. It appears that the *changwat* authorities in the area made very little effort to administer to the needs of the *tambon*; in fact there is the suggestion that the representatives of the various technical Ministries at the *changwat* level did not pass on to the *tambon* the full quota of financial and technical assistance which was the latter's due. It also appears that the inhabitants of the *tambon* made no great effort to seek out the assistance of the authorities or to use the institutions such as the hospitals and the high school which were in fact available. On the other hand the officials were very rarely seen in the *tambon*; villagers reported that the only officials they had ever seen were policemen and agents of the Excise Department.

The Political Process

If it is true, as many writers contend, that Thailand's constitutional arrangements are to a great extent designed to impress those countries with whom she especially wishes to remain on good terms, one must clearly be careful when scrutinising the Thai political process not to confuse appearance with reality. There is for instance a good deal of enlightened labour legislation on the statute books in Thailand, but one would be naive indeed if he supposed that the laws about minimum wages and the employment of juveniles were observed with any great strictness. One would also be wrong if he supposed the Thais do not care about such abuses: they do, but their reaction is liable to be coolly realistic. They do not call for vengeance on the wrong-doers: they merely express the hope that one day economic conditions will match up with political and social aspirations.

Conservatism and patience are the two features of the Thai attitude to political matters which most readily strike the foreign observer. The Thais, while never entirely satisfied with things as they are, are content to make haste slowly. Theirs is the way of evolution not revolution. Such an attitude to life may irritate the frenetically active Westerner, but the Thai sees no advantage to be gained by radically changing it. It seems that each one of us carries within himself a kind of psychic metronome which sets the pace at which we do things and the speed with which we expect things to get done in domestic, business and national life; the Thai metronome is set at *lento* rather than *allegro*.

The Thais are accused of being "apathetic" and "not interested in democracy". Their critics point to the twenty per cent turn-out in the Bangkok-Thonburi municipal elections of September 1968. One could, however, equally well point to the municipal elections held elsewhere in the country in December 1967 and quote the seventy per cent turn-out which was to be found there. Describing that occasion a foreign correspondent noted the interest the voters had in "participatory democracy". Again, "apathetic" is hardly the word to describe the attitude of the thousands who filled one of Bangkok's longest and widest streets in order to listen to the speeches of the leaders of the Democrat Party just before the general elections of February 1969. The crowd on this occasion was so great that more than twenty loudspeakers had to be set up at intervals down the street so that everyone could hear what was being said. According to all accounts the audience was very attentive and this is certainly borne out by the fact that the Democrats swept the board in Bangkok.

What people really mean by the lack of interest in democracy is perhaps the deference which is such a feature of the social system. Without question a very large number of Thais subscribe to the view that a man is what he deserves to be. The verse of the nineteenth century Christian hymn which goes:

> The rich man in his castle,
> The poor man at his gate,
> God made them, high or lowly,
> And ordered their estate.

describes the situation quite neatly. Thai society is markedly stratified. For example, foreigners who come to Thailand to help start a factory or to instal an electricity generating plant and who are charged with training Thais to take over supervisory and management positions, often find themselves unable to promote the most suitable candidates simply because the latter refuse to be placed above those whom they consider to be their social superiors. This atmosphere of deference is to be found everywhere and reaches its apogee in the royal court where ceremonial obeisance is still very much the order of the day. There is no widespread criticism of the social structure and the ordinary person's acceptance of it is just as real and unselfconscious as was that of the average Englishman in relation to society in mid-Victorian England.

In these circumstances it is not surprising that really radical political parties are hard to find in Thailand.

In the 1969 elections, the three groups with the best representation in the House of Representatives were:

United Thai People's Party	75
Independents	72
Democrat Party	57

The remaining fifteen seats were shared between the Democratic Front (7), the United Economist (4), the People's Party (2), the Farmers (1) and the Free Democratic (1).

The United Thai People's Party or *Saha Pracha Thai* was the Government's party led by the Prime Minister, Thanom Kittikachorn. Prominent in the party were General Prapas, the Deputy Prime Minister and Minister of the Interior, Mr Pote Sarasin, the Minister of National Development, Police-General Prasert, the Deputy Minister of the Interior, and as its Secretary-General Air Chief Marshal Dawee Chullasapya, Field Marshal Thanom's deputy at the Ministry of Defence. The party did not obtain a majority in the House of Representatives but this did not unduly alarm its leaders who confidently expected to receive the support of the independent members, who were not organised as a political party.*

---

* This confidence was not entirely justified. In 1970 the Budget was only approved by a majority of one.

The Democrat Party did very well, especially in the Bangkok and Thonburi areas where they won all the seats. They also did well in certain country areas and one can be fairly sure that their strategy between now and the next election will be to concentrate their attention on the most promising areas in the hopes of getting the fifty-three more seats they require in order to be the majority party in the lower house.

In spite of its name the Democrat Party does not have a radical programme. Led by Seni Pramoj, whose title Mom Rajawong indicates that he has royal blood in his veins, and backed by fairly substantial businessmen, the party is not seeking to promote a social revolution. Its objectives are more modest: the elimination of corruption, a gradual civilianisation of the top echelon of government, and constitutional changes which would entail either the elimination of the Senate or its conversion into a fully elective chamber. But above all the Democrat Party believes in moderation and gradualism. Aware that it has to operate in a country which is situated very near the edge of the Indo-Chinese volcano, it has no desire to raise the political temperature or to create an atmosphere in which the electorate's hopes might be unduly raised and in which the wilder parties of the Left might flourish more vigorously.

Return to Bureaucracy

The truth of D. A. Wilson's dictum about the evanescence of Thai constitutions was clearly demonstrated on November 17, 1971 when Thanom Kittikachorn announced that the 1968 Constitution had been annulled and that, for the time being, the country was to be governed by a Revolutionary Council consisting of a mixed group of military and police officers and civilians. Thailand thus formally returned to the bureaucratic constitutional format which, in various guises, had been her system of government ever since the Chakri dynasty first came to power nearly two centuries before.

References

1. M. SMITH, A *Physician at the Court of Siam*, Country Life, London, 1948, p. 26.
2. *Ibid.*, p. 34.
3. F. W. RIGGS, *Thailand: The Modernisation of a Bureaucratic Polity*, East-West Center Press, Hawaii, 1966.
4. D. A. WILSON, *Politics in Thailand*, Cornell University Press, Ithaca, N.Y., 1962, p. 262.
5. F. W. RIGGS, op. cit., p. 323.
6. K. JANLEKHA, *Saraphi*, Geographical Publications Ltd., Bude, Cornwall, 1968.

CHAPTER FIVE

Laos

Introduction

Of Thailand we said that she owed her independence to her ability to adapt her internal affairs to foreign pressures: Laos unfortunately could not even if she had wanted to, for the simple reason that she did not even exist. Of all the products of colonial map-making in Southeast Asia the most artificial must be Laos: even the name is a French invention and is a misleading one in that it suggests that its inhabitants are mainly ethnic Lao, which is very far from being the case.*

Laos is faced with most of the problems which could conceivably confront a new nation: uncertain boundaries, disunity, ethnic problems, the gap between *élite* and mass, insolvency, communist insurgence, powerful external pressures, corruption, bad communications, illiteracy . . . the list is almost endless. Such however is its strategic position—landlocked and sharing borders with China, Burma, Thailand, Cambodia and the two Vietnams—that there are many urgent reasons why the great powers should wish to keep her alive with constant transfusions of money, material and men. It seems unlikely that Laos will manage to survive indefinitely on this basis let alone grow into an integrated political unit, but whatever happens one thing is certain: the main factors determining the future of Laos will be, as so often in the past, external ones.

Historical Background

De l'ancien Grand Lanxang au petit Laos nouveau,
La défense de ton sol nous a coûté très cher.
Pour relever ta gloire effacée depuis hier
Ton élite d'aujourd'hui bâtit ton renouveau.

From *A Ma Patrie*
by Khamchan Pradith

---

* J. M. Halpern[1] puts the percentage of Laotian Thai in Laos at just over 50.

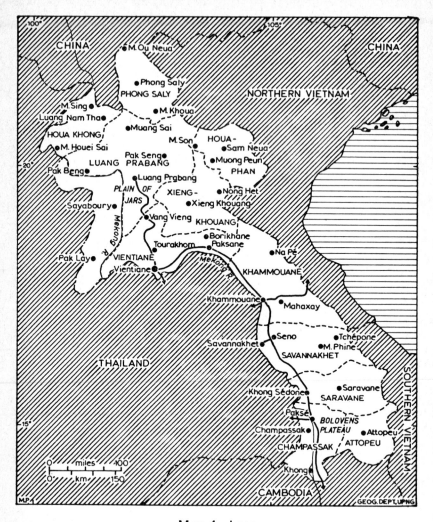

Map 4. Laos

In Vientiane, the capital of Laos, the main hotel and the main boule-
vard share the same name: Lan Xang. Lan Xang is to the Laotian
what Madjapahit is to the Indonesian, a reminder of the days, centuries
before the French appeared on the scene, when the country was united
and ruled by a single monarch.

It was in the middle of the fourteenth century that Fa Ngoum with
the help of a Khmer army established Lan Xang, "the country of a
million elephants".* In doing this he deposed his grandfather who ruled

---

* In 1957 there were said to be 1,200 elephants in Laos.[2]

in Muong Swa. Fa Ngoum enlarged the boundaries of his grandfather's kingdom so that it eventually included the three lesser kingdoms of Xien Khouang, Vientiane and Champassak: his writ thus ran over most of present day Laos as well as parts of Thailand and Northern Cambodia. Fa Ngoum brought with him a famous golden statue of the Buddha known as Pra Bang. Two hundred years later King Setthathirat renamed the town Luang Prabang in honour of the Buddha. In 1778 the Siamese general Praya Chakri took Vieng Chan (Vientiane) and removed both the Pra Bang and the Pra Keo. The former was returned to the Laotians in 1782 and King Anurut subsequently built a pagoda, Wat May, to enshrine it. The Pra Keo, or Emerald Buddha, was kept in Siam and is now housed within the precincts of the Royal Palace in Bangkok where the direct descendant of General Chakri reigns.

Lan Xang remained intact for two reigns but in the fifteenth and sixteenth centuries was under constant pressure from its neighbours, particularly Burma. By the beginning of the eighteenth century there were two kingdoms: one ruled from Luang Prabang, the other from Vieng Chan. Vieng Chan, sacked by Chakri in 1778 was again sacked in 1828 by another Siamese general and its population transferred to Siam. Luang Prabang was not much more fortunate. It came under the protection of Burma in 1752—having been invaded by the Burmese —and then under the suzerainty of Siam in 1778 at the time of the fall of Vieng Chan. A further encroachment was made in 1826 when the Annamese took over an area which included the present province of Xien Khouang, which had been under the suzerainty of Luang Prabang.

By the time the French arrived the Siamese ruled Vientiane directly and exercised suzerainty over the other two kingdoms of Luang Prabang and Champassak, though in competition with Annam over some areas, including Xien Khouang. The French, who now controlled Annam, took over the latter's claims to suzerainty and exploited them to such good effect that by the end of the nineteenth century they had displaced Siam as the ruler or "protector" of the area.

Though the French gave the name "Laos" to the area they made no particular effort to promote unity or nationhood. On the contrary they divided the area into three regions which were each treated differently. Phongsaly province was administered by the Army; the kingdom of Luang Prabang was ruled by its King with the assistance of French advisers; and the remainder was divided into eight provinces, each administered by a hierarchy of French civil servants with a *résident supérieur* in Vientiane, which was the administrative headquarters.

The nature of the terrain, the bad communications—no railways, few roads and these impassable in the wet season—the small number of administrators, the fact that Vientiane was virtually cut off from Saigon, Hanoi and the rest of French Indo-China: factors such as these meant that the main impact of the French was upon the small *élite* with whom, and through whom, the French ruled rather than upon the masses, whose lives were virtually untouched, for there were few plantations and no large industries.

That French culture made a very deep impression on the Lao *élite* there can be no doubt. Most of the present ruling class have had a French education: Souvanna Phouma's daughters have all been to France for their schooling and one of them has married a French *Comte*. Even today it is virtually impossible to get a secondary education in Laos except in French and from French-speaking teachers (Belgians are apparently in demand for this purpose).

The ties with France were not even entirely broken when the Japanese became the "suzerains" of Laos from 1941 to 1945. Sisavang Vong, King of Luang Prabang and a good friend of France, hesitated to declare the independence of Laos at the behest of the Japanese and only eventually did so under pressure. The pressure was exerted not only by the Japanese but by Laotians, for as soon as political independence became a possibility a struggle developed between the various, mainly princely, contenders for the positions of power.

At first there were two main groupings: the pro-French which included the King, the heir apparent Savang Vatthana and Prince Boun Oum of Champassak; the anti-French or Free Laos (Lao Issara) which contained the Princes Phetsareth, Souvanna Phouma and Souphanouvong, all sons—though not by the same mother—of the regent of Luang Prabang, Bhoun Khong.

When the French, spurred on by events in Vietnam, had conceded most of the demands of the Lao Issara, the latter disbanded and unity under a, by now, constitutional monarch would have prevailed but for the decision of Souphanouvong, expelled from the Lao Issara in May 1949, to set up in 1950 the Pathet Lao movement with the strong encouragement of the Viet Minh. The original object of the Pathet Lao (whose name merely means Lao State) was to make Laos truly independent of the French and not to tolerate any compromise. By 1964 the aim was still anti-colonial but the target had changed. The programme of the Pathet Lao's political party the *Neo Lao Hak Sat* now spoke of "the struggle against the United States imperialists and their followers—the traitors— . . ." The situation after 1950 became further complicated by the fact that the Pathet Lao was increasingly infiltrated by Communist cadres, some of whom were concurrently members of North Vietnam's Lao Dong Party. Souphanouvong, the "Red Prince", the nominal head of the Pathet Lao married a North Vietnamese, who is said not only to have been a fervent Communist but to have served as Ho Chi Minh's secretary. Whether the Prince shares her views is not entirely clear. Certainly the Neo Lao Hak Sat's manifesto advocates far-reaching socialistic measures, but it also recommends its readers to "respect the throne", to "respect freedom of belief" and to "protect pagodas and respect Buddhist priests". The

Prince is rumoured to prefer the ancient Greek classics to Marx and Lenin.

Thailand, as we have seen, managed to survive by adapting its internal politics to external pressures. In Laos the man who has for nearly twenty years tried to play the role of adapter is Prince Souvanna Phouma. A half-brother of Phetsareth and Souphanouvong, he, like them, was given a French education first at the *Lycée Albert Sarraut* in Hanoi and then at the Universities of Paris and Grenoble where he graduated in architectural and electrical engineering respectively. A remarkably durable politician, Souvanna Phouma has been Prime Minister, officially and sometimes unofficially, on and off since 1951. His constant objective has been to produce a "neutral" Laos which will give no offence to any of her powerful neighbours. The story of post-war Laos is in a sense the story of the Prince's efforts to play the part of the "judicious bottle-holder". It is to this story that we now turn.

In October 1953 Souvanna Phouma had been Prime Minister for nearly two years. France, weary by now of *la sale guerre* in Vietnam, decided to lighten her load by granting full independence to two parts of her former Indo-Chinese empire, Laos and Cambodia. Unfortunately, this magnanimous gesture which should have marked the beginning of a new era for Laos, nearly led to her undoing. For it was in a quixotic effort to defend Laos against the large-scale incursions of the Viet Minh that the French decided to launch "Operation Castor" which ended in France's defeat at the hands of General Giap at Dien Bien Phu. The battle took place while the great and small powers were gathered at Geneva in early 1954. The result was that the hand of the Pathet Lao was greatly strengthened and the organisation which Sananikone, a previous Prime Minister, had described at Geneva as "representing nothing" ended up by being given two provinces within which to "regroup". Having made an auspicious start the Pathet Lao now proceeded to press home their advantage. Their constant military forays split the non-Communist Laotian politicians into "hard-liners", such as Sananikone and Sasorith, and those who were prepared to do a deal with the Pathet Lao; this latter group included Souvanna Phouma the current Prime Minister and Kou Voravong the Minister of Defence, a member of the family into which, ironically, the "rightist" Phoumi Nosavan married. When, in November 1957, Souvanna Phouma eventually reached agreement with Souphanouvong it looked as if the moderates had won. As a result of these agreements the Pathet Lao were allowed to form a political party and campaign in competition with the other parties for an extra twenty seats, which were created for the purpose. The Pathet Lao's party, Neo Lao Hak Sat, won nine seats; their allies the Santiphab led by Quinim Pholsena (also a friend of Souvanna Phouma's) won four seats and Souphanouvong himself won the most votes of any candidate in the election. This alarming victory for the left had three major consequences: the temporary eclipse of Souvanna Phouma and his "neutralist" policy, the exclusion of the Pathet Lao from the government (into which they had briefly been admitted by Souvanna after the November 1957 agreements) and the rise in influence of the CDIN (*Comité de la Défense des Intérêts Nationaux*). Founded in June 1958 the CDIN was a group of younger soldiers and civilians, among whom was the then Colonel Phoumi Nosavan, who were politically ambitious and strongly anti-Communist. Tradition has it that *Les Jeunes*, as they were sometimes called, were the puppets of the CIA, working through an organisation known as the Program Evaluation Office which was part of the American aid structure. According to this version the CDIN was thus an American invention. Michael Field, in *The Prevailing Wind*, suggests that this is not so and that the CDIN was of wholly Lao origin even if it later received heavy American subventions.

The new Prime Minister, Sananikone, now came under pressure from both political wings. From the left the Pathet Lao, excluded from the Government, increased their military activities: from the right the CDIN demanded and received representation in the Government and then did their best to suppress any further parleys with the Pathet Lao. For a time Sananikone leant heavily towards the right and even, mostly at the insistence of the CDIN, dissolved the Assembly in which the Neo Lao Hak Sat formed so vociferous a group. The Pathet Lao now redoubled their activities, having no legitimate means of making their demands known.

Under pressure from the Pathet Lao and subsequently from the United Nations, whose aid he had invoked, Sananikone decided to alter course. He jettisoned the CDIN on December 15, 1959 intending presumably to embark on a more "neutralist" course. A fortnight later Phoumi Nosavan showed his—and the CDIN's—strong displeasure by organising a show of armed strength in Vientiane: a few days later Sananikone resigned and the CDIN installed the ageing Kou Abhay (the father of Kouprasith Abhay) as Prime Minister until elections could be held.

The year 1960 was a turning point in the history of post-war Laos. It was the triumph and downfall of the forces of the right, represented by the CDIN and their American backers; it saw also the staging of the *coup* which exposed the weakness of the rightists and set Laos once again on the path of neutrality which it has followed ever since.

The 1960 elections were quite blatantly "rigged" to produce a rightist Assembly. The Pathet Lao were allowed to participate but as their leaders were under arrest and their likely candidates mostly debarred from standing, as a result of specially drafted regulations governing the qualifications required of a candidate, the Neo Lao Hak Sat won no seats at all. Even where they were able to sponsor a candidate the results showed that the ballot had been interfered with. In Sam Neua, one of the Pathet Lao strongholds, the NLHS candidate, a former governor of the province, received thirteen votes against the winning candidate's 6,508. There were numerous other similar results. It was even alleged that CIA agents had been seen distributing money to village headmen.

At this particular moment when many in Laos were filled with cynicism and distaste at the tactics of the CDIN and their allies, Prince Souphanouvong escaped with eight of his fellow detainees from his place of custody in Vientiane. Eleven weeks later while Prince Somsanith, the new Prime Minister, and most of the government were in Luang Prabang to make final arrangements for the state funeral of the lately deceased King Sisavang Vong, Captain Kong Le, commanding the Second Parachute Battalion decided to stage his own protest at the decomposition in the state of Laos. Piqued it is said* by a decision to send his battalion into action against the Pathet Lao instead of meeting his men's grievances at the inadequacy of their barrack accommodation in Vientiane, and taking advantage of the absence of senior soldiers and civilians, Kong Le took over the few important buildings of Vientiane and announced the end of the current régime and the inauguration of a new one in which there was to be no corruption, no interference by foreigners, a purge of the administration and a reorganisation of the parliamentary system. Foreign aid was to be accepted "provided no strings are attached". For political guidance—for he was not well versed in these matters—Kong Le looked to Souvanna Phouma who gave him his backing, but managed to persuade him not to take measures that were too extreme. The National Assembly passed a vote of no confidence in Prince Somsanith's government (with the parachutists and the mob outside they had little choice) and the King asked Souvanna Phouma to form a new one.

The new government, which did not include any of the "rightists" had a very short life. The King withheld his approval and Souvanna was forced eventually to come to terms with the Right and form a new cabinet which included Phoumi Nosavan, now a General, as Vice-Premier and Minister of Defence. The leading Leftist, Quinim Pholsena, was demoted from the Ministry of the Interior to that of Information. But the Right and their backers were still not appeased. Phoumi went straight to his home town Savannakhet to make preparations for the *coup* which he staged in December and which brought down the Government and sent Souvanna Phouma into exile in Cambodia.

By the end of 1960 there were three forces in the field: those of the Left led by Souphanouvong; those of the Centre, whose leaders Souvanna Phouma and Kong Le were being pushed further leftwards under pressure from men like Pholsena and by the actions of the

---

* This account of his motivation has been denied by Kong Le. (See H. Toye, *Laos*[3]).

Rightists; and those of the Right, led by Phoumi and Boun Oum and backed by the United States.

Phoumi's *coup* in December 1960 came as no surprise. His forces had been moving towards Vientiane for some time, and Souvanna had plenty of warning. Prince Boun Oum of Champassak became Prime Minister and his régime was immediately accorded diplomatic recognition by the West, while the East continued to recognise Souvanna Phouma as the *de jure* head of government.

Phoumi's main objective, namely the crushing of the Pathet Lao once and for all, was never achieved. He met his Waterloo (or Dien Bien Phu) in May 1962 at Nam Tha when his forces were routed by Pathet Lao troops, heavily reinforced by North Vietnamese "volunteers". The parallel with Dien Bien Phu is quite apt because the nations were again met together in Geneva to try to solve the problem of Laos, largely at the instigation of Prince Sihanouk of Cambodia, Souvanna Phouma's temporary host. The defeat of the forces of the Right simplified matters and once more, after much negotiation, Souvanna Phouma emerged as the only acceptable head of a "neutralist" government in which he was Prime Minister and Minister of Defence; Souphanouvong was a Deputy-Premier and Minister of Economic Affairs and Planning, and Phoumi Nosavan was Deputy-Premier and Minister of Finance.

The coalition did not last long. First one of Kong Le's Colonels was assassinated by the Pathet Lao and then Quinim Pholsena, now Foreign Minister, was murdered in revenge by one of Kong Le's men. By this time part of Kong Le's forces had defected to the Pathet Lao under the leadership of a Colonel Deuane, who had been Kong Le's right-hand man at the time of the August 1960 *coup*. Within ten days of Pholsena's death on April 9, 1963 both Souphanouvong and Vongvichit left Vientiane for the headquarters of the Pathet Lao in Khang Khay. This move left the cabinet virtually without Pathet Lao representation for although Souphanouvong left deputies behind they had no real power and were for the most part totally out of touch with their masters. This state of affairs has remained unaltered to the present day.

A year later Souvanna made another attempt at reconciliation. He and Souphanouvong and Phoumi met on the Plain of Jars on April 17 and 18. The talks broke down and Souvanna announced his intention of resigning. Next day the commander of the Vientiane area, General Kouprasith, the son of the former Prime Minister Kou Abhay, staged a *coup* with the aid of Police-General Siho. Their object was apparently twofold: first, to stop Souvanna Phouma from drifting to the left; second, to reduce the power of General Phoumi. In the long run they were able to achieve both these aims.

Souvanna Phouma did not resign but he agreed to certain changes, the chief of which was the merger of the armed forces of the "right" and "centre". The new Royal Laotian Army was now under the command of General Ouane Rattikone with Kouprasith as a prominent member of the General Staff. There was now no separate "rightist" force commanded by Phoumi and the latter also had his lucrative import firm Sogimex closed down and the Bank of Laos, which he controlled, was no longer allowed a monopoly of the import of gold. From that time on General Phoumi's power and influence waned rapidly. The US government no longer backed him and he lost the support of the Army to such an extent that by February 1965, when he and Siho attempted a *coup,* he found himself so isolated that he left the country and went into exile in Thailand.

The other leading figure who began to go into eclipse was Kong Le. Deserted by his chief subordinate, Deuane, and many of his troops, Kong Le came under increasing pressure from his superiors on the General Staff who had not forgotten or forgiven him his insubordinate actions in 1960. In November 1966 Kong Le resigned his command and left the country, complaining that the "rightists" would no longer allow his troops to have a separate identity.

On the constitutional front the life of the CDIN-dominated Assembly came to an end in 1965 and elections were held on a franchise restricted to about 22,000 soldiers, civil servants, company directors and village headmen. These elections were boycotted by the NLHS which said they were illegal. The major new force which emerged in the new House of Assembly was a group of younger deputies centred round Sisouk na Champassak, a kinsman of Boun Oum's. The new deputies were elected for a special two-year term but in fact only served for a year as the House was dissolved towards the end of 1966 as a result of its refusal to approve the government's budget. Elections on a wider basis were held in January 1967 and this time Souvanna Phouma made no mistakes. Lacking a personal following among the electorate Souvanna ensured that he made the right deals with the princes, the regional military commanders and the aristocrats who could "deliver" the vote in their respective areas of influence.

The composition of the Cabinet reflected Souvanna's resolve to please everybody. For Souphanouvong and Vongvichit of the Pathet Lao there were the customary two places reserved. Representing the Phoumi/CDIN faction were Leuam Insisiengmay, a member of the Voravong family and an anti-neutralist, and Inpeng Suryadhay, whose expulsion from the cabinet Kong Le had demanded in 1960; while the old-guard neutralists were well represented by the Prime Minister himself and the Minister of Health, Interior and Social Affairs, Pheng Phongsavan. The rising generation, *les jeunes,* were represented by Sisouk, who was given the Ministry of Finance and had no trouble getting his budget approved by the new Assembly.

On the military front the situation improved slowly. The Pathet Lao's main efforts were directed at keeping open the "Ho Chi Minh trail" from North Vietnam through Laos to South Vietnam. The trail was bombed by US aircraft flying from bases in Thailand and elsewhere but Souvanna Phouma refused to allow American ground forces to operate in Laos.* There was an upsurge of Pathet Lao activity in mid-1968 and again in early 1970 and some observers thought the Communists might be staking out their territorial claims in anticipation of a further Geneva-type settlement. Meanwhile Souvanna Phouma complained frequently to the International Control Commission about the incursions into Laos of the North Vietnamese but could get no satisfaction as the diplomatic fiction of the tripartite neutralist government was still being preserved and the ICC could take no action without the approval of the representatives of the Pathet Lao.

There is at present an uneasy equilibrium in Laotian politics. At the point of balance stands Souvanna Phouma, the only person in the whole of Laotian politics who seems capable of maintaining a genuine neutrality without incurring the enmity of either side in the Cold War. He accepts without demur the American aid without which the economy would founder and at the same time manages to remain *persona grata* with Russia. He has even accompanied the King, by nature a "rightist", on visits (one journalist called them "tribute-bearing missions") to Moscow and Peking. Although he describes his half-brother Souphanouvong as entirely in the clutches of North Vietnam, he has still not lost hope of eventual reconciliation with the Pathet Lao. Now nearing his seventieth birthday the Prince no doubt wishes to retire from politics to his property in France and it is difficult to see who could successfully succeed him. Souvanna is in a sense unique: a man with no particular territorial affiliations and no personal popular following, he can serve as the centre round which the other great Laotian families such as the Sananikones and the Voravongs and the Champassaks, can revolve. He also remains, it is said, uncorrupted in a country in which huge quantities of foreign largesse have made heavy inroads on personal integrity. It is said that Sisouk na Champassak is being groomed for the succession but Sisouk is closely identified with the South and Boun Oum, and there is no doubt that other families would dispute his title. Souvanna Phouma is anxious to preserve unity at all costs and is apparently deliberately building up the royal house of Luang Prabang for this purpose. He has accompanied the Crown Prince on tours of the countryside and shown him to the people. Whether this will have the desired effect one cannot say but two things are certain: one is that the royal house has historically only ruled part of Laos until very recently and cannot expect to command much loyalty outside the Luang Prabang area; and the other is that the continued dominance of a small *élite* composed almost exclusively of ethnic Lao cannot in the

* Secret state papers published by the *New York Times* and other American newspapers in June 1971 suggest that American, South Vietnamese and Thai ground forces were operating in Laos as early as 1964 without the knowledge of Souvanna Phouma.

long run provide a permanent political solution for a country in which other ethnic groups form fifty per cent of the population.

The Constitution, Government and Administration of Laos

Laos is a constitutional monarchy: the King reigns but he does not rule. Theoretically this state of affairs first came into being when the new post-war constitution was promulgated by King Sisavang Vong on May 11, 1947. In fact, however, the workings of the new constitution do not represent a radical departure from time-honoured practice.

Writing of England, Walter Bagehot[4] once argued that there were two parts to the English Constitution: the *dignified* and the *efficient*. The *dignified* parts were those "which excite and preserve the reverence of the population" and the *efficient* parts are those "by which it, in fact, works and rules". Under the new constitution of Laos there is no doubt that the King represents the *dignified*, and the President of the Council or Prime Minister the *efficient* part; but this arrangement is by no means alien to Laotian tradition. It used in fact to be the practice for a King to leave the day-to-day administration of the Kingdom to a *Maha Oupahat* or Viceroy, who was also of royal blood. In fact if one looks at the genealogy of the Royal Family of Laos one can see that Prince Souvanna Phouma is the senior member of the cadet branch of the royal family from which the Maha Oupahat would normally be chosen. The last person to be actually designated by this title was Souvanna Phouma's eldest brother, Prince Phetsarath, who died in 1959. The division between the dignified and the efficient parts of the Constitution are symbolised by the fact that the King resides in the royal capital of Luang Prabang while all the administration and government is carried out in Vientiane, where all the government offices are situated.

The Constitution

The general principles are laid down in the Preamble and first Section of the Constitution. There is a reference to the "role handed down" to Laos by "history" and the hope is expressed that the unity and independence which is the natural condition of the country will be restored. Article 6 states that the official language "shall be the Laotian language"; there is no mention of the languages of the ethnic minorities. In Article 7 Buddhism is stated to be the established religion and the King its "High Protector". The Buddhism referred to here is Theravada, the "Way of the Elders", sometimes also called Hinayana or "Lesser Vehicle", a version regarded by its adherents as more "primitive" and "pure" than Mahayana, "Greater Vehicle", which is the Buddhism of China and North Vietnam. Theravada, which is also the version to be found in Cambodia and Thailand, stresses the responsibility of the individual for his actions and their consequences.

In Section 2 the powers of the Monarch are defined. Although the King's powers have decreased greatly since the days of Lan Xang, he is still something more than the constitutional monarch of Western Europe. He presides over the Council of Ministers and although he has to act through "the intermediary of Ministers whom he shall nominate when they have received the confidence of the National Assembly", his power to nominate is a real one and has been used to introduce into the cabinet, or Council of Ministers, men whom the Prime Minister (President of the Council of Ministers) would not otherwise have chosen.

In normal circumstances the country is run, like any constitutional monarchy, by the President of the Council and his Ministers who need not be drawn from the National Assembly. Article 19 however makes it possible for the King, at the initiative of the Government and with the consent of the King's Council and the National Assembly, personally "to exercise the functions of government or himself to appoint a Government of his own choice" when "there is a need to safeguard the vital interests of the Kingdom".

Except in the situation outlined in Article 19 a new government has to have the approval of the National Assembly, from which it must obtain a vote of confidence. A new government must also have the approval of the King. In 1960 the King withheld approval of the Kong Le regime and Souvanna Phouma was obliged to put forward an alternative, compromise cabinet.

The Council of Ministers is responsible to a National Assembly "composed of members elected every five years by universal suffrage" (Article 24). The Assembly "shall pass laws specially relating to the Budget, National Loans, the Administrative Accounts, the status of persons, the revision of the Laotian Codes, the organisation of the Kingdom, Amnesties, the ratification of treaties" (Article 28). Laws passed by the National Assembly have to be submitted for approval to the King's Council which consists of six members chosen by the King and six elected by the National Assembly. Article 33 states that "the King may dissolve the National Assembly on the proposal of the Council of Ministers after the agreement of the King's Council has been signified. In that event the new election shall be held within ninety days." This seems to conflict somewhat with the provisions of Article 22 which states that if the National Assembly "refuses to give its confidence to the Government or if it passes a vote of censure the Government as a whole shall resign". On the whole National Assemblies are fairly faithful followers of the government and have not caused much trouble. Even the 1965 Assembly, which was dissolved under the provisions of Article 33 when it refused to approve the Budget, did not take its duties over-seriously. The London *Times* of March 11, 1966 said: "As yet the Assembly is far from mature or aware of its responsibilities. In a recent confidence vote Prince Souvanna Phouma got 28 votes with two against and five abstaining. The rest (of the 59) were absent—attending festivals or otherwise enjoying themselves on family occasions."

In April 1965 a joint session of the National Assembly and the King's Council recommended that the Constitution be amended so as to empower the King "when elections cannot be held" to do one of three things: to extend the life of the existing Assembly; to order a new election with limited suffrage; to appoint new deputies after a "limited population consultation". The King in fact adopted the third course on this particular occasion. It should be noted here that the words "when elections cannot be held" refer to the sort of situation when security is bad or the NLHS refuses to co-operate with the government.

Section 6 gives a brief outline of the structure of local government and then makes a brief reference to the judiciary, not giving its structure but saying that "the independence of the judicial power and its relationship to the legislative and executive shall also be laid down by law" (Article 42).

Finally, Section 7 makes it impossible for certain features of the Constitution to be altered—namely "the monarchical form of government, the unitary and indivisible character of the State, the representative nature of the regime and the principles of liberty and equality guaranteed in this Constitution" (Article 43).

The Government and Administration

The key figure in the government is the Prime Minister, or rather the President of the Council of Ministers. He, with his Ministers—all of whom are required to receive a vote of approval and confidence from the National Assembly before being confirmed in office by the King—not only direct the everyday business of the realm but also have the lion's share in devising the legislation which has to be passed by the legislature. The legislature's powers are not in practice very great; we have already seen how in recent times it has been dissolved by the King on the instructions of the Prime Minister when it has displayed too much independence.

Occupying the middle ground between the King and the National Assembly is the King's Council which acts not only in an advisory capacity to the Monarch but also as an Upper House which examines measures passed by the lower chamber and advises the King whether to sign, veto or amend them. The Council consists of twelve men, usually elder statesmen, six of whom are nominated by the King and six by the Assembly. The consent of the Council is mandatory on certain occasions such as the dissolution of the National Assembly.

Beneath the Prime Minister are the usual Ministries—Interior,

National Defence, Education, Health, Finance and so on—each of which has its administrative headquarters and staff in Vientiane.

Provincial and local administration come under the general aegis of the Ministry of the Interior which in these troubled times is assisted and sometimes frustrated by the Ministry of Defence.

Laos is divided into sixteen provinces (*Khoueng*), each of which is headed by a Governor or *Chao Khoueng*. Each *Khoueng* is then sub-divided into three, four or five *Muong*, each under a *Chao Muong*. The *Chao Khoueng* and *Chao Muong*, it should be noted, are public servants under direct control of the Minister of the Interior, and appointed by him. The first elected officials appear at the sub-district or *Tasseng* level. The *Tasseng* himself—the unit and the official share the same appellation—is elected but once elected receives a stipend from the Ministry of the Interior. At the lowest level of the administration is the *Ban* or "village" (though it may not be one) whose head the *Nai Ban* is also elected. On January 1, 1967 Laos was divided into sixteen *Khoueng* in which there were 115 *Muong*, 18 *Kong*, 922 *Tasseng* and 11,782 *Ban*.*

In the *Khoueng* and *Muong* are also to be found officials of the various Ministries: Education, Agriculture, Health, Information and so on. Although these officials owe their allegiance to the heads of their departments in Vientiane they are also under the general direction of the *Chao Khoueng* and *Chao Muong*. On paper the system appears heavily centralised but in practice there is a good deal of *de facto* decentralisation and local autonomy; when to this is added poor security and bad communications one can imagine the difficulties confronting anyone who wishes to put any kind of overall economic plan into operation.

In a country like Laos, which has been in a state of war for many years, one might expect to find the military controlling the civilians, yet there are only two provinces with military governors and it seems generally agreed that civil functions in the other provinces are largely carried out by civilians. That this is the case is largely due to the fact that the civil and military *élites* are largely drawn from the same sources and there is usually some close connection between the military and civilian chiefs. If we examine the five military regions into which Laos is divided we find that in 1970 the first region, centred on Luang Prabang, was commanded by a half-brother of the King; the second, centred on Sam Thong, was commanded by the Meo leader Vang Pao; the third, centred on Savannakhet, was commanded by General Boun-pone, who had married once, if not twice, into the Champassak family, the ruling family of the South; the fourth, centred on Pakse, was com-

---

* It should be noted that in some areas where there are existing tribal groups, some of the groups have been designated *Kongs* and the heads of them *Nai Kongs*—the status of a *Nai Kong* being about that of a *Chao Muong*.

manded by Phasouk Somly who was also connected by marriage with the Champassaks; while the fifth, centred on Vientiane, was commanded by General Kouprasith Abhay, who had strong links with the powerful Sananikone family, whose fief this particular area is. All in all, one might say that the civilians and the military co-exist in a symbiotic state, each drawing power and influence from the other.

External Forces

Of all the forces bearing upon the political life of Laos the two most significant are those which come respectively from the United States and Vietnam. In this and the next section we propose to deal with the civil rather than the military aspects of the results of these influences, asking the reader to bear in mind that the North Vietnamese are said to have at least forty-five thousand members of their armed forces in Laos and that the Americans were alleged in 1969 to be spending between $135 million and $145 million a year on military aid to the Royal Lao Government's forces, in particular those under the command of General Vang Pao.[5] This assistance was increased greatly in the following year and one estimate of the value of the total aid, both military and civil, given by the United States to Laos in 1970 was $500 million or approximately $200 for every man, woman and child in the recipient country.[6]

United States' Aid Programme*

The aims of United States economic assistance, which was expected to reach forty-eight million dollars in the fiscal year 1970, have been described as:

1. Stabilisation of the economy and of the value of the Kip (the local unit of currency);
2. Humanitarian relief of the suffering of the Lao people;
3. Development of the economy to improve the living standard of the people.

For the fiscal years 1955 through 1970 the sum of United States economic assistance amounted to seven hundred million dollars. What has this vast expenditure achieved?

The programme has been remarkably successful in realising its first two aims. The currency is certainly stable: in 1970 there was no evidence

---

* Much of this section is based on
  (a) "Four Questions on American Economic Aid to Laos", an address given in Vientiane on November 12, 1969 by the Director of the USAID Mission to Laos;
  (b) "United States Aid to Laos", a pamphlet published in May 1968 by the US Embassy in Vientiane.

of any black market in the Kip; there was only one rate, the official one.

In the field of humanitarian relief much has been achieved. A striking example of the sheer scale of United States aid is the town of Sam Thong in the province of Xieng Khouang, whose capital town of the same name is in the hands of the Pathet Lao movement. In 1969 Sam Thong was the third largest town in Laos and was inhabited very largely by refugees from the town of Xieng Khouang supplemented by others drawn in from the surrounding countryside.*

In November 1969 the Director of USAID said that the number of refugees then requiring assistance was nearly three hundred thousand. This is perhaps more than a tenth of the entire population of Laos. The proper care of such a vast number is a burden which even a rich country might find financially onerous. For a small, poor country the burden would be crippling and there is no doubt that without the assistance of the United States the lot of these displaced persons would be extremely unpleasant.

USAID's third objective, the development of the economy, will be much harder to achieve. The primary aim in this area is to improve, expand and develop agriculture. To this end a great deal of money and effort has been expended on irrigation schemes; encouragement of the use of fertilisers and insecticides; improvement of transportation and marketing systems and the introduction of new, improved seeds. In some areas solid gains have been made: for example whereas in 1967 5,411 tons of rice were procured locally to help feed refugees and the military, in 1968 this figure had risen to 12,644 tons. The main, and all too human, failing of the USAID programme is that in general it only operates in areas where there is every chance of success. This means in practice that aid goes mostly to those who live in secure areas where the forces of the Pathet Lao are not likely to undo in a week all that the Americans and the Laotians have taken months to build up. In terms therefore of the ideological war, the Americans are only preaching to the converted or those whose minds are not so likely to encounter hostile propaganda. It also means that in those border areas which are sometimes under Royal rule and sometimes under the Pathet Lao, the latter may even get some of the credit for the work done under the USAID programme because the local Pathet Lao commander may suggest that it can only be carried out by his permission.

Laos is part of the battlefield of the Indo-Chinese war and it would be very surprising in these circumstances if there were not a strong element of ideological motivation behind USAID. That this is the case can be seen quite clearly in the pronouncements of the programme's leading officers.

---

* In March 1970 Sam Thong was overrun by Pathet Lao forces, but the latter only occupied it for a short time and the town was then reoccupied by the forces of General Vang Pao and his American advisers.

Like the Marxists the Americans are wedded to an economic interpretation of politics and it seems that one of their basic aims is to build a "property-owning democracy", a society in which the citizens have such substantial political and economic stakes that they would not let the "enemy" take the whole concern over without a great and spontaneous struggle. As the Americans see it, the average Lao peasant is totally unconcerned about the nature and identity of his current rulers and it is this state of affairs that the Americans are anxious to alter. To combat this indifference American field workers are striving to promote economic activity, both individual and co-operative and to "strengthen democratic decision-making processes at the local level and consequently strengthen the ability of local governments to identify the problems and work with the rural people effectively for their resolution". For these purposes training has been given to individual farmers in new techniques, the purchase of equipment, seeds and fertilisers has been facilitated through the setting up of an Agricultural Development Organisation, while on the administrative front a fair number of *Tassengs* and *Nai Bans* have received in-service training and one or two more senior administrators have been sent to Thailand for courses in public administration.

Inasmuch as the Americans have succeeded in implementing their programme they have solved certain economic problems at the expense of raising new political and social ones. USAID apologists point with pride to the new awakened citizen who is now not afraid to march into the office of the *Chao Muong* and to demand that his particular case be attended to—an action which the said citizen would have considered suicidal a few years back. The change of attitude is no doubt admirable but it also heralds social strife: antagonism between generations, the loosening of ties and the undermining of traditional authority.

Another leading objective of American policy is to encourage national unity and in this area the Royal Lao Government gives its wholehearted co-operation.

Laos has a grave problem of integration. The Government has evidently decided to promote cohesion by promoting the symbols of unity such as the monarchy and the revived memory of Lan Xang and the days when Luang Prabang, Vientiane and Champassak were under one ruler. The Government has also decided to cut the ethnic Gordian knot by going all out to spread the use of the Lao language. In both these fields the Americans have given invaluable help. They have helped to pay for the production and distribution of thousands of posters bearing photographs of the King and they have made an immense contribution to the extension of education, and the spread of textbooks in the Lao language. In the period 1955-1969 2,903,395 elementary school textbooks in the Lao language were written, printed and distributed by USAID in conjunction with the appropriate government agencies.

One intended by-product of this campaign for the promotion of Lao will be the gradual elimination of French as the language of instruction of some primary and all secondary and tertiary education. There is no doubt that the Americans feel some antipathy towards the French in this and other parts of the former Indo-China and that they are consciously trying to diminish the influence of the former colonial power on her former subjects. In a speech delivered in Vientiane in November 1969 the Director of USAID said " . . . I believe that you must increasingly turn your attention away from Europe and America and learn to look to the geographical region of which you are a part as the real economic and political sphere in which you live and work. For a nation only recently (as historical time goes) divorced from the tutelage of a European power, this will be painful in two ways: it means the loosening of some ties of a cultural and economic nature which are comfortable but inhibiting: it means at the same time a coldly realistic view of some aspects of national sovereignty as they may inhibit participation in the economic life of the region." What this means precisely in practice is not entirely certain but it clearly entails a loosening of the ties with France. The reference to the "region" suggests that the Americans would like to see the Laotians turn to Thailand for assistance and co-operation. The Lao have cultural and ethnic ties with the Thai and the languages are sufficiently alike to make it feasible for Lao-speaking students to pursue their tertiary studies in Thai universities, in subjects for which there is not already adequate provision in Laos. Whether such regional co-operation would conflict with the neutralist policy which Laos professes is a question which only Lao politicians are in a position to answer.

Life with the Pathet Lao*

From the reports of refugees from the "enemy"-held areas of Xieng Khouang province a picture has been built up of life under the Pathet Lao, or Neo Lao Hak Sat. The NLHS seems to have three main objects: to raise the level of productivity in agriculture and animal husbandry to a point at which the needs of the military can be satisfied and the general standard of living improved; to transform, by example and indoctrination, the whole way of life of the people; and above all to recruit enough soldiers, front-line or auxiliary, and porters to keep up the pressure on the Royal Laotian Government forces.

The reaction of the people to these demands has been to accommodate themselves as best as they can to the new situation. The most unpopular measures imposed by the NLHS have predictably been those

---

* Much of this section is based on *Life Under the P.L. in the Xieng Khouang Ville Area* by Edwin T. McKeithen, an undated publication of the U.S. Embassy in Vientiane.

which have involved taxation and conscription. Males are liable to be called for military service at any age between thirteen and fifteen. Practically all eligible males are in the Army; the older ones being in auxiliary and "home guard" units, the younger being in the regular front-line units. Taxation mostly takes the form of levies on rice. After certain "family allowances" have been deducted the tax-payer has to give fifteen per cent of his rice product to the state. In certain areas a second levy of ten per cent was made which required a man to sell this percentage at a fixed price to the co-operative. A further contribution called "rice from the heart" was also asked for. Although this was supposed to be voluntary, a good deal of moral pressure was brought to bear on possible donors to outdo one another in the generosity of their contributions. Further gifts were also called for, for certain purposes such as supporting teachers and doctors.

Another unpopular feature of NLHS rule is the compulsory stint which practically everyone, male or female, has to do as a porter. People are expected to make several "short trips" and at least one "long trip" a year. A long trip usually involves thirty days of actual *hauling* so that a man or woman may be away for much longer than a month as no account is taken of the time taken to get to or from the place of work.

The NLHS hopes of course that some of these measures will be short term ones and can be gradually abandoned as success is achieved in the field of battle. The long term measures are those which are concerned with redirecting the minds and hearts of the people under its care. For this purpose the NLHS has infiltrated its cadres into the normal administrative structure of the province. The posts of *Chao Khoueng, Chao Muong*, Tasseng and Nai Ban are all occupied by "Patriotic Neutralists" who represent the "ordinary" government. Alongside all these officials are NLHS men who are designated *Neo Khoueng, Neo Muong* and so on. In addition there are North Vietnamese advisers to the top three levels of government.

An interesting development of the last three or four years is the "Awakening Group", an unofficial but influential ginger group consisting mainly of dedicated trustworthy single men who "have a nominal role as community development advisers" but whose "prime responsibility is to check on villagers' industriousness and political reliability".

Like all true Communists the NLHS officials wish to receive wholehearted, not merely grudging, support from the people. Unfortunately for the people, this involves an attack on almost everything which goes to make up the received ideas and conventional wisdom of the typical Laotian-Buddhist society. Buddhism is constantly under criticism and monks are portrayed as parasites who "eat the people's rice". Traditional festivals and family celebrations are discouraged because they involve unnecessary consumption of scarce commodities. Expensive cremations are out of favour. In short all the principles and practices of the older generation are under attack. When people deviate from the true path they are required not only to be tried and punished but to make public confession of the error of their ways. It is also reported that all adult citizens have to carry or be able to produce at short notice "merit books", in which all their successes and failures are recorded. An impressive number of "good marks" in the merit book is a *sine qua non* for promotion or selection as a candidate for an elective office.

Summing up the effects of the Pathet Lao regime, an American observer talks of the difficulties confronting the NLHS officials in their attempt to change the mode of life of the people. "Much of the P.L. political machinery" he writes "is based on group loyalty and dedication to organisations, but the Lao have had almost no experience with such groups or societies in the Western sense of the terms. There is simply no precedent for a 'youth organisation' devoted to lofty principles and dedicated to the advancement of long-range goals. Similarly the traditional Lao tolerance of practically everything (work habits, personality deviations, individual beliefs, etc.) has made the introduction of a new morality particularly difficult." If this analysis is correct it follows that the Americans must have an equally difficult row to hoe. Indeed the Director of the USAID Mission, in another part of a speech already quoted, says "The concepts of co-operative self-help to improve the level of living and of participating democratically in the process of national government and nation-building are not prevalent among the rural people."

The contest between the Royal Lao Government, backed by the United States, and the Pathet Lao, backed by the North Vietnamese, for the allegiance of the people will be a close one. The Royal Lao Government has more money at its disposal and is less harsh in its dealings with the populace; on the other hand there is a good deal of corruption in its ranks, whereas refugees from Pathet Lao rule "spoke favourably of the virtual elimination of official corruption".

References

1. J. M. HALPERN, in F. M. Lebar, G. C. Hickey and J. K. Musgrave (Eds), *Ethnic Groups of Mainland Southeast Asia*, Human Relations Area Files, New Haven, 1964, p. 215.
2. *Geographie du Laos*, Vientiane, 1963.
3. H. TOYE, *Laos*, Oxford University Press, London, 1968, p. 141.
4. W. BAGEHOT, *The English Constitution*, Fontana Library Edition, London, 1963 p. 61.
5. Senator Fulbright before Senate Foreign Relations Committee, October 1969.
6. *Far Eastern Economic Review 1971 Yearbook*, Hong Kong, 1970, p. 215.

CHAPTER SIX

Khmer Republic (Cambodia)

Historical Background

South of Laos and sharing a border with her and Thailand and South Vietnam lies the kingdom of Cambodia. Unlike Laos she has a coastline and a seaport, Kompong Som (formerly Sihanoukville), capable of taking ships of up to 10,000 tons or much larger ships if they are not fully laden. Like Laos her political fortunes are very much bound up with those of her neighbours and of course China, whose shadow is cast over all Southeast Asia.

In two important respects, however, Cambodia has a great advantage over Laos: she has a near-homogeneous population—eighty-five per cent to ninety per cent Khmer—making for ethnic unity while her comparatively high degree of political unity is in large part derived from a proud history which is based not on vague memories of Lan Xang but—until 1970—on the living reality of an active monarchy with one of the longest pedigrees in the world.

In the second half of the eighth century when central Java was witnessing that flowering of Buddhist art whose most famous product was the great monument called Borobudur, Cambodia was under the suzerainty of the Javanese dynasty known as Sailendra or "Lords of the Mountain". It was from Java at the beginning of the ninth century that the man later known as Jayavarman II sailed to Cambodia to found the kingdom of Angkor whose base was to the north of the great lake, Tonle Sap, in the modern province of Siem Reap on the borders of Thailand. To demonstrate his independence of the Sailendra Jayavarman II became a "Lord of the Mountain" himself and started a cult of himself as a *deva-raj* or "god-king" whose power, virility and fertility were symbolised by a stone linga placed on top of a hill.

The Angkor kingdom reached its zenith in the twelfth century under Suryavarman II (1113–1150) and Jayavarman VII (1181–1218) whose kingdom included most of present-day Laos and much of Thailand. Suryavarman II built Angkor Wat, the great funeral monument which was rescued from the clutches of the jungle by the French and which is now the symbol of Khmer greatness. Significantly it was also Suryavarman II who acknowledged China as his suzerain and obtained her protection and favour in much the same way as his distant successor Norodom Sihanouk was to do in modern times.

Angkor went into eclipse in the fourteenth century after a blaze of constructive activity which perhaps left it drained of energy and resources. Under Jayavarman VII roads, hospitals, rest houses, libraries and schools were built and there is no doubt that the king, megalomaniac though he may have been, did much for the welfare of his people. D. G. E. Hall[1] says ". . . modern research has established the significant fact that each Khmer king, upon taking office, was expected to carry out works of 'public interest', particularly works of irrigation before starting upon his own temple-mountain. Indeed M. Groslier goes so far as to say that the labour bestowed upon the ever-developing irrigation system is 'far more impressive than the building of temples, which were merely chapels crowning a Cyclopean undertaking' . . .". In assessing the relationship of the monarchy to the people in modern Cambodia one should bear in mind that even in the highly undemocratic days of the god-kings of Angkor monarchs were expected to give as well as receive.

With the death of Jayavarman VII the kingdom started to decline in power and Angkor eventually fell to the Siamese, who destroyed the city in 1431. A further period of independence was enjoyed under the great Ang Chan and his successor but once again the capital city, Lovek, fell in 1594 to the Siamese who have continued to play an important role in the life of Cambodia ever since.

The other great influence in Cambodian affairs, Vietnam, first appeared on the scene about thirty years after the fall of Lovek when a Khmer king married a Vietnamese princess. It was about this time that the Vietnamese, ever driving southward, first colonised the area around the modern Saigon.

By the beginning of the nineteenth century the fortunes of Cambodia were very low. She had lost two provinces—Battambang and Siem Reap —to Siam and with them the site of Angkor Wat. In Coedes' graphic words: "the descendants of the kings of Angkor received their crowns at the hands of the kings of Siam and paid tribute to the emperors of Vietnam".[2]

Events then followed a course similar to those in neighbouring Laos. The Cambodian king tried to play Vietnam off against Siam but only succeeded in incurring the militant wrath of the same General Bodin who had earlier sacked Vieng Chan. The Cambodians then turned to

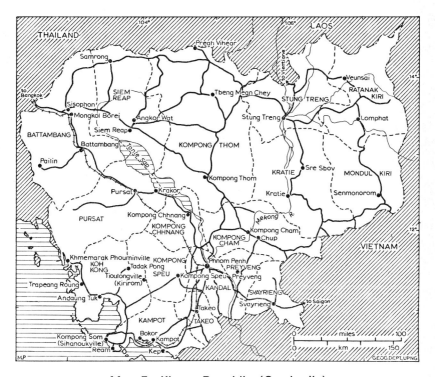

Map 5. Khmer Republic (Cambodia)

the French who were about to interfere in any case on the familiar pretext of taking over Vietnam's rights of suzerainty in the area. In due course Cambodia accepted France's protection and this time the new king, Norodom, received his crown from the French. The provinces which she had earlier lost to the Siamese were not, however, recovered until forty years later: so it was not until 1907 that Angkor Wat stood once more on Khmer soil.

In Cambodia, as in Laos, the French wrought no great changes. They

ruled through the monarch and indeed attempted to increase his prestige in the land. The country, unlike Laos, was ruled as a unit and there
were no contentious minorities to be dealt with. The French, however,
sowed the seeds of ethnic conflict by importing several thousand Vietnamese to work in the offices and rubber plantations, in much the same
way as the British imported Indians for similar work in Burma and
Malaya. The Vietnamese today form something like five per cent of the
population and are viewed with a good deal of suspicion by the Khmers
who differ from them both ethnically and linguistically.

Until the arrival of the Japanese in 1941 the Cambodian *élite* was
happy to imbibe French culture, receive French education and remain
on good terms with their new suzerains. This relationship was severely
damaged by the arrival of the Japanese. Very soon the leading Cambodians were divided into pro-Japanese, pro-French, and plain nationalists. When, in March 1945, the Japanese deposed the French,
compelled King Sihanouk to declare the independence of Cambodia
and set up an independent government composed of their own nominees, the whole political situation was in a state of flux.

The subsequent departure of the Japanese left, as in Laos, two main
factions: those who welcomed the return of the French and those who
demanded immediate independence. As in Laos, the pro-French faction
was led by the King, but there was one vital difference: Sihanouk, then
in his early twenties, was a young man cast in a much sterner mould
than Sisavang Vong of Laos. He realised that Cambodia badly needed
French administrative and financial assistance but he was at the same
time quite as keen as any of his fellow countrymen that Cambodia
should retain the independence she had received from Japan. He
determined therefore to try to have the best of both worlds. He welcomed the French back, but outflanked the Khmer Issarak (Free
Khmers) by insisting that the French recognised Cambodia's changed
status. This was done on January 7, 1946 when a so-called *modus
vivendi* or agreement was arrived at by which Cambodia was described
as an autonomous kingdom within the French Union.

For the next seven years King Sihanouk fought a running battle on
two fronts: against the French for fuller independence; and for political
power against the Democratic Party, which formed the government
under the constitutional monarchy set up by the 1947 Constitution.
Far too much of an activist to be content with being a Sisavang Vong
or a Savang Vatthana, Sihanouk was determined not to have all his
moves blocked by a succession of quarrelling and indecisive politicians.

His first tactic against the politicians was to dispense with them
altogether or at most only to deal with his own nominees. For two
years from September 1949 to September 1951 he did without the
National Assembly, which he dissolved, and ruled through a nominated
cabinet. A new National Assembly was elected in September 1951, but
again the Democratic Party won a majority of the seats and resumed

its old blocking tactics. In June 1952 Sihanouk assumed dictatorial powers and in January 1953 the Assembly was again dissolved.

For the next two years Sihanouk's main aim was to gain complete independence from the French, who by virtue of their presence in all the key administrative, military, financial and policy making sectors still controlled the country's affairs.

So successful was the King in his mission—he called it his Crusade for Independence*—that his country was effectively and not just nominally independent by early 1954. An important consequence of this was that, unlike Laos, Cambodia could afford to take a very firm line with the Viet Minh at the Geneva Conference in mid-1954 and was thus spared the appalling problems of being saddled with a Khmer version of Pathet Lao. Sihanouk, unlike his Laotian counterpart, was in a position to tell both the Viet Minh *and* the French troops to leave his country.

Sihanouk had asked his people to give him three years in which to achieve political independence and internal security. In early 1955 he held a referendum in which he won overwhelming popular approval for his actions since June 1952. He now set about consolidating his political power. He at once encountered problems but solved them with his customary flair.

Sangkum

Sihanouk's first problem was a constitutional one. The Cambodian delegates at the Geneva Conference had promised that there should be free elections at the earliest opportunity. Sihanouk however had no intention of allowing affairs to return to the 1952 situation with the Democratic Party once again impeding progress. Since neither his political opponents nor the International Commission would allow him to assume dictatorial powers and since as a constitutional monarch he was relatively powerless, he made a surprising but wholly logical move. He stepped down from the throne and became a private citizen. He made his father King and then set about defeating his opponents on the electoral battle-field.

Having resigned, Sihanouk founded his own political party which he called the Sangkum Reast Niyum (Popular Socialist Community) or Sangkum. A few months later, on September 11, 1955, elections were held and Sangkum won all the 91 seats in the new National Assembly and polled eighty-three per cent of the popular vote. There were three further elections in 1958, 1962 and 1966 and on each of these occasions the Sangkum again swept the board. What was the secret of the party's success? To begin with, Sangkum was no ordinary political party; it was more a movement, a rally, a *rassemblement*. It was not just *a* party, it was

---

* The official account is given in "L'action de S.M. Norodom Sihanouk pour l'indépendence du Cambodge 1941-1955".[3]

the party—the only party to which anybody could belong without feeling
that he was indulging in un-Cambodian activities, so to speak.* Second,
Sangkum had no ordinary leader. To many of the sophisticated peasants
who supported his party Sihanouk still had the supernatural aura of
the *deva-raj* about him. The peasant's feeling of awe about the monarchy may not have been shared by the sophisticated French-educated
élite in Phnom Penh but these men, too, realised that it paid to be a
supporter of Sangkum.

Sihanouk held many valuable assets. By Southeast Asian leadership
standards he was young: born in 1922, he was twenty-one years younger
than Sukarno, thirty-one years younger than Ho Chi Minh, and about
16 years the junior of his neighbour Prince Souvanna Phouma. He
thus appeared to have many years of active political life ahead of him.
His trump card, of course, was that he was "the Prince who had been
the King". As ex-King he had tremendous prestige with all ranks of
the Cambodian electorate. As head also of Sangkum he was the fount
of all political honour and could make and unmake cabinet ministers
and civil servants alike. He had, furthermore, a firm grip on most of
the media of communication in Cambodia—the Press, the broadcast-
ing, and even the cinema. He was an extremely versatile man: a writer,
an orator, a film-maker, a musician, a diplomatist, and above all an
astute politician who knew how to put all his considerable talents to
their best use.

The National Congress

Sangkum was not the Prince's only political creation. There was also
the National Congress. The National Congress was designed to be a
forum held twice a year at which the electorate could meet their rulers
and hold a dialogue with them. "It is not sufficient" said Sihanouk,
"that the ministers and deputies meet with the people once every four
years when they are up for re-election. They should meet here to render
an account of their activities every six months, to answer the questions
of the people, to listen to their advice, to explain their actions."

The National Congress became quite an important political institution in Cambodia. It was a six-monthly rally for which an official holiday was given and which was attended by peasants, Sangkum members
and even members of opposition parties. It was an occasion at which the
people was given a chance to listen to and applaud the President of
Sangkum while the latter—Sihanouk—demonstrated to friend and foe
alike the strength of his popular support *outside* the National Assembly.
Resolutions—in many cases sponsored by Sihanouk himself—passed
by the Congress were handed down to the Assembly for conversion
into law. The Assembly was not, in fact, bound to do any more than

---

* The adjective "un-Sangkumian" was in fact coined for just this purpose.

"take notice" of these resolutions, but in practice found it expedient to follow the leader.

The picture that Prince Sihanouk liked to project to the world was that of a strong, independent and neutralist Cambodia united behind her "Comrade Prince", conscious of her ethnic unity and glorious Khmer past. The reality was somewhat different. Undoubtedly, Sihanouk was by far the most important political figure in Cambodia, and the people genuinely revered him not only for his god-like attributes but for his successful "crusade for independence" against France. They applauded his neutralist stand and even the way he dared to spurn American aid—although they may have regretted the economic consequences of this particular action. But among the *élite* all was not well. There was a growing number of leading politicians and soldiers who disapproved both of the Prince's policies and of his attempts to monopolise the political stage.

The Growth of Opposition

Until 1966 Sihanouk had kept the National Assembly well under control by ensuring that only one person was nominated to represent the Sangkum in each constituency. As his nominees were almost certain to be elected, the Prince could thus virtually hand-pick the Assembly.

In 1966 the Prince made his first concession to the critics. He allowed his monopoly to be broken by letting more than one member of the Sangkum stand as candidate in a constituency. To his dismay the Assembly which emerged from the elections was much too conservative for the taste of the Prince, who believed that left-wing opinion should be given a fair, if well-controlled hearing. Alarmed by this imbalance, the Prince decided to give dissenters a voice by forming a *contre-gouvernement* with a "shadow-cabinet" the main function of which was to criticise the men in office. The *contre-gouvernement* was given a fine house and offices in Phnom Penh and published a news-sheet in the columns of which bureaucrats were accused of bumbledom, sharp practice and even fraudulent behaviour; politicians were assailed and there were also attacks on the business ethics and standards of performance of Chinese and Vietnamese manufacturers and merchants— presumably as a counter to adverse criticism by right-wingers on the conduct of state enterprises. On the whole the experiment of the *contre-gouvernement* was not a great success. The official government was angered by what it regarded as an attempt to undermine its authority and considerable dissension arose. In the end Sihanouk dismissed the government and for a while resumed his personal rule. From this time onwards there was a gradual polarisation of the political forces of Cambodia. The two main issues on which sides were taken were the Vietnam war and economic policy.

For years the pivot of Sihanouk's foreign policy had been neutralism which he had practised with great skill and considerable consistency. His main object was to keep Cambodia intact territorially and to avoid becoming involved in the Vietnam war. At Geneva in 1954 he had managed to avoid the fate of Laos by getting the Viet Minh forces expelled from Cambodia before they could set up a "Pathet Khmer". Ever since Geneva there had been subversive activity in the border provinces but the problem did not become really serious until the stepping-up of the Vietnam war during and after 1965. Sihanouk now found himself in a dilemma. His reason told him that the Americans would one day tire of fighting *la sale guerre* just as the French had done before them; after the departure of the Americans, South Vietnam would inevitably fall under the domination of the Hanoi Communists who would then wish to complete the operation by bringing Laos and Cambodia under their rule. To the Communisation and unification of Vietnam Sihanouk had no particular objections but nobody with his sense of Khmer history could possibly have looked favourably upon the prospect of Cambodia's being ruled by her ancient enemies. It was precisely at this point that the dilemma arose. His experience in Geneva told the Prince that the best way of avoiding Vietnamese rule was to ensure that there were as few enemy troops as possible in the country when the cease-fire was sounded and no provinces which the Vietnamese or their allies could possibly claim to have "liberated". Unfortunately it was quite clear that the Cambodian army, then about thirty thousand strong, was not equal to the task of dealing effectively with any really determined Vietnamese attacks. It was equally clear that the Americans, with whom Cambodia now had no diplomatic relations, were the only people who were willing to dispense large-scale military aid for use against the intrusive NLF and North Vietnamese forces. Yet if Sihanouk resumed diplomatic relations with the United States and accepted massive military aid there was no doubt in his mind that he would have to hand over the government to the rightists, led by Lon Nol and Sirik Matak, with the result that Cambodia would inevitably become part of the battle-field of the Vietnam war. She would lose her status as a neutralist and, after the war's end, would become part of a Communist Indo-China. To avoid this fate the Prince deliberately turned a blind eye to the activities of the North Vietnamese, the NLF, the Americans and the South Vietnamese within Cambodia's borders. For a while the compromise worked. In 1967, however, Vietnamese activities increased so greatly that they could no longer be overlooked and the Cambodian army leaders began to press for action.

Pressure, of a different kind but mainly from the same quarters, was brought to bear on the Prince to change his economic policy. The 1960s saw a great expansion in the activities of state-run and "mixed" enterprises. In 1960 the Republic of China gave Cambodia a large grant with which to establish state enterprises of various kinds. There were textile factories in Kompong Chom and Battambang, a paper mill in Chhlong, a cement factory in Chakrey Ting and a glass factory in Stung Meanchey. There was also a petrol refinery in Kompong Som, a large distillery, a tyre factory, a fertiliser plant and various other enterprises financed by donations from countries like Yugoslavia, Czechoslovakia, France and other friendly powers with whom Sihanouk wished to remain on good terms. Unfortunately, the management of these state enterprises was inefficient and corrupt and their contribution to the economy was not great. Nor was this the only weak sector of the economy; production everywhere dwindled—both of goods and foodstuffs. Rice had to be imported and the reserves of foreign exchange were drained away.

On July 31, 1969 the twenty-seventh meeting of the National Congress of the Sangkum was held in Phnom Penh. In his opening speech Prince Sihanouk drew attention to Cambodia's economic plight. He announced that a special congress of the chief political institutions of the country would be called to discuss the formation of a new government charged with salvaging the nation's economy. From Sihanouk's point of view the most ominous feature of the National Congress was the widespread criticism of the state enterprises; in particular Sonaprim (the State Import Distribution Company), SKD (the State Distillery) and Sonexperior (the State Gemstone Export Company) came under heavy fire.

On August 4, 1969 a special congress of both houses of parliament, the Youth Assembly, representatives of the Press and the *contre-gouvernement* met to choose a new government. In the ensuing ballot General Lon Nol received the most votes, closely followed by Prince Sirik Matak. On August 14 the new Prime Minister, Lon Nol, presented his programme to the National Assembly. He made it quite clear that Sihanouk's economic policy was going to be abandoned. He proposed to reform certain sectors of the economy by liberalising them "in the over-riding interests of the country and the people".[4] There would be no further nationalisation and the existing state enterprises would be examined to see how they could be made more profitable. Foreign investments would be encouraged.

To this swing to the right in economic policy was added a political swing in the same direction, with the re-establishment of diplomatic relations with the USA. This was the second indication that the Prince's influence was on the wane. It was he who had broken off relations with the USA when he had called for an end to American aid, and many felt that Cambodia's present economic troubles were in no small measure due to the Prince's action on that occasion. There was now a general expectation that American aid would be resumed.

The third set-back for the Prince was the increase in both insurgent and Viet Cong activity in the country; the one weakened the authority of the central government and the other gave Sihanouk's opponents the opportunity to accuse the Prince of tacitly aiding and abetting the Vietnamese, the traditional enemies of the Khmers.*

For some time now Hanoi had been using the border areas of Cambodia as a supply route for their allies in the south, and the Viet Cong had been using other areas for recuperation and regrouping. Sihanouk's policy was one of live and let live. From time to time he protested against violations of the border by Americans and Vietnamese, but he was not anxious to press the matter too far. He calculated that none of the parties concerned wished to invade and occupy the whole of Cambodia; they merely wished to use part of it for their own limited purposes. In these circumstances it seemed wiser to tolerate a partial infringement of Cambodia's sovereignty than to risk Cambodia's becoming the cockpit of an extension of the war. In addition Prince Sihanouk anticipated that the day would come when the National Liberation Front would be playing a leading role in the government of South Vietnam and he had no wish to antagonise them unnecessarily now.

Troublesome as these border incidents were they were perhaps not such a threat to the internal unity of the nation as the growth of banditry, insurgency and inter-ethnic strife in several of Cambodia's provinces.

The tendency for the provinces to seek to acquire autonomy was nothing new; it was a product of the geography of Cambodia as much as of the historical tradition that provincial governors should be "eaters of provinces" in the Burmese style. Such an attitude was certainly adopted by Dap Chuon, a former leader of the Khmer Issarak, who, until his death at the end of the 1950s, was an extremely independent governor of Siem Reap with his own private army. Such provincial independence and *de facto* decentralisation had been accepted by Phnom Penh in the past and had posed no great threat to the state, but from 1967 the situation started to get out of control.

In 1967 the Khmer Serai (Free Khmers) became very active in the province of Battambang. The Khmer Serai was a group formed in 1959 in opposition to Sihanouk; it was alleged to receive support from Thailand, South Vietnam and the American Central Agency (CIA). Son Ngoc Thanh, its leader, had been appointed Cambodia's first Foreign Minister by the Japanese when the latter gave the country its independence. Shortly after his appointment Thanh staged a *coup*, imprisoned many of his colleagues and made himself Prime Minister, thereby antagonising many of the royal family, who resented this challenge to their authority. The returning allies removed Thanh from office and eventually deported him to France. When he returned to

---

* By 1970 many people, including Sirik Matak, were convinced that the Prince and his wife Monique were receiving money from the Viet Cong; this slur on the Prince's integrity undoubtedly contributed to his downfall.

Cambodia he promised to refrain from taking part in politics, but soon broke his word. Although driven into hiding to escape the police, he still managed to build up quite a strong challenge to Sihanouk in the 1955 elections. When the Sangkum won its overwhelming electoral victory Thanh set about creating a republican national liberation force which was initially largely composed of former members of the Khmer Issarak. About 1959 this movement became known as Khmer Serai and continued to receive support from various foreign powers. Its alleged connection with the CIA and its ceaseless anti-Sihanouk propaganda were partly responsible for the breach in diplomatic relations between Cambodia and the USA in 1963. The renewed activity of the Khmer Serai in 1967 caused General Lon Nol to take stern measures against them. At the same time he sought out and attacked Khmer Communist groups which were operating in the area and were said to be supporting the Khmer Serai, or at least taking advantage of the general disorder to pursue their own subversive ends. General Lon Nol's vigorous action earned him the enmity of the left-wing politicians, who subsequently had the satisfaction of seeing him removed from the Prime Minister-ship and replaced by someone more pliant.

The troubles in Battambang were followed in 1968 by reports of widespread attacks by Khmer Loeu tribesmen on Khmers in the province of Ratanak Kiri on the borders of Laos. Ratanak Kiri and Mondul Kiri were two new provinces which had been in existence for about a decade. They were the responsibility of the Army, which had the task of developing them economically and trying to bring the Khmer Loeu into the wider community. The highlanders evidently resented "Khmerisation" and their hostility eventually turned into armed resistance. By the end of 1968 similar troubles were reported from Mondul Kiri; in both cases the rebels were said to be receiving assistance and encouragement from North Vietnamese operating in the area.

The *Coup* of March 1970

The changed economic policy, the resumption of diplomatic relations with the USA, the increased Communist and insurgent activity: all these factors made for a polarisation in Cambodian politics which left the neutralist Sihanouk in an ambiguous and isolated position. In March 1970 anti-Communist demonstrations, sometimes violent, were held in Svay Rieng and, three days later, in Phnom Penh where the building housing the mission of the Provisional Revolutionary Govern-ment of the Republic of South Vietnam was attacked and badly damaged. At this juncture a series of telegrams was despatched to Prince Sihanouk, then in France, telling him of the situation and pre-sumably asking him to make a public statement denouncing the Viet Cong. The Prince however refused to listen and threatened to "act with the greatest severity in dealing with those deputies, members of the Government and the military, who were revealed as opposed to his policy vis-a-vis the Viet Cong and North Vietnamese".[4] Shortly after this reply had been received the National Assembly and the Council of the Kingdom held a joint meeting and decided to withdraw their confidence in Prince Sihanouk as Head of State. A new government was formed with General Lon Nol as Prime Minister, Sirik Matak as Deputy Prime Minister and Cheng Heng, the President of the National Assembly, as acting Head of State.

Prince Sihanouk now flew by way of Moscow to Peking where he called on all loyal Khmers to oppose the new regime.

Sihanouk's deposition was the signal for the South Vietnamese and their American allies to seek and to obtain permission to cross the border into Cambodia, in order to pursue and destroy Viet Cong strongholds and supply depots and strategic headquarters in Svay Rieng province and areas adjacent to it. In the course of the fighting which ensued untold damage was done to Cambodia's already fragile economy. Many of the great French-owned rubber plantations—including the famous one at Chup*—were burned down or defoliated, and the processing plants utterly destroyed. The loss of foreign exchange resulting from the drastic fall in rubber exports, the sudden cutting off of rice shipments to China, North Vietnam and the NLF, coupled with the meteoric rise in defence expenditure meant that Cambodia now became entirely dependent on foreign, mainly American, aid. Cambodia's fragile neutrality was at an end and most of Prince Sihanouk's worst forebodings were now a reality. The final blow fell on April 23, 1971 when the Prince's lifelong adversary, Son Ngoc Thanh, now politically rehabilitated, was named as one of three deputy premiers when Lon Nol became ill and could not sustain the full burden of leadership.

The Political Process

On October 9, 1970 the National Assembly and the Council of the Kingdom voted unanimously to declare Cambodia a republic, thus bringing to an end the oldest monarchy in Southeast Asia. The change from constitutional monarchy to republic was not, in fact, as radical a constitutional change as it appeared. The Monarchy as an effective institution suffered its first setback in 1955 when Sihanouk resigned from the throne to take part in the wider political arena as a "Comrade Prince". True, there was still a King—Sihanouk's father Suramarit— but Sihanouk constantly reminded his audience that he was the "Prince who had been the King" and the Monarchy thereby lost a good deal of its legitimacy. "There cannot" as the Chinese say, "be two Suns in the sky".

The next blow to the Monarchy came on April 3, 1960 when King

---

* 18,000 hectares (44,450 acres).

Norodom Suramarit died. Sihanouk himself came under considerable pressure from the Royal Council to resume the throne but he had no intention of complying with the wishes of the other members of the Royal Family. Eventually the dilemma was solved by adding a new Article (122) to the Constitution which read "Where circumstances do not permit either the appointment of a new sovereign nor of the Council of Regency . . . the two chambers . . . may . . . confer the powers and prerogatives of Head of State on a person expressly and incontestably appointed by the vote of the nation." Shortly afterwards Sihanouk became the first Head of State to be appointed in this fashion. Although it may not have seemed so at the time, Article 122 was clearly a double-edged weapon: what the two chambers and the people could make they could also presumably unmake.

In theory the King or Head of State plays an important part in the political process. In the legislative field the Head of State can initiate legislation and has the right to demand a reconsideration of a Bill even if it has already passed through both chambers. In the executive field the Head of State, after consultation, appoints the President of the Council (Prime Minister) and also acts as chairman of the Council of Ministers when it meets in plenary session. He may also dissolve the Assembly if asked to do so by the Council of Ministers (Cabinet).

The Legislature is bi-cameral and consists of a popularly-elected National Assembly and a partly appointed Council of the Kingdom.

Assemblymen are elected by direct universal suffrage and must be Cambodian citizens of at least twenty years of age but not serving members of the armed forces or monks.

Article 65 states that "the National Assembly alone shall pass the laws. It may not delegate this right." In this sentence "pass" is the key word because both the Head of State and the Council of the Kingdom have considerable powers to propose, delay and amend legislation.

The Council of the Kingdom used to consist of two members of the Royal Family, two members elected by the Assembly from outside its ranks, ten members elected on a restricted franchise to represent the administrative regions, ten elected members to represent the professions and four elected members to represent the bureaucracy. When Cambodia became a Republic and royal titles were dropped the reference in Article 75 to the two members to be appointed from the Royal Family became due for amendment but otherwise the composition of the Council remained unchanged. The Council's duties are to examine all Bills submitted to it by the National Assembly and to consider "all questions submitted to it by the government". Amendments proposed by the Council to Bills must be wholly accepted or rejected by the Assembly but not further amended. The Council may also delay the passage of legislation but not block it altogether.

During Sihanouk's regime the most distinctive feature of the constitution was the National Congress. This body, which was scheduled to meet at least twice a year, was designed to "give the people the opportunity to become directly acquainted with affairs of national interest".* In Sihanouk's hands meetings of the Congress, of which he was soon elected President, became festive occasions when a national holiday was declared and suitable peasants were given a free outing to Phnom Penh to have a welcome break from their work and to be given a chance to applaud their President. At the same time they could hear Sihanouk's opponents, both within and without the government and Assembly, ridiculed. The National Congress proposed and passed numerous resolutions of which the National Assembly had to take serious note.

After an initial burst of enthusiasm, interest in the Congress slowly waned and meetings became less regular and less well attended as Sihanouk's popularity and grip of public affairs weakened.

On March 18, 1970 the National Assembly and the Council of the Kingdom, the very bodies which had conferred the powers of Head of State on Sihanouk, agreed unanimously to withdraw confidence in the Prince. Pending further elections Cheng Heng, President of the National Assembly, took over the functions of Head of State. From that moment the locus of power shifted from the Palace to the Council of Ministers and in particular to its President and Vice-President, respectively General Lon Nol and General—formerly Prince—Sirik Matak.

The President of the Council of Ministers is normally the leader of the majority party in the Assembly and is appointed to his position by the Head of State. Once appointed the President then selects his Ministers who may be, but need not be, members of the Assembly. After nomination every President must present his Ministerial team and his political programme to the Assembly for approval.

In Sihanouk's time it was possible to write the "really important affairs of state are rarely discussed in the cabinet". Today, although important affairs may not be discussed by the cabinet as a whole, the most important decisions are taken by cabinet ministers. The advent of the Republic has thus transferred power from the Monarch or Head of State to men who are, in theory at any rate, subject to democratic control by elected representatives of the people. This is a process which Sihanouk and his government-in-exile will find difficult to reverse.

References

1. D. G. E. HALL, *History of South-East Asia*, Macmillan, London, 1966. 2nd Edition, p. 125.
2. G. COEDES, *The Making of South-east Asia*, Routledge and Kegan Paul, London, 1966, pp. 199-200.

* Article 92.

3. "L'action de S. M. Norodom Sihanouk pour l'indépendence du Cambodge 1941-1955", Ministry of Information, Phnom Penh, 1959.
4. "Etudes Cambodgiennes No. 19", July-September 1969. Ministry of Information, Phnom Penh.
5. *Asian Almanac*, 1970, p. 4006.

CHAPTER SEVEN

Vietnam

Historical Background

A Country Divided

The key to the understanding of the situation in Vietnam today is a knowledge of her past history.

Vietnam today is divided, torn by political strife and civil war. The North is pitted against the South; elements in the South are fighting each other while the Great Powers aid and abet their respective protégés.

A person listening to talk about the re-unification of Vietnam might pardonably suppose that unity was the natural state of affairs in that country. This is very far from being the case. In fact it has only been the case for about thirty years in the last five hundred.

In the days of French colonial rule Vietnam was divided into three parts: Tonkin in the north, with Hanoi as its capital; Annam in the middle, with its capital at Hue; and in the south, Cochin-China administered from Saigon. Hanoi also served as the administrative capital of the whole of French Indo-China which beside the three Vietnamese territories included Laos and Cambodia.

The heartland of Vietnam at the beginning of the Christian era was in the area we have called Tonkin. From 111 B.C. to about 939 A.D. Tonkin was under Chinese rule. That is, it was administered by Chinese who may or may not have used the local native notabilities as subordinates.

It was apparently during this long period of Chinese rule that the Vietnamese began to acquire a separate identity and a feeling of nationhood. Although their whole culture and language became very closely akin to China's they never became wholly Chinese, mainly because their territory was so very much a fringe province of the Chinese Empire.

The Vietnamese acquired their independence from China in the tenth century, and were never again under direct Chinese rule except for a brief interlude between 1408 and 1427.

The Vietnamese acquired their independence from the Chinese more by default on the part of China than by any gigantic military effort of their own. It is commonly believed that after 939 A.D. the Vietnamese frequently repelled massive attacks by Chinese armies. There is a good deal of truth in this but it seems that the Chinese, in making these military interventions, were not attempting to re-impose their rule: they were mainly interested in re-establishing a deposed ruler who was entitled to his overlord's protection, for Chinese Emperors were the suzerains of Vietnamese princes and the latter continued to send tribute to China until 1877 A.D. These military interventions frequently failed in their purpose but the Chinese were realists and usually gave the successful usurper official recognition after a decent interval had elapsed.

Nam Tien—The Drive to the South

It was in the fifteenth century that the Vietnamese began their remarkable *Nam Tien* or "Drive to the South".*

When the Nam Tien started, the areas which we have described as Tonkin, Annam and Cochin-China were, very approximately, occupied by the kingdoms of Nam Viet, Champa and Funan respectively.

By the end of the fifteenth century the Vietnamese had taken the Champa capital, Vijaya (Binh Dinh) and penetrated into those very provinces of Laos, namely Sam Neua and Phong Saly, where today the Vietnamese-sponsored Pathet Lao forces are most active.

In 1650 the Khmers, who were the heirs of Funan, lost control of the Mekong delta and were forced back into present day Cambodia. They were then compelled to acknowledge the Vietnamese Emperor as their suzerain.

Although by this time Vietnamese had, so to speak, completed their "drive to the south" the land was not united under one ruler. The Emperor whom the Khmers recognised as suzerain was not the ruler of all Vietnam, but only of that part which lay south of the Song Gianh river. For the Nguyens ruled in the south with their capital at Hue and the Trinh dynasty ruled in the North.

There was a brief interlude when three brothers from Tay Son, whose surname was Ho, changed their name to Nguyen, seized power and divided the whole of Vietnam between them. Their co-operation was short-lived and the youngest brother had succeeded in taking over two parts of the kingdom when he was in turn ousted by Nguyen Anh who was the legitimate Nguyen heir. The latter, after years of fighting

---

* See p. 21.

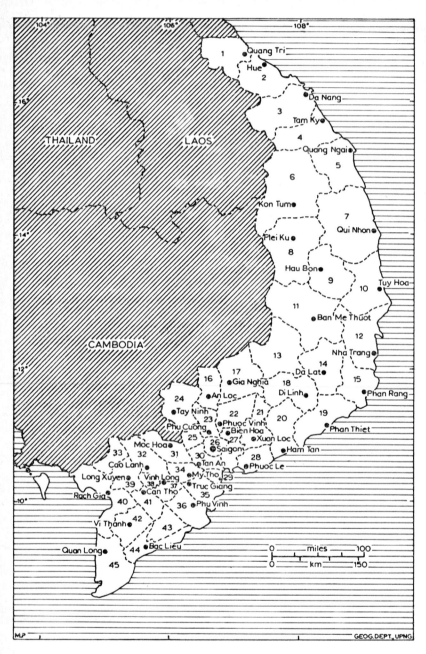

Map 6. South Vietnam

and frequent set-backs, eventually conquered the country—this time from south to north—and became the Emperor of all Vietnam under the name of Gia Long.

The Country United

Gia Long ruling from his capital at Hue celebrated his accession by getting his subjects to carry out a number of extensive public works projects. The most famous of these was the Mandarin Road, in some places more a path than a road, which ran nearly the whole length of the country from Hanoi to Saigon, a visible symbol of Vietnam's newly-found unity.

Gia Long, who had been helped by Frenchmen to win back his throne, was on the whole friendly towards Europeans and western ideas. It is possible that if his successors had pursued the same policy Vietnam might have escaped being colonised or at least been colonised much later. However, Gia Long's son and successor, Minh-Mang, who reigned from 1820 to 1841 attempted to put the clock back.

Minh-Mang and his two successors Thieu-Tri (1841-1848) and Tu-Duc (1848-1883) were all strict Confucians, very Chinese in their outlook and determined to keep their country free of contamination from barbarous western influences.

Internally they organised the country on Chinese bureaucratic lines. Vietnam was divided into three main parts roughly corresponding to the Tonkin, Annam and Cochin-China as previously described. These three areas were the subdivided into provinces, divisions, districts, subdistricts and villages. Government was by officials right down to subdistrict level: the villages chose their own officials.

The Vietnamese Emperors' hostility to western ideas drove them to persecute Christian missionaries. This led to their downfall.

At first the French, aided in the early stages by the Spanish, mounted a series of expeditions designed to procure the release of imprisoned

---

Key to Map 6: Provinces in South Vietnam

1. Quang Tri	13. Quang Duc	25. Hau Nghia	37. Vinh Long
2. Thua Thien	14. Tuyen Duc	26. Gia Dinh	38. Sa Dec
3. Quang Nam	15. Ninh Thuan	27. Bien Hoa	39. An Giang
4. Quang Tin	16. Binh Long	28. Phuoc Tuy	40. Kien Giang
5. Quang Ngai	17. Phuoc Long	29. Go Cong	41. Phong Dinh
5. Kontum	18. Lam Dong	30. Long An	42. Chuong Thien
7. Binh Dinh	19. Binh Thuan	31. Kien Tuong	43. Bac Lieu
8. Pleiku	20. Binh Tuy	32. Kien Phong	44. Ba Xuyen
9. Phu Bon	21. Long Khanh	33. Chau Doc	45. An Xuyen
10. Phu Yen	22. Phuoc Thanh	34. Dinh Tuong	
11. Darlac	23. Binh Duong	35. Kien Hoa	
12. Khanh Hoa	24. Tay Ninh	36. Vinh Binh	

missionaries. Later, as the anti-Christian pressure mounted, the French began a long campaign of forceful annexation, which resulted in the whole of Vietnam's coming under their rule in 1883. Four years later Vietnam became, with Laos and Cambodia, part of the Indo-Chinese Union.

French Colonial Rule

The impact of the French administration varied in its intensity. Cochin-China was ruled directly by the French: Tonkin partially so: Annam even less so. The result was that in Cochin-China, which is today the heartland of South Vietnam, the native inhabitants had very little chance to acquire administrative skills and it is no coincidence that the most energetic men in South Vietnamese politics and government today, come, on the whole, from Annam and Tonkin.

Throughout their period of rule the French met with opposition which they suppressed with speed and severity. The early nationalist movements were concerned to restore the power of the Emperors and were led by mandarins who had themselves also lost power and prestige. The later and more important movements were of a more revolutionary character.

The VNQDD (Viet Nam Quoc Dan Dang) was the Vietnamese version of the Chinese Kuo Min Tang (or KMT) and was concerned to overthrow the French regime and then to set up a republic in its place. This organisation was formed in 1927 but was crushed a bare three years later by the French after an incident in Yenbay, where a military garrison mutinied and murdered its French officers.

The suppression of the VNQDD came in 1930, and in the same year the Vietnamese Communist Party was formed by Ho Chi Minh, who was then working for the South Seas Bureau of the Russian-led Communist International or "Comintern". In 1931 the title of the party was changed to the Indo-Chinese Communist Party (ICP) so that its operations could be extended into Laos and Cambodia. It is interesting to note that the modern descendant of the ICP is called the Dang Lao Dong Viet Nam (usually shortened to "Lao Dong") which means "Vietnamese Workers Party"; the reference to Indo-China has been dropped in order to avoid giving offence to the Communists in Laos and Cambodia, who would not like it to be thought that their parties were run by Vietnamese, though there is strong evidence that members of the Lao Dong do, in fact, direct these parties.

It was the intention of Ho Chi Minh at this time, as always, to promote a genuine, and not necessarily Communist, nationalist movement in order eventually to bring it under Communist control. For this purpose he was quite ready to betray non-communist nationalists to the French secret police. A number of Vietnamese who refused to join a Communist organisation, such as the Association of Vietnamese Revolutionary Youth the forerunner of the Indo-Chinese Communist

Party, were in fact imprisoned or executed by the French as a result of information given to the police by Ho's agents.

Ho Chi Minh's big chance came after the almost bloodless French surrender to the Japanese in July 1941. Two months earlier Ho had formed a broad nationalist movement called the Viet Nam Doc Lap Minh Hoi ("Viet Nam Independence League") or Viet Minh for short which contained hardened Communists like Vo Nguyen Giap (later the Commander of the North Vietnamese Army) and Pham Van Dong (the present Prime Minister of North Vietnam) in key positions.

The Viet Minh, like so many other communist infiltrated movements in other parts of Southeast Asia at the time (in Burma, Malaya, Indonesia and the Philippines), served as the focus of both nationalists and anti-Japanese "resistance" fighters. As such the American and British military commanders aided and abetted the work of such organisations because they were generally the best source of information about Japanese troop movements and other vital intelligence data. The strong suspicion, however, remains that the leaders of, for instance, the Viet Minh and the Malay Anti-Japanese Peoples League were gratefully accepting arms and ammunition for eventual use against the returning colonial power rather than immediate use against the Japanese.

On March 9, 1945 the Japanese who had so far ruled through the existing French administration, ousted the French. On the following day they announced that Indo-China was now liberated from colonial rule. On March 11, Bao Dai, the last of the Nguyen Emperors declared the independence of Annam and Tonkin. In the days that followed the Kings of Cambodia and Laos followed suit.

The fact that the Japanese refused to give Cochin-China independence underlined the essential weakness of their puppet Bao Dai's position. Bao Dai as Emperor of Annam could command a certain amount of allegiance in the area of Hue but much of Tonkin was under Viet Minh control and the Japanese were still in command in the south.

On August 6, 1945 the first atomic bomb dropped on Hiroshima. Eight days later the Japanese conceded independence to Cochin-China. On August 26, 1945 Bao Dai ceremoniously handed over the symbols of his kingly authority to an emissary of Ho Chi Minh. A week later Ho Chi Minh declared the independence of all Vietnam.

In Indo-China, as the name implies, Hindu ideas of kingship and the Chinese concept of the "mandate of heaven" meet together and reinforce each other. There is no doubt therefore that Vietnamese who witnessed or subsequently heard about Bao Dai's ceremonious and voluntary abdication would immediately be sure that authority and divine favour has passed from him to the Viet Minh in general and Ho Chi Minh in particular. This goes far towards explaining why subsequent French attempts to regain Bao Dai's authority for him met with such little success.

The impression is sometimes given in accounts of post-1945 Vietnamese history that Vietnam was in fact united behind Ho Chi Minh and that this unity was forcibly shattered by the French. This is not true. The fact is that although the Viet Minh was the only movement which at any time looked likely to unite Vietnam, its leader was unable to achieve this unity in spite of being—until 1949—as supple and accommodating in his diplomacy as he possibly could be.

Ho Chi Minh was never able to consolidate his position in Cochin-China. Here he had not only to contend with the greatest concentration of French administration and culture but also other vigorous local opposition in the form of the so-called United Front of Cao Dai, Hoa Hao and Trotskyites. The latter were supported by the Japanese and later the French but it would be idle to pretend that the Vietnamese nationalist movement was ever as solidly behind Ho Chi Minh as, say, its Indonesian counterpart was behind Sukarno and Hatta. There was always a split in the South between the Viet Minh and the various elements of the United Front, with the Binh Xuyen and supporters of France thrown in for good measure.

For three weeks Ho Chi Minh stood at the head of a hastily "united" Vietnam but on September 23, 1945 the French took over the government offices in Saigon. A month later General Leclerc began the reconquest of Vietnam.

While the French were reasserting themselves in the South, Ho Chi Minh tried his utmost to consolidate his base in the North.

On March 6, 1946 an agreement was reached between Ho Chi Minh and Jean Sainteny, the French Commissioner in North Indo-China. By this agreement the French recognised the Democratic Republic of Vietnam as a free state within the French Union (the French equivalent of the (British) Commonwealth); there was to be a referendum to decide whether Tonkin, Annam and Cochin-China should be united, and full independence would come in 1952, by which time the last French soldier would have left Vietnam. Ho Chi Minh made generous concessions, in for instance allowing French troops to relieve the Chinese but the good work was all undone in subsequent conferences held in France and Vietnam. The situation was not made any easier by men like Admiral d'Argenlieu the French High Commissioner who said he was amazed that "with such a fine expeditionary force there were those who preferred to negotiate rather than fight".[1]

On November 23, 1946 after an incident in the port of Haiphong the French bombarded the Vietnamese quarter and reportedly killed 6,000. The first phase of the Vietnamese War had started.

The French needed a base for their operations and this they made in Cochin-China where already on June 1, 1946 a "free Republic" had been set up with a President and a Vice-President who, though ethnic Vietnamese, were both French citizens.

Over the next two years it became increasingly obvious that a military solution would not be forthcoming and that some kind of political arrangement must be made. There were divisions and dissensions in the North and a succession of feeble and unrepresentative governments in the South. Eventually all parties started looking towards Bao Dai, who was visited (in Hong Kong) by the Viet Minh, the French and the United Front.

Bao Dai was in an impossible position. It seems that he was himself slightly in favour of backing Ho Chi Minh, to whom he had after all transferred his authority, but his close advisers including Ngo Dinh Diem, would not allow him to take this course. He also realised that if he agreed to be the head of a truly national government he could not settle for anything less than the Viet Minh was now offering the nation. This made it very difficult for him to come to any agreement with the French. Another grave handicap was that although there were many honest patriots who were not willing to support the Viet Minh very few of them were willing actively to serve an alternative regime in an official capacity. The main cause of this reluctance was the fact that the French continued to occupy all the key posts in administration and the economy, not to mention Norodom Palace, the traditional seat of Government in Saigon. In such circumstances all Vietnamese ministers and government officials were bound to look like puppets of the French and collaborators with the colonial enemy. This is very much the situation today with Americans replacing the French. It may not be a fair comment on American intentions but such considerations do not weigh heavily with men like Ho Chi Minh.

In the event Bao Dai did not become head of the State of Vietnam until June 14, 1949 by which time the Communists under Mao Tse Tung were well on the way to victory over Chiang Kai Shek in China and the Viet Minh was becoming more and more a purely Communist movement.

By February 1950 China and Russia had recognised the Democratic Republic of Vietnam headed by Ho Chi Minh; while the British and Americans had recognised Bao Dai's State of Vietnam.

Any kind of agreement such as Sainteny had reached in 1946 between the French and the Viet Minh was now no longer a possibility.

Vietnam was now part of the "Cold War" between East and West. Bao Dai was already being represented as an *American* (not French) puppet. The Chinese were now supplying arms to the Viet Minh in fairly large quantities and more and more posts in the Viet Minh's higher ranks were being taken over by Communist Party members.

The Bao Dai area was hopelessly divided. There was no strong central control: instead there were zones controlled respectively by the Cao Dai, Hoa Hao, Binh Xuyen in the South and by the Dai Viet (a nationalist mandarin-led organisation) and the Catholic bishops of Phat Diem and Bui Chu in the North with an area around Dalat containing Bao Dai's personal supporters.

In 1953 two things became clear to many Frenchmen. First, that the war was very costly: up to the end of 1952 it had cost twice as much as France received in Marshall Aid. Second, that the war had become an anti-Communist crusade rather than a fight for the preservation of the French Union: indeed Bao Dai's supporters made it quite clear in September 1953 that *they would not join the Union even if they did win the war*. These two factors were perhaps the most important among those which drove France to the conference table at Geneva. The fall of the great French stronghold of Dien Bien Phu heavily underlined the necessity for a settlement.

The 1954 Geneva Agreements

In the light of what has happened since it is important to understand that the hard core of the Geneva Agreements was a cease fire the most important provisions of which were:

1. Partition of the country into two roughly equal parts at the seventeenth parallel with a demilitarised zone in the middle. The purpose of the partition was to enable the opposing forces to disengage and re-group on their own side of the boundary.
2. The promise of national elections in two years' time in preparation for the eventual reunification of Vietnam.
3. The setting up of an International Control Commission consisting of representatives from India, Canada and Poland whose task would be to ensure that the conditions of the agreement were observed.

This part of the agreement was signed only by the French and the Viet Minh.

There was also a "Final Declaration", not signed by anybody, which amongst other things repeated the hope that free elections would duly be held.

Throughout the conference the Bao Dai delegation protested against the partition of the country and their protests were underlined a year later by Ngo Dinh Diem, Prime Minister of the State of Vietnam, when he said: "We did not sign the Geneva Agreements. We are not bound in any way by these Agreements, signed against the will of the Vietnamese people." It was quite clear by this time that the Democratic Republic of Vietnam, as the Viet Minh was now called, did not expect elections to be held and that the State of Vietnam would not permit them to be held. South and North Vietnam were likely to remain divided at least as long as North and South Korea and East and West Germany and for much the same reasons.

The Rule of Ngo Dinh Diem: 1954-1963

While the agreements were being reached in Geneva in June 1954, Bao Dai appointed Ngo Dinh Diem as his Prime Minister.

A little over a year later Diem became President of the independent Republic of Vietnam as a result of a referendum in which he asked the people to choose between himself and Bao Dai as head of state. In the years that followed Ngo Dinh Diem consolidated his position as virtual dictator of South Vietnam.

Denis Warner calls Ngo Dinh Diem "The Last Confucian"[2] in his excellent book of that name. The title is deliberately paradoxical in that Diem was a fervent, even bigoted, Roman Catholic whose religion coloured many of his actions. Warner's title is nevertheless well chosen because Diem was above all a mandarin of the old Confucian school: upright, incorruptible, scholarly, aloof, expecting obedience and above all convinced of his own superior intellectual and moral worth.

Diem was a man of the North from the Nghe An province of Annam, a poor, over-populated area famous for its revolts and rebellions. Nghe An's other, even more famous son was Nguyen Tat Thanh, who in 1942 took the name of Ho Chi Minh. Diem became a Province Chief at the age of thirty and subsequently served under Bao Dai (Emperor of Annam) in 1932 as Minister of the Interior. He later quarrelled with the Emperor and disappeared from public life. When the Viet Minh killed his elder brother Ngo Dinh Khoi in 1945, Diem became an implacable enemy of the Communists as did his brothers Nhu and Can who had been with Diem in Viet Minh prisons.

Coming from the North it was perhaps inevitable that Diem should lean heavily on northerners and particularly the hundreds of thousands of Roman Catholics who had fled from north of the seventeenth parallel in the period of "regrouping" allowed by the cease fire agreement.

His choice of northerners and Roman Catholics for important positions and his intolerant mandarin ways were only two of the things which made his rule eventually intolerable in the South. The other two main factors were the conduct of his immediate family and his—and their—treatment of the Buddhists.

The dictatorship which arose under Diem was not the dictatorship of a single man but of a family, whose most important members were his brothers Nhu, Can and Thuc and his sister-in-law Tran Le Xuan, the wife of Nhu and better known as Madame Nhu.

Diem had two immediate tasks in mind: to get rid of his rivals for power, and to fight the Communists with their own weapons. In achieving his first objective Diem removed Bao Dai from the political scene by declaring Vietnam a Republic and getting himself chosen by referendum as President; he also ruthlessly crushed the "sects" as they were known, the Cao Dai and Hoa Hao and the gangster organisation known as the Binh Xuyen which had control of most of the gambling and opium dens and was alleged to be virtually running the police force. These victories were not won without making Diem many personal enemies.

Against Communism Diem used Communist weapons, namely ideology and a combination of cadre party and secret police.

Diem's ideology, which he borrowed and adapted from French writers, was called Personalism and was a kind of Catholic Confucianism which put the accent heavily on the place of the family in the State. The State itself was seen as a large family with everyone in it owing filial obedience to its head, namely Diem. Erring children were to be soundly chastised as indeed were Diem and his brothers in their childhood, in a strict Confucian household.

Diem's equivalent of the Communist Party was the Can Lao, outwardly a movement for the propagation of the Personalist gospel, but in fact a body of well-selected people in key positions who would act both as agents of Diem's anti-Communist policy and as a secret network of spies who could inform Diem of any plots against his government. The Can Lao was run by Diem's brother Ngo Dinh Nhu, whose wife organised amongst other things a semi-military women's association known as the Women's Solidarity Movement.

One of Diem's first moves after becoming Prime Minister was to ask America for aid in resettling the refugees, who were pouring in from the North. President Eisenhower responded generously and he made it clear that it was not only the plight of the refugees which motivated him. "The purpose of this offer is to assist the Government of Vietnam in developing and maintaining a strong, viable state, capable of resisting attempted subversion or aggression through military means."[3]

American aid in men and materials was both the salvation and in the end the undoing of Diem.

There is little doubt that in the chaos following the partitioning of Vietnam, the South would have foundered but for the support which America gave Diem. It enabled him to resettle the homeless, pacify the countryside and increase food production. Indeed at one time it looked as if the 1954 position was going to be reversed, with the Viet Minh in retreat and the North in turmoil.

It was in 1959 and 1960 that the tide began to turn. The North had got over the reign of terror which accompanied its land reform and Ho Chi Minh had begun to re-activate the many Viet Minh agents who had remained in the South and had access to hidden caches of arms and ammunitions which had been quietly and carefully laid by for a suitable occasion.

As the Viet Minh agents became active again there was unrest in the Army and an unsuccessful attempt at a *coup* in 1960.

After this incident and until his assassination in 1963, Ngo Dinh Diem's regime became more and more harsh and suppressive and the Ngo Dinh family more and more suspicious of people outside the family circle. Nhu's Can Lao agents infiltrated and informed and sowed distrust until they became at least as unpopular as the Viet Cong; the latter, in fact, soon realised that one of the ways in which they could win support was to make such men the earliest targets for selective assassination.

Thus discontent built up in the South against the oppression, the favouritism and the corruption of the Diem regime. The President himself was never accused of corruption but became so aloof and so concerned with manipulating people that he lost touch with reality.

The crisis came when the government came into open conflict with the Buddhists particularly in Hue where one of Diem's brothers Thuc was Archbishop and another, Ngo Dinh Can, the local warlord. A number of incidents, including the first suicides by burning, culminated in the events of May 6, 1963 when police and soldiers fired on a crowd in Hue, which had met to protest against an order forbidding the local Buddhists to display their flag in processions in celebration of the anniversary of the Lord Buddha's birthday. The Buddhists felt particularly aggrieved because the Catholics had only a few days before been allowed to process with flags and banners to celebrate another anniversary.

Nine people were killed in this incident in Hue. It was followed by others in Saigon and elsewhere. In the end Ngo Dinh Nhu planned moves to suppress the Buddhists in the same way as he had helped previously to tame the Binh Xuyen and the "sects".

Before Nhu's plan could be carried out there was a successful military *coup*, led amongst others by General Duong Van Minh.

The *coup* took place on November 1, 1963, and although Diem and Nhu escaped from the Presidential Palace they were caught and shot the next day.

The deaths of Diem and Nhu and the removal of the influence, and activity, of the dreaded Can Lao was the signal for the revival of all the divisive forces which had been kept suppressed. The Cao Dai, the Hoa Hao, the VNQDD and of course the Catholics and the Buddhists, all began to clamour for a place in the sun. In addition the Cochin-Chinese saw an opportunity for them to replace the many Annamites and Tonkinese who had been given preferential treatment by the Ngo Dinhs.

The Post-Diem Era

The story of the next nineteen months is one of *coup* and counter-*coup* as military group after military group seized power. There were occasional interludes of civilian rule as when Tran Van Huong and Phan Huy Quat were Prime Ministers but the interludes were very brief.

Meanwhile outside Saigon, the situation deteriorated so badly that by 1965 five northern provinces of South Vietnam were on the point of secession, the Viet Cong were masters of a greater part of the countryside and American and Vietnamese strongpoints were islands in a Communist sea.

As 1965 opened, South Vietnamese fortunes were at a very low ebb, but by the end of the year dramatic changes had taken place. During 1965 America stepped up its participation in the war and two men came to power—General Nguyen Van Thieu and Air Force Brigadier Nguyen Cao Ky—who were still the leading figures on the South Vietnamese political scene six years later.

In February 1965 American arcraft first bombed North Vietnam and two months later the first American combat division was in operation on South Vietnamese soil. These moves were made because the Americans were convinced that nothing else could prevent the Communists, whether in the shape of the Viet Cong or the North Vietnamese, from taking over the South.

In the years that followed a certain stability was achieved. The South Vietnamese government—the Government of the Republic of Vietnam, to use its proper title—was confident enough of its grip on events to risk holding elections in the secure areas of the country. A Constituent Assembly was elected in September 1966 and was charged with the task of drawing up a new constitution. The document was duly produced in March 1967 and the new Constitution was promulgated on April 1, 1967. On September 3, 1967 Nguyen Van Thieu and Nguyen Cao Ky were elected President and Vice-President respectively.

The new government had been in office just under five months when the NLF launched the greatest military offensive in its history. Taking advantage of the holiday atmosphere and relaxed vigilance of Tet, the great festival of the lunar New Year, the NLF attacked, during the night of January 29/30 and succeeding nights, most of the major cities and towns of South Vietnam. There was widespread damage to life and property. Probably the worst damage was done in Hue, the ancient capital of Annam, much of which was totally destroyed in the course of three weeks of savage fighting. Saigon itself suffered considerable damage and there was a dramatic assault on the American Embassy which had a great psychological effect on the public back in the United States.

Whether the Tet offensive achieved everything its sponsors hoped for one cannot say without being privy to the inner councils of the NLF. If, for example, the Front expected a general uprising, or *khoi ngia*, to take place in accordance with its theory, it was mistaken; there was remarkably little response in this direction from the general public. The Front also sustained, according to most accounts, far more battle casualties than it had expected. On the other hand, if the NLF's main intention was to drive the enemy to the conference table it achieved its purpose.

The Tet offensive was, in a sense, America's Dien Bien Phu. Dien Bien Phu was not an irretrievable military disaster but it *was* the straw that broke the French public's back. The Tet offensive was still less a military disaster for the Saigon government and the Americans; on the contrary, many experts saw it as a grave defeat for the NLF. Nevertheless, to a great section of the American public the events of early 1968 seemed to indicate that the war was unwinnable and that the final victory, which the generals were always saying was just round the next corner, was just a mirage.

At the end of March 1968 President Johnson announced that the bombing of North Vietnam would be partially halted. In May, apparently in response to the President's gesture, talks opened in Paris between the Americans and the envoys of the Democratic Republic of Vietnam. In October the bombing of North Vietnam came to a complete halt, and in March of the following year the NLF and the Saigon government joined the Paris talks. In June 1969, doubtless in anticipation of an eventual peace settlement, the NLF announced the establishment of a "Provisional Revolutionary Government of the Republic of South Vietnam", which was promptly accorded diplomatic recognition by various Communist and neutralist countries, including Cambodia.

If, at the beginning of 1971, the negotiators had still reached no agreement in Paris, there were great changes under way in South Vietnam. American troops were being withdrawn with a rapidity which could be interpreted as a sign either of the USA's total disenchantment with the war or of its confidence that the Saigon regime could survive militarily without the help of American combat troops. The material and financial aid was, of course, expected to continue indefinitely.

In the opinion of some military experts, the war in the south of South Vietnam, where the bulk of the population lived, was now virtually over. The NLF was, however, expected to continue to operate in the hills in the north and west and to establish its main base somewhere in the forested highlands in the triangle where Laos, Cambodia and Vietnam meet and where the ethnic minorities could be expected to give its troops food and shelter.

If there were those in Saigon and the Pentagon who were optimistic about the military situation, there was no such confidence about the prospects for survival of the current political regime. Before 1970, indeed, few people would have given the anti-Communists any chance of beating an NLF-backed presidential candidate in a free election. After the passage of the land reform legislation, however, the government's prospects looked much better, particularly as the NLF and its North Vietnamese allies had apparently received a further military drubbing over the border in Cambodia. President Thieu, indeed, felt confident enough to offer the NLF a chance to test its strength in an electoral contest. The NLF, however, refused to co-operate in any way until the Thieu-Ky-Khiem triumvirate was replaced by a more acceptable set of leaders—possibly headed by the more flexible General Duong Van Minh. The NLF presumably did not rate very highly its chances of winning any election, however "fair", which took place under the auspices of the current regime.

By the beginning of 1971, then, an uneasy equilibrium had been reached, with deadlock in Paris, a lull in the battlefield and uncertainty on the political scene. In the absence of accurate and unbiased reporting it was difficult to guess at the shape of the future, but there were certain features of the situation which must have given the historically-minded a feeling of unease. Few, for instance, could have missed the parallels between the Thieu regime in 1971 and the last days of the Diem government in 1963. Then, as now, power was concentrated in the hands of an ever-narrowing circle of men tending to rely exclusively on the support of the Army, the Catholics and the Americans. Then, as now, there had been savage and, at times, undiscriminating campaigns to eliminate all those suspected of supporting the Communist cause in any way. In Diem's day there had been the campaign for the denunciation of the Communists; in Thieu's time there was the "Phoenix Programme", which by May 1969 was said to have resulted in the elimination of over 35,000 members of the NLF's infra-structure. Moreover, in 1971, as in 1963, there were signs that the Americans were about to withdraw their support from the government in power. "A policy of continued unqualified support for Thieu is inconsistent with a successful American strategy" wrote Robert H. Johnson in Foreign Affairs in July 1970. The writer then went on to suggest that the Americans should take advantage of the next change of Ambassador to jettison Thieu, just as they had abandoned Diem when Mr Lodge replaced Mr Nolting as American Ambassador at Saigon. To complete the parallel, General Duong Van Minh, who had led the coup against Diem in 1963, was the man most confidently tipped to replace Thieu—with American and NLF approval—in 1971. On the earlier occasion Minh had lasted three months in office; it was an open question how long he might survive if given a second chance.

In the event—and in spite of all the efforts of the American Embassy in Saigon to promote a democratic contest—both Duong Van Minh and Nguyen Cao Ky withdrew their candidatures in the Presidential elections for which polling took place on October 3, 1971. Nguyen Van Thieu, now the only candidate, was duly re-elected. Outwardly the situation was unaltered, but the refusal of Thieu's two main political opponents to take part in what they claimed to be "rigged" elections cast doubt both upon the validity of the democratic process and upon the legitimacy of Thieu's leadership.

The Constitution

The formal framework within which the political process is designed to take place is described in the 1967 Constitution. Designed very much for its times the Constitution gives wide powers to the President. Popularly elected, the President is head of state and government as well as being Commander-in-Chief of the Armed Forces.

There is a Prime Minister and a Ministry which is appointed by the

President on the Prime Minister's recommendation, but since the President is a genuine chief executive and not a mere constitutional monarch the Prime Minister's role is definitely a subordinate one. The Prime Minister and the Cabinet are responsible to the President, not to the legislature.

The Vice-President is given no specific duties beyond serving as Chairman of various Councils: Culture and Education, Economic and Social, and Minorities; he is in fact forbidden to take any other Ministerial post. The first Vice-President, Nguyen Cao Ky, a powerful personality, chafed under this constitutional restraint and soon found ways of building up his political prestige, notably by taking a prominent part in the Paris peace talks.

The legislature is bi-cameral. There is a Senate which consists of sixty Senators elected at large for a six-year term; elections for half the Senate take place every three years.

There is a House of Representatives whose Deputies are elected for four-year terms from constituencies on the level of the province and the autonomous city; the number of members in each constituency is proportionate to the population and is based on the ratio of one deputy for every fifty thousand registered voters. The number of Deputies elected in 1967 was one hundred and thirty-seven but the elections were not country-wide and the Constitution provides for up to two hundred Deputies to be elected. Seats are reserved in the House of Representatives for the ethnic minorities: the Khmers and the *Montagnards* are given six each and the Chams two. These fourteen seats may be compared with the sixty or so seats occupied by the *Montagnards* in the Democratic Republic's legislature. On the other hand one should note that the Vice-President is the head of a Council for Ethnic Minorities which is charged with the promotion of the interest of the minorities; there is also a Ministry of Ethnic Development.

Members of the Supreme Court are elected for a six-year term by members of the legislature from a list submitted by various professional legal associations. The Supreme Court has powers of judicial review and may pronounce on the constitutionality of any particular legislative measure. It also has the unusual power of being able to dissolve any political party whose "policies and activities are judged incompatible with the republican form of government". This particular provision should be read in conjunction with a passage in the opening chapter of the Constitution which declares that "the Republic opposes Communism in any form and every activity designed to publicise or carry out Communism is prohibited".

For the purpose of local government the country is divided into forty-four provinces and six autonomous cities. In theory the province chiefs are elective but the Constitution provides that they may be appointed during the first four years of the Constitution. In practice all the provincial chiefs in 1971 were army officers of the rank of colonel. The province chiefs are advised by provincial councils whose members are elected by village councils acting as electoral colleges. Provinces are subdivided into districts whose heads are appointed by the province chiefs; in 1971 they were all army officers of the rank of major or captain.

The smallest unit of local government is the "village", consisting of several hamlets, whose chief is chosen by the directly-elected village council.

The 1967 Constitution was devised and promulgated against a background of war and siege which was not the ideal environment for democratic experiment. It was produced largely in response to heavy pressure from the Americans. The Army, however, was not willing to take any chances and made sure that there were provisions, such as that allowing for the appointment of province chiefs, which would safeguard its position. In 1971 the Army, and in particular the President, combined civil and military power and most important appointments had to have the personal approval of General Nguyen Van Thieu.

Political Parties

There are nearly thirty political parties operating in South Vietnam. Most of them are generals without armies: groups, cliques, personal followings and factions which form and reform temporary alliances with each other or combine to make the ever-popular "fronts" (Mat Tran) which have played such a prominent part in the political history of Vietnam.

Many of the parties are clustered round a single man: some have religious affiliations either to sects like the Hoa Hao or the Cao Dai or to a Buddhist group attached to a particular pagoda such as An Quang or to the Catholic Church in a particular diocese.

There are also the remnants of the pre-war nationalist parties like the VNDQD (the Kuomintang Party) and the Dai Viet, both of them broken up into several factions.

Overshadowing all these are the two organisations which are the main contenders for power in South Vietnam: the Army led by General Thieu and the National Liberation Front led by Nguyen Huu Tho.

In 1971 General Thieu's main aim was to be re-elected. The President is the most powerful and prestigious man in the country and it is the Presidency rather than the National Assembly which is the main political prize for which the groups contend. As in the Philippines support for a particular Presidential candidate is mustered by means of wheeling and dealing, patronage and the skilful use of "pork-barrel". Unlike the Philippines, however, there is very little of the symbiotic *utang na loob* relationship between the classes to be found in South Vietnam and the government's lavish "self-development" funds which have been made available to village councils to spend on rural reconstruction do not have the political impact of the cheques handed over personally to the *barrio* captains by Ferdinand and Imelda Marcos.

The government and the NLF work in opposed but complementary ways. The government as befits an organisation brought up in the mandarin tradition works from the top downwards; the NLF on the other hand works from the bottom upwards. The government helps the villager to do his duty; the NLF helps the villager to obtain his rights. Until fairly recently the government thought of politics as the "business of the city"; not unnaturally, perhaps, in a country where over a third of the population live in urban areas.

It became however increasingly clear as 1971 approached that the election was going to be won by whichever candidate or party could "deliver" the rural vote. It was in the towns that the opposition to the government was best organised and where the Buddhists and the "peace" candidates were most effective, but none of these groups had roots in the rural areas.

As long as there was no prospect of a Communist party's being allowed to contest the elections the government could count on being able to get electoral support in the countryside. Elections in Vietnam are not, as the *Economist* once said: "the sort of thing that maiden aunts at Bournemouth would recognise", and there is no doubt that the party in office is able to exercise a good deal of influence upon the voter through the provincial, district and village chiefs, most of whom owe their position directly or indirectly to the favour of someone in Saigon.

After the Tet offensive in 1968 the scene started changing rapidly. The withdrawal of the American forces brought about a "Vietnamisation" not merely of the battlefield but of the political process; politicians as well as soldiers were required to stand on their own feet. It was precisely at this moment that many people began to realise for the first time that NLF's purely military effort was only part and ultimately by no means the most important part of its total effort. Its main impact and its main message over the years had been political and social. Its main aim had been not merely to promote an anti-colonial revolution but a social revolution. Its ultimate object was not just to eject the Americans or the French but to transform Vietnamese society. It chose to use the "countryside" to defeat the "city" not merely because this was a winning guerilla formula but because the greatest social injustice was to be found in the countryside. Land reform was the first action of the Viet Minh in French times. In the North, where there was little landlordism, land reform may well have been a convenient excuse for eliminating political opponents; in the South, however, in the immediate post-Japanese period about two per cent of the landowners owned forty-five per cent of the land, while small-holders representing seventy-two per cent of the total number of landowners owned only fifteen per cent of the land.[4] In the years up to the Geneva Conference the Viet Minh made a drastic redistribution of land and issued new ownership certificates to thousands of tenants. Continued ownership was admittedly conditional upon appropriate political and military support but there was no questioning the fact that a social revolution had taken place in the countryside.

The Viet Minh land reform was, however, regarded as unofficial by Ngo Dinh Diem who instituted an official programme of his own. Unfortunately the programme frequently entailed the handing back to its rightful owner of land which had already been transferred to the tenant by the Viet Minh. To add insult to injury the official pegging of the rent to a reasonable percentage of the harvest was often made an excuse for absentee landlords to collect several years' back rent. Measures such as these, designed to aid the peasants, merely served to arouse strong anti-government feelings.

It was not until 1970 that the government and its American advisers were driven to take action in what was now seen to be a matter vital not only politically but militarily. In that year, after much opposition, the so-called "Land to the Tiller" Law was promulgated.

The objective of the Law was to give ownership of land to those who were actually cultivating it. The legislation did not apply to holdings of less than fifteen hectares. Persons owning more than this would be compensated swiftly and adequately and the land would be transferred to the "tiller" without charge for registration.

What long-term political effect this legislation will have it is difficult to say. At worst the peasants may not be grateful for the mere legislation of a Viet Minh-NLF achievement. On the other hand the NLF's main crutch has been removed and the resulting loss of psychological advantage may damage their political and military performance quite seriously.

The significance of the Land Reform Law of March 1970 in relation to the electoral scene was that it may have confirmed President Thieu's resolve to do without the help of political parties as such and to rely mainly on building up public goodwill towards himself and his government by producing progressive legislation and concrete social benefits.

In mid-1969 Thieu made an effort to build up civilian support by means of a "front". The National Social Democratic Front was a loose alliance of six quite disparate parties with no common ideology, programme or administrative structure. There were elements of Dai Viet, VNQDD, Hoa Hao and Catholic groups. The Front was not a success. Vietnamese tradition prefers clandestine to open organisations and as the electoral test approached Thieu preferred to divide and confuse his enemies while building up his support among the two blocs with whom he felt most at home, the Catholics (mainly from the North) and the Army.

Another group from whom Thieu may have been expecting support were the village and hamlet officials who were brought to Vung Tau for short training courses. The President is said to have addressed every intake and no doubt wished them to act as government propagandists when they returned to their home areas.

Whatever foreign observers and some Vietnamese politicians said about the existence of a "third force" which was neither pro-American nor pro-Communist there appeared in 1971 to be no effective contenders for power besides the NLF and the Army led by Thieu. The NLF's recognition of this fact was shown by its incessant demand that the Thieu-Ky-Khiem triumvirate be replaced by a "neutral" team before elections took place.

The Thieu government in turn recognised that the NLF was its main adversary. Hence its genuine and partially successful attempts to cut the political ground from under the NLF's feet.

The exact role and objects of the NLF were a good deal more difficult to define in 1971 than they were in earlier years. The "Viet Cong"— to use the government's opprobrious label—was originally seen as the heir to the Viet Minh, carrying on the anti-colonial struggle against the Americans rather than the French. When this role became difficult to sustain the NLF chose to put its accent on the class struggle. This line of propaganda made an effective impact so long as the government could be seen as serving the land-owning interest, but as soon as the land reform measures began to bite it started to lose its effectiveness.

But social inequality is not the only bone of contention in South Vietnam. There is, amongst other things, the ever-present fear on the part of Southerners, especially in the Highlands and Cochin-China, of the *nam tien*, the eternal "Drive to the South" of the Vietnamese. People in the South are well aware that the establishment of a Communist government in South Vietnam would be the prelude to the unification of all Vietnam under the rule of the Northerners in Hanoi. In this connection it is interesting to note a discrepancy between the programmes of the NLF and the People's Revolutionary Party (PRP), established in January 1962, as the arm of the Lao Dong in the South. Whereas the PRP looks forward to the reunification of all Vietnam, the NLF—the vast majority of whose members are Southerners—lays much greater emphasis on obtaining what it conceives to be a just solution for the problems of Vietnam below the seventeenth parallel.

North Vietnam Since 1954

The representatives of the Democratic Republic of Vietnam were highly disappointed by the outcome of the Geneva Conference. Under pressure from Russia and China they had been forced to accept half a loaf in place of the full loaf, to which they had been looking forward after the dramatic defeat of the French at Dien Bien Phu. There are those who maintain that the men of Hanoi were surprised that the elections promised in the agreement signed by the Viet Minh and the French were not held in 1956, yet it seems unlikely that men as realistic as Ho Chi Minh would have thought that a foe as implacable as Ngo Dinh Diem* would have allowed an election to have been held which would almost certainly have given the whole country over to the rule of Hanoi and the Lao Dong.† The elections after all were to decide who should rule all Vietnam and not just the South: with its greater population and the efficiency of its party machine the North would only have required modest support in the South to have achieved success. The South undoubtedly won an undeserved reprieve in 1954 and its leaders were not likely voluntarily to throw away their unexpected gains. The real surprise was not that the elections were not held but that the Diem regime lasted so long.

Whether in anticipation of a possible election or not the government in the North now set about consolidating its grip on the population under its immediate control. The first move was the so-called agrarian reform of 1955.

North Vietnam, unlike Cochin-China, had no serious land problem. In Tonkin less than two per cent of the land holdings at the time of the reform were greater than five hectares (twelve acres) and in Annam there were also scarcely any large landholders. There was thus in North Vietnam no class of rich, and often absentee, landlord such as existed in the South. Nevertheless in 1955 Truong Chinh, the Lao Dong's Secretary-General, launched a campaign of agrarian reform which though in theory dedicated to the eradication of landlords in the collectivisation of agriculture on the Chinese pattern turned out in practice to be a programme of denunciation and terror aimed mainly at eliminating possible opponents of the regime. The technique used was to get the people in every village to classify each other into five grades: landlord, rich peasant, middle peasant, poor peasant and landless labourer. Having done this the people were encouraged to denounce class enemies; the latter were then tried by people's courts and punished or put to death, generally in full view of the assembled villagers. So indiscriminate was the process and so ruthless its execution that a violent reaction set in and rioting broke out in several areas, notably in Ho Chi Minh's own home province of Nghe An.

The campaign was called off. Its author, Truong Chinh, was temporarily disgraced and Ho Chi Minh himself admitted that errors had been committed "in the implementation of unity in the countryside". However, the news that "those who have been wrongly classified as landlords and rich peasants will be correctly classified" in most cases came too late to achieve any but a posthumous rehabilitation for the persons concerned.

The agrarian reform may not have increased North Vietnam's

---

* Diem's brother Ngo Dinh Khoi was assassinated by the Viet Minh in 1946.
† According to P. J. Honey,[5] Pham Van Dong said at Geneva "You know as well as I do that there won't be any elections".

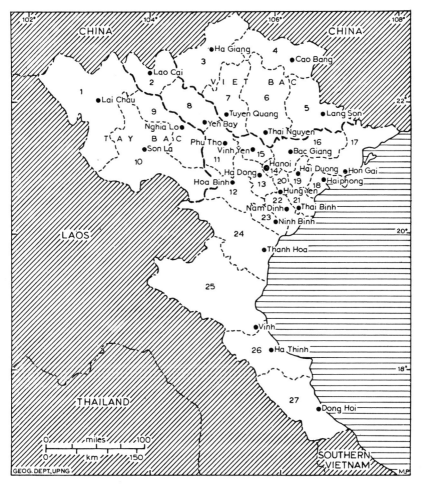

Map 7. North Vietnam

Key to Map 7 : Provinces in North Vietnam

1. Lai Chau	8. Yen Bay	15. Phuc Yen	22. Nam Ha
2. Lao Bay	9. Nghia Lo	16. Ha Bac	23. Ninh Binh
3. Ha Giang	10. Son La	17. Quang Ninh	24. Thanh Hoa
4. Cao Bang	11. Phu Tho	18. Kien An	25. Nghe An
5. Lang Son	12. Hoa Binh	19. Hai Duong	26. Ha Tinh
6. Bac Thai	13. Ha Tay	20. Hung Yen	27. Quang Binh
7. Tuyen Quang	14. Hanoi	21. Thai Binh	

agricultural efficiency but it undoubtedly contributed greatly to the achievement of the Lao Dong's main aim, the "unification" of "the countryside" and the removal of actual and potential opponents of the regime.

"Intervention" in the South

An important year in the history of the Democratic Republic was 1960. It saw the promulgation of a new constitution, the launching of a Five-Year Plan and the beginning of active intervention in the affairs of the South.

For those who wish to find support in international law for the massive intervention of the USA on the side of the Republic of Vietnam it is of great importance to prove that Hanoi has breached the Geneva Agreements by sending men and supplies to the South— an action which the North could not and would not deny. The legal argument will not be resolved here but it should be pointed out that there are not two countries or nations or states in Vietnam, but two *governments* both of which claim to be the legal government of *all* Vietnam. The Democratic Republic dates its reign from August 1945 when Ho Chi Minh declared the independence of Vietnam while the Republic of Vietnam regards itself as the legitimate successor to the State of Vietnam to which France transferred sovereignty in 1950; and which was given international diplomatic recognition at that time by the United States and Great Britain among many others. One should moreover note that the Final Declaration of the Geneva Conference stated quite specifically in paragraph 6 that "the military demarcation line is provisional and *should not in any way be interpreted as constituting a political or territorial boundary*" (Author's italics). It can, of course, be argued that the parties to the Agreement agreed that "no person, military or civilian, shall be permitted to cross the provisional demarcation line unless specifically authorised to do so by the Joint Commission" and that the Viet Minh broke this agreement; on the other hand one of the parties to the agreement, namely the French Union Forces, was no longer on the scene and its "successor in its functions" was not a signatory and had stated quite clearly that it did not feel itself bound by the terms of the agreement. If such a declaration from Saigon was not enough to weaken Hanoi's resolve to observe the terms of the agreement, all such scruples must finally have been removed when July 1956 came and went without any attempt to hold the nation-wide elections which the Final (unsigned) Declaration had promised for that date.

Douglas Pike[6] in his book *Viet Cong* states quite bluntly that Hanoi "embarked on a new and more aggressive course" as soon as it realised that elections were not going to be held and Diem's government was not going to collapse. Lao Dong cadres, says Pike, went South and helped to found the National Liberation Front of South Vietnam, a front which was by no means a purely Communist affair but one which included groups like the Cao Dai whom Diem had treated with such great severity.

If we do not regard the seventeenth parallel as an international frontier the question of who in fact was responsible for the setting up of the National Liberation Front in the South in 1960 is an academic one; yet even if one concedes that the decision was made in Hanoi and that many of the top cadres came from the Lao Dong one must also agree that the NLF was in the main an autonomous Southern movement. Pike points out that many of the cadres from the North were "regrouped Southerners and in any case the NLF would never have been as successful as it was if thousands of Southerners had not been willing to join it or at least have been the willing 'sea' in which the cadres and the guerilla units could 'swim' unmolested."

The unexpected success and longevity of the Diem regime—as well as its extremely harsh treatment of its political enemies—threatened to wipe out all the military and political gains which the Viet Minh had so painfully won in the years up to 1954. Hanoi was now forced, both for its own prestige and for the sake of the nationalist-communist cause, to turn from economic and social development to the development of a military and industrial potential sufficient to cover both the needs of self-defence and the active reinforcement with men and materials of their fellow countrymen in the South.

The decision to give all necessary support to the NLF came at a most inopportune moment for 1960 was also the year in which the First Five-Year Plan was launched.

The main aim of the Plan was to build up heavy industry in the North in order to give the country greater self-sufficiency. The Plan presented Hanoi with a very great challenge. The long war against the colonial power—the heaviest fighting took place in Tonkin—and the subsequent rapid withdrawal of French knowledge and equipment left the North in a sorry state, with hardly any industrial capacity to use the mineral resources which it possessed in rather greater quantities than did the South.

In spite of all the difficulties which lay in its path the executing of the plan was quite successful. There was only one major disappointment. The great Thai-Nguyen iron and steel combine, the construction of which had been put in hand in 1958, had been scheduled to begin operations in 1960 in time to get the Plan off to a good start. Unfortunately this Chinese-backed project upon which the success of the Plan was for a fair part based was still not completed by February 1965 when the first American bombs fell upon North Vietnam.

The enormous increase in the intensity of the battle in the South and the decision of Washington and Saigon to carry the fight to the North meant that Hanoi had to revise its economic strategy radically. The Democratic Republic felt compelled to increase dramatically its

contribution in materials and men to the NLF; it also had to put its
economy on a war footing. Heavy and light industry could no longer
be concentrated so as to invite quick destruction by bombs: factories
had to be relocated and manufacture dispersed and fragmented. A
great deal of the economic resources of the country had to be devoted
to such essential but unproductive tasks as repairing bombed roads,
bridges, houses, factories, schools and hospitals. Manpower had to be
diverted from the rice fields to the army to the detriment of agricultural
production. Visitors to North Vietnam were unanimously of the
opinion both that the citizens were coping magnificently with all their
new troubles and that the bombing had stiffened rather than weakened
their resolve to carry on the fight against the imperialist foe; but it
was quite clear that the economic price for this diversion of effort was
very great and would set back the North's material progress by several
years.

The Political Process

In 1960 the new constitution for the Democratic Republic of Vietnam
was announced. Like its rival, the constitution of the Republic of Vietnam, it begins with a bold declaration that "The Territory of Vietnam is
a single indivisible whole from the North to the South"; any further
ambiguity is removed in the preamble which speaks of a "single entity
from Lang Son to Camau".

The constitution as a whole has much in common with the 1945
Constitution of Indonesia. As in Indonesia the theoretical source of
authority lies with an elected Assembly whose functions are delegated,
when it is not in session, to a smaller body, the Standing Committee.
The National Assembly elects the President and Vice-President for a
four-year term. The President, again on the Indonesian pattern, has
very wide powers and is able to nominate the Prime Minister and other
members of the Council of Ministers.

For administrative purposes "the country is divided into provinces,
autonomous zones and municipalities directly under the central authority. Provinces are divided into districts, cities and towns. Districts are
divided into villages and townlets."* In all these administrative units
there are People's Councils and Administrative Committees to which
the Councils delegate authority.

One of the most interesting features of the administrative framework is the provision of "autonomous zones" for the minorities.

Originally there were three of these zones but one of them, in the
Upper Red River area proved unworkable. The two remaining ones,
Tay Bac and Viet Bac are located in the north-west and north-east
respectively of North Vietnam. Tay Bac borders on Laos and is
adjacent to the Pathet Lao province of Sam Neua; its inhabitants are

---

* Article 78.

mostly Thai and Meo. Viet Bac which comprises the provinces of Ha Giang, Cao Bang, Tuyen Quang, Bac Thai and Lang Son shares a long common border with the Chinese province of Kwangsi in Southeast China; it has a multiplicity of ethnic groups within its boundaries and its administrative centre is at Thai-Nguyen, the site of the Democratic Republic's great iron and steel combine.

The Constitution itself is silent about the degree of autonomy to be enjoyed by Tay Bac and Viet Bac but in practice it seems to have been limited to the recruitment of administrators from among natives of the area. Otherwise as the Constitution makes clear the autonomous zones are "directly under the central authority".

However small the actual degree of autonomy the solicitude of the government for the hill-tribes and the relative success of its policy of wooing the minorities is of great importance. The *Montagnards* of Vietnam, like hill peoples everywhere else in Southeast Asia, have an ingrained distrust of lowlanders and do not easily tolerate incursions into their territory by aliens. On the other hand they occupy about half the entire surface area of Vietnam, including some of the most strategically important areas in the region. Practically all the *Montagnard* zones straddle international borders, are perfect terrain for guerilla actions and are highly suitable for use as secure bases from which to launch "wars of liberation" in South Vietnam, Laos and Cambodia. Despised by the ethnic majorities in all these countries and ignored or tactlessly handled in the past by the French and the Americans, the *Montagnards* may yet play a decisive role in the future of Indo-China. If they do, it will very likely be on the side of the successors to the Viet Minh.

The Judiciary under the Constitution consists of a Supreme People's Court which "supervises the judicial work of local People's Courts, military courts and special courts".* There are also People's Organs of Control headed by a Supreme People's Organ of Control which "controls the observance of the law by all departments of the Council of Ministers, all local organs of State, persons working in organs of State, and all citizens".† The Organs of Control are apparently the equivalent of the "office of the procurator" in the USSR. In Russia procurators act partly as public prosecutors and partly as a kind of "Ombudsman" for the redress of the grievances of citizens against the bureaucracy. They are also able to institute appeals against judicial decisions which they deem to be contrary to public interest. The procurators are independent of the Ministry of Justice and are ultimately responsible to the Supreme Soviet. It seems that in the Democratic Republic of Vietnam one of the Organ's main duties is to ensure that the spirit of the law is carried out in cases where the letter of law proves inadequate for the purpose of bringing an enemy of the people to book.

---

* Article 104.
† Article 105.

Dang Lao Dong (Workers' Party)

As in all Communist regimes the thread which runs through the entire constitutional apparatus from the Presidential Palace to the village council is the Party: in this case the Dang Lao Dong or Workers' Party.

It is not so much that the Lao Dong is a "parallel hierarchy" making the official structure redundant; it is that Lao Dong cadres are in key official positions all through the country while members of the Party's Politburo like Pham Van Dong, Le Duan, Nguyen Vo Giap and Truong Chinh also occupy the top places in the government. The Lao Dong not only permeates the civil bureaucracy but also has its political commissars and cells in the People's Army in whose operations political decisions are often as important as military ones.

The Dang Lao Dong was formed in February 1951 as the successor to the Indo-Chinese Communist Party which was dissolved in November 1945.

Between 1945 and 1951 the Viet Minh required the support of patriotic non-Communists, landlords and the *bourgeoisie* in its anti-colonial struggle for independence. It was therefore thought prudent not to put too much emphasis on the Communist nature of the leadership.

After the withdrawal of the Chinese Nationalist troops from north of the sixteenth parallel and the subsequent defeat of Chiang Kai Shek by the Chinese Communists in 1949 caution was no longer so necessary; the leaders of the Viet Minh could now proclaim their membership of the newly-formed Workers' Party.

The Party is a relatively large one having in 1966 a reported membership of 760,000.[7] Its structure is similar to that of its offshoot the People's Revolutionary Party in the South. At the head of the structure is the Central Committee from which is elected the eleven-man Politburo, the most powerful body in the organisation. Beneath the Central Committee are the zone, province, district, village and hamlet organisations and city, town, ward and street committees, not to mention the three-man cells in, for example, industry, schools, and the army. Although in theory an exclusively workers' party the Lao Dong draws its cadres mainly from the *petite bourgeoisie* and the intellectuals;[8] its function is not so much the articulation and aggregation of interests from the grass-roots upwards but rather the dissemination of information, instruction and doctrine from the top downwards. The Lao Dong runs on the principle of "democratic centralism" according to which "the lower echelons obey the decisions of the upper echelons, all elements of the Revolution obey the Central Committee. . . . There is one shout and a thousand echoes."[9]

The Lao Dong's activities are not confined to North Vietnam. It is represented in the South by the People's Revolutionary Party (PRP) which was founded on January 1, 1962 as the successor to the Lao

Dong and which is the most important political element of the National Liberation Front. Although one cannot thereby infer that the NLF's activities are wholly directed by Hanoi, it is undoubtedly true that important PRP cadres are also members of the Lao Dong.

In Laos too the heart of the "national liberation" movement is an emanation of the Lao Dong, namely the Phak Khon Ngan Lao or Lao Labour Party. The PKNL is said to have been formed in 1952, and became the specifically Communist element in the Neo Lao Hak Sat. Of the best-known leaders of the Pathet Lao, Kaysone and Nouhak are said to be also members of the Lao Dong and it was estimated in 1968 that there were in all about one hundred and fifty members of the Lao Dong actively engaged in the work of the Pathet Lao.[10]

In Cambodia the Viet Minh infiltrated the Khmer Issarak movement and tried to set up a national liberation movement and a provisional government substantial enough to take part in the Geneva Conference. Although they did not achieve their main objective of obtaining a Laos-type settlement for Cambodia, they did manage to establish a lasting communication system between Hanoi and the various liberation movements in Cambodia, Laos and South Vietnam; at the centre of this system was the Lao Dong.

References

1. ELLEN HAMMER, *The Struggle for Indochina 1940-55*, Stanford University Press, California, 1966, p. 155.
2. D. WARNER, *The Last Confucian*, Penguin Books, Harmondsworth, 1964.
1. MARVIN E. GETTLEMAN (Ed.), *Vietnam*, Penguin Books, Harmondsworth, 1966, p. 215.
4. B. FALL, *The Two Vietnams*, Frederick A. Praeger, New York, 1964, p. 308.
5. P. J. HONEY, *Communism in North Vietnam*, Massachusetts Institute of Technology, Cambridge, Mass., 1963, p. 15.
6. D. PIKE, *Viet Cong*, Massachusetts Institute of Technology, Cambridge, Mass., 1966, p. 74.
7. M. W. NORMAND, "The Party System in North Vietnam", *J. S.E. Asian Hist.*, March 1967, 8, No. 1, p. 72.
8. J. C. DONNELL, "North Vietnam" in R. Scalapino (Ed.), *The Communist Revolution in Asia*, Prentice-Hall, Englewood Cliffs, N.J., 1965, p. 142.
9. *Ibid.*, p. 149.
10. *Far Eastern Economic Review*, March 28, 1968.

CHAPTER EIGHT

Burma

Historical Background

Colonial Rule

To those who think of Southeast Asia purely in terms of the "Impact of the West" and who see "modernisation" as being the goal of all right-thinking Southeast Asians, Burma must come as something of a shock.

We are told that when the first Council of Chiefs was held in Kuala Kangsar in the State of Perak in Malaya in 1897 an old chief told the British Resident of Pahang: that "until we visited Perak we were like unto the frog beneath a coconut-shell not dreaming there were other worlds than ours." We infer that this Malay chief was grateful for the enlightenment: it is not at all certain that the Burmese were grateful for the "enlightenment" brought by the West. Today, in any case, they seem to prefer the coconut shell to the "other worlds".

The British invaded and annexed the territory that today makes up the Union of Burma in three stages. In 1826, after two years of hard fighting, they annexed Arakan on the borders of India, and Tenasserim which has a long coastline on the Bay of Bengal and a border with Thailand. In 1852 Pegu was annexed and with it Rangoon. In 1862 British Burma became a Province of India under a Chief Commissioner in Rangoon. In 1885 the British marched on Mandalay and Thibaw, the last of the Burmese Kings, surrendered. The annexation of Burma was now complete.

The society which the British disturbed was a relatively stable one. The social pyramid, with its broad base of peasant cultivators, tapered sharply upwards through the village and "circle" headmen, the myothugyis and the myosans or "eaters of provinces" to the King. The mass of the people—cultivators, fishermen, boatbuilders—paid tribute to the chieftains and performed services for them as soldiers or labourers when required.

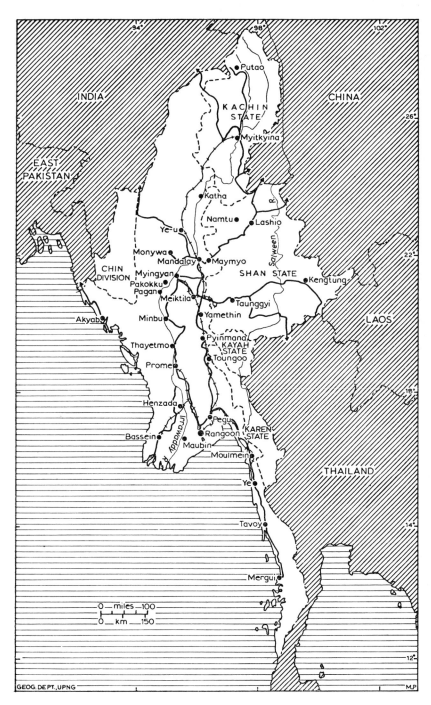

Map 8. Burma

There was nothing in those days that future British administrators fresh from India would recognise as a proper legal system, clear and codified. Disputes were mostly settled by chieftains and headmen in accordance with custom and the moral precepts of Buddhism.

The land, except that which was carved out of the jungle, belonged to the King and was cultivated on a leasehold basis. The export of rice was forbidden and no more was grown than was necessary for subsistence and the payment of taxes.

The whole social structure was permeated—and to a great extent kept together—by religion. Buddhism supported and was supported by the King. At all times—including of course the period of British rule —the authority and quality of a government was judged by its "merit" in the Buddhist sense. The ruler, national or local, who did not build pagodas or in some other way further the cause of religion was deemed deficient in "merit" and liable to receive lukewarm support, if not open hostility.

The position of the Monarch in this scheme of things was of crucial importance. He was the lynch-pin, the Defender of the Faith, the person in whom spiritual and temporal power met.

The Monarchy and Buddhism were thus the two pillars which upheld Burmese life. The British, without much thought for the consequences, removed one pillar (the Monarchy) and seriously weakened the other.

Education was supplied by the monks. In the monasteries opportunity was given for every male to learn enough to be able to read, write a little and commit to memory the main precepts of Buddhism. Such an education may seem inadequate from a modern viewpoint but in its own setting it was entirely effective in that it fitted the individual for society and taught him his role in it; it was only when the setting changed and the demands of society grew more complicated that its weaknesses were exposed. One of the great shortcomings of the British was that they failed to provide a satisfactory alternative; instead of giving the Burmese a suitable training they preferred to rely either on their own countrymen or on Indians or Chinese who already possessed the necessary degree of learning and sophistication.

By 1869 the British had done very little to alter the face of the land. "There are" said the Chief Commissioner "but five incomplete roads in Arakan, Tenasserim and Pegu . . . and beyond the mere fact of our military possession of the country beyond the existence of a police, most inadequately paid, there is hardly anything . . . to testify to the presence of any rule superior to that from which the country has been wrested."[1]

But already an agricultural and economic revolution was gathering momentum in the hitherto uncultivated and depopulated lands of the Irrawaddy delta. More and more peasants began descending on this area to hack down the jungle and plant rice. The movement had begun well before the opening of the Suez Canal in 1869 but there is no doubt that the shortening of the trade route to Europe by 4,000 miles gave an impetus to it.

The country as a whole began to grow rich and its exports expanded greatly. There is no doubt that some—not much—of this prosperity brushed off on to the Burmese peasant, who was certainly better off than most of his opposite numbers in India; but some would say that the price, in terms of demoralisation and the indebtedness that invariably followed high spending, was too great.

Whatever one's view of the results, the facts are reasonably clear. The British had already lifted the age-old embargo on the export of rice; the opening of the Suez Canal had brought one of the markets nearer and the imposition of a certain measure of law and order enabled economic exploitation to take place.

The first wave of peasants soon took the best land. Thereafter, it had to be reclaimed from the jungle. This required capital, since the prospective cultivator needed to subsist until the land was fit for planting. Since there were no Burmese money-lenders, the peasants were soon in the hands of the Indians. High interest rates led to indebtedness; indebtedness to sale of land, and eventually two-thirds of the area was owned by absentee landlords. By 1930 the total agricultural indebtedness was reckoned to be forty million dollars.[2]

Out of the original multiplicity of small holdings arose larger estates. Agriculture became industrialised and large rice-mills were established. This process had two important consequences. First, the jobs which should have been available for the Burmese in the new mills were in fact mostly taken by large numbers of immigrant Indian coolies, willing to work for near-starvation wages and in appalling conditions. The resulting unemployment was made worse because work on the paddy fields became largely seasonal when factory techniques were applied to the rice culture.

The second consequence was the demoralisation which we have already mentioned: perhaps spiritual uprooting would be a better description. J. S. Furnivall tells us that in 1891 there was in Upper Burma a monastery in nearly every village; in Lower Burma, the centre of the new rice industry, three out of every four villages had no monastery.[3] The people were also separated from the circle headmen who had been their temporal rulers.

When Thibaw surrendered in 1886 and was exiled to India the British could find no suitable successor and decided to do without the monarchy.

Having removed the King—and with him the upper ranks of native rulers—the British proceeded to weaken the Buddhist organisation by curbing the powers of its head.

In place of the traditional administrative structure in which allegiance to a chieftain might often be based on personal rather than territorial ties, the British imposed what they considered to be a neater system based on a division of the countryside into the familiar pattern of "villages", sub-districts, districts, divisions and so on—a pattern which has largely survived to this day.

In place of Buddhist precepts and the Hindu Code of Manu the British brought the Rule of Law. A very distinguished Burmese, Maung Maung, was of the opinion that this was one of the three most important contributions of British rule.[4] J. S. Furnivall on the other hand relates how the law was at first unread or misunderstood and often administered by men who had no knowledge of English, and sometimes not even a copy of the laws. Later, when the judges could understand the law and speak English there was a rising tide of litigation, greater opportunities for corruption and a wasteful flow of the best Burmese talents into the legal profession.

It is very important to note that all we have said so far has referred to Upper and Lower Burma, the heartland of the modern Union of Burma. British rule in the Shan States, Kachin and the Chin Hills was imposed indirectly under the general supervision of superintendents or residents. The State of Western Karenni was theoretically independent, but in practice was also a protected state, paying annual tribute to the superintendent of Shan States. Life then in these areas proceeded much as before and the British cannot be said to have made much impact.

This unwillingness or inability of the British to bring the whole area under unified and uniform rule certainly had a bearing on the problems of disunity facing post-colonial Burmese governments.

About twenty-five per cent of the total population of Burma consists of minority tribes such as the Karens, Kachins, Chins, and Shans; the rest are Burmans. Only three times in the known history of Burma have the Burmans managed to dominate the entire country and there has always been this built-in divisive factor in Burmese politics. The British as we have seen took no steps to minimise it. They merely accepted it as the natural state of affairs and even institutionalised it by allotting special places in representative bodies, such as Parliament and local government councils, for the main ethnic groups.

Even the nationalism in colonial Burma was not all directed against the British. In 1881 for instance the Karen National Association was founded with the objects of promoting co-operation with the British; advancing the education and prosperity of the Karens *and* protecting Karen rights against the Burman majority.

Nationalism of the more conventional anti-colonial kind started with a Buddhist revivalist movement. In 1906 the Young Men's Buddhist Association was formed. It was not originally a subversive movement. Its main aim was to discuss, refine and reform Buddhism in the light of modern learning and Western concepts.

A crucial year in the history of Burmese nationalism was 1918. It was the year of the so-called "no-footwear" outcry—a protest against the refusal of some foreigners to take their shoes off when entering pagodas—and of the publication of the White Paper on Indian Constitutional Reform in which Burma was excluded from the operations of the new and more liberal scheme. It was also the year when the central body of the Young Men's Buddhist Association changed its name from the Grand Council of Buddhist Associations to the Grand Council of *Burmese* Associations and became a political as well as a religious organisation.

In 1920 came the strike at the newly founded University of Rangoon in protest against the allegedly too high standards set there. The strike spread to all the Government schools and several aided schools. This was followed by the foundation of "national" schools run by Burmese by themselves: the movement met with success at first but subsequently lost support. Among the future nationalist leaders who received part of their education at one of the three national schools was U Nu.

In 1923 great constitutional changes were made. Certain subjects like defence, external affairs and income tax remained in the hands of the Indian Government; others like law and order and land revenue remained in the hands of Ministers in Burma, responsible only to the Governor; but a third category which included matters of considerable importance such as agriculture, health, public works and education were in the hands of Ministers responsible to a largely elected Legislative Council.

In harmony with previous practice what were known as the "Scheduled Areas" (Karenni, Shan States, Kachin and Chin tribal areas) were given special treatment: they were outside the scope of the new Constitution and were legislated for by the Governor.

The world-wide depression sparked off by the Wall Street crash of 1929 brought much economic distress to Burma and indeed all the countries of Southeast Asia. There was much political agitation in Burma. There were anti-Indian and anti-Chinese riots and there was the unsuccessful but bloody rebellion of Saya San.

The British had at last decided to separate Burma from India. The Burmese politicians immediately became suspicious of British intentions. They thought it might mean that Burma would advance at a slower pace than India along the road to self-government. There were riots against "separation" and the Legislative Council voted against it but the British overrode their objections. The tumult died down surprisingly quickly and separation became an accomplished fact.

About this time a new movement was born in Rangoon University which was to produce most of the men who led Burma into independence.

The new young politicians called themselves the "Thakins", a term equivalent to "Sahibs" and normally allotted to Europeans and others of high rank. They consisted mainly of the poorer and less bright students who were not destined to join the ranks of the administrative *élite*. They were enthusiastic readers of left-wing literature, had much closer contacts with the masses than the honours graduates and generally acquired a name for troublesome behaviour. Their leaders were "Thakin" Nu and "Thakin" Aung San, respectively President and Secretary of the Students' Union. In spite of Nu's subsequent reputation as a pious Buddhist, this was a secular movement.

The Thakins first achieved fame by organising in February 1936 a strike at the University over the alleged immoral behaviour of a lecturer. The whole affair caused the Government considerable embarrassment. One of the people who made political capital out of the strike was U Saw, a young journalist-cum-politician who demanded—against the wishes of Dr Ba Maw, the Education Minister—that a commission be appointed to investigate the students' grievances.

Three men, Ba Maw, Aung San and U Saw dominated the political scene from 1936 until the Japanese took over in 1942.

Ba Maw was the first Prime Minister under the new Constitution and the coalition which he headed lasted until 1939. He returned to power in 1943 when Burma was given independence by the Japanese. His cabinet on that occasion included U Nu as Foreign Minister and Aung San as Minister of Defence.

In 1940, after the outbreak of World War II in Europe, U Saw had rather cynically helped the British to imprison many of the "Thakins" but although U Nu was arrested, Aung San escaped and later returned to gather volunteers to join the group known as the "Thirty Heroes" or "Thirty Comrades". The group went to Japan for training and then returned to Burma to form the Burma Independence Army. Among the "Thirty" was a certain "Thakin" Shu Maung who adopted the name *Ne Win* signifying "Sun of Glory" and in due course became Prime Minister and then military dictator of his country.

Even now, as the war drew to a close and independence from Britain must have seemed a near-certainty, Burma was not united. A resistance group composed largely of Karens and including Communist Thakins held out not only against the Japanese but against Aung San's Burma Independence Army.

Aung San himself did his utmost to rally as many of the different forces, political and military, around him as he could. The Burma Independence Army became the Burma National Army (BNA) and the latter then became part of the Anti-Fascist Organization.

When the British returned the BNA was officially disbanded but reappeared as the People's Volunteer Organization (PVO) which Aung San subsequently used as a pressure group to hasten the granting of independence.

To go with his private army, the PVO, Aung San built up the political organisation known as the Anti-Fascist People's Freedom League (AFPFL) which grew out of the Anti-Fascist Organization but was now directed against the British rather than the Japanese.

In July 1947, just when independence had been conceded and only the details remained to be discussed, Aung San and several of his colleagues were shot and killed by a gang of assassins acting under orders from U Saw.

U Saw had hoped to take Aung San's place but was arrested and later executed; and it was U Nu who became Burma's new Prime Minister.

Civil War and the Fight for Unity

Five months before his death Aung San made a plea for unity at a conference held in Panglong to discuss the terms on which the peoples of the "frontier areas" might join the proposed Union of Burma.

"In the past," said Aung San, "we shouted slogans 'Our race, our religion, our language'. These slogans are obsolete now. What is race after all? What are its tests? We have in Burma many indigenous peoples: the Karens, the Kachins, the Shans, the Chins, the Burmese and others. In other countries too, there are many indigenous peoples, many races. China, Japan and the Soviet Union provide examples. In America, though the many peoples speak a common language, they spring from many stocks; there are the British, the Italians and other peoples but they have become assimilated and they identify themselves as 'American'. Thus race does not have rigid values. Religion is no test either, for it is a matter of individual conscience. In Burma the majority are Buddhists but there are those who freely accept Christianity, Islam or animism."[5]

It is possible that Aung San with his force of character and magnetic appeal might have made Burma what it was called, a Union, but the task proved too difficult for U Nu, his successor.

In 1947 and 1948 almost every organisation of political significance split into two or more factions. The PVO was asked to disband but was split into those who complied (Yellow Band) and those who did not (White Band). The Burmese Communist Party split into two groups: the so-called White Flags (Burma Communist Party) and the Red Flags (Communist Party of Burma). The Karens divided into those who were willing to work with the Government and those who wanted to fight for an independent Karen State. The latter formed the Karen National Defence Organization (KNDO) which at the end of 1948 launched a military attack on the Government. They were joined in due course by the Communists and other disaffected groups such as the "White Band" PVO members.

The civil war which began in 1948 is still in progress today. General Ne Win, the current Chairman of the Council of Ministers of the Revolutionary Government, is still confronted by some of the same enemies as he was twenty years ago, when he was Deputy Prime Minister and Minister of Home Affairs and Defence under U Nu.

Faced with the problem of disunity U Nu's remedy was to try to divorce the political from the military issues and tackle them separately. Under Aung San the Army, which under the Japanese had expanded greatly and now contained a large proportion of ethnic Burmans, was rapidly becoming a "citizen army"—a political rather than a military body. U Nu, "a civilian through and through",* wished to change all this and preserve the old British tradition that the Army should be "on tap" and not "on top". He wished to use the Army for the purely military purpose of defeating insurgency and not for any civilian "nation building" operations.

Politically U Nu had two main tasks: to keep the Left Wing politicians within the fold of the main political party, the AFPFL, and to heal the rifts between the majority ethnic group the Burmans and the minority groups, in particular the Karens.

As part of a campaign to entice the support of both Socialists and Communists U Nu produced a policy of mild Socialism which included a programme of land nationalisation and the setting up of a more democratic form of local government. U Nu also produced a rather vague political philosophy which was a mixture of Buddhism, Marxism and British Socialism which he hoped would have a universal appeal. Aung San had been careful not to use religion as his main political weapon for fear of arousing the wrath of minorities and to begin with U Nu followed the same policy.

As regards the rebellious ethnic groups U Nu could only press forward with military action while at the same time offering promises of greater measures of self-government, if the groups gave up the armed struggle.

On the military front the Government managed to roll back a concerted attack by the Red Flag Communists. Unfortunately, in the free-for-all which followed, various incidents involving clashes between Karens and military police and Burman units of the Army led to a violent renewal of traditional Burman-Karen enmity, and the Karen regiments who were part of the hard core of the regular Army deserted and began the long insurgency which is still part of the Burmese scene today.

Hampered by the desertion of some of his best troops Ne Win had to build up a new and effective Army. This he did with a fair measure of success over the next few years. By doing this and by giving his officers opportunities for further education and indoctrination at the Defence Services Academy at Maymyo and the National Defence College in Rangoon, Ne Win was also building up a group of political supporters and possible future military administrators.

By 1952 enough of the countryside was militarily secure for there to be a greater concentration on civilian political matters. From 1952 to 1956 U Nu's Anti-Fascist People's Freedom League was at the height

---

* The description is Dr H. Tinker's.

of its success. It carried through parts of its programme of socialisation and land reform and although as is the case with most one-party regimes there was a good deal of favouritism—membership of the Party was the key to advancement—the electorate seemed to be fairly content.

In 1956 an opposition group calling itself the National Unity Front shook the complacency of the AFPFL by winning forty-eight seats and capturing thirty per cent of the popular vote.

U Nu chose this moment to step down from his leadership of the AFPFL. He handed it over the leading socialists in the League, Ba Swe and Kyaw Nyein, who became Premier and Deputy Premier respectively.

U Nu returned as Prime Minister in March 1957 but a year later the AFPFL split into two factions, one known as the "clean" AFPFL led by U Nu and the other as the "stable" AFPFL, led by Ba Swe. By now U Nu's faction had only a small majority in the Chamber of Deputies and effective government was being sacrificed to party bickering.

Both factions then agreed to hand over the government of the country to Ne Win and the Army while they regrouped and reorganised themselves in preparation for the elections which should have been held in 1958 but were now postponed for a year.

From September 1958 to February 1960 the Army was in power and the people felt the impact of firm government. They did not like it very much. As Ba Maw said: "They just want to be left alone by the Government. Progress means change and all sorts of rules and regulations they cannot understand and so it is interference with their lives or fascism as it is called in Burma nowadays."

In 1960 U Nu swept back into power at the head of the "clean" AFPFL with 159 seats out of a total of 237. Both leaders of the "stable" AFPFL, Ba Swe and Kyaw Nyein lost their seats.

By now U Nu had abandoned his old tactics of reconciliation. He offended the Socialists by saying that Marxism was no longer his guiding philosophy and he openly exploited Buddhism as a vote-catcher. He had already acquired great merit by promoting the Sixth Buddhist Council, held in Rangoon in 1956 and he pressed home his advantage by arranging for all the ballot boxes for his party to be painted the Buddhist colour, a deep yellow. He further made a promise that if elected he would make Buddhism the state religion.

This move antagonised some of the minorities but others, especially the Mons and the Arakanese, were soothed by promises of a measure of self-government.

His most important enemy was the Army which had clearly backed the "stable" AFPFL led by Ba Swe a former Defence Minister. The fact that Ba Swe's faction performed so poorly in the elections and that Nu had played on popular anti-Army feelings did not help matters.

Over the next two years Burma was beset by all its usual political and economic problems, but with this difference: that U Nu seemed progressively more unwilling or unable to exercise control over the political sector. During this period he made it clear firstly that he intended to resign from the Presidency of the "Pyidaungsu" or Union Party (as the "clean" AFPFL had been renamed) and subsequently that he wished to retire from politics altogether when his term of office came to an end in 1964. Neither of these statements contributed to the maintenance of political stability. As soon as his impending resignation from the Pyidaungsu's Presidency was known all the old rivalries were reborn and the party like its predecessor the AFPFL was split into factions, each sponsoring different candidates for office. When, afterwards, it was known that U Nu was thinking of leaving politics altogether to devote himself to the cause of Buddhism the struggle grew more intense.

The situation in the countryside also deteriorated. The Shans, in particular, who had had brushes with Ne Win's Burmese troops during the period of military rule, greatly increased their insurgent activities. They were motivated not only by a hatred of Ne Win's soldiers but by U Nu's laggardly behaviour in face of their demands for a fairer share of the national cake and a greater degree of self-government.

The Karens, who had been fighting for independence for so many years, kept up their struggle, their enthusiasm made all the greater by the passing of the State Religion Act, for the Karens contain a fair proportion of Christians as do the Chins who also joined the struggle although they had previously been loyal to Rangoon.

Many people were surprised when the Army handed back power to the civilians in 1960: they thought this showed how strong the idea of democracy was in Burma. But fewer people were surprised when on March 2, 1962 General Ne Win stepped back into power and brought democratic rule to an end.

Ne Win's Coup

From Ne Win's point of view the country was in an appalling mess. The rebels were gaining ground on every side, the so-called "Union" of Burma hardly existed with every group wishing to have self-government. The civilian government was falling apart of its own accord and now that U Nu was known not to wish to stay in office there seemed to be no logical successor to whom the country would respond. Ne Win himself had been Deputy Premier to U Nu and had been asked to take over in 1958 by him and he now very likely thought that he was not only Nu's logical successor, but the only man with the only organisation that could save the country.

Ne Win moved quickly and ruthlessly. He tore up the constitution, and imprisoned many political leaders including Nu, Kyaw Nyein and Shwe Thaik, the Shan who had served as Burma's first President.

Parliament was dismissed and in its place Ne Win set up a Revolutionary Council consisting of himself and a group of Brigadiers and

Colonels. The Revolutionary Council in turn appointed a Council of Ministers who controlled the various departments of State. Most of the members of the Council of Ministers also belonged to the Revolutionary Council and all but one of the Ministers was a member of the Armed Forces. The exception was U Thi Han who was given the joint appointment of Minister of Foreign Affairs and National Planning.

The Death of Party Politics

With the advent to power of General Ne Win, for the second time, politics in the Western democratic sense came to an end. Only one of the political parties existing at the time of the takeover wanted to (or was allowed to) co-operate with the military. Even that party disappeared soon afterwards. There was a thorough purge of AFPFL members, many of whom lost their jobs or were put in detention. The General himself said that he admired parliamentary democracy but in his opinion the circumstances in which it could flourish were not present in Burma. In particular, he mentioned "the absence of a mature public opinion".

Faced with the necessity to mobilise public opinion, Ne Win tried to form a national political party or movement to which all could aspire to belong. It was called the Burma Socialist Programme Party (BSPP) or "Lanzin". Although open for membership to all except "those who live by exploitation of their fellowmen", it was in fact a "cadre" party like the Communist party and its full members were trained, hand-picked men.

The trouble with the old parties, it was said, was that they were not real parties at all but merely separate groups of people with varied interests whose only link was the temporary friendship which might exist between their leaders. Thus the AFPFL had men in it whose followers represented every shade in the political spectrum from deepest blue to brightest red. When the leaders disagreed they hived off from the main group to form a separate party. The AFPFL endured two major splits, the 1958 "clean"-"stable" split and the 1961-62 dissension over the succession to the leadership, but apart from these two major divisions the composition of the AFPFL "confederation" had not stayed the same for more than a year at a time.

In order, therefore, to get more cohesion and discipline into his new party, Ne Win decided that it would be heavily centralised and be controlled from the top downwards in the manner of what the Communists would call "democratic centralism"—indeed much of the organisation and methods of the BSPP was borrowed from the Communists.

The growth of the BSPP membership was far from swift. Three and a half years after its launching it was estimated to have twenty full members, 99,638 "candidates" and 167,447 "sympathisers". By

1969 the full membership had risen to one hundred and there was a waiting list of nearly 300,000.[6]

All the top posts in the organising and disciplinary committees of the Party went to senior military officers and it was clear that unless something drastic was done to "civilianise" it the BSPP would never become a popular movement.

The Army had made a conscious effort to keep in touch with the people and to aid them with civic action projects but the traditional Burmese attitude to authority was too deep-seated for these moves to meet with much success.

The country was run in conditions of martial law. Local government of the old type was replaced by a system of Security and Administrative Councils run by men selected by the Government.

It was the intention that these should be replaced by Peasants' and Workers' Councils but progress in this direction was slow. The inaugural meeting of the Central People's Workers' Council (CPWC) was not held until May 1968 and the people had to wait until February 1969 for the first meeting of the Central People's Peasants' Council. These Councils were the two institutions which, with the Burma Socialist Programme Party, now renamed the People's Party, would serve as the three pillars of the new democratic socialist society. By the beginning of 1970 it was said that 8,256 of the 14,250 villages of Burma and 207 of its townships had Peasants' Councils. In the absence of hard information it is difficult to say how effective these councils were and to what extent they were genuine grass-roots institutions rather than organs of "democratic centralism". Certainly the tone of Ne Win's references to them suggested that they served a tutelary, educative function in the fields of agricultural extension work and the promotion of the regime's political philosophy. Members of the Councils were paid by the government and showed the usual bureaucratic tendency to be at least as much concerned with their own organisational problems as with the problems of the peasants.[7]

Ne Win's lack of a mass base, apart from the Army, was a source of constant anxiety to him. The new society was to have been built by and for the peasants and the workers; yet it was precisely the peasants and the workers who had failed to "accept the goals, sacrifices and orders" of the revolution.[8]

Preserving the Union

Ever since Independence Burma has been fighting to preserve the Union. U Nu attempted to do it by being all things to all men and by conciliation and endless negotiation. In the end he was driven to make divisive moves in order to keep the majority in the fold. He repudiated Marxism and made Buddhism the state religion.

Ne Win's tactics were precisely the opposite. From the start he went all out for unity and would not admit the possibility of any alternative. He rescinded the State Religion Act and dissolved the various State Councils and replaced them by Councils headed by the military. He offered amnesties to all the rebel groups and for a while there were great hopes that the insurgency might at last be brought to an end. Leaders and representatives of all the major rebel groups came to Rangoon for talks but in the end they all returned without reaching any agreement. Their demands for autonomy were too great and the price of their co-operation too high.

In one case, however, agreement was reached. The Karen National Defence Organisation agreed to call off their war: in return the Karen State was officially re-named Kawthoolei (The Flowery Land) which had been its unofficial "rebel" name before.

Some Communists took advantage of the amnesty and were given posts in the government, but most of the White Flags and the Red Flags went back to the mountains and jungles to carry on their disruptive work.

Before very long, after a promising start, the security position in the countryside was as bad as ever. Even the KNDO resumed its activities though under a new leader, Bo Mya. Previously the Karen rebels had been split between those who supported the Communists (the Karen National United Front) and those who did not (the KNDO). The KNUF was not a party to the 1964 agreement with Rangoon and had carried on with the insurgency. In 1967 however, their leader, Mahn Ba Zan, broke off relations with the White Flags and joined a so-called National Liberation Council which had been formed in 1965 by Bo Mya and some renegade senior Burmese soldiers and civilians, prominent among whom was said to be Bo Yan Naing, one of the original "Thirty Comrades", the son-in-law of Dr Ba Maw, and a former Brigadier on Ne Win's staff.

There was also trouble in the north-east. In this area there were two, possibly three, forces operating. There was the Kachin Independence Army, a nationalist non-Communist force, and a newcomer: the Kachin Liberation Army, a Communist-led force sometimes also referred to as "Northeastern Command". This force was first reported active in early 1968 and was said to have been a Chinese-trained band of ethnic Kachins with some Shans and possibly also Chinese, led by a former Burma Rifleman and ex-Commander of the KNDO "General" Naw Seng who had left Burma for China in 1949. The Command's headquarters were said to have been on the Yunnan Border about fifty miles north of Lashio.

The reported active support of China for an anti-government group was significant in two respects: it marked a deterioration in Sino-Burmese relations and it also showed China's contempt for the pro-Peking "White Flags" whom it might perhaps have been expected to support but did not. The "White Flags" were in fact also having internal ideological troubles in the course of which their long-time leader Than Tun was executed.

The deterioration in Sino-Burmese relations dated from June 1967 when there were widespread anti-Chinese riots in Rangoon and Mandalay following demonstrations by Chinese students against a government decision forbidding them to wear Mao Tse Tung badges.

After these riots, during which much Chinese property including the Embassy was damaged or destroyed and many people were killed or injured, diplomatic relations between Peking and Rangoon were broken off. For the next eighteen months Peking encouraged "liberation" movements such as Naw Seng's and mounted a long campaign of propaganda against Ne Win and his "fascist" regime. China's hostility abated somewhat in 1969 and on October 12, 1970, an agreement was reached between the two countries to restore full diplomatic relations by the exchange of ambassadors.

The rift between China and Burma was an extremely serious matter. Ne Win's task of unifying the country was a very difficult one but it would obviously have become quite impossible if China had decided to throw her weight behind one of the rebel groups or to start a war of "liberation". In particular Ne Win did not wish to have to rely on the West, particularly the USA, for arms, thus becoming the capitalists' puppet which Chinese propaganda portrayed him as being. The constant threat from China along the thousand-mile border also prevented Ne Win from adopting a federal solution to Burma's political problems; the prospect of having nothing but a series of weak, uncontrolled semi-autonomous states between him and a potential enemy did not appeal to him.

Ne Win's long-term policy therefore was two-fold: to keep on friendly terms with China and to build a centralised unitary system of government in Burma.

At the very moment when Burma's relations with China were improving a new disruptive force appeared. U Nu, the former Prime Minister, who had been released from detention in 1966, on condition that he did not take part in political activities, announced from London on August 29, 1969 that he intended to stage a comeback. On October 21 he said in Hong Kong that he was prepared to plunge Burma into civil war in order "to restore parliamentary democracy". He said he would accept arms from the Devil himself for this purpose. In August 1970 U Nu was said to have signed an agreement with Mon and Karen rebels whereby the latter would join an anti-government front under his direction.

Ne Win had no choice but to oppose U Nu's every move. Everything which U Nu proposed directly contradicted all Ne Win's plans for Burma's future. Where Ne Win wanted centralisation and unity U Nu held out the promise of federation and regional autonomy; where Ne Win wished to run a socialist democratic state under one-party rule

U Nu proposed a return to multi-party parliamentary democracy; and although U Nu talked of asking Peking for arms it was clear that his policy towards China was not as conciliatory as that of Ne Win; finally there was the suspicion that U Nu's "liberation front", launched as it was from Thailand, had clandestine support from the USA.

The Political Process

The Burmese Way to Socialism

The political philosophy of the Ne Win regime was summed up in the document known as "The Burmese Way to Socialism".

Socialism has always played a large part in the thinking of Burmese political intellectuals right from the days when the Thakins read the publications of Britain's Left Book Club. U Nu himself was a co-founder with Than Tun (later Leader of the "White Flag" Communists) and Ohn Khin of the Red Dragon Book Club, which published, in Burmese versions, many socialist classics including parts of Karl Marx's *Das Kapital* and John Strachey's *Theory and Practice of Socialism*.

The Socialism of the "Burmese Way to Socialism"* is no half-hearted affair; it has little room in it for the enlightened capitalism of Lee Kuan Yew's Singapore. The Manifesto of the Revolutionary Council as published on April 30, 1962 is uncompromising. In its opening sentence it states that "pernicious economic systems" are the prime cause of man's misery. These systems must therefore be replaced by a socialist economy in which "such vital means of production as agriculture and industrial production, distribution, transportation, communications, external trade etc., will have to be owned by the State or co-operative societies or collective unions". Private enterprise is mentioned but only in a highly ambiguous way: ". . . national private enterprises which contribute to national productive forces will be allowed with fair and reasonable restrictions." Exactly what "national" private enterprises are is not made clear.

The "Burmese Way to Socialism" is intended to herald a clean break with the past and with the politics of the U Nu-AFPFL era. "The nation's socialist aims cannot be achieved with any assurance by means of the form of Parliamentary Democracy that we have so far experienced." There is also an ill-concealed thrust at U Nu's use of Buddhism in politics. "Attempts must be made by various correct methods to do away with bogus acts of charity and social work for vainglorious shows, bogus piety and hypocritical religiosity. . . ."

The Revolutionary Council was as good as its word. The economic scene was soon transformed. Foreign businessmen were dismissed

---

* The full text may be found in W. C. Johnstone's *Burma's Foreign Policy*.[9]

and soon there were no foreign firms left unnationalised, including those owned by Indian and Chinese nationals. All banks were taken over by the State, even the three "Red" Chinese ones—a sign of Burma's impartiality as between East and West.

Ne Win's drive against the foreigner resulted in the wholesale flight of Indians from the country. In pre-war and to a certain extent in post-war days the Indians played an important part in the business and professional life of Burma. Before the war Rangoon was in fact an Indian city. Indians formed the majority of its citizens and it is said that one had to be able to speak Hindustani in order to use the telephone.

When the Japanese invaded Burma thousands of Indians took the terrible road to India as refugees. After the war some returned and there were thought to be about six hundred thousand Indians in Burma in 1953. After Ne Win's *coup* the Indians were so badly harassed that they emigrated in their thousands: one hundred thousand are said to have emigrated in 1964 alone.[10] Among those refugees were many doctors who performed a vital function in Burmese life but were now debarred from carrying on their profession, except in charity hospitals. This restriction applied to all foreign doctors but it hit the Indians particularly hardly as they were predominant in the profession in Burma.

The socialisation of big business did not bring any economic benefits to the men in the street and the paddy-field. Two years after the *coup* drastic demonetisation measures were taken in order to halt inflation. As in Indonesia three or four years before, the Government called in all the higher-denomination notes and only handed back, in the form of low-denomination notes, a small proportion of the money thus collected. The intention was to catch the profiteer and the black market operator and all other "economic criminals" who dealt in cash transactions only and avoided bank accounts and income-tax returns. As in Indonesia the main sufferer was the "little man" who also avoided the banks, preferring to put his savings into high-denomination notes which he kept at home.

The move was not successful and caused much undeserved distress. The distress was aggravated by the shortage of the necessities of life in the village stores, whose shelves soon became bare following the nationalisation of the retail trade. The Army, acting in a civilian role, tried to make good the deficiency but eventually the stores were handed back to their original owners, who were better able to manage the process of retail distribution.

Burma's economic troubles were not confined to the domestic front. In 1961-62 Burma exported 1,600,000 tons of rice; by 1969 this figure had dwindled to about 345,000 tons.[11] The dramatic decline in her chief export contributed greatly towards Burma's trade deficit; it also made her short of the foreign exchange which was so badly needed to reanimate her dying factories. The epitaph on Burma's economy was pronounced by Ba Nyein, Burma's leading planner: "Government people are just not as efficient in running the enterprises . . . as the previous owners. . . ."[12]

Education

In his drive towards "Burmanisation" and national unification Ne Win tried to make full use of the educational system. In 1920 and 1921 the students of Rangoon University started a strike, which spread to the schools and brought education to a temporary halt. They were acting in protest against what they considered to be unnecessary official interference with the running of their new University.

In July 1962 the students protested again, this time against undue interference by the military. The soldiers moved in and in the ensuing battle about fifteen students were killed and the students' Union was deliberately destroyed by the Army.

The students had lost their first battle, and the University was closed. When it reopened it was well under the control of the military who amongst other things opened, as an Institute of the University, the "Central School of Political Science" at Chawdwingon in July 1963: this was a place where students could study Marxist thought and be trained to become political cadres and eventually full members of the Burmese Socialist Programme Party.

It is generally agreed that standards in the University have declined sadly. Apart from military interference, one of the main factors has been the insistence on Burmese as the sole language of instruction in both lower and higher education.

Until fairly recently English was the medium of instruction in many mission schools as well as being widely used at the University, where so many of the text books were in English. Ne Win changed all this and ordered that English, if it was taught at all, should only be taught as a foreign language. At the University lecturers whose mother tongue was English soon disappeared and their places were taken either by Burmese or academics of other nationalities, who had to work through interpreters.

Meanwhile a great drive was initiated to translate text books into Burmese, a language at present ill-fitted to be a vehicle for the new technology which Ne Win was so keen to propagate.

The ruling that matriculation examinations had to be written in Burmese put the brighter students in the non-Burmese speaking States at a considerable disadvantage and increased the ever-present hostility towards the central government.

Constitution Making

After nearly a decade of army rule Burma still had no new constitution to replace the one which had been, figuratively speaking, torn up in

March 1962. In the post-*coup* period the Army supplied the administrative framework and the basic ideology was set out in the "Burmese Way to Socialism".

This latter document made it quite clear that the soldiers had no intention of returning to the previous constitutional arrangements. The scornful reference to parliamentary democracy indicated that the days of "free-fight liberalism" were over and Ne Win's known aversion to any form of regional autonomy offered little hope to those who had looked forward to a federalisation of the Union.

In early 1968 about two hundred political prisoners were released. Among them were many of the top politicians of the pre-*coup* period: U Ba Swe, Kyaw Nyein, Ba Maw, Aung Gyi, Bo Let Ya and Mahn Win Maung. About nine months later some of these men were invited by General Ne Win to be members of a thirty-man Internal Unity Advisory Board which was to make recommendations for a new constitution. The appointment of this Board and the membership of it of men like U Nu and the former President Mahn Win Maung, may have caused people to expect some liberalisation of Ne Win's autocracy. If so they were disappointed. It soon became apparent that the General wished to legitimise rather than alter his regime.

The Board's findings were published in June 1969. There were three main streams of opinion. U Nu, in a report submitted by himself alone, suggested that power be transferred from the present government to a provisional one led by himself. Parliament would then be reassembled and would elect Ne Win as President and give him the sort of powers possessed by the Chief Executive of the Philippines. Thus would parliamentary democracy be restored and Ne Win's position legitimised. U Nu, it should be noted, claimed that his proposal had the support of "President U Win Maung and the majority opinion among the committee. . . ."[13]

A second group, comprising eighteen out of the thirty members, recommended a return to parliamentary government and to a modified type of socialist economy in which there should be private and mixed businesses, state enterprises and co-operatives.

The third group, which had eleven members, recommended the setting up of a strong unitary government, a National Unity Congress, a single political party and a fully socialist economy—in fact the preservation of the *status quo*.

Predictably it was the recommendation of the third group which won Ne Win's approval. Equally predictably U Nu, who had left the country in April 1969, gave great publicity to Ne Win's rejection of the Board's majority proposals for a return to parliamentary government. Ne Win's regime, said U Nu, was a fascist one and he, U Nu, proposed to attempt to overthrow it at the earliest opportunity.

Perhaps in answer to accusations that his regime lacked a broad base Ne Win announced in November 1969, on the occasion of the fourth seminar of the BSPP, that the Party was no longer to be an exclusive cadre party but a "party of the masses". By the middle of the following year the Party was reported to have 859 full members, 295,471 candidates and 734,167 aspiring candidates. These figures, though a great advance on those for 1969, still did not suggest that the oligarchical nature of the regime was undergoing any great transformation.

As 1971 opened General Ne Win was reported to be suffering from a serious illness and there was much speculation as to what would happen if he had to withdraw from the political scene. On balance it seemed unlikely that the military would willingly loosen its grip on the political system and equally unlikely that U Nu and his followers would be able to force them to do so.

If a continuation of the present somewhat barren state of affairs is unpalatable to many observers it must be remembered that the British left their successors a well-nigh impossible task, namely that of forging a nation out of an assortment of peoples who had neither race, nor religion, nor language, nor political institutions in common. U Nu tried the way of persuasion and compromise; he failed. Ne Win's more authoritarian methods of military rule and the single party have met with no greater success. It is indeed a measure of the hopelessness of the situation that U Nu, the apostle of Buddhist pacifism, should now feel obliged to threaten to resort to force to overthrow the military regime. Force may have solved Nigeria's problems but it will not solve those of Burma.

Burma has two handicaps: disunity and authoritarian government. U Nu, the self-proclaimed democrat, deems the latter the greater evil. If, however, the only way to overthrow the authoritarian government is to accentuate the inter-ethnic hostilities U Nu's remedy may well prove to be worse than the disease.

References

1. J. S. Furnivall, *Colonial Policy and Practice*, Cambridge University Press, London, 1948, p. 49.
2. *Ibid.*, p. 89.
3. *Ibid.*, p. 103.
4. Maung Maung, *Burma in the Family of Nations*, Djambatan, Amsterdam, 1957, p. 77.
5. Maung Maung, *Aung San of Burma*, M. Nijhoff, The Hague, 1962, p. 123.
6. *The Economist*, April 5, 1969.
7. *Far Eastern Economic Review*, March 26, 1970.
8. Josef Silverstein, "The Burma Socialist Program Party and Its Rivals: A One-plus Party System", *J. S.E. Asian Hist*. March, 8, No. 1, p. 16.
9. W. C. Johnstone, *Burma's Foreign Policy*, Harvard University Press, Boston, 1963, pp. 313-17.

10. G. HUNTER, *South-east Asia: Race, Culture and Nation*, Oxford University Press, London, 1966, p. 19.
11. *Far Eastern Economic Review Year Book for 1971.*
12. *Far Eastern Economic Review*, January 2, 1969.
13. *Far Eastern Economic Review*, September 4, 1969.

CHAPTER NINE

Malaysia

Kingdoms and Traders

The Federation of Malaysia comprises Western Malaysia, which we shall call Malaya, and Eastern Malaysia which consists of Sabah and Sarawak. Malaya is in turn divided into eleven States namely Perlis, Kedah, Kelantan, Trengganu, Perak, Selangor, Pahang, Negri-Sembilan, Johore, Malacca and Penang.

In 1937 Professor Emerson used the then somewhat unfamiliar term "Malaysia"[1] to denote the area occupied today by Malaya, Singapore and Indonesia. Although the term cannot be used today in this sense without causing confusion, it nevertheless serves to draw attention to the fact that the history and fortunes of the peninsula and the archipelago have been very closely linked.

The first major link was forged in the three hundred years starting at the end of the seventh century A.D. when the empire of Sri Vijaya flourished. Based on Palembang in Southern Sumatra, Sri Vijaya at its height claimed overlordship over the east coast of Sumatra, the west coast of Borneo and the western extremity of Java. It thus commanded the Sunda Straits and the Straits of Malacca.

Sri Vijaya was not the only power in Indonesia. In the eighth and ninth centuries the Sailendras or "Lords of the Mountain" were well established in Central Java and were building great Buddhist monuments of which the most famous is Borobudur.

The Sailendras, who ruled an inland kingdom, were not rivals of the maritime Sri Vijayan Empire, and in the ninth century a member of the Sailendra dynasty became king of Sri Vijaya when the Sailendra territory was taken over by an East Javanese kingdom.

Under physical attack by the seafaring Cholas of South India and spiritual attack by the spread of Islam which had taken root in the western end of Sumatra by the end of the thirteenth century, the power of Buddhist Sri Vijaya declined.

By this time the Thai were encroaching on the northern states of present-day Malaya and some of the other states were paying tribute to China.

The vacuum left by the decline of Sri Vijaya was partially filled by the central Javanese kingdom of Majapahit whose rule under the famous chief minister, Gadjar Mada, was alleged to extend over most of Malaya, Sumatro, Java, and the west coast of Borneo. Although it is now thought that Majapahit's actual territorial possessions did not extend much beyond a large area of east and central Java, there is no doubt that she exerted a certain amount of intermittent control over the Straits of Malacca.

It was fitting that the first great maritime empire to operate from Malay soil should have been founded by a Sailendra prince married to a princess of Majapahit. After an unsuccessful attempt to make a base in Singapore the prince eventually settled in Malacca in the closing years of the fourteenth century and founded the Sultanate. "Sultan" is a Moslem title and one of the most important events in the life of Parameswara, the Sailendran prince, was his conversion to Islam, after which he took the Moslem name of Iskandar* Shah. Under Iskandar Shah's successors the Sultanate of Malacca extended its rule until most of Malaya and much of Sumatra's east coast was subject to it.

When Malacca was founded, Islam was already beginning to spread through Indonesia and Malaya and no doubt the rise of Malacca to power and the fairly rapid spread of Islam in the area were complementary processes.

The Portuguese captured Malacca in 1511 but were not powerful enough entirely to take over Malacca's role in the area. After many trials and tribulations the descendants of the defeated Sultan of Malacca founded a new Sultanate in Johore and it was this Sultanate together with the Sultanate of Acheh in northern Sumatra which eventually shared control of the Straits with Portugal.

The next century saw a succession of changing alliances as different combinations of Portugal, Johore and Acheh strove against each other for mastery. At the end of the sixteenth century two other competitors, England and Holland, arrived on the scene and a combined attack by Holland and Johore drove the Portuguese out of Malacca in 1641. If the Sultan of Johore had been hoping that the Dutch would reinstall him in Malacca he was disappointed. In the event the Dutch managed to establish a far greater control on shipping and trade than the Portuguese had ever done.

In 1619 the Dutchman J. P. Coen founded the town of Batavia on

---

* After Alexander the Great. Until recently it was thought that his new name was Megat Iskandar Shah, but Professor Wang Gungwu asserts that this was the name of his son who ruled from 1414-1424.[2]

the north coast of west Java on the site of the Javanese port Djakarta. Having failed in 1606 to take Malacca which dominated the Straits of Malacca, Coen turned to Djakarta which was close to the other main shipping route, the Sunda Straits. Thus when Malacca was captured in 1641 the Dutch were in a position to dominate the trade of the waters around the Malayan peninsula and the Indonesian archipelago.

At this stage Holland was strictly a maritime power and had no great territorial possessions in the area. In Malaya her only foothold was the port of Malacca and the rest of the peninsula was divided into areas ruled or indirectly controlled by Siam, Acheh and a new power, the Johore-Rhiau Sultanate, which by 1722 had become the property of the Bugis.

The Bugis, who at different times in the eighteenth century managed to control most of the southern half of Malaya, were remarkably adept sailors and fighters, who had been driven from their home in the Celebes by the Dutch only to become the latter's chief enemy in the fight for the control of the Malacca Straits.

The end of the eighteenth century saw the collapse of the Dutch East India Company and the taking over of Malacca and Java from the Dutch by the British to forestall French moves after the Netherlands had come under Napoleonic rule. Both these places were later restored to the Dutch after the defeat of Napoleon at Waterloo.

In 1786 the British occupied and leased the island of Penang and by 1800 the Sultan of Kedah had ceded Penang and sold an area of the mainland opposite, subsequently named Province Wellesley.

In 1819 Sir Stamford Raffles, who had served as Lieutenant-Governor of Java from 1811-1815, negotiated the purchase of Singapore from a virtually British-appointed Sultan of Johore and founded a new free port which was to grow with astounding rapidity.

In 1824 by the Treaty of London agreement was reached between the British and the Dutch as to their respective spheres of influence in the area. The British ceased to occupy territory in Sumatra while the Dutch ceded Malacca and gave the British an assurance that they would not establish themselves anywhere in Malaya or make any treaty with "any Native Prince, Chief or State therein. . . ."

The only area which remained undefined was Borneo and it was not until late in the nineteenth century that the lines were drawn with Sabah, Sarawak, Labuan and Brunei in the British sphere and the remainder of the island within the orbit of the Dutch East Indies.

It will be recalled that the British invaded Burma in 1824 and had to fight for two years before they could force the Burmese King to cede Assam, Arakan and Tenasserim. Siam shared a long border with Burma and the British were naturally anxious to come to a good understanding with the Siamese. For this purpose an embassy was sent to Bangkok led by a Major Burney.

By an Anglo-Siamese treaty of 1826 it was agreed that the Siamese should not extend their control beyond Kedah and in particular that they should not intervene in Perak or Selangor provided the British guaranteed to protect Perak against an invasion by Selangor and provided the Sultan of Perak did not continue to acknowledge the suzerainty of Siam by sending the *bunga mas* (gold flower) which was the symbolic tribute of a vassal to a suzerain.

The acknowledgement of Siamese control over Kedah did the British very little credit. In ceding Penang to the British the Sultan of Kedah had made it quite clear that he expected protection from Siam. When the time came, however, the British did nothing. After Kedah had been forced to invade Perak on Siam's behalf the Siamese in 1821 took over both states and the Sultan of Kedah fled to Penang.

The Siamese did not occupy Perak for very long. They were driven out in 1822 by the inhabitants with the help of the Sultan of Selangor and his army.

As a result of this episode and a clause of the Burney treaty, Britain initially took the place of Siam in regard to Perak and Selangor, if not as suzerain then at least as arbiter.

The state of affairs created by the 1826 treaty remained more or less undisturbed for the next eighty years with one exception, namely that in 1842 the Siamese agreed to the restoration of the exiled Sultan of Kedah. The fact that the Sultan was still in receipt of a pension from the British and had proved a staunch opponent of the Siamese meant that the *status quo* was disturbed even though the Sultan agreed to send the *bunga mas* to Bangkok.

Johore and Pahang

One of the by-products of the Anglo-Dutch treaty of 1824 was the splitting of the Johore-Rhiau Sultanate into two, Rhiau being on the Dutch, and Johore on the British, side of the line of demarcation. There were now also two Sultans. Hussein the British-sponsored Sultan lived in Singapore while Abdul Rahman the Dutch candidate lived in Rhiau.

Hussein was the nominal ruler of Johore and Pahang. How nominal his and his successors' rule was became clear over the next forty years during the course of which there were struggles for power in Johore and a civil war in Pahang, which began in 1868 and lasted five years. These two events led to both of those areas becoming independent states: Johore under a *Temenggong* and Pahang under a *Bendahara*. Both these titles dated from the days when the Sultan of Johore was the overlord of Johore and Pahang but in fact neither the *Bendahara* nor the *Temenggong* thought of themselves as being subservient to the Sultan although the connection between the two states was never completely severed.

Kelantan and Trengganu

The exact position of Kelantan and Trengganu was not made explicit by the Burney treaty. In the 1860's Cavenagh the British Governor of the Straits Settlement considered them independent[3] while the India Office thought they were paying tribute to Siam,[4] although it seems that the autocratic Sultan Omar of Trengganu did not send the *bunga mas* to Bangkok during his reign which lasted from 1839 to 1876.[5]

British Intervention and Expansion

Until 1873 and in spite of all the actions taken by men like Cavenagh, the official British policy was one of non-intervention in Malay affairs. Neither the India Office up to 1867 nor the Colonial Office* until 1873 wished to increase British commitments either territorially or by treaty in the Malay peninsula.

In 1873 British policy changed. Looking back one can see a number of forces converging on one spot to bring pressure to bear upon the Colonial Office in London.

There were the demands of the Chinese business community in Penang, Malacca and Singapore whose investments in tin mines in Perak, Selangor and Sungai Ujong were at risk following riots and minor wars in those states. Many of these Chinese were British subjects, or regarded themselves as such, and demanded British intervention to establish law and order.

There was also pressure from British businessmen, though these were not as heavily committed as the Chinese, and from senior members of the administration of the Straits Settlements who favoured a "forward" policy of expansion.

The pressure that finally turned the scale was the threat of foreign, specifically German, intervention in the Peninsula and it was to forestall this as well as to remedy the other ills that the new Governor Sir Andrew Clarke was asked "to consider whether it would be advisable to appoint a British officer to reside in any of the States". The instructions made it clear that while Britain had no wish to "interfere in the internal affairs of the Malay States" she did not on the other hand wish to see "these fertile and productive countries" go to rack and ruin for want of someone to check "the present disorders".[6]

"The Present Disorders"

The Chinese merchants and others who wished Britain to intervene in Malaya had a vested interest in trying to paint the picture as black

---

* The Straits Settlement was transferred from the India Office to the Colonial Office in 1867.

as possible. They not only suggested that Germany might forestall Britain but that Holland, France, the United States of America and even Italy might be plotting to make a move if Britain delayed too long. They also tended to exaggerate the degree of disorder into which the Malay States had fallen. In this they were naturally followed by those officials and Ministers in the Foreign and Colonial Offices in London and those officials in the Straits Settlements who sought to justify a "forward" policy in the peninsula.

It was of course not difficult for people living in the Straits Settlements at the time to get the impression that the Malay States were in disorder. The fighting in the area of the Larut River in Perak was getting dangerously near the borders of Province Wellesley. There was violent gang warfare in Penang itself between rival Chinese Secret Societies, an extension of the struggles between similar factions in the tin-mining area of Larut. There were also riots in Singapore.

In these circumstances it was easy to jump from the particular to the general and to assume that because conditions were bad in parts of Perak, Selangor and Sungai Ujong the same must be true of the rest of Malaya. Though not accurate, this assumption was nevertheless freely made and coloured much of the thought and writings of people then and for a long time afterwards.

While it would be absurd to pretend that maladministration and civil disturbances did not exist in the Peninsula before official British intervention it would be equally unjust to the Malays to suggest that their troubles were entirely of their own making.

Sir Richard Winstedt has said: "It was Chinese immigration on a large scale that finally broke down Malay administration"—a remark which has not lost much in significance even today. The Chinese came mainly for the purpose of engaging in tin-mining, an activity which had been going on for many centuries in Malaya. Up to about 1840 the Malays had done the mining themselves but thereafter the Chinese arrived in great numbers and set about taking over the industry.

The local Malay administration was simply inadequate to cope with such an influx. Although from the beginning the Sultans and their Chiefs were heavily involved with the Chinese—even inviting them to exploit resources in the areas which they controlled and from which they could now expect dramatically increased revenues—the latter never became integrated into the community. It was not surprising. They were a race apart, separated from the Malays by their clannishness, their language and above all by their customs such as pork-eating which were abhorrent to a Moslem. Lured by the prospect of acquiring great wealth the Malay chiefs sought to exploit the Chinese, but they generally ended by losing both their authority and their money, which they frequently borrowed from Chinese businessmen in the Straits Settlements. They also became heavily embroiled in the battles which broke out between the rival secret societies, to which the miners were compelled to belong. At best these societies were welfare organisations providing accommodation, food and clothing and generally looking after the workers' interests; at worst they were glorified "protection" clubs run on Chicago gangster lines.

The largest societies such as the Hai San and the Ghee Hin quickly became kingdoms of their own and as rivalry between them increased in intensity the Malay chiefs became powerless to control them and merely tried to align themselves with the faction most likely to win.

The advent of tin-mining on a large scale and especially in areas which the Malays had never worked meant that many petty non-royal chiefs who had hitherto been relatively poor relations living on the perimeter of the Sultanate found themselves suddenly rich and powerful and able to challenge the authority of the Sultan and even to make a bid for the succession in advance of men of much higher birth. Such a person was Mantri Ngah Ibrahim in whose district, Larut, one of the richest tin-bearing areas was located. It was precisely the bitter struggles of men like the Mantri, aided and abetted by merchants and secret societies both inside and outside the State, which precipitated the crisis which led to British intervention in Perak and the installation of a British Resident in 1874.

The Chinese were not the only ones who interfered in the internal affairs of the Malay states; the British were equally active. A brief account of the activities of one of the most prominent contemporary Englishmen may serve to illustrate the extent to which business and politics were intertwined.

A leader of the business community in Singapore W. H. Read had played a prominent part in the campaign to transfer the Straits Settlement from the care of the India Office to the Colonial Office.[7] In 1866 he and Tan Kim Ching, a wealthy businessman and philanthropist of Singapore, lent money first to Sultan Abdul Samad of Selangor and then to his son-in-law, Zia-ud-Din, whom he had appointed his *wakil* or deputy. At about the same time J. G. Davidson, a Singapore lawyer, obtained from Zia-ud-Din an extremely generous tin-mining concession over a very large area of Selangor. Read then joined Davidson and others and floated the Selangor Tin Mining Company.

When this great tin-mining venture looked as if it might be frustrated by the insecurity which accompanied the civil war between Zia-ud-Din and various other contestants for power and influence, Davidson and Read decided to attempt to press the British Government to take action.

Davidson's London solicitors wrote to the Secretary of State, Colonial Office, describing conditions in Selangor and suggesting that the Government should either take Selangor under its protection or else allow the Selangor Tin Mining Company to raise its own military force.

This move met with no success. W. H. Read's brother-in-law, Seymour Clarke, who also acted as Davidson's agent in London, wrote to the Permanent Secretary at the Colonial Office and told him that an "old resident of Singapore" had warned him that if Britain offered no protection the smaller Malay States would probably look to some other European Power—"he had heard Germany mentioned"—for assistance.[8] Seymour Clarke went on to say that the promoters of the Company had had a letter from Zia-ud-Din in which the *wakil* had specifically asked whether Britain "or any other government" would be ready to preserve law and order so that the economic development of the State could go ahead in peace.

This time Read and Davidson were more successful. It would appear that Seymour Clarke's letter was instrumental in changing the Colonial Secretary's mind on the subject of intervention. At any rate the new Governor Sir Andrew Clarke was instructed to look into the possibility of appointing British officers to reside in the disturbed Malay States —with, of course, the prior consent of the Rulers.

This was not the end of Read's political activities. When the situation in Perak had got so serious that Clarke had made up his mind to take action Read managed to persuade Abdullah, the Sultan whose title was in dispute, to sign a letter which Read himself had drafted asking Clarke to send him someone "to show him a good system of government" and expressing the wish to "settle under the protection of the British flag" when all the troubles were over.[9]

This letter led to a meeting between some, but not all, of the Perak chiefs and Clarke on the island of Pangkor at which agreement was reached on the appointment of a "British Officer, to be called Resident who shall be accredited to his (the Sultan's) Court, and whose advice must be asked and acted upon on all questions other than those touching Malay Religion and Custom".[10]

The precedent was now established and it made the next move easier. In the next twelve months Read and Davidson achieved what they had originally been working for, namely British intervention in Selangor to protect the tin-mining venture: and not only this but Davidson himself was appointed Resident. This appointment, which shocked the Colonial Office, meant that Davidson was working hand in glove with the very man, Zia-ud-Din, who had given him the tin-mining concession.[11]

It might be argued that the Sultan of Selangor and his "deputy" genuinely wished the British to assist them to keep law and order and to establish a sound system of government and tax collection: one could not say the same of the Perak Malay chiefs.

It seems that Abdullah and Sir Andrew Clarke had very different ideas about the role of a Resident. Abdullah wanted a Resident mainly as a symbol of official British recognition of the legitimacy of his title of Sultan: a sign that anyone who disputed the title would have the British to reckon with as well as any forces which Abdullah could command from among his followers. Sir Andrew Clarke and Birch, the first Resident, had a much more positive role in mind.

Birch indeed set about his work with such energy and single-mindedness and with such a disregard for Malay susceptibilities that he managed to alienate the sympathies, not only of Abdullah but also of the latter's previous enemies and rivals. So outraged was Abdullah by the high-handed way in which Birch attempted to take over the entire running of Perak that he eventually connived at the murder of Birch by an agent of the Maharajah Lela.

Although Birch's assassination demonstrated precisely what Abdullah and the others thought of the Residential system it nevertheless made Britain's task much easier. The succession problem was neatly solved since most of the contenders were executed or banished leaving the way open for the British to appoint Yusuf, who had just as good a claim to the throne as Abdullah.

Interestingly enough Davidson was appointed to succeed Birch but found the task uncongenial and resigned the next year to go back to his legal and other work in Singapore.

The third Resident was installed in the small state of Sungai Ujong which is now part of Negri Sembilan ("Nine States"). Here again there was a connection with Singapore. We find that one of the directors of the Sungai Ujong Tin Mining Company was R. C. Woods, a partner of J. G. Davidson:[12] while another partner was Hoo Ah Kay known as Mr Whampoa (after his birthplace near Canton) who was, with W. H. Read, one of the first unofficial members of the Legislative Council formed in 1867.[13]

Such was the origin of the Residential System and such the part played in its formation by Chinese miners and financiers and British businessmen.

The system, after initial difficulties, was a success from the British point of view and probably also from the point of view of the Sultans who now had assured incomes and secure titles to their throne. It spread to Pahang whose Ruler acted on the advice of the Sultan of Johore who had close ties with both Pahang and Singapore.[14]

Very soon the Advisers became Rulers and the Rulers Advisers. In 1893 the Rulers lost even more power when the four States became a Federation under the first Resident-General, Sir Frank Swettenham.[15]

In 1909 a series of moves which had begun in the 1890's culminated in the Treaty of Bangkok by which the Malay States formerly under Siamese protection were brought under British control. Profiting by the experience of their less fortunate brothers, the rulers of Kedah, Perlis, Kelantan and Trengganu refused to join the Federation. They accepted Advisers but managed to ensure that a good deal of the administration remained in Malay hands.

These four Unfederated Malay States, as they were called collectively, provide an interesting contrast to the four who originally accepted Residents.

In July 1873 Governor Ord described the situation in the Peninsula as follows: ". . . the richest part of it is in the hands of the lawless and turbulent and with the exception of Johore, it is only in those States dependent in a certain degree on Siam that order is preserved".[16]

Even at this distance in time it is difficult to find out how accurate this observation was.

W. A. Graham, an Englishman who was appointed as the Siamese Government's Adviser in Kelantan in 1902, described Trengganu as a place where "there were no written laws, no courts and no police. All manner of crime was rampant, the peasantry was mercilessly down-trodden, but the land was full of holy men and the cries of the miserable were drowned in the noise of ostentatious prayer. In fine, Trengganu presented in the beginning of the year 1909 the type of untrammelled Malay rule which had fortunately disappeared from every other State in the Peninsula."[17]

Graham's description certainly has a ring of exaggeration about it and is difficult to reconcile it with Sir Harry Ord's assessment which we quoted a little earlier. A recent investigation[18] into the state of affairs in Trengganu at this time, however, suggests that the truth is nearer to Ord's version than Graham's.

There seems in fact to have been very little oppression. A previous Sultan had abolished *penghulus*, who would normally have transmitted his orders to the villagers, with the result that the leaders in the villages tended to be the religious leaders, the *sayyids* and the *Hajis*, who no doubt prayed ostentatiously but who also had a reputation for opposing unjust rule.

As for the chaos produced by "untrammelled Malay rule", a British investigation into alleged misrule revealed that there was only one district in which the allegations could be justified and that while rule was satisfactory in the others there was at least one district which could be held up as a model of good administration.

Of Kelantan, Graham speaks of the "chaos" which preceded his appointment as Siamese Adviser. The chaos appears to have been mainly in the area of revenue-collection and does not seem to have taken Graham very long to put right. A much more serious problem was one created not by the Malays but by an Englishman, Robert Duff, who secured a concession from the Rajah in 1900 which gave him almost unlimited powers of exploitation and even government over about a third of the total area of Kelantan. The subsequent history of this concession will not be told here:[19] suffice it to say that the State of Kelantan was eventually burdened with a debt which impeded its progress for years to come. In 1937 for instance it was noted that "Kelantan had a debt of $5,182,734 most of it borrowed from the

Straits Settlement and the Federated Malay States to settle the claims of the Duff Development Corporation".[20]

Of Perlis there is not much to be said beyond that it was a small (316 square miles) state, predominantly agricultural and predominantly Malay. Like Kelantan it had an Adviser appointed by Siam whose main task was to supervise its finances and in particular the uses to which a Siamese development loan was put.

In Kedah there was a powerful royal family and firm government. Up till two years before the British took over the suzerainty of Kedah from the Siamese in 1909 the effective administration of the State had been for over twenty years in the hands of the *Raja Muda* Abdul Aziz, the uncle of Tunku Abdul Rahman, the man who became the first Prime Minister of independent Malaya. As in Kelantan and Trengganu there were financial troubles which led in 1905 to the appointment of an Englishman named Williamson, himself the financial adviser to the Siamese Government, to Kedah as Adviser. Siam made a loan and it was understood that the Adviser would be withdrawn as soon as the loan was repaid.[21]

In 1909 all the Siamese protected states came under British control. In due course they all received British Advisers whose precise duties varied from State to State.

It was apparently the intention of the Governor at the time of the take-over that these states should eventually join the Federation. There are various reasons why this never happened. One important one was the very nature of these States. Unlike their Federated brothers they were predominantly Malay, predominantly agricultural and lacking the large foreign element in their population, which had undermined the traditional basis of society elsewhere.

Another important factor in the preservation of a certain amount of autonomy in the Unfederated States was that their Rulers had seen what had happened to their fellow-Sultans after Federation. They had seen how their power had been eroded, even if their position and their incomes had been stabilised. They had seen the growth in the power of the Residents and had no wish to have history repeated in their own states. Kedah in particular made this quite clear in 1910 when its civil servants went on strike *en masse* as a protest against the Adviser's autocratic behaviour.[22] Incidents like this not only gave Kedah a reputation for independent behaviour but made its accession to the Federation even more unlikely.

It has rightly been said that the determination of the "unfederated" Sultans to resist encroachments on what remained of their sovereignty had important results. It stood as a substantial obstacle on the path to centralisation and the ultimate goal of a unitary state. It also helped to underpin the position of the Malay Sultans and reminded the Governors and Colonial Secretaries to practise what they were so fond of preaching, namely the desire of the British not to diminish "in the slightest degree the powers and privileges which they (the Sultans) now possess" nor to curtail "the rights of self-government which they at present enjoy".

Decentralisation

Sir Frank Swettenham attacked Emerson for devoting so much of his book "Malaysia" to the question of "decentralisation". He wrote: "To give this local and embittered controversy—which began in 1920 and we all hope ended in 1932—the dignity of a record in the shape of a large volume, itself full of highly contentious writing, seemed needless, and naturally raises the question of what was the author's object in writing it."[23]

In retrospect it certainly seems strange that Swettenham, the architect of the 1895 Federation of the Malay States and the chief advocate of the further extension of the Federation to include the ex-Siamese States, should think the issue of "decentralisation" of so little moment.

In any case one cannot escape the fact that in the early 1920s and early 1930s "decentralisation" was the main topic of debate in high business and political circles in Malaya.

The Proposal

On the face of it "decentralisation" was merely a proposal that the Federation should become truly federal. Ever since 1895 the tendency had been for more and more power to be concentrated in the hands of the Resident-General* (as Swettenham had no doubt intended) and the Federal Council which between them had bid fair to usurp the functions of the Residents and the State Councils.

In the early 1920s there was an economic recession and this seemed to be an appropriate occasion to cut back the federal bureaucracy, thus avoiding unnecessary duplication of function, and at the same time to restore to the Sultans (or more realistically the Residents) some of the powers which the British were in theory so anxious to preserve.

As a further sop to the States it was also proposed to abolish the post of Chief Secretary and to make the Residents responsible only to the Governor in his role as High Commissioner to the Federated Malay States.

The Background

At the time when the proposals were made Malaya was divided into three parts:

1. *The Straits Settlement* (SS) a Crown Colony consisting of Singa-

---

* After 1910 Chief Secretary.

pore, Malacca and Penang administered directly by the British. Racial composition of the population in 1931:

Chinese 59·6%; Malay 25·6%; Indian 11·9%.*

2. *The Federated Malay States* (FMS) consisting of Selangor, Perak, Negri Sembilan and Pahang. In each State there was a British Resident, controlling a civil service whose senior members were mostly British. Above the Residents was the Chief Secretary who became the chief executive of what was more nearly a Union than a Federation. He was in turn responsible to the Governor in the Straits Settlement in the latter's role as High Commissioner. Racial composition of the population in 1931:

Chinese 41·5%; Malay 34·7%; Indian 22·2%.

3. *The Unfederated Malay States* (UMS) consisting of Johore, Kedah, Perlis, Kelantan and Trengganu. In each of these States was a British Adviser whose role in State affairs was in practice—if not in theory—much less pervasive than that of a Resident in the FMS. It is also true that the Advisers were much freer than the Residents in that they had no Chief Secretary to contend with but this freedom was usually exercised on behalf of their own State rather than in the interests of any outside or alien body. Racial composition of the population in 1931:

Chinese 21·7% Malay 69·2%; Indian 7·3%.

N.B. It should be noted that the figures for Johore are:

Chinese 41·4%; Malay 46·4% Indian 10·1%.

Reactions to the Proposal

Reactions to the proposal to decentralise were strong and varied. Each of the three groups viewed the matter from a different angle and within each group there were different reactions from at least three interested parties: the Sultans, the civil servants and the businessmen.

The Interested Parties

If we accept as a rough rule of thumb the proposition that the level of business activity in any given State was in direct proportion to the size of the Chinese community we may deduce that the sharpest reaction came from businessmen in the FMS, SS and Johore. They did not speak with one voice. Businessmen in the great free port of Singapore were mainly middlemen, not producers, and their interests were by no means the same as those of their colleagues in the FMS and the UMS, who were mainly engaged in the production and sale of primary products such as rubber and tin. In times of economic depression the

---

* All figures in this section are taken from Reference 25.

producers looked for salvation to schemes which would restrict trade, a course of action which was anathema to the free traders of Singapore. Any scheme therefore which contained any suggestion that the SS and the FMS might be united was bound to be suspect. This was precisely how the business community saw the proposals for decentralisation. Far from thinking of it as a mere restoration of the old pre-Federation state of affairs they suspected that the removal of the Chief Secretary was only the prelude to direct rule of both SS and FMS by the Governor from Singapore. On the other hand, even if it was to be a genuine decentralisation the businessmen in the FMS were also against it on the grounds that it would lead to loss of efficiency in administration stemming from increased Malay participation.

The Sultans as we might expect were not unanimous in their reactions. On the whole the FMS Rulers were in favour of any move which gave them more power. The Rulers in the UMS on the other hand wondered if the removal of the Chief Secretary was the first step in the direction of a Malayan Union since it put all the States in more or less the same relationship to the High Commissioner. Their fears must have been confirmed when eventually the Chief Secretary was replaced in 1935 by a Federal Secretary, whose sphere of action covered all the States and not just the Federated ones.[25]

The civil servants were also divided. There were on the one hand those who thought only of efficiency and therefore supported the business community's opposition to decentralisation; others—particularly those who had served in the predominantly Malay States—were in favour of preserving the Malay character of Malaya and thus supported decentralisation.

In one sense the whole decentralisation controversy was about the future of Malaya, although perhaps it was only the Malays who looked at it in that light. The question to which the British never gave an unambiguous answer was whether Malaya was to be a Malay or a Malayan* country. It might be argued that the British with their continual emphasis on the unimpaired sovereignty of the Malay Rulers followed a consistently pro-Malay line. If so they went about it in a strange way. In practice the British, from the moment they installed advisers, did almost everything they could to make the Sultans mere figureheads. They also encouraged immigration of Chinese and Indians to the point where the latter heavily outnumbered the Malays in several States and only just failed to outnumber them over Malaya as a whole.† In 1946 they even went so far as to abandon the Malays

---

* We use the term "Malayan" to denote a person of whatever ethnic origin who resides in Malaya. The term "Malay" denotes a person who speaks Malay and "conforms to Malay customs", a phrase which usually means that he wears Malay dress and in most cases is a Moslem.
† The figures for the whole of Malay in 1931 were: Malays 44.7%; Chinese 39.0%; Indians 14.2%.

altogether by forcing a Union on them which would have stripped the Sultans of their authority and given full Malayan citizenship to a body of "aliens equal in number to her (Malaya's) indigenous population".[26]

Sir Richard Winstedt once said that the history of Singapore was written mainly in statistics;[27] he was referring to its trade figures: one might with equal accuracy say that the history of Malaya is written in her census returns.

The Outcome

The great fight over decentralisation ended quite tamely with a victory for the decentralisers. The Chief Secretary was replaced by a Federal Secretary, who, though junior to the Residents, nevertheless had all the States, Federated and Unfederated, within his purview.

Thus for the time being were both sides satisfied. The decentralisers thought they had restored power to the States and the Sultans, while the centralisers regarded the abolition of the post of Chief Secretary as a necessary step on the path towards direct and unified rule by the High Commissioner. The events of 1945 and 1946 suggest that the latter view may have been the correct one.

Nationalism in Malaya

The Malays

"We have made Italy," said Massimo D'Azeglio;[28] "now we must make Italians". The Malay nationalists were faced with the problem in reverse: they did not need to "make Malays", but they needed to make Malaya.

The outlook of the average Malay was both too parochial and too inclusive. It was too parochial in that it never envisaged a world greater than that ruled by the Rajah and normally no greater than that ruled by the district chief; it was too inclusive in that anyone who professed Islam and conformed to custom was regarded as Malay whether he was actually born in the peninsula or had come over from Sumatra, Java, Borneo or even the Philippines.

"Nationality" was not a term of much significance to a Malay. The Malay equivalent of nationality was a compound of being a Moslem and owing personal allegiance to the Rajah: it was a personal rather than a territorial matter and took no account of modern artificial boundaries. Until the Anglo-Dutch Treaty of 1824 drew a line between the Peninsula and the Archipelago all previous large-scale political structures had straddled the Straits of Malacca and made no distinction between the Malays, say of Negri Sembilan and those of Minangkabau in Central Sumatra.

The British, as we have seen, maintained at all times that no action of theirs was designed to impair in any way the sovereignty of the

Malay Rulers. The British also, though economically pro-Chinese and pro-Indian, were politically pro-Malay.

By this we mean that British policy was designed to maintain the *status quo ante*. Inasmuch as the Malay peasant received any education it was primary education only and conducted in Malay not English. It was calculated to produce "a vigorous and self-respecting agricultural peasantry, such as must form the backbone of every nation".[29]

For the peasantry there were vernacular schools. For the aristocracy there was the Malay College at Kuala Kangsar where a select body of pupils drawn from the ranks of the upper classes received an English education which fitted them for lower to middle grade jobs in the public service. The rajahs and their immediate circle of courtiers of course continued to reign, if not rule, with or without the benefits of education.

In these circumstances perhaps the one factor which might have induced an awareness of nationality in the Malays was the vast and menacing influx of Chinese and Indians. In 1911, for instance, only just over thirty-six per cent of the population of Perak, Selangor and Negri Sembilan was Malay, compared with about forty-three per cent Chinese and eighteen per cent Indian.

For much of the period of British rule it was thought that the Chinese were not a permanent feature of Malayan life: they were merely birds of passage who stopped for a while in Malaya to make money and then returned to China. When, in the 1920s and 1930s, it slowly dawned on the Malays that this was not the case they also realised that it would be rash to press for the withdrawal of the British. As Abdul Majid put it in 1928: "It is dangerous for fatherless young chickens like ourselves . . . to move about above where there are hawks and eagles hovering about ready to pounce. . . ."[30]

The Malays, then, in the *kampong* looked to their rulers for a lead and the rulers for the reasons given were not anxious to press for the withdrawal of the British protectorate. They were content instead to make sure that their powers were not further eroded and that more opportunities were given to Malays to qualify for posts in the administration.

RELIGIOUS REFORM

Up to 1938 there were virtually no specifically anti-colonial Malay movements, but this is not to say that there were no political movements of any kind.

There was first the Islamic reform movement. As Islam embraces both the religious and the political any movement to reform, "modernise" or purify Islam was bound to have political repercussions in the Malay community. This, as in Indonesia, took the form of a battle of words between *Kaum Muda* (The Young Generation) and *Kaum Tua* (The Old Generation). *Kaum Tua* regarded the whole modernist movement as an attack on the authority of the established social order. *Kaum Muda* was especially hard on the rural establishment in which the *ulama* (those learned in Islam) played an important role. The latter were held up as charlatans who had very little knowledge of Islam and who took advantage of the illiterate peasants.[31]

However, in Malaya, unlike Indonesia, Islam never became the rallying point of a nationalist, anti-colonial movement. But then in 1930 "Foreign Asiatics" (mostly Chinese) were only 2·2% of the population in the Netherlands East Indies whereas they were 53·2% (Chinese 39%: Indians 14·2%) of the population of British Malaya.

CULTURAL NATIONALISM

If the promotion of one's own culture is a form of a nationalism there were several examples of this in Malaya both before and after the British "Forward Movement" of the 1870s.

People became increasingly aware of the need to consolidate the Malay language and to standardise its spelling and grammar. Dictionaries were compiled in the early years by Malays; in the later years by Malays in conjunction with European scholars like Wilkinson and Winstedt.

The growth of vernacular schools revealed the sad lack of suitable Malay texts and an effort was made on the lines of the Balai Pustaka (Institute of Culture) in Indonesia to produce books in Malay dealing with the history, legends and folk stories of Malaya. Text books in Bahasa Indonesia, the Indonesian variant of Malay, were also imported from the Dutch East Indies and used in Malay schools.

The nearest this cultural drive got to reaching national proportions was in the Sahabat Pena (Pen Friend) which at one time had about 2,000 members over the Peninsula. Starting life as a children's pen friend organisation it became popular and soon became something more serious, a society to promote Malay literature, with branches in every State. It was sometimes suspected of being a cover for clandestine political activity but there is no reason to believe that the suspicion was ever justified.

The Chinese

THE NATIONALISTS

Most of the Chinese who lived in the "Nanyang", as the area we know as Southeast Asia was called, came from two provinces of China which were noted for their general hostility to the rule of the Manchu dynasty (1644-1912). Their feelings therefore towards their mother-country were ambivalent and some of them were inclined to regard the lands to which they had emigrated as the focus of their loyalty.

By the turn of the century, however, the picture had changed considerably. Rebellions had broken out in various parts of China and the Manchus' position began to look very insecure.

It was at this time that Sun Yat Sen started to go round the Far East and Southeast Asia founding societies whose main function was to collect money to finance the rebel movements in China, many of which had been organised by Sun himself. In the early 1900s Dr Sun visited Malaya and formed branches of the T'ung Meng Hui in several towns. General hostility to the Manchus ensured that the Chinese community was quite generous in its donations to Dr Sun's cause.

All these efforts were crowned in 1912 by the forced abdication of the last Manchu Emperor, P'u Yi—then a boy of about six years of age—and the proclamation of a republic.

These events had a great effect upon the Chinese of the Nanyang. It resulted in a new flowering of pride in their mother-country and a growing sense of detachment from the country of their adoption. In Malaya and Indonesia they became nationalistic, not in the sense of wishing to promote the independence of Malaya and Indonesia, but in the sense of wishing to promote the interests of China and all things Chinese.

The integration in China of various societies in 1912 into a new organisation known as the Kuomintang (KMT) led to the formation of KMT branches throughout Southeast Asia.

The KMT was suspect in Malay for various reasons. It directed Malayan Chinese patriotism towards China rather than Malaya; it was under strong Communist influence (Sun Yat Sen worked with Michael Borodin and Ho Chi Minh) and it was anti-colonialist, although the anti-colonialism was mostly directed at the exploiters of China rather than the Southeast Asian colonial regimes.

In 1927 Chiang Kai Shek expelled the Communists from the KMT causing a split in the movement which was paralleled throughout the Nanyang. The KMT was now in power in China and Chiang's regime was given diplomatic recognition by the West. The British authorities in Malaya, who had banned the KMT, were now compelled to change their policy and a compromise was reached whereby the Chinese could be members as individuals of the KMT of China but were not allowed to form branches in Malaya.

Perhaps the most significant by-product of the events of 1912 in China was the renewed interest in education. A wave of enthusiasm for education engulfed the Chinese of Malaya and Indonesia; and in both countries scores of new schools were set up. The schools were mostly supported by voluntary contributions and the instruction in them was not often of a high standard but because they multiplied rapidly and because they used Chinese as the medium of instruction they were of great political significance. Through the use of Chinese rather than Malay or English they stressed the alienness of the Chinese and through the use of textbooks published in Shanghai they spread anti-colonial propaganda among the pupils.

The British authorities eventually censored the textbooks and demanded that they be replaced, but apart from this they actively encouraged the Chinese by giving government grants to the schools. By thus encouraging the growth of Chinese education for the Chinese and Malay education for the Malays the British did a great deal to ensure that the two communities would grow further and further apart. It is not surprising therefore, that the Malays should lay on Britain much of the blame for the present communal strife.

THE COMMUNISTS

Until 1927 the fortunes of the Chinese Communists in Malaya were bound up with those of the KMT; after that date they went into eclipse but revived in 1937 when Chiang Kai Shek came to an agreement with the Communists after the latter had only just failed to remove him from power.

In the same year Japan began her undeclared war on China and Chinese Communities in the Nanyang whether KMT or Communist had another reason for making common cause against the new enemy.

But the Communists were not content merely to mirror events in China. They were also concerned to promote the social revolution in Malaya. One of their successes was the rubber tappers' strike in 1937 as a result of which the workers were awarded higher wages by the Government.

In Indonesia the Communists were very much part of the general nationalist anti-colonial movement. In Malaya their efforts in this field misfired. They were unable to kindle much enthusiasm among the Malays for an anti-British movement and the Chinese were either entirely content with the present state of affairs as compared to the chaotic pre-British days or were too engrossed with events in China to pay much attention to local politics.

It was as the driving force behind the anti-Japanese movement that the Communists finally came into their own. When the Japanese invaded Malaya in 1941 the Chinese were their first and chief victims and the Communists were in the forefront of those who resisted. Eventually even the British were driven to co-operate with them and give them arms and military training.

One commentator[32] maintains that by 1945 the Malayan Communist Party was in an excellent position to capture the Malayan nationalist movement and "block the return of the British". There are various good reasons why they failed to make the most of this opportunity. The most convincing of these is that the Communists lacked firm leadership. In the absence of this they were apt to rely on directions from Moscow, which were none too clear at this time. In any case they decided to try to build up a large following among the ra'ayat (the people) and to foment labour unrest and strikes. In the two or three years they were doing this the nation's attention was shifted to the battle between the Malay Rulers and the British over the formation of a Malayan Union.

The new constitution threatened to make a "Malayan" Malaya with common citizenship for all its permanent residents regardless of race. The Malays therefore rallied behind their traditional leaders and were in no mood to follow the lead of the Malayan Communist Party with its almost exclusively Chinese membership.

In 1948 the unpopular Malayan Union was replaced by a Federation and the Malay Rulers were back in their old places but with somewhat greater powers than they had enjoyed before the war. The initiative had now passed to the traditional leaders and it was they and not the Communists who led Malaya to independence in 1957.

Background to Politics after 1945

Part One: *The Malays*

THE ANTECEDENTS OF UMNO

In 1926 a group of middle-class, mainly English educated, Malay lawyers, journalists, religious functionaries and merchants founded the Kesatuan Melayu Singapura or Singapore Malay Union. Its objects were to promote the welfare of Malays living in Singapore politically, socially and educationally. The need for such an organisation must have seemed quite obvious in a city whose population in those days was over eighty-seven per cent non-Malay.

This example was not followed anywhere else in Malaya until 1937 when branches were formed in Malacca and Penang. In 1938, however, there was a new phenomenon: the organisation of a political society under the patronage not of the middle class Malay but of the aristocracy. This was the Persatuan Melayu (Malay Association) of Pahang, one of whose founders was Dato Husain the father of Tun Abdul Razak, a leading figure in independent Malaysia.

Similar associations were set up in Selangor, Johore, Kelantan, Perak, Sarawak and Brunei in the course of the next two years. Attempts were made to unite all these movements into one great Union of Malay Associations but they failed. Loyalty to the State and its Ruler prevailed over any interest which the Malays might have had in common.

The history of these associations clearly demonstrates that as far as mobilising Malay opinion was concerned the traditional aristocrats were still the most effective leaders. It was not, however, until their corporate existence was threatened that they were willing to co-operate with each other across the State boundaries.

THE FORMATION OF UMNO

The threat to the rulers came in 1945 after the surrender of the Japanese when the British returned to Malaya and announced their plans for the setting up of a Malayan Union. In this new unitary system the citizens would no longer owe their allegiance to the Rulers of their State but to the British Crown, in preparation for the day when there would be a united independent Malaya. In this new scheme of things the traditional Malay rulers would lose most of their powers and the Malays would no longer enjoy privileged status but would have to be content to be equal citizens with the Chinese and the Indians. In March 1946, a few weeks before the official inauguration of the Malayan Union, Dato Onn, the son of a former Prime Minister of Johore, called a meeting of all the Malay Associations and succeeded in amalgamating them into one body, the United Malay Nationalist Organisation. The main object of UMNO was to oppose Malayan Union and to fight for a restoration of the rights and privileges of the Malays in a Malay country. As the first President of UMNO, Dato Onn was able in his campaign against the Union to use the experience he had gained as an editor of a Malay newspaper in the 1930s, when he was fighting for Malay rights during the arguments over "decentralisation".

Part Two: *The Chinese*

THE MALAYAN COMMUNIST PARTY

The formation of a Federation whose constitution was biased in favour of the Malays made it inevitable that post-Federation politics would be conducted in racial or "communal" terms. It was therefore doubly unfortunate that the Malayan Communists, the vast majority of whom were Chinese, should choose this moment, not only to try to take over the leadership of the anti-Federation, anti-Malay movement, but to launch a terrorist movement designed to bring down the colonial regime.

The Communist insurgency which lasted from 1948 until the middle of 1960 and is generally referred to as the "Emergency", divided the Chinese community into at least three factions: those who supported the Communists; those, including members of the KMT, who opposed them and those—the majority—who sat on the fence awaiting the outcome.

For Communist activity in Southeast Asia 1948 and 1949 were peak years. There are strong reasons for supposing that delegates to the Communist Youth Conference of 1948 in Calcutta were encouraged, if not ordered, to step up their activities at the earliest opportunity. In any case Communist subversion increased in every country and Communists everywhere were given an additional boost by the victory of Mao Tse Tung over Chiang Kai Shek and the inauguration of a Communist People's Republic in mainland China on October 1, 1949.

THE MALAYAN CHINESE ASSOCIATION

The Malayan Communist Party claimed to be waging a war of national liberation on behalf of all Malayans. However its membership was so overwhelmingly Chinese that it received little sympathy from the Malays who were mostly content to work gradually and constitutionally towards independence. The MCP also put the non-Communist Chinese in a very embarrassing position: the latter wished on the one hand to be dissociated from the Communists but on the other hand to fight for their rights in a Malay-oriented Federation. At this juncture Tan Chen Lock, a pre-war member of both the Straits Settlement Legislative and Executive Councils, founded the Malayan Chinese Association. He had support in this venture from the High Commissioner, Sir Henry Gurney, who was also anxious that Malayan Chinese should have some non-Communist outlet for their legitimate political demands. The British gave their support because they could see the dangers inherent in a situation where "terrorist" and "Chinese" might be thought of as synonymous terms. In fact the MCA was able to do valuable work during the "Emergency" by giving aid of all kinds to the many victims of terrorism and to those who were compulsorily removed from remote spots and re-settled in "new villages" where they could no longer be blackmailed into giving food and sustenance to the Communists.

The MCA was not a "popular" party in the strict sense of the word: it was mainly a party of well-to-do Chinese who acted as spokesmen for Chinese interests in the Federation. Its main contact with the "masses" was through its welfare work and it no doubt expected recipients of aid to remember the party at the next elections. But even in the early years it was never *the* party of the Chinese. It was not "communal" enough. In 1957 for instance when the final details of the Federal Constitution were being worked out, the MCA refused to support widespread Chinese demands for the recognition of Chinese as an official language and for the abolition of discrimination against non-Malays in matters like the acquisition of Malayan citizenship.

Part Three: *The Non-Communalists*

THE IMP AND THE PARTY NEGARA

A significant year in the history of post-war Malayan politics was 1951. In that year Dato Onn, the founder of UMNO and a Malay nationalist of long standing, decided to launch a new party which was to be genuinely multi-racial. His attempts at widening the membership of UMNO had failed and he was convinced that Malaya needed to present a united multi-racial front to the world in order to earn the right to independence.

To this end Dato Onn left UMNO, where his place was taken by Tunku Abdul Rahman, and formed the Independence of Malaya Party (IMP), membership of which was to be open to all races.

The experiment failed, just as the Malayan Union had failed, and for the same reason: at this time no political programme which included the promise of equal citizenship rights for Malays, Chinese and Indians had any hope of success.

Three years later Dato Onn tried to get back into politics. This time his new organisation, the Party Negara, was implicitly for Malays only. It was left to his successor as leader of UMNO to launch the one and only multi-racial venture which ever met with any real success.

THE ALLIANCE PARTY

In 1952 the holding of local government elections as a preparation for further instalments of self-government gave UMNO and MCA a chance to make an electoral arrangement by which each would support the other's candidates in selected constituencies.

The success of this arrangement led to its institutionalisation in 1953 as the Alliance Party. In 1955 the Malayan Indian Congress joined the Alliance.

It is important to stress that the Alliance Party has throughout its existence been more an alliance than a party. Lennox Mills has described it as a marriage of convenience between the Malays, who had the votes, and the Chinese, who had the funds. The description is a useful one in that it helps one to understand the changes that were bound to occur within the Alliance when the Malays started to aspire to the money and the Chinese acquired the vote.

After its successes in the 1952 local government elections members of the Alliance Party then went on to win fifty-one out of the fifty-two elective seats in the general elections for the Legislative Council in 1955. The Alliance's leader, Tunku Abdul Rahman, was now in a position to head the independence movement and acquire most of the kudos which rightly came his—and his party's—way when independence was achieved on August 31, 1957.

The Federation of Malaya 1957-1963

Throughout the colonial period the British maintained what one might call the legal fiction that Malaya was a Malay country ruled by Malay Sultans. In 1957 the fiction became a fact: Malaya retained its Sultans and the Malay Head of State, himself a Sultan, was given the responsibility in Article 153 of the Constitution of safeguarding "the special position of the Malays and the legitimate interests of other communities . . .". He also had to provide for "the reservation for Malays of such proportion as he may deem reasonable of positions in the Public Service (other than the Public Service of a State) and of scholarships, exhibitions and other similar educational or training facilities given or accorded by the Federal Government and when any permit or licence for the operation of any trade or business is required by federal law then subject to the provisions of that law and this Article, of such permits and licences."

Article 153 ruled out the possibility of Malaya's ever being a "Malayan" Malaya—a phrase which can only imply the loss by the Malays of their "special position". If this point was not at first clear to the Chinese in Malaya it soon became clear over the next few years.

When the Alliance fought its first general election in 1955, eighty-four per cent of the electorate was Malay and eleven per cent Chinese and there was a majority of Malay voters in all but two of the fifty-two constituencies.

In the first post-Independence elections in 1959 the position had changed considerably. The Malays now formed only fifty-seven per cent of the electorate while thirty-six per cent of the voters were Chinese and in only sixty-three out of the one hundred and four constituencies was there a majority of Malay voters. In the absence of vital external issues the 1959 elections were fought on the government's domestic record and the result was by no means the vote of confidence which the Alliance later claimed it to be. The Alliance in fact won seventy-four out of the one hundred and four seats and suffered severe defeats in the predominantly Malay areas of Kelantan and Trengganu. Even more significant than these losses was the quite bitter struggle within the Alliance's National Council over the number of constituencies in which each of the three partners would be allowed to put up the official Alliance candidate. In particular the Chinese demanded a greater share of the official candidatures in view of their greatly increased representation in the electorate. A compromise was eventually reached but the chairman, Lin Chong Eu, and some of the younger element of the MIC left the Alliance to seek their political fortunes elsewhere. This quarrel and the poor performance of the party in Kelantan and Trengganu showed that both the Chinese and the Malays were beginning to lose faith in the Alliance as a party which could advance their sectional interests.

In the next elections the Alliance regained much of its lost ground and it looked as if a victory had been won for the politics of non-communalism; however the circumstances in which this victory was won were by no means normal, as will appear.

The Transition to Malaysia

On May 27, 1961 at a meeting of foreign correspondents in Singapore, Tunku Abdul Rahman made the first open move towards the formation of Malaysia. He said that the time had come for a plan to be formulated whereby Malaya, Singapore, North Borneo, Brunei and Sarawak could be "brought closer together in political and economic co-operation". Though received with great enthusiasm by Singaporeans present at the meeting the Tunku's announcement must have come as a great surprise to those who remembered the general antipathy in Malaya towards any close association with Singapore. In truth the Tunku's

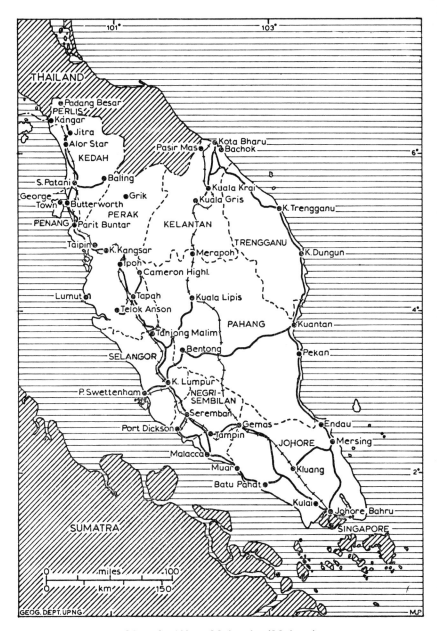

Map 9. West Malaysia (Malaya)

attitude to Malaysia differed quite widely from that of Singapore's Prime Minister, Lee Kuan Yew; where the latter was looking to the creation of a genuinely multi-racial society where no particular ethnic group would have a "special position" but all would acquire a common "Malaysian" identity, the Tunku was still thinking in much less radical terms. For him the concept of Malaysia with its inclusion of the large non-Chinese populations of the Borneo territories was a neat solution of the problem of how to "merge" with Singapore without being swamped by the latter's large Chinese population. It is an irony of history that the Borneo territories, which were least enthusiastic about entering Malaysia, are still within it whereas Singapore, which was soon to be its main champion, was a member state for only two years.

At this point we turn to a consideration of the political atmosphere in each of the three British colonies which were about to achieve independence through incorporation within Malaysia.

Singapore

By the time the British returned to Singapore after the final surrender of the Japanese it had already been decided that the island was going to be politically separated from the Malay Peninsula. If the Malayan Union, with its promise of common citizenship, was unpopular with the Malays and their Sultans one can imagine how much less acceptable would have been the prospect of a Union which included the large Chinese population of Singapore. Singapore was therefore declared a Crown Colony with a Governor and provision for a Legislative Council which was to include six popularly elected members.

The first two elections, in 1948 and 1951, did not arouse much enthusiasm. Registration was voluntary and only a small number of people took the trouble of getting themselves enrolled and not all of these actually voted.

In 1954 the Rendel Commission published its recommendations on constitutional reform. There were no startling changes. There was to be an Assembly with greater popular representation but the Council of Ministers, of which the Governor was chairman, still had officials in the most strategic positions.

Of rather greater importance was the foundation in 1954 by Lee Kuan Yew, a brilliant lawyer, of the People's Action Party (PAP), which distinguished itself in the following year by winning three of the four seats for which it put up candidates in the 1955 elections to an enlarged Assembly.

From 1955 to 1959 the main focus of attention was the dialogue between the United Kingdom and Singapore on the subject of self-government. Since these negotiations took place when the "Emergency" was still a grim reality in neighbouring Malaya it was not surprising that the whole question of security, against both internal and external foes, was uppermost in the minds of the British. At a time when all Chinese were being regarded with suspicion and when it looked as if the People's Action Party, a good proportion of whose membership was Communist, stood a fair chance of winning the next election, the British were most anxious to retain some measure of control over defence and internal security. Eventually, after the first Prime Minister, David Marshall, had resigned and his successor, Lim Yew Hock, had demonstrated his political soundness by having various prominent left-wingers arrested and detained, agreement was reached. A defence committee was set up with the British Commissioner as chairman. The committee had equal numbers of British and Singaporeans on it but also had a representative from Malaya who had a casting vote in the event of a deadlock. With the problem of defence solved Singapore achieved self-government with Lee Kuan Yew as Prime Minister at the head of the PAP which won forty-three out of the fifty-one seats in the Legislative Assembly in the 1959 elections.

For Lee Kuan Yew self-government was but a step on the road to independence: independence as part of a larger Malayan whole. The British separation of Singapore from the mainland seemed to Lee an artificial state of affairs which should not be allowed to continue. Singapore and Malaya were natural and complementary economic partners while politically Lee Kuan Yew had for some time dreamed of building a genuinely multi-racial society in which Chinese and Malay could mix on equal terms. Such ideas were not welcomed at this time in Malaya. The Malay leaders realised that if Singapore was merged with Malaya the Chinese would be the largest single ethnic group in the new Federation. They also disagreed on the question of citizenship. The Sultans had stoutly resisted the idea of a common citizenship without special rights for the Malays in the days of the short-lived Malayan Union and they were not willing to change their opinions now to suit Lee Kuan Yew's concept of what he had once called a "Malayan society, not Malay, not Malayan Chinese, not Malayan Indian, not Malayan Eurasian, but Malayan, one that embraces the various races already in the country".

Tunku Abdul Rahman's thoughts about a wider federation were given at the press conference of May 27, 1961. Lee Kuan Yew was naturally greatly in favour of the proposal and by September of that year had come to a general agreement with the Tunku on the terms of Singapore's entry. Enthusiastic as Lee Kuan Yew was about Malaysia he still had to have the proposal approved in the Legislative Assembly where he could now no longer command a majority since the ultra-left wingers had deserted the PAP to form the Barisan Socialis. The latter, as well as other left-wing groups, were known to be opposed to merger and it was very much an open question as to whether Lee's views would prevail. The Prime Minister decided to find out the views of the general public by means of a referendum. Lee Kuan Yew afterwards referred to the holding of the referendum as a "calculated risk"[33] but as the voters were asked to choose not between merger and non-merger but between three different conditions for merger there was perhaps more calculation than risk attached to the enterprise. In the event seventy-one per cent of the voters declared themselves in favour of the PAP's merger conditions while twenty-five per cent returned blank ballots. The opposition parties complained bitterly but Lee had won a great political victory. Singapore was now committed to Malaysia; it only remained for the Borneo territories to follow her lead.

Sarawak

With an area nearly as large as Malaya but only a tenth of Malaya's population, Sarawak at the time of its entry into the Federation of Malaysia in 1963 was under-developed both economically and politically. For all but seventeen of the previous one hundred and twenty-two years Sarawak had been under the personal rule of the Brookes, the so-called "White Rajahs". There can be no doubt that the Brooke family was able, brave and conscientious, not to say colourful; but its achievements in the field of the political education of the people in its care were so small as to be hardly noticeable. The one and only concession to modernity came in 1941 when, in commemoration of a hundred years of Brooke rule, Sir Charles Vyner Brooke gave his people a new constitution in which the Council Negri, a lower house of twenty-five members, was given legislative powers and a measure of control over public expenditure. Since the Council had a majority of official members and the Rajah had a hand in appointing the unofficial members, it could not be said that the new constitution marked any great advance towards responsible and representative government. In any case the Japanese intervened before the new system had had a chance to function for any reasonable length of time.

As soon as the war in the Pacific was over and the winds of anti-colonialism were beginning to blow strongly, the British Government took over responsibility for Sarawak from the Brooke family, mainly on the grounds that the latter did not have the resources to finance the rapid economic and social development which the post-war situation demanded.

From 1946 to 1963 there was heightened activity in Sarawak, but the main effort was in the economic and administrative fields. As far as political development was concerned the new administration concentrated on the setting up of local government bodies and by the end of 1957 most of Sarawak was covered by these councils. The intention was that these councils should be the basic building blocks upon which a structure of representative government would be built. Sarawak was, and still is, divided into five divisions: each of these divisions was administered by a Resident who had a Divisional Advisory Council to

assist him. At the apex of the pyramid was the Governor, advised by
the Council Negri. There were no general elections for all these bodies:
there were only elections for the district councils. Once elected, the
district councillors then chose representatives for the Divisional Advisory Councils and members of the latter in turn acted as the electorate
for twenty-one of the forty-five members of the Council Negri. Of the
remaining twenty-four members of the Council Negri, three were
elected by the members of the three most important town councils and
twenty-one were appointed by the Governor-in-Council.

When Tunku Abdul Rahman first mooted the idea of a Federation
of Malaysia which might include the Borneo territories of Brunei,
Sarawak and Sabah (British North Borneo), the Sarawakians had had
no experience of general elections except those held for District
Councils in 1959, and only a brief and very slight introduction to the
intricacies of representative government at any but the lowest level. In
these circumstances it is not surprising that the idea of federation
with the much richer and more politically sophisticated Malaya and
Singapore met with a cold, not to say hostile, reception in Sarawak.
The Sarawakians, after years of *laissez-faire* under the Brookes and a
short period of gentle progress under the British Crown, found the new
pace of political advancement altogether too fast. They were also
suspicious of the Malays and it needed all Tunku Abdul Rahman's
considerable diplomatic skill to persuade them that they were not
merely exchanging British for Malay colonialism.

Sabah

Three-fifths the size of Sarawak and with a proportionately smaller
population Sabah in 1963 was even more politically backward than
Sarawak. It had a Legislative Council, it is true, but its powers were
very limited and its members were all nominated and unlike the
Council Negri there was no majority of unofficial members until April
1961. At the time when the Malaysia proposals were being discussed
Sabah had had no elections at all and there was, not surprisingly, not
a single political party in existence. There were town councils in
operation but their members were all nominated and it was not until
December 1962 that the first elections were held to choose people to
serve on the district councils.

Previously known as British North Borneo, the territory now called
Sabah was administered by the British North Borneo Company from
1878 to 1946, when it became a Crown Colony like Sarawak. The
territory had formerly been partly under the rule of the Sultan of Sulu
—in the present-day Philippines—and partly under the rule of the Sultan
of Brunei. The two sultans ceded the territory to a certain Baron von
Overbeck in 1878, in return for an annual payment of five thousand
Straits dollars. At intervals ever since 1878 this transaction has been the

subject of controversy and diplomatic battles. The Spanish, then the colonial rulers of the Philippines, disputed the validity of the cession almost as soon as it had been made but eventually agreed to recognise its legality. The argument was revived after the Second World War by the government of the Republic of the Philippines which based its arguments on the ambiguity of the Malay text of the bargain made between von Overbeck and the Sultan of Sulu: the Filipinos claimed that the word which the British—and the Malaysian Government— translated as "ceded" really meant "leased". The Malaysian Government has so far declined to take the matter to the International Court so the ownership of Sabah still remains in dispute.

Like their neighbours in Sarawak, the people of Sabah, or rather those few who had any knowledge of what was involved, reacted hostilely to the idea of inclusion in the new Federation of Malaysia. With no political parties and no ready-made machinery for representation or the testing of public opinion, the role of spokesman was assumed by Mr Donald Stephens, the leader of the unofficial members in the Legislative Council. Stephens's first move was to join Ong Kee Hui of the Sarawak United People's Party (SUPP) and A. M. Azahari, the leader of Brunei's solitary political party the Party Ra'ayat, to form the United Front to represent the Borneo territories in discussions about Malaysia. Two weeks after Tunku Abdul Rahman's announcement about the possibility of forming a Federation which would include the Borneo territories the United Front announced that "any plan in accordance with the pronouncements made by Tunku Abdul Rahman in Brunei and Sarawak would be totally unacceptable to the people of the three territories". The main fear seemed to be that the Malays would take advantage of the relative educational backwardness of the Borneans and take over all the top administrative posts as soon the British had left. They also evidently thought that the Tunku was assuming rather too readily that the indigenous races of Borneo—the Ibans, the Kadazans, the Muruts and all the others—could be counted on for political purposes as "Malays". At this stage, the general consensus of opinion was that the territories should achieve independence first and then decide whether or not they wished to join a wider federation.

Considering that not only the Bornean leaders but also the British Governors of Sarawak and British North Borneo and the High Commissioner for Brunei were initially antagonistic to the idea of Malaysia, it is surprising how quickly opinions changed over the following few months. Of the various factors which might account for this change three stand out for special mention: the Tunku's diplomacy, the threat of Communism and the sheer economic logic of the situation.

Tunku Abdul Rahman spared no effort in his attempt to win over the Bornean leaders. Sensing that the latter might be nervous at the prospect of venturing into the uncertainties of Independence the

Tunku made sure that his guests were shown all the economic and political achievements of Malaya. The visitors were suitably impressed by the rural development schemes, the very healthy balance of payments and the success with which the Alliance Party had managed to keep the peace between the various racial groups. The prospect of sharing in this prosperity was quite an alluring one.

The threat of Communist expansion and infiltration played an important part in the formation of Malaysia. Abdul Rahman had always been averse to any kind of merger with Singapore on the grounds that Lee Kuan Yew's People's Action Party had an important Communist element and it was only when Lee showed his ideological soundness by managing to win a general election—admittedly by a very small margin—without the help of the Communists, who had now been expelled from the PAP, that the Tunku was willing to listen to Lee's argument that Singapore and Malaya could fight Communism better together than apart. The Communist presence in Singapore was more of an immediate threat to Malaya than Borneo but the threat that hung over all the would-be Malaysian territories came from Indonesia which was allying herself more and more openly with Peking. Sabah and Sarawak both had long common borders with Indonesian Kalimantan, while both in Brunei and Sarawak there were people and parties who were known to be supporters of Indonesian expansionist ambitions in the area. In December 1962, A. M. Azahari, the leader of Brunei's Party Ra'ayat, organised a revolt in Brunei in protest against the formation of Malaysia. His cause was soon taken up by the Indonesian government which now labelled "Malaysia" a neo-colonialist plot. Azahari's revolt was quickly suppressed and his scheme for the formation of a separate federation of the three Borneo territories met with little support from Sabah and Sarawak, whose inhabitants remembered the old days when the Sultans of Brunei had lorded it over them with an iron hand.

Azahari's revolt and the readiness with which their neighbour Indonesia supported it merely confirmed what had been fairly plain already to the leaders of Sabah and Sarawak that the only alternative to joining Malaysia was being swallowed up by Indonesia.

Third, there was the economic argument. Lacking the resources to finance their own development, Sabah and Sarawak looked forward to sharing in Malaya's prosperity and getting the same sort of assistance as the poorer rural areas of Malaya were apparently getting. They also saw trade advantages in joining a Malaysian Common Market.

Negotiations between Borneo and Malaya

Once they had decided, in principle, to join Malaysia the Borneo territories concentrated on the task of negotiating the best possible terms. Tunku Abdul Rahman's oft-repeated assurance that the new members would have exactly the same privileges as the other eleven states of Malaya was not regarded as at all adequate. It was clear to the Borneo delegates that their countries would have to have more independence of action and more safeguards against direction from Kuala Lumpur than was enjoyed by the states of the present Malayan federation.

In July 1961 during a meeting of the Commonwealth Parliamentary Association in Singapore a "Malaysian Solidarity Consultative Committee" (MSCC) was formed, consisting of delegates from all the prospective members of the proposed new federation. The MSCC's function was not only to discuss the shape of the new federation and various important constitutional issues but to publicise the idea of Malaysia and encourage public debate. It did its work so well that by the end of its fourth and last meeting in Singapore in February 1962 it was able to announce that there was such unanimity among the delegates that the formation of Malaysia was now only a matter of time. The delegates from Borneo were now clearer about the safeguards which would have to be written into the constitution of the federation when their countries joined it and their thoughts on this subject were submitted to the Commission of Enquiry which was set up to "ascertain the views of the peoples of North Borneo and Sarawak" and to make recommendations.

The main anxieties of the Borneo delegates were in the fields of religion, language, migration and education.

There was considerable opposition to the idea of making Islam the religion of the new Federation but eventually non-Moslems were persuaded to agree to this proposal when it was pointed out that this provision had in no way endangered religious freedom in Malaya.

On the question of language the delegates had no objection in principle to the choice of Malay as the national language; there had, however, to be safeguards and the actual decision to put such a proposal into effect should be in the hands of the State and not the Federal legislature.

The delegates from Borneo were also anxious that their sparsely populated countries should not be over-run by migrants from Singapore and Malaya; they were anxious to preserve opportunities for employment in commerce and the civil service for local residents. They were anxious to retain the services of British civil servants until "their places can be taken by qualified people *from the Borneo territories*".

The future of education in the Borneo territories was very much bound up with the use of English as a medium of instruction. The Borneans were quite happy to use Malay as the national language and lingua franca but they were alarmed at the prospect of its replacing English as the chief medium of instruction.

All these and other matters were discussed fully by the parties concerned and appropriate amendments and additions were later made to the constitution of Malaya, which was to serve as the basis of the constitution of the new federation.

Malaysia 1963-1965

The federation of Malaysia came into being on September 16, 1963. It consisted of Malaya, Singapore, Sarawak and Sabah (lately British North Borneo). In the event Brunei decided against joining. Her reasons for this included her confidence in her ability to go it alone on the strength of her very considerable oil revenues; her confidence in the protective arm of Britain which had saved her from the Indonesian-backed Azahari; and her general reluctance to share her wealth with her less fortunate neighbours.

The federation faced great external pressures from the very beginning. The Philippines was still pressing its claim to Sabah and the Indonesians were embarked on their "confrontation" with Malaysia, making full use of such allies within the Malaysian camp as Azahari of Brunei, who claimed to be head of Kalimantan Utara (North Kalimantan) and the Clandestine Communist Organisation (CCO) of Sarawak whose members had infiltrated the Sarawak United People's Party. But the greatest danger came from within, from the clash between the Tunku and Lee Kuan Yew over the nature of Malaysia. This ideological battle became particularly intense during the first Malaysian elections of 1964.

The Elections of 1964

Under the new constitution each of the four partners in the Federation was allotted a certain number of seats in the Federal House of Representatives: one hundred and four from the States of Malaya, sixteen from Sabah, twenty-four from Sarawak and fifteen from Singapore. On the basis of the 1961 census figures this gave the States of Malaya one representative per 70,000 inhabitants; Sarawak one per 32,500; Sabah one per 11,900 and Singapore one per 113,000. The excuse for the over-representation of the Borneo territories was the same as that used for the weighting of the rural areas in Australia, namely that the constituencies were so large and the communications so bad in these areas that account should be taken of the physical size of the constituency as well as of its population. The same principle, it should be noted, had been applied in the original federation of Malaya where the sparsely inhabited rural areas were favoured in comparison with urban areas. One could observe in passing that this principle not only worked in favour of the rural areas but also worked against the Chinese, the greater part of whom lived in the more heavily populated —and relatively less well-represented States. The under-representation of Singapore in the federal parliament was not a unilateral act of discrimination but the price paid by Lee Kuan Yew for a number of important concessions: these included control over education and labour policy, no "special rights" for Malays in Singapore and permission for Singapore to remain a free port for the purposes of external entrepôt trade.

In 1964 elections were held to choose representatives for Malaya in the federal house; the representatives for Singapore, Sabah and Sarawak had already been chosen indirectly and none of these states was expected to take any part in the election. Lee Kuan Yew himself had gone on record in September 1963[34] as saying that the PAP would not intervene and it was understood that truly federal parties would not for the time being be allowed to develop. Nevertheless the PAP *did* put up nine candidates in Malayan constituencies and although only one of them, Devan Nair, was elected the intervention caused much controversy and ill-feeling and was one of the major causes of the subsequent secession of Singapore from the federation. What was the reason for Lee's action? Various explanations have been given. The one advanced by Lee himself was that he wished to give former supporters of the MCA a pro-Malaysia and progressive alternative to vote for in place of the extreme left-wing anti-Malaysia parties. He felt it necessary to provide such an alternative since the 1959 elections had shown that the MCA was losing a lot of its supporters. Another explanation is that the PAP was merely following the lead of the Alliance Party which had definitely backed certain candidates in the 1963 elections in Singapore and was now represented in that State by the Alliance Singapura.

Whatever the reason for it, the PAP's intervention did not pay many electoral dividends. The 1964 elections were a triumph for the Alliance Party, which won eighty-nine out of the one hundred and four Malayan seats in the federal House of Representatives. Nevertheless the PAP's action was the signal for the outbreak of a war of words between the Alliance and the PAP or more specifically between Lee Kuan Yew and the Moslem "ultras" led by Syed Ja'afar Albar, the Indonesia-born Secretary-General of UMNO. The verbal battle was fought in Parliament, television, radio, and the press and thus achieved maximum publicity. The already acrimonious atmosphere was made worse by the activities of President Sukarno of Indonesia, who was conducting a virulent anti-Malaysia campaign which was designed amongst other things to widen the rift between the Malays and the Chinese of Malaysia.

Lee Kuan Yew countered the Alliance's onslaught by inviting four opposition political parties from Malaya and Sarawak to join the PAP to form the Malaysian Solidarity Convention. In May 1965 members of the Convention stressed that they stood for a Malaysian Malaysia in which the "Nation and the State could not be identified with the supremacy, well-being and the interests of any one particular community or race".[35]

In June 1965 Tunku Abdul Rahman left Malaysia to attend a Commonwealth Prime Ministers' Conference in London. His return was delayed by illness but he kept in touch with the developments at home. It was apparently while he was in hospital that he decided that Singapore would have to leave the new Federation unless the PAP could be persuaded to "call off the heavy politicking which, he feared, would lead to racial bloodshed".[36] On or about August 7 Abdul Rahman confessed to Dr Toh Chin Chye, the PAP's Chairman, that he was not "strong enough and able to exercise complete control of the situation" and that in his opinion there was "absolutely no other way out"[37] but for Singapore to leave Malaysia. On Monday August 9, 1965 Parliament met and was told of the decision to sever the connection with Singapore.

Lee Kuan Yew was now on his own but his battle for a Malaysian Malaysia was carried on in the truncated Malaysia both by PAP supporters, who soon formed themselves into the Democratic Action Party, and by men like Dr Lim Chong Eu, Dr Tan Chee Khoon and Dr Alatas who fought under other political banners.

Singapore Since 1965

The Decline of the Barisan Socialis

On Monday August 9, 1965 Lee Kuan Yew declared Singapore a "sovereign democratic and independent nation". His dream of a Malaysian Malaysia had been shattered and he now set about the important but less grandiose task of building a prosperous multi-racial society in Singapore's two hundred and forty square miles.

On the domestic political front the most important development in the ensuing sixteen months was the disappearance of Barisan Socialis from the parliamentary scene and the consolidation of the PAP as the sole effective political party.

Barisan Socialis was formed in 1961 out of the left-wing members of the PAP who deserted the party in July of that year. The defection was a grave short-term blow to the PAP which, it has been estimated, lost eighty per cent of its membership and of its paid organising secretaries and seventeen out of its forty-three members in the Legislative Assembly.[38]

Having opposed Singapore's entry into the Federation in 1963 and having instructed its followers to cast blank votes in the referendum, Barisan Socialist was still not satisfied when Singapore was expelled from Malaysia two years later. Its members started to boycott the Assembly and in December 1965 announced that they were taking this action because the PAP Government was using Parliament "as a platform for propaganda to cheat the people and confuse them".[39]

Over the next ten months, four members of Barisan Socialis left the

Assembly either by resigning their seats or by resigning from the Party, which amounted to the same thing since the Constitution requires anyone who changes his party affiliation to resign from Parliament and submit himself for re-election. In October 1966 the remaining nine Barisan Socialis members resigned and announced that they were going to carry on their fight outside Parliament. All the seats vacated by men of the Barisan Socialis were quickly filled by members of PAP which thus by the end of 1966 was the only party represented in the Legislative Assembly. The PAP's pre-eminent position was confirmed again in the 1968 general election when it won all the seats in Parliament.

Problems of the One-Party State

For more than five years now Singapore has been a one-party state. Many of Lee Kuan Yew's political opponents are still in prison awaiting trial and there is very little prospect that an effective legal opposition party will appear in the next few years. Lee Kuan Yew's own views on the matter are pragmatic and ruthless: he would like to have an opposition but it must be a "loyal" one; anything else would endanger the whole delicate equilibrium of Singapore's multi-racial society.

In the absence of an opposition Lee Kuan Yew has taken great care and some unusual steps to ensure that his government neither lacks critics nor loses touch with the voters.

Formal criticism comes from various quarters. From time to time Parliament has "self criticism" sessions in which members of the PAP are asked to air their views frankly. More interestingly the Constitutional Commission of 1966 suggested that there should be a Council of State, consisting of non-elected but eminent persons, which would have the special function of ensuring that proposed legislation did not threaten the legitimate interests of minorities. The Council's deliberations were to be held in private.

The proposed Council, now called the Presidential Council, was set up in December 1969. Its members were all appointed by the President acting on the Government's advice. The Commission made it quite clear that they did not intend the Council to be an Upper House or Second Chamber with powers to thwart the will of the elected representatives of the people; it was not, however, intended to be a mere piece of window dressing; it was designed to act as a channel for the articulation of interests which in the circumstances of a PAP monopoly of the Legislative Assembly might otherwise remain unvoiced.

The Presidential Council has not been an unqualified success. In the first place it has no real power or influence: its discussions are not made public and its proposals can be negatived by a two-thirds majority in the Assembly. In the second place the Government, by its actions, has made it clear that it will not give the Council much freedom of manoeuvre. In mid-1970 the Council voiced objections to certain clauses of the Enlistment Bill, which gave the Minister powers to exercise discrimination in his choice of persons to be called up for national service. The Government replied by proposing an amendment which would have the effect of removing subjects of this "sensitive" nature from the Council's scrutiny. Mr David Marshall, who had been appointed a permanent member, resigned from the Council in protest but his resignation made little impression on the Government.

Although the one institution which was charged with the protection of minorities appears to have been given very few "teeth", the position of the Malays in Singapore is protected in a manner which must have surprised those who thought Lee's devotion to the idea of a Malaysian Malaysia was not genuine. Not only are Malays given a "special position" in the Constitution but the Malay language is one of Singapore's four official languages—the others being Tamil, Chinese and English—and the first head of state (Yang di-Pertuan Negara) was a Malay.* These valuable concessions have no doubt been made partly with an eye to the hypothetical day when Singapore is once again part of the Federation of Malaysia.

More effective than the Council in the function of interest articulation are the Citizens' Consultative Committees which were set up in each electoral district in 1965. These committees consist of the chairmen of the Street and Kampong Committees and act as both a channel downwards for explanations of government policy and a channel upwards for complaints and criticism.

If any of these complaints concern material shortcomings such as poor roads or bad street lighting, such defects can sometimes be put right without too much delay, by calling on a fund specially set up for that purpose by the Government, somewhat on the lines of the Barrio Development Fund of the Philippines.

Singapore, by Lee Kuan Yew's own definition, is a "rugged" society in which the citizens are asked to lay aside any impediment which may hinder them from running the race that is set before them. Lee describes himself as a socialist and a democrat but his concepts both of socialism and of democracy are flexible. Socialism for Lee is not something static involving a mere redistribution of existing wealth; it is something dynamic, a vision of an expanding economy in which everyone can take a hard-working and well-paid part and which will be able to generate enough surplus to take care of the needs of the less fortunate. Lee's democracy is rather more difficult to assess. So far Singapore has had regular elections and if there is no effective opposition party one could plausibly argue that Barisan Socialis has gone into voluntary rather than compulsory liquidation. On the other hand Lee has said that the Westminster system and one-man-one-vote are not institutions which can be transplanted without modification into Asian societies.

---

* His successor, Dr Benjamin Sheares, was a Eurasian.

At heart Lee is an elitist with some of the intellectual arrogance of the brilliant academic. Aware that most of his constituents are poorly educated and therefore unqualified to take a responsible part in decision making, Lee Kuan Yew has taken it largely upon himself to formulate and give concrete expression to the General Will. Whether such an autocracy, however benevolent, can survive depends largely on whether the proposition that the Chinese value economic efficiency above political participation is true or false.

Malaysia 1965-1969

Singapore left the Federation on August 9, 1965. In the early hours of October 1, 1965 the "Gestapu" *coup* took place in Djakarta and thus set off a train of events which was to have profound implications for Malaysia. At the end of August 1967 it was announced that full diplomatic relations had been resumed between Malaysia and Indonesia. This marked the end of the "confrontation" which had made its contribution towards Singapore's secession.

Improved relations between Kuala Lumpur and Djakarta had several effects on Malaysian domestic politics. It removed the outside threat which had proved so powerful an electoral aid to the Alliance; it made the problem of dealing with the guerilla fighters on the Sarawak-Kalimantan borders somewhat less intractable; it made the Malayan Communist Party revert to its previous role of aggravating inter-ethnic tensions; and it strengthened the hand of the PMIP and the "ultras" of the right wing of the Alliance, who had always been advocates of closer co-operation with Indonesia, a policy which frightened the Chinese and was not warmly welcomed by those in the Alliance leadership who did not favour the growth of pan-Islamic sentiment or the creation of a new Indonesia-led Sri Vijayan Empire.

Two other events of importance in 1967 were the enactment of the National Language Bill and the riots which took place in Penang following the devaluation of sterling.

On September 1, 1967 Malay became the sole official language in West Malaysia. In spite of this, English still played a very important part. English could continue to be used in the Federal and State legislatures and in the courts of law; laws and ordinances would continue to be published in both Malay and English. English continued to be the medium of instruction in many primary and secondary schools as well as being the main language used in the University of Malaysia.

On November 19, 1967 the Federal Government announced that the "new" dollars would retain their value but that the "old" Malayan and Straits dollars would follow the pound sterling and be devalued by fifteen per cent. This measure, which hit the Chinese rather harder than it did the Malays, was the pretext for a total shut-down of shops and businesses in Penang on November 23. This was followed by riots during which, according to Tunku Abdul Rahman, "clashes took place, with Malays and loyal supporters of the Government becoming targets for attack". The Tunku asserted that Chinese members of the Mao Tse Tung Youth Movement were the instigators of the shut-down and the riots.

Whatever the truth of the matter the Malayan Communist Party was certainly busy in other directions. There was renewed activity in the Malay-Thai border areas where Chin Peng was able to capitalise on the anti-government sentiments of the fervent Moslems in Kelantan, and the anti-Thai sentiments of the Malay population in the Thai provinces.

Six months before the May 1969 elections the government arrested a large number of people suspected of subversive activities. Among those arrested were several members of the Labour Party and the Party Ra'ayat, both of which promptly announced that they would boycott the elections. It was shortly after this that Dr Tan Chee Khoon, formerly of the Labour Party, helped to form the the new Gerakan Ra'ayat Malaysia. Dr Tan was by all accounts a moderate and cannot have been pleased by the Tunku's account of the genesis of the GRM. "As it turned out," wrote the Tunku, "Dr Tan's new party, of which he became Secretary-General continued to receive solid support from members of the now non-contesting Labour Party and from all those others who were in backdoor sympathy with the Communist cause."[37]

Another factor which the Alliance Government hoped might assist their cause in the general elections was the growing hostility of the government of the Philippines towards Malaysia in respect of Sabah's membership of the Federation. About a year after Indonesia had resumed diplomatic relations with Malaysia the Philippines broke them off. Attempts of the Alliance to rally the nation behind them in the face of the perils of Communism subversion and Filipino aggression did not, however, succeed. Manila appeared to be less than whole-hearted about its desire to claim dominion over Sabah and the electorate was still not convinced that the Communist menace was as serious as the government made out.

The 1969 Elections

Voting for the election of representatives both to the Dewan Ra'ayat or Federal House of Representatives and in most States legislative assemblies took place on May 10, 1969. On May 12, the newspapers showed that with thirty-one results still to come the Alliance had won seventy-six out of the one hundred and forty-four seats in the House, the DAP had won thirteen, the PMIP twelve, the GRM eight and the People's Progressive Party four. Voting was scheduled to be completed in Sabah by June 7, and the result of the Sarawak polling was due to be announced on May 25. Preliminary reports from Sarawak indicated that the Sarawak Alliance's constituent parties had decided to run under their own names and that results could not be expected to be very favourable to them.

The results came as a shock to the Alliance Party which had lost twenty-two of its seats in West Malaysia and had polled less than fifty per cent of the total vote. With bad news expected from Sarawak it now seemed highly unlikely that the party would have the two-thirds majority in the Federal legislature which it had enjoyed before and which was necessary for making amendments to the Constitution.

There were further set-backs for the Alliance in the States. It lost control of Penang and Perak, failed to regain Kelantan from the PMIP and was in trouble in Selangor where the Alliance had fourteen seats and the opposition parties together had the same number.

Disappointing as these results were the Alliance leaders were not at first inclined to indulge in any public lamentations or accusations. Both Abdul Rahman and his deputy Abdul Razak spoke of democratic processes and healthy opposition parties.

The May 13 Incident

On May 13 the picture suddenly changed. What had always been a possibility became a reality. Riots broke out in the train of "victory" processions first by the largely Chinese Gerakan Ra'ayat Malaysia and then by the Alliance. After days of burning, stabbing, looting and curfews, the government issued on May 17 an ordinance proclaiming a state of emergency and placing the country under martial law and the rule of a National Operations Council, in which Abdul Razak was named the Director of Operations. The elections were suspended indefinitely and the country was governed without the assistance of parliament.

It is difficult at this stage to make a reasoned assessment of the so-called "May 13 Incident". The official version was that the riots were deliberately provoked by crypto-Communists who had infiltrated the opposition parties. It was suggested that these extreme left-wingers came from the banned MCP or from the Labour Party which had first boycotted the elections and then decided to "sabotage" them. There is no doubt that all the apparatus which was set up to deal with the post-Incident scene was borrowed from, and designed to recall, the days of the "Emergency", when the chief enemy was the Chinese Communist.

The official version also claimed that the government's drastic action was necessary in order to preserve the spirit of non-communalism for which the Alliance had fought so consistently. The forces of communalism had been let loose—by the opposition—during the election campaign and had been responsible for the events of May 13: it was clearly the duty of the government to keep these forces under control, if necessary by force.

The anti-government version of May 13 was quite different. It suggested that the processions which led to the riots need not have been allowed to take place: that the trouble could have been dealt with, with more efficiency and far less bloodshed, if the government had given the police a freer hand; and that the use of Malay troops against Chinese civilians was deliberately provocative.

The most damning charge which the opposition parties brought against the government was that it had used the May 13 riots to regain by force for the Alliance the dominating position which it had lost by the operation of the ordinary democratic process.

Whatever the true explanation of May 13 may be, the fact is that a Malay-led Alliance government was confirmed in office by the decree of May 17 and did not look like relinquishing its great powers for some time to come.

The Political Process

West Malaysia: The Chinese

MALAYAN CHINESE ASSOCIATION

Hardest hit of all the Alliance's partners in the 1969 elections was the MCA: its twenty-seven seats in the 1964 House dropped to a mere thirteen in 1969. Its performance was so poor that its leader Tan Siew Sin took the fateful step of announcing that the MCA would not participate in any cabinet whether at Federal or State level. Tun Tan was subsequently co-opted by the National Operations Council to serve as a Minister "with special duties" but the damage had been done and the MCA had publicly owned that it no longer considered itself truly representative of the Chinese community.

This development cannot have come as a great surprise; rather was it the inevitable outcome of a process which had been going on ever since the "Emergency" had begun to fade away and the Chinese could at last survey the political scene more coolly.

Over the years three main adverse criticisms were gradually gaining wider and wider currency. The first was that the MCA's influence in the higher councils of the Alliance was in no way proportionate to the ever-increasing number of Chinese in the electorate. The second was that the MCA leaders were all "Establishment" figures; wealthy men who were out of touch with the ordinary voter and who were quite content to maintain the *status quo* even if it meant making very considerable concessions to the Malays. Finally, many Chinese—and Malays too for that matter—felt that the whole social system needed drastic revision. The rich Chinese *towkays* and the Malay Sultans were all seen as part of an out-moded way of life. The concern of the Sultans for the "sons of the soil" was seen as a device for perpetuating the institution of the Sultanate; while the MCA's support of an UMNO-dominated Alliance was regarded as a means of buying economic privileges for its wealthy supporters.

DEMOCRATIC ACTION PARTY

Chinese voters who deserted the MCA were offered three main choices: the DAP, the GRM and the PPP. The first of these, the Democratic Action Party was a reconstituted version of the People's Action Party (of Singapore) which had won one seat in the 1964 election. Branded by the Alliance as a puppet in the pay of a foreign power the DAP sought to provide the Chinese—and hopefully Malay—elector with an independent and more radical alternative to the MCA Alliance.

In the 1969 elections the main points made by DAP candidates were in the fields of land reform, education and foreign policy. They wanted more land to be made available to the peasants—without political discrimination. They wanted a big expansion in higher education with a heavy emphasis on technology and business management. They did not wish Malay to be made the sole medium of instruction; they agreed that Malay should be a compulsory subject but they advocated the establishment of a multilingual society such as existed in Singapore, one in which education would be available in all the main languages at all levels. They would establish, for instance, a Tamil University for the Indian Community.

As to foreign policy the DAP wanted to see diplomatic relations established with all countries regardless of ideology; the party also hoped that one day Singapore might be allowed to rejoin the Federation on suitable terms.

GERAKAN RA'AYAT MALAYSIA

The GRM, though also an advocate of a Malaysian Malaysia, occupied a position near the centre of the political spectrum. If it had no clear programme to put in front of the electorate this was not too surprising as it was itself a compound of three different groups, headed respectively by the Chairman, Professor Syed Hussein Alatas, the Vice-Chairman, Dr Lim Chong Eu and the Secretary, Dr Tan Chee Khoon. Dr Alatas came from the Party Negara; Dr Lim was an ex-President of the MCA and came to the GRM via his own United Democratic Party which he formed after his resignation from the MCA; Dr Tan came from the Labour Party, which boycotted the 1969 elections and was later blamed for all the racial disturbances. Since Dr Tan was at the head of a procession which was the occasion of one of the riots his political background is of significance.

A multi-racial party with a non-Chinese Chairman, the Gerakan believed in a Malaysian Malaysia but was quite ready to concede that the Malays needed to be given greater opportunities for advancement.

It criticised the Alliance for channelling a good deal of Government aid exclusively to its own supporters. On the language issue it was more conformist than the DAP; it upheld the use of Malay as the national language (*bahasa kebangsaan*)* but was against its use as the only medium of instruction. Like the DAP it was in favour of a system in which education on all three levels was available in all the major languages.

PEOPLE'S PROGRESSIVE PARTY

The third choice for Chinese anti-Alliance voters was the PPP but this was a choice only open to electors in Perak where the party was born under its original name of Perak Progressive Party. Led by two Indian brothers named Seenivasagam, one of whom died shortly before the 1969 elections, the party was supported mainly by the lower ranks of Chinese society. Its political platform was socialist, and it advocated the creation of a multi-lingual state and the abolition of special rights for the Malays.

THE FUTURE OF CHINESE REPRESENTATION

The MCA has not left the Alliance but its leaders have as good as admitted that it has lost the confidence of the Chinese community. The Alliance leaders have frequently stated that they have no intention of replacing the MCA by either the Gerakan or the DAP. What then is the future of Chinese representation at Government level? This is a difficult question to answer; all that one can say with any assurance is, that much will depend on the extent to which the opposition parties —particularly the DAP and the Gerakan and possibly the PPP—can co-operate in the re-animated Parliament.

West Malaysia: The Malays

PAN-MALAYAN ISLAMIC PARTY

Although the PMIP put up candidates in well over half the federal parliamentary constituencies its main strength lay in Kelantan, Trengganu and Kedah where it drew its support from the conservative Malay farmers and local religious leaders.

As its name suggests the PMIP's political platform had two main planks of which the more important was the building of a Malay Islamic state in Malaysia; the other was the alignment of Malaysia with other Malay and or Moslem countries both in Southeast Asia— which meant Indonesia—and elsewhere. On the main domestic issues the PMIP wished to establish a unified educational system, presumably taught in Malay, with compulsory instruction in Islamic subjects. It also advocated an extensive programme of nationalisation of essential

---

* Also commonly known as Bahasa Malaysia.

industries as well as state encouragement and aid for co-operatives. It wished foreign bases to be removed from Malaysian soil and alliances, if necessary, to be entered into with friendly Moslem neighbours.

The PMIP did well in the 1969 elections, winning twelve federal seats and forty state seats and increasing its total vote by more than half compared with the previous election. Its triumphs were however a sad blow for the cause of multi-racialism and multi-lingualism to neither of which, unlike thee other opposition parties, did it pay even lip-service.

UNITED MALAY NATIONALIST ORGANISATION/ALLIANCE

In spite of the successes of the PMIP the first choice of the vast majority of Malay voters was still the UMNO/Alliance. The UMNO was originally formed, as we have seen, to fight the formation of a Malayan Union in which all citizens, regardless of ethnic origin, would eventually have equal status. The UMNO's fight was successful and the Malayan Union was replaced by a Federation which was firmly based on the institution of the Sultanate and the entrenched superiority of the Malays.

When the UMNO first made its electoral pact with the MCA the Chinese were in such a weak and suspect condition that the basic incompatibility between the aims of the two organisations was not immediately apparent; the Chinese who supported the Alliance were merely grateful that they could not be confused with their brethren in the MCP. Later, however, as the Emergency receded and the number of enfranchised Chinese grew rapidly there was increased friction between the UMNO and the MCA.

During 1959 the disagreements between these two partners became public knowledge. After an argument over the apportionment of official nominations as between UMNO and MCA candidates the MCA leader Dr Lim Chong Eu resigned in order to form or assist in the formation of parties—first the United Democratic Party and later the Gerakan Ra'ayat Malaysia—which, according to one's point of view, one could call either more truly multi-racial or more pro-Chinese.

The results of the 1959 elections in which the Alliance won seventy-four out of one hundred and four seats as compared with fifty-one out of fifty-two in 1955 revealed not only that the Chinese were beginning to desert the Alliance but that the rural Malays, particularly in the north-east, were looking for a more uncompromising alternative to the UMNO. In 1964, in the days of "confrontation" with Indonesia, the Alliance could work not only on anti-Chinese sentiment—Indonesia's foreign policy at the time was heavily influenced by Peking—and thus discredit the non-Alliance Chinese opposition parties; but also on anti-Indonesian sentiment and thus discredit the PMIP which had Indonesian ties and whose leader Dr Burhanuddin had a background tinged with Communism and Indonesian nationalism. In these more favourable circumstances the UMNO regained some of the lost ground; the PMIP representation in the Dewan Ra'ayat fell from fifteen to nine while the UMNO's rose from fifty-two to fifty-nine.

In 1969, with no external threat to bind the nation together behind it, the Alliance made its appeal in the predominantly Malay rural areas in terms of the issues which were closest to the electorate: religion, education and the Chinese peril. To those who might be considering voting for the PMIP it pointed out that the UMNO/Alliance had achieved everything that the PMIP was claiming as its sole prerogative —Malay rights, the position of the Malay language and the institution of Islam as the official religion. To those who might argue that it was their religious duty to vote for the uncompromisingly Islamic PMIP the UMNO/Alliance alleged that the PMIP had made an "unholy" electoral pact with the infidel DAP and had even received funds from that Singapore-backed party. To the Chinese in these areas the Alliance's essentially negative message was that they would undoubtedly be much worse off under the racist PMIP than the multi-racial Alliance.

The fact that the Alliance should make its appeal on an essentially communal basis is not surprising. The Alliance Party was always much more of an alliance than a party; indeed the Alliance until recently never had a *direct* membership—membership of the Alliance went automatically with one's membership of one of its three constituent elements. There was no Alliance organisation at the branch level; only at the level of the constituency or higher was there official liaison between the parties. In these circumstances the man in the street or field voted for the UMNO, the MCA or the MIC rather than the Alliance and since the candidate was nearly always of the same ethnic group as the majority of his constituents it was inevitable that the message to the voters would have a strong communal element.

We have said that the Alliance Party was more of an alliance than a party; by 1969 the complaint was that it had become more of a party than an alliance—the party in this case being the UMNO.

East Malaysia: Sarawak

THE SARAWAK UNITED PEOPLE'S PARTY (SUPP)

The exclusion of Singapore from the Federation of Malaysia must have initially come as a great shock to Sabah and Sarawak, particularly as they were not consulted before the event. The Borneo Territories, however, soon recovered from their surprise and it was only the Sarawak United People's Party, a mainly Chinese organisation, which registered a protest and demanded a referendum to decide whether Sarawakians wished to continue to be part of a Singapore-less Federation.

SUPP was founded in June 1959 for the purpose of contesting the local government elections in that year. Its leadership was mainly Chinese as was over half its membership. The main issue which rallied

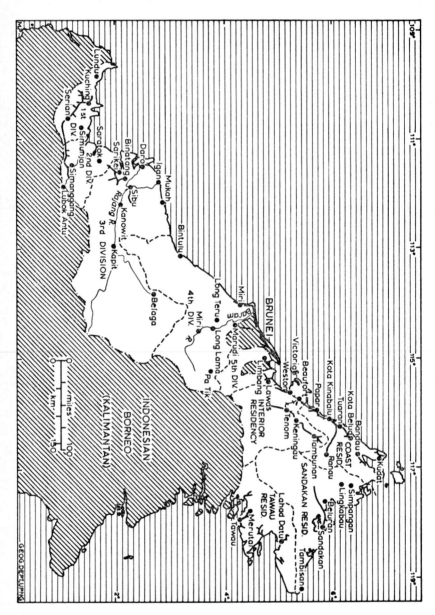

Map 10. East Malaysia (Sabah and Sarawak)

the Chinese was much the same as that which was the concern of their fellow-Chinese in Malaya, namely the prospect of having to live in an increasingly Malay- or *Bumiputra*-dominated country. Bumiputrans were being given priority in the apportionment of land and there was increasing discrimination against schools whose medium of instruction was Chinese.

Unlike the MCA, however, the SUPP was infiltrated by Communists and was officially extremely suspect. In a White Paper entitled "The Danger Within" the Government said there was evidence that the "Clandestine Communist Organization" or CCO* was using the SUPP for its own purposes". The Communists were said to be particularly strong in the rural areas and in the schools where they could make much of the threat to Chinese education. An extract from a Communist Party Manifesto of January 1965 reads "All the people who love Chinese education realise that if they do not unite now and resolutely engage themselves in the struggle it will be too late."

One should, however, make it quite clear that the SUPP was not a Communist or even a particularly radical party; as the CCO itself admitted, it was basically "an organ led by the propertied class" and its members lived mainly in the towns of Kuching, Sibu and Miri or ran small trading, cash-cropping and timber businesses out in the *ulu*.

Originally an opponent of Malaysia the SUPP swung now to supporting the Federation on the basis of its being a "Malaysian Malaysia". In this matter the party took its lead from Singapore; in 1965 the SUPP joined the Malaysia Solidarity Convention† which was formed by Lee Kuan Yew in answer to the growing Malay nationalist propaganda of the Alliance's Secretary-General Albar. The formation of the Convention had a polarising effect in Malaysian politics and the threat of an impending lethal clash between Malay and non-Malay was a key factor in the formation of Tunku Abdul Rahman's decision to expel Singapore from the Federation.

When Singapore declared its independence on August 9, 1965, hopes for a Malaysian Malaysia dwindled and the Chinese parties of Malaysia and the Borneo Territories were compelled to face a future in which Malay interests were likely to dominate the political and, increasingly, the economic scene.

Branded by its opponents as a Communist infiltrated party, the SUPP has lived nearly all its life in political opposition to the ruling Alliance group. Over the years, however, it has been purged of many of its Communist elements: one estimate is that about 800 of its members were arrested during the period 1959-1968 and leading officials

---

* This is a blanket term used in the White Paper to cover various Communist organisations.
† The other members of the Convention besides Lee Kuan Yew's PAP, were the mainly Chinese UDP and PPP of Malays and Sarawak's MACHINDA, a small and new multi-racial party.

were still being arrested in the period immediately preceding the abortive 1969 elections.*

Although much of the SUPP's membership was drawn from the Chinese—comparatively few of whom voted for the official Alliance Chinese party, the Sarawak Chinese Association—the party claimed there was growing support for it from the non-Chinese community after 1965. This is not so surprising when one considers that only about eighteen per cent of the non-Chinese population of Sarawak are normally classed as Malays,† there are therefore likely to be many non-Chinese who have some interests in common with the Chinese—in particular those relating to the too-rapid imposition of the Malay language in education as well as general hostility to the idea of increased central control of the Federation from Kuala Lumpur.

SARAWAK NATIONAL PARTY

Also in opposition to the ruling Alliance was the Sarawak National Party (SNAP) which though not an ally of SUPP co-operated with the latter to the extent of making an electoral pact in 1969 on the lines of those made between the opposition parties in West Malaysia.

Largely composed of Ibans living in the Third Division SNAP's leader ever since its beginnings in 1961 has been Dato Stephen Kalong Ningkan. In 1963 SNAP joined all the other parties, with the exception of SUPP, to form the Sarawak Alliance with Temenggong Jugah of PESAKA as Chairman and Ningkan as Secretary. Both chairman and secretary were Ibans and the PESAKA, formed in 1962, was composed largely of Ibans from the Second Division.

When the Sarawak Alliance won a comfortable majority of the seats in the Council Negri Dato Stephen Kalong Ningkan became the first Chief Minister of non-colonial Sarawak and led the government until 1966 when he found himself unable to command a majority in the Council.

Ningkan's fate demonstrates the shifting nature of the Sarawak Alliance. Unlike its counterpart in West Malaysia the Sarawak Alliance has changed its composition more than once. When the Alliance was only about four months old the Malay party, PANAS, left it only to rejoin it in 1966 when SNAP left the Alliance and followed its leader Ningkan into opposition.

The main plank in SNAP's platform is "Sarawak for the Sarawakians", a slogan which appeals to all those who look for the "Bor-

---

* Chung Kwok Chuan, the Executive Secretary of the central committee was arrested in January 1969 and Toh Geoh Choon, the Vice-Chairman of the party in Sibu and Deputy Chairman of the Sibu Urban District Council, was arrested in the following April.
† June 1967 estimates give: Chinese 33.9%; Iban 29%; Malay 18%; Other indigenous 19% (Melanau, Land Dayaks, etc.).

neanisation" rather than the "Malayanisation" of the political and economic structure of Sarawak. In a nine-page manifesto issued in 1969 SNAP's four main points were these: that it was anti-Communist, that it was multi-racial and believed in racial harmony, that it believed "in a Malaysia that honours the spirit of the London agreement whereby Sarawak achieved independence from Britain within Malaysia", that it was dedicated to the cause of Sarawak for the Sarawakians.

Such a programme, combined with SNAP's proposal that the English should continue to be the official language for an indefinite period after 1973, was hardly calculated to please the Alliance's leaders in Kuala Lumpur and it is not surprising that SNAP has remained outside the Alliance's fold.

SARAWAK ALLIANCE

The Sarawak Alliance in 1970 consisted of Bumiputra, Pesaka and the Sarawak Chinese Association.

Of the three, the Sarawak Chinese Association was by far the smallest and least effective. The SCA was a pale imitation of its counterpart in West Malaysia and was unable to compete for membership among the Chinese with the far more active SUPP.

Party Bumiputra drew its support mainly from Malays and Melanaus and was therefore by nature Malaysia-minded. Among its leaders were Abdul Rahman Ya'akub the Federal Minister for Lands and Mines until May 1969, Abang Ikhwan Zainie and Enche Abdul Taib bin Mahmud. A largely Moslem party, the Bumiputra placed a good deal of emphasis on the promotion of Islam and no doubt claimed credit for the several new mosques which have been built in recent years, including the resplendent one in Kuching.

In contrast to Bumiputra, Party Pesaka was primarily an Iban party whose members were mostly Christian or pagan. Their most prestigious leader was Tan Sri Temenggong Jugah who was in 1969 Federal Minister for Sarawak Affairs and also Chairman of the Sarawak Alliance National Council. While Temenggong Jugah was a traditional Iban leader and may have felt at home anyway among the Malay rulers in Kuala Lumpur, it was reported that the younger elements of the Pesaka were inclined to follow a course more independent of West Malaysia.

The Sarawak Chinese Association, Bumiputra and Pesaka were strange bedfellows and it, therefore, came as no surprise when Tun Abdul Razak announced in March 1969 that the Sarawak Alliance would not campaign as a single party, but that each member-party would contest the elections in its own name and under its own separate symbol. The Sarawak Alliance nevertheless received massive support from its counterpart in West Malaysia which was reported to have contributed ten tons of election posters and sixty thousand badges.[41]

"MAY 13" AND THE SUSPENSION OF ELECTIONS IN SARAWAK

On Thursday May 15, 1969 it was announced that "all elections to the Dewan Ra'ayat and State Legislatures which have not been completed are suspended until further notice".

The announcement drew a strong protest from SNAP condemning the "totally inexcusable and dastardly action by the Central Government of Malaysia in suspending the General Elections in Sarawak and Sabah without any legal excuse except that of extending the power of a government which is not acceptable to the majority of Malaysian people must be condemned not only by the peoples of Malaysia but indeed by the whole free world. Democracy is dead. . . ."

A few days later Tun Ismail, the Federal Minister of Home Affairs, echoed these words when he was reported as saying that democracy was dead in Malaysia. "The country could not afford the democratic process in its present chaotic state."[42] The affairs of Sarawak were then put in the hands of a Local Operations Council whose Chairman was the existing Chief Minister, Dato Penghulu Tawi Sli—Dato Stephen Kalong Ningkan's successor—and whose other members included senior military and police officers.

In June 1970 the long-delayed elections were finally held. The results were initially a grave disappointment for the Alliance. The three parties nominally fighting under the Alliance banner—the Bumiputra Pesaka and SCA—won twenty-three out of the forty-seven seats in the Council Negri and thus did not have even a bare majority until an Independent joined the ranks of Pesaka. When it looked as if the Alliance had been beaten an agreement was apparently reached between Pesaka, SNAP and SUPP that they, with an assured thirty-one seats between them, should form a government. At this point Ya'akub made a strong bid for SUPP's support and managed to persuade Stephen Yong to bring his party into a coalition with the Alliance. The wooing of SUPP represented a dramatic break with the Alliance's previous policy of depicting SUPP as a crypto-communist movement. The announcement that SUPP had joined the Alliance came as a great shock to SNAP whose leader Ningkan immediately asked to join the Alliance. He was told, however, that there would be no places available to SNAP in the cabinet. SNAP went once more into opposition where, it was predicted, it might be joined by disillusioned members of SUPP and Pesaka.[43]

The new government of Sarawak was announced in July and contained Ya'akub as Chief Minister, Stephen Yong (SUPP) and Simon Dembab Maja (Pesaka) as deputy chief ministers.

In the Federal Parliament the Alliance-SUPP Coalition won forty-one seats. Tun Abdul Razak made it quite clear that the SUPP members would be expected to support the "Grand" Alliance in Federal Parliament: "You cannot join the Alliance in the State and not vote for the Alliance here."[44]

East Malaysia: Sabah

In May 1961 when Tunku Abdul Rahman first put forward the concept of Malaysia, there were no political parties in Sabah: a year later there were five main parties in the field, each largely based on ethnic group or religion.

UNKO For the Kadazans, who constitute about thirty-two per cent of the population and are in the main rice-growing non-Christians, there was the United National Kadazan Organisation (UNKO) founded by Dato Donald Stephens, a Roman Catholic of mixed Australian and Kadazan parentage.

PM The United National Pasok Momogun Organisation was originally founded in rivalry to the UNKO and also consisted of non-Moslem Kadazans but from a different area. Politically the party was more conservative than UNKO and was not as ready as the latter to let go of the British Government's guiding hand.[45]

USNO Mainly for the Moslems was the United Sabah National Organisation founded by Tun Dato Mustapha, currently Chief Minister and previously the first Head of State or Yang di-Pertua Negara. It drew its membership mainly from the Moslem Bajans, Bruneis and Malays and had close ties with the UMNO of West Malaysia.

SANAP The Sabah National Party (SANAP) was formed out of two earlier parties. The Democratic Party which catered for the Chinese and Sino-Kadazans in smaller businesses and manual employment, and the United Party whose greatest support came from the more affluent Chinese.

SIC In 1960 the total Indian, Pakistani and Ceylonese population of Sabah was 3,180. The number of Indians in the community was thus very small and it was for these that the Sabah Indian Congress was formed. It was proportionately smaller and a good deal less effective than its counterpart in West Malaysia.

SABAH ALLIANCE

These five parties joined together to form the Sabah Alliance. In contrast to Sarawak, Sabah had no opposition party. There were moments in 1964 and 1965 when it looked as if Dato Stephens was about to lead UPKO out of the Alliance but the danger passed. UPKO had been formed in 1964 as a result of a merger between UNKO and PM and consequently represented a natural non-Moslem counterweight to the Moslem UMNO-oriented USNO. In 1964 there was trouble over the political activities of the Yang di-Pertua Negara, who in the eyes of Dato Stephens should have been politically neutral as befitted a constitutional monarch. Dato Mustapha, on the other hand, was the President of USNO and found it impossible to sustain an apolitical role. Dato Stephens resigned to take up a post in the Federal Cabinet but found himself in further controversy when Singapore left the

Federation in August 1965. Stephens argued that Singapore's departure created a new situation, the balance of Malaysia had been disturbed and it was no longer the Federation which Sabah had agreed to join three years before; he demanded a "re-examination" of Sabah's terms of entry into Malaysia. Dato Stephens no doubt feared that with the "Malaysian" Lee Kuan Yew out of the way Malaysia's politics would become increasingly Malay and Moslem dominated; as the head of a non-Moslem party, he had no wish to see fulfilled his prophecy of July 1961: "If we join Malaya the people who will come and take over most of the top jobs will be from Malaya." When the UNKO had asked the Cobbold Commission in 1962 that "everything possible should be done to encourage British officers to remain in North Borneo after Malaysia, until the indigenous peoples are qualified to take their place" it was plain that the term "indigenous peoples" did not include Malays who had not been born in Sabah.

Tun Dato Mustapha, who had just resigned from the position as Yang di-Pertua Negara and was now back as President of USNO, attacked Stephens for trying to break up the Sabah Alliance. He denied that the secession of Singapore made Malaysia "incomplete". He went on to say that there was no chance of rights of Sabahans being eroded by Kuala Lumpur: "Our agreement with the Central Government and the 'Twenty Points' safeguards, which we have requested, have not been changed."[46]

Mustapha then referred to the fact that the Constitution could not be amended "except with the approval of a two-thirds majority of Members of Parliament"; he did not mention that the Alliance now commanded such a majority. It was also true that amendments regarding certain vital matters affecting citizens of Sabah could not be made without also obtaining the consent of the Governor—that is the Yang di-Pertua Negara—but Mustapha's recent performance in that role can hardly have reassured Stephens that the position of the Kadazans would necessarily be protected by this provision.

On November 2, 1965, after a long meeting with members of his Executive Committee, Stephens resigned as President of the UPKO in order to save the Alliance. He asked the new leadership of UPKO to "do everything possible to bring about closer understanding between the UPKO and the USNO . . .".

In December 1967 UPKO was absorbed by USNO and the Sabah Alliance now consisted of USNO, SCA and SIC. Stephens's successor as President of UPKO, Dato Ganie Gilong, was appointed Minister of Justice in the new Federal Cabinet announced shortly after the 1969 riots.

As in Sarawak, the elections to the Federal Parliament were postponed for just over a year. Held eventually in June 1970 the elections resulted in a total victory for the Sabah Alliance. Eleven of the sixteen candidates were returned unopposed; the constituencies which were clustered round the main five towns were contested but here again the Alliance candidates were victorious.

Dato Stephens's fears that Sabah might be increasingly dominated by Malays and Moslems seemed to be justified in 1970 and 1971 when Tun Mustapha's government initiated an Islamic "forward policy" which resulted in the expulsion—mainly by non-renewal of permits— of a large number of Christian missionaries; at the same time it was alleged that preferential treatment was being received by Moslems in business and politics. Peter Mojuntin, a member of the State Assembly, protested to the Malaysian Prime Minister about this policy of "Islamisation" but received no official reply.

Meanwhile many prominent non-Moslem politicians publicly announced their conversion to Islam, the climax being reached when Dato Donald Stephens himself, then High Commissioner for Malaysia in Canberra, announced that he had left the Roman Catholic fold and embraced Islam. He wished henceforth to be known as Muhammad Fuad Stephens. His statement that he regarded his conversion as an important step "towards bringing about greater Bumiputra* unity" seemed to indicate that the move had as much political as religious significance.

The Federal Constitution

Malaysia is a Federation whose constituent members are the eleven States of Western Malaysia (Malaya) and the two Borneo States— Sabah and Sarawak.

Islam is the religion of the Federation; "but other religions may be practised in peace and harmony in any part of the Federation".†

The Supreme Head of the Federation is called the Yang di-Pertuan Agong who is elected for a term of five years by the Conference of Rulers, a body composed of the Rulers, or Governors as the case may be, of the various States.‡

The Yang di-Pertuan Agong is a constitutional monarch who acts on the advice "of the Cabinet or of a Minister acting under the general authority of the Cabinet".

The Yang di-Pertuan Agong selects as Prime Minister (Perdana Mentri) "a member of the House of Representatives who in his judgment is likely to command the confidence of the majority of the members of that House . . .";§ the Prime Minister then nominates the rest of his Ministry for approval by the Head of State. The Cabinet is collectively responsible to Parliament which consists of the Senate (Dewan Negara) and the House of Representatives (Dewan Ra'ayat).

---

* Bumiputra means "native" or "son of the soil" and refers in Malaysia to locally-born non-Chinese, non-Indian, non-expatriate people.
† Article 3(1).
‡ Article 32(3).
§ Article 43(2).

The Senate contains two elected members for each State and thirty-two members appointed by the Yang di-Pertuan Agong.* The term of office of a Senator is six years. The Cabinet must be drawn from Parliament and the power of appointment to the Senate enables the Head of State to enable a suitable person to be included in the Cabinet without necessarily going through the electoral process. Tan Sri Ghazali Shafie, formerly Permanent Secretary of the Ministry of Foreign Affairs was given a Ministerial post in Tun Razak's first Cabinet in just this fashion.

The House of Representatives has one hundred and forty-four members: one hundred and four for West Malaysia; sixteen for Sabah and twenty-four for Sarawak.† Representatives are elected from single-member constituencies for a term of five years.

All Bills must be assented to by both Houses and may originate in either House. The only exception to this rule is the case of a Money Bill, which may only originate in the House of Representatives and which may be passed with the assent of the House of Representatives alone, in cases where the latter is in conflict with the Senate over all or part of the Bill.

The relations between the Federation and the States are set out in Parts V, VI and VII of the Constitution. Each State has a Ruler or Governor and a Legislative Assembly. The constitutions of the States are guaranteed by the Federation. There are three schedules or categories of legislation: Federal, State and Concurrent. The Ninth Schedule lists the areas in which the Federal and State legislatures may operate. Any inconsistency between a State and a Federal law is to be resolved in favour of the Federal law.

Part VII, taken in conjunction with the Tenth Schedule deals with financial provisions including grants to States and the allocation of certain taxes, fees and duties to the States. One may mention here that among "additional sources of revenue assigned to the Borneo States" is "import duty and excise duty on petroleum products". This item promises to be a bone of contention between Sarawak and the Federation particularly as the latter has claimed all but the first three miles of Sarawak's continental shelf as Federal property.

Part VIII deals with elections. Its most interesting provision is contained in the Thirteenth Schedule which is to be read in conjunction with Section 116(1). The Thirteenth Schedule provides that "having regard to the greater difficulty of reaching electors in the country districts and other disadvantages facing rural constituencies, a measure of weightage for area ought to be given to such constituencies, to the extent that in some cases a rural constituency may contain as little as one half of the electors of any urban constituency". This provision

---

* Article 45(1).
† Article 46.

which came into force in June 1962, replaced the previous one which allowed for a deviation of only fifteen per cent from the norm in any rural constituency. Article 116 and its attendant Schedule clearly give an advantage to the predominantly Malay rural areas. It is of help to the UMNO but is of equal use to the PMIP.

The Judiciary is set up under Part IX. It consists of a Federal Court in Kuala Lumpur, two High Courts—one in Kuala Lumpur and one in the Borneo States—and "such inferior courts as may be provided by federal law".*

The Federal Court, whose Judges hold office until they reach the age of sixty-five, has appellate jurisdiction as well as the power of judicial review. It may pronounce on the validity or otherwise of laws passed by either Federal or State legislatures and it may adjudicate on disputes between States or between the Federation and any State.†

Part XI covers legislation against subversion, proclamations of emergency and restrictions on preventive detention. Section 150 is the section under which "emergencies" were declared in Sarawak in 1966 and the Federation in 1969.

The most contentious provisions of the Constitution are to be found in Articles 152 (National Language) and 153 (Reservations of quotas in respect of services, permits, etc., for Malays).

Article 152 asserts that the national language shall be Malay. It also provides that for a period of ten years after Merdeka Day (1957) "and thereafter until Parliament otherwise provides" the English language may be used for certain purposes. Legislation in accordance with the provisions of this Article was passed in 1967.‡ This Article should be read in conjunction with Article 161 which provides that no Act of Federal Parliament "terminating or restricting the use of the English" for certain purposes "shall come into operation . . . until ten years after Malaysia Day", that is until 1973.

Article 153 provides that the Yang di-Pertuan Agong, subject to certain provisions, "shall exercise his functions . . . in such manner as may be necessary to safeguard the special position of the Malays and to ensure for the reservation for Malays of such proportion as he may deem reasonable of positions in the public service (other than the public service of a State) and of scholarships, exhibitions and other similar educational or training privileges . . . and, when any permit or licence for the operation of any trade or business is required by federal law, then, subject to the provisions of that law and this Article, of such permits and licences." This Article may not be amended without the consent of the Conference of Rulers.§

Article 153 and its underlying philosophy has been under attack

---

* Article 121.
† Article 128.
‡ See p. 160
§ Article 159.

from non-Alliance parties for some time. The Alliance government's policy hitherto has been highly ambiguous: on the one hand it has defended the "special rights" of the Malays as being part of the cost of Federation; on the other hand it has taken considerable pains to explain to the non-Malays that the provisions of Article 153 have not been fully implemented. The NOC's booklet "The May 13 Tragedy" gives figures which show that Division One of the government services is anything but a Malay preserve. For instance, of the total number of officers in Division One (excluding Armed Forces and the Police) 63·74 per cent were Chinese and 36·26 per cent Malays on November 1, 1968.[47]

Article 161A extends the provisions of Article 153 to the "natives", as defined in subsection 7, of the Borneo States.

Article 159 lays down the procedure for amending the Constitution. With certain important exceptions, amendments may not be passed in either House without a two-thirds majority of the total number of members of that House. The most important exceptions are that no Articles relating to the position of the Malay Rulers and the special position of the Malays may be passed without the consent of the Conference of Rulers. One can see, in the light of this Article, why the Alliance was so anxious to achieve a two-thirds majority in the 1969/70 elections and why the NOC in its turn recommended that legislation should be passed making it impossible for Article 159 itself to be amended without the consent of the Conference of Rulers.

On February 19, 1971 the National Operations Council was dissolved. Four days later Parliament was reconvened on the explicit condition that it would pass the proposed constitutional amendments by the necessary two-thirds majority. The debate duly took place and the amendments were passed by a handsome majority which included members of the Gerakan. It was now sedition to question Malay rights, the position of the Rulers, citizenship and the national language.

The Basic Problem

In August 1963 on the eve of the inauguration of the new Federation of Malaysia a small booklet was published entitled *Questions and Answers on Malaysia*. It set out to "answer fundamental questions asked about the Federation" and it achieved its objective with a frankness which is unusual in official publications. No percipient person who reads this booklet can be left in any doubt as to the basis on which the Federation was built; misconceptions only arise when people try to gloss over the simple reality.

The Federation was formed on the basis of the numerical and political superiority of the Malays. It was indeed the only basis on which the Federation could have been formed at all. This is made quite clear in the booklet: "The main factor impending the union has been the fact that the one and a quarter million Chinese in Singapore would upset the racial balance of the country by creating a Chinese majority. . . . By bringing in the Borneo territories the racial balance is preserved because the majority of Malays in Borneo balance the Chinese of Singapore and provide a ratio acceptable to all partners."[48]

The authors of this booklet thus make it quite clear that "racial balance" in the context of Malaysia means a preponderance of Malays or "Bumiputra"; this is the norm; anything else is abnormal and would remove the fundamental presupposition on which the concept of Malaysia rests.

Along with the notion of the numerical superiority of the Bumiputras goes the implicit assumption of their political hegemony. Precisely what this means in practice has never been explicitly formulated but among the institutions which embody the concept of Malaysia for the "sons of the soil" are: the Rulers, the Malay language, the preferences given to Bumiputras in certain trades and professions—in short, the recognition of the "special position" of the Bumiputras.

There is nothing new in any of this. From the very beginning of British "indirect rule" in Malaya it was made clear that the sovereignty of the "Rulers" of the Malay States was to be unimpaired.

Even if the Rulers' sovereignty was more of a legal fiction than a reality any move to alter their constitutional and legal position always met with resistance. The Duff Development Corporation case made the legal position of the ruler of Kelantan quite clear even if in this instance it worked to his disadvantage. Again, after the Second World War, when the British tried to set up a Malayan Union which would have severely restricted the Rulers' powers, they were forced to abandon the scheme in favour of an arrangement which safeguarded the position of the Malay Rulers and recognised the special position of the Malays. When Malaya accepted independence from Great Britain she did so on the strict understanding that the protection which the Malays had received under the British would continue to be enjoyed by them even if they should one day become numerically a minority in their own country.

In an address given to an Australian audience in 1965 Lee Kuan Yew said: "Had the British been more far-sighted and seen that it was not possible to hold Singapore separately from Malaya, many of these problems need not have arisen. But these problems have. Because for eighteen years Malaysia was so accustomed to Malay predominance, when the awful moment of truth that it could not go along to the utter disregard of Singapore came, they found Singapore so unpalatable and indigestible a unit that they insisted that Sabah, Sarawak and Brunei should go along with it."[49]

This comment of Lee Kuan Yew's does not accord with historical reality. It is certain that any proposal for a Malayan Union which included Singapore on an equal footing with the Malay States would have been fiercely opposed by the Sultans. Moreover, by 1945 the British were morally and legally unable to resist the wishes of the Malay Rulers; this particular point was made quite clear in 1945 and the following year by UMNO and the Rulers.

Attempts have been made several times by different politicians to change these basic presuppositions. Dato Onn tried in 1951 to found a genuinely multi-racial party which would stand for a "Malayan" rather than a "Malay" Malaya. He failed.

In the 1960's Lee Kuan Yew made by far the longest and most sustained attack on Malay supremacy that has yet been attempted. He also failed.

In 1969 the issue was raised again. This time it aroused so much passion and hatred that the Malay leaders decided to place the whole subject of Malay special rights and the position of the Rulers beyond dispute and even discussion.

In his book about the May 13 riots Tunku Abdul Rahman, reputedly the apostle of non-communalism, stated quite bluntly: "Let me repeat that this nation had been accepted by all the other races living here as being fundamentally a Malay country. . . ." The point was made again in the report of the National Operations Council a few weeks later. The compilers of the report reminded their readers that as far back as 1946 the British Secretary of State had "accepted the principle that the special position of the Malays shall be safeguarded". The NOC then chose to draw attention to the fact that the Working Committee in 1946 had been reminded that "the Malays have no alternative homeland whilst the remainder of the population, with few exceptions, retain in varying degrees a connection with their country of origin and in many cases regard that country and not Malaya as the primary object of their loyalty". The undisguised anti-Chinese tone of this extract and indeed of the whole report underlined the fact that the spirit of a Malaysian Malaysia was now well and truly laid.

The rejection of the "Malaysian" solution does not, however, imply that there is no alternative to "Malaysia for the Malays". Until 1969 a compromise had always been reached between the Malays and the Chinese on the basis that the Chinese would be allowed to maintain their grip on the economy at the price of conceding political supremacy to the Malays.

The events of May 13, 1969, however, indicated that this compromise was no longer acceptable to the parties concerned. The Sino-Malay bargain had been struck under the pressure of impending independence and at a time when the Malays greatly outnumbered the Chinese on the electoral roll. Things had changed a great deal since then. Most of the Chinese had the franchise and had political ambitions; the Malays were now anxious to play a more important role in the economy; and the generation which struck the original informal bargain was giving way to a new, better-educated, more emancipated generation which was not afraid to question the attitudes of its elders.

During the whole of Tunku Abdul Rahman's Prime Ministership politics were conducted in an air of benign hypocrisy. The Tunku's style was to strike a strongly Malay attitude verbally while in practice allowing great freedom in the implementation of seemingly pro-Malay policies. Such a policy could only be successful if the general public was kept in ignorance of the true state of affairs and if the Malays and the Chinese followed non-competing courses in a segregated, genuinely "plural" society.*

Since independence in 1957 there have been great social changes, in particular a great increase in education. British educational policy was elitist and tended to keep the various ethnic groups in separate streams directed towards separate destinations in the economy and the public service. The first independent Malayan governments decided in principle to make education freely available to all. In doing so they unwittingly gave many Malays, and to a lesser extent Chinese, the impression that there would be matching career opportunities waiting for them at the end of their schooldays. In a sense then May 13, 1969 was the day when the revolution of frustrated expectations broke out. It was the day which marked the end of the plural society. The new Chinese and Malay generations had decided to enter on competing, collision, courses. As the NOC's report put it: "The eruption of violence on May 13 was the result of an interplay of forces that comprise the country's history. These include a generation gap and differences in interpretation of the constitutional structure by the different races in the country, and consequently the growing political encroachment of the immigrant races against certain important provisions of the Constitution which relate to the Malay language and the position of the Malays. . . ."[50] The report did not mention the growing desire of the indigenes to encroach on the economic preserves of the immigrant races.

The resignation of Tunku Abdul Rahman marked the end of the era of "the politics of ambiguity".† Both major ethnic groups had to be confronted with two basic facts: that the Constitution meant what it said about the special position of the Malays; and that the bargain which had been struck by an older generation of Malays and Chinese was preferable to its anarchic alternative. To put the first matter beyond doubt was the task of the 1971 Parliament in which the government hoped to have the two-thirds majority required to amend the Constitution. As to the second matter, it was decided to "institutionalise" the bargain by making the National Consultative Council (now the National Unity Council) the only place where the controversial

---

* Defined by J. S. Furnivall as a society in which "different sections of the community" live "side by side, but separately, within the same political unit".
† Cynthia H. Enloe's phrase.[51]

topics concerning "inter-racial co-operation and social integration" might be discussed freely but without the publicity attendant upon the proceedings of Parliament.

When the reconvened Parliament duly passed the Sedition Bill early in 1971 the political balance became permanently tilted in favour of the Malays. The government now set about correcting the economic balance which had for years been heavily weighted in favour of non-Malay Malaysians and Europeans. This was a task which required very delicate handling. The line of least resistance would have been the negative one of taking over the non-Malay sector by more or less forcible tactics; the more difficult but in the long run much more rewarding policy was to encourage new Malay enterprises and to step up the training of Malays in production and managerial techniques. This was the policy officially favoured not only by the government but also, understandably, by many of the Chinese liberals such as Dr Tan Chee Khoon of the Gerakan.*

References

1. R. EMERSON, *Malaysia*, University of Malaysia Press, Kuala Lumpur, Reprinted 1964.
2. WANG GUNG-WU, "The First Three Rulers of Malacca", *J. Malayan Branch R. Asia Soc.* July 1968, **XLI**, Part 1, pp. 11-22.
3. R. EMERSON, op. cit., p. 100.
4. C. D. COWAN, *Nineteenth Century Malaya*, Oxford University Press, London, 1961, p. 41.
5. J. KENNEDY, *A History of Malaya*, Macmillan, London, 1967, p. 119.
6. R. WINSTEDT, *Malaya and its History*, Hutchinson, London, 1966, 7th Edition, p. 65.
7. C. B. BUCKLEY, *An Anecdotal History of Old Times in Singapore 1816-67*, University of Malaya Press, Kuala Lumpur, Reprinted 1965, p. 368.
8. C. D. COWAN, op. cit., p. 167.
9. R. EMERSON, op. cit., p. 119.
10. R. EMERSON, op. cit., p. 121.
11. C. D. COWAN, op. cit., p. 210.
12. C. D. COWAN, op. cit., p. 142.
13. C. B. BUCKLEY, op. cit., p. 659.
14. J. KENNEDY, op. cit., p. 73.
15. R. EMERSON, op. cit., p. 139.
16. R. EMERSON, op. cit., p. 114.
17. R. EMERSON, op. cit., p. 225.
18. J. DE V. ALLEN, "The Ancient Régime in Trengganu 1909-19", *J. Malayan Branch R. Asia Soc.* July 1968, **XLI**, Part 1, pp. 23-53.
19. R. EMERSON, op. cit., pp. 252-62.

---

* For a forceful statement of the Malay case see Mahathir Bin Mohamad, *The Malay Dilemma*.[52]

20. L. A. MILLS, *British Rule in Eastern Asia*, Oxford University Press, London, 1942, p. 105.
21. J. DE V. ALLEN, "Anglo-Kedah Relations 1909-1915", *J. Malayan Branch R. Asia. Soc.* July 1968, **XLI**, Part 1, pp. 54-94.
22. R. EMERSON, op. cit., pp. 236-37.
23. Quoted by J. Bastin in Introduction to R. Emerson, op cit.
24. R. EMERSON, op. cit., p. 22.
25. R. EMERSON, op. cit., p. 335.
26. R. WINSTEDT, op. cit., p. 142.
27. R. WINSTEDT, op. cit., p. 60.
28. R. EMERSON, *From Empire to Nation*, Harvard University Press, Boston, 1960, p. 95.
29. W. R. ROFF, *The Origins of Malay Nationalism*, University of Malaya Press, Kuala Lumpur, 1967, pp. 138-39.
30. W. R. ROFF, op. cit., pp. 196-97.
31. W. R. ROFF, op. cit., pp. 85-86.
32. F. STARNER, "Communism in Malaya", in R. Scalapino (Ed.), *The Communist Revolution in Asia*, Prentice-Hall, Englewood Cliffs, N.J., 1965, p. 224.
33. A. JOSEY, *Lee Kuan Yew*, Donald Moore Press, Singapore, 1968, p. 236.
34. R. S. MILNE, *Government and Politics in Malaysia*, Houghton-Mifflin, Boston, 1967, p. 98.
35. A. JOSEY, op. cit., p. 96.
36. A. JOSEY, op. cit., p. 404.
37. A. JOSEY, op. cit., p. 411.
38. ROBERT E. GAMER, "Parties and Pressure Groups", in Ooi Jin-Bee and Chiang Hai Ding (Eds), *Modern Singapore*, University of Singapore, Singapore, 1969, p. 202.
39. A. JOSEY, op. cit., p. 433.
40. ABDUL RAHMAN, *May 13*, Utusan Melayu Press, Kuala Lumpur, 1969, pp. 13-14.
41. *Sarawak Vanguard*, March 14, 1969.
42. *Straits Times*, 20 May, 1969.
43. *Far Eastern Economic Review*, July 16, 1970.
44. *Straits Times*, July 8, 1970.
45. *Cobbold Report*, Report of the Inter-Governmental Committee, published in Kuching, Sarawak and Jesselton (Kota Kinabalu) Sabah, 1962.
46. *Daily Express*, October 11, 1965.
47. *The May 13 Tragedy*, The National Operations Council, Kuala Lumpur, October 9, 1969.
48. *Questions and Answers on Malaysia*, Ministry of Information, Kuala Lumpur, August 1963.
49. *Malaysia—Age of Revolution*, Singapore Ministry of Culture, 1965.
50. *The May 13 Tragedy*, op. cit., p. ix.
51. CYNTHIA H. ENLOE, "Issues and Integration in Malaysia", *Pacific Affairs*, **XLI**, No. 3, 1968.
52. MAHATHIR BIN MOHAMAD, *The Malay Dilemma*, Donald Moore, Singapore, 1970.

CHAPTER TEN

Indonesia

Kingdoms and Sultanates

The Sailendras and Sri Vijaya

We have spoken already of the antithesis between the maritime and mainland; between the mobile sea-faring empires and those based on a static rice-growing peasantry. We have spoken, too, of the Sailendras or "Lords of the Mountain", god-kings who presided over an earthly replica of the eternal cosmos. We have spoken of Hindu splendour, Buddhist quietude and the evangelical fervour of Islam. In Indonesia all these ingredients of Southeast Asian civilisation are to be found.

It is not our purpose here to give a detailed narrative of Indonesian history, rich and interesting though it is. For this the reader must go to the acknowledged authorities. We shall be content to pick out one or two episodes.

Some modern writers, notably Palmier,* have seen recent Indonesian history as a struggle between Java and the Outer Provinces (to use Dutch parlance) or more specifically between Java and Sumatra. Although one should not place too much reliance on it there is much to support the generalisation that there is and always has been a certain tension in Indonesian history between the sea-faring, out-going, largely Moslem states which have arisen mainly in Sumatra and the inward-looking, Hinduised, bureaucratic polities of inland Java. It is as well to stress that these are only stereotypes. There have, for instance, been sea-faring Moslem states, like Banten, in Java, just as there have been empires like Madjapahit which were rice-based, bureaucratic *and* sea-faring.

Of the many empires and city-states which have come and gone we intend arbitrarily to nominate five to represent the historical and

---

* See Leslie H. Palmier, *Indonesia and the Dutch*.[1]

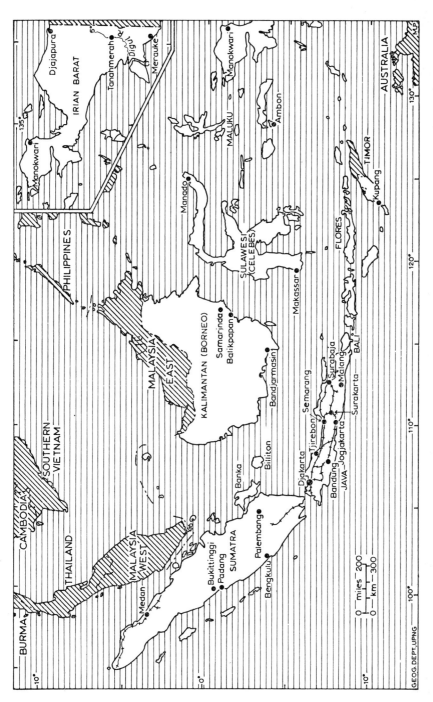

Map 11. Indonesia

cultural background of which all educated Indonesians are aware today. The five are the Sailendras, Sri Vijaya, Madjapahit, Mataram and Atjeh.

The Sailendras or "Lords of the Mountans" reigned in central Java and were responsible for the building of the immense monument of Borobudur on a site near the modern Jogjakarta. The Sailendra kings were followers of the Hindu cult of the *deva-raj* or god-king about which we have already written in greater detail elsewhere in this book.

Sri Vijaya, though an offshoot of the Sailendras with the same *deva-raj* cult, was a sea-going empire based on a city near the modern Palembang, which lies some forty-five miles up the tidal waters of the River Musi in south-eastern Sumatra. At its height Sri Vijaya exercised control over an area which included the western end of Java, the east coast of Sumatra and most of the coast of Malaya. One cannot be sure of the precise dates of Sri Vijaya but it seems to have reached its zenith at the beginning of the eleventh century.[2] Then in about 1028 it was attacked by a Chola king from South India and took some years to recover from this savage assault. It was still influential in Malaya up to the last quarter of the twelfth century but thereafter seems to have been eclipsed by new forces emerging from Thailand and Java.[3]

Madjapahit

The empire of Madjapahit occupies a central point in the consciousness of the Indonesian nationalist. In the thirteenth and fourteenth centuries this great central Javanese empire ruled or exerted a dominant influence over an area which some Indonesians claim to have been at least co-terminous with the boundaries of the former Dutch East Indies. We may doubt the validity of the claim but it is taken seriously by Indonesian politicians and has served to prove that the Republic of Indonesia is not a mere successor to the Dutch colonial government but the rightful heir to an ancient indigenous kingdom. It should also be noted, in passing, that the empire of Madjapahit is claimed to have included West Irian, formerly Dutch New Guinea.

The most famous names in the history of Madjapahit are King Hayam Wuruk and his chief minister Gadjah Mada under whom the empire flourished greatly in the latter part of the fourteenth century.

Mataram

There have been two kingdoms of Mataram in central Java. The earlier one was Hindu and flourished in the period of the Sailendras. The second one was Moslem with a strong undercurrent of Hindu culture and is the one with which we are now concerned.

Of all the great Indonesian empires Mataram is the only one of which more than just monuments and memories remain. It is represented today by the Sultanates or "special regions" of Jogjakarta and Solo (Surakarta).

Founded in the seventeenth century, Mataram was a rice-based inland kingdom in the style of Madjapahit and its rulers though nominally Moslem enjoyed the status of the old Hindu *deva-raj*. Great names in the history of Mataram were Senopati, its founder, and Sultan Agung its most powerful monarch.

Sultan Agung attacked the Dutch fort at Batavia (now Djakarta) in 1629, but lacked the sea-power needed to defeat the Dutch. For this exploit, and other harassments of the Dutch, the great Sultan is regarded as one of the fathers of Indonesian nationalism.

After Sultan Agung's death the fortune of Mataram declined and by the beginning of the nineteenth century parts of it had been ceded to the Dutch and the remainder divided between the kingdoms of Solo, ruled by a Susuhunan (Sunan) and Jogjakarta, ruled by a Sultan. These rulers were obliged to acknowledge the suzerainty of the Dutch and to accept the latter's arbitration in the case of a disputed succession. It was out of just such a dispute that the costly Java War of 1825-1830 arose, and provided another Indonesian nationalist hero.

Apart from his natural dislike of alien, non-Moslem rule Prince Dipo Negoro had at least two good reasons for leading a revolt against the Dutch. In the first place the Dutch had overlooked his claim to the throne of Jogjakarta. Second, the Dutch had antagonised the local Javanese aristocracy by requiring them to terminate leaseholds given to aliens and to make cash refunds. The Dutch were trying to protect the peasants but only succeeded in making enemies of the nobility who now rallied to the side of Dipo Negoro.

The war lasted five years and is estimated to have cost the Dutch twenty million guilders and fifteen thousand lives. The Javanese were eventually defeated and Dipo Negoro exiled to Makasar in Sulawesi (Celebes) where he died in 1855.

The Indonesians today look back on the Java War as an event of great importance. They have good reasons. Dipo Negoro showed that the Dutch were by no means invulnerable. He also gave his countrymen a rallying-cry and a symbol: Islam and the red-and-white flag, "Sang Merah-Putih". Nearly a century later the Indonesian nationalist movement grew out of Serikat Islam and the "Merah-Putih" flag adopted by the nationalists now flies over a free Republic.

Jogjakarta itself became a symbol of resistance and in a land where symbolism counts for so much, it was fitting that this city should be chosen as the temporary capital of the besieged infant Republic of Indonesia in its struggles with the returning Dutch in the late 1940s.

Atjeh

Atjeh, in the northern extremity of Sumatra, was the cradle of Islam in Indonesia. Marco Polo found Moslems there at the end of the thirteenth century. Later, as we have seen, it became a great trading power and a rival to Malacca and Johore.

It was not until the last quarter of the nineteenth century that the Dutch made a serious attempt to bring the fierce and independent Atjehnese under their rule. The ensuing war lasted for over thirty years and marked a turning point in Dutch colonial history.

In 1871, after some years of friction between British traders and the Dutch Government, concerning the freedom of trade in the ports of Sumatra's east coast, the British and the Dutch entered into negotiations which led to the signing of the so-called Treaty of Sumatra. In return for various concessions elsewhere the Dutch were given *carte blanche* to deal with the Atjehnese "pirates", and if necessary to bring Atjeh under their rule.

In 1873, exactly the same year that the British started their "forward" movement in Malaya, the Dutch began their war against Atjeh. After initial successes the Dutch found themselves involved in interminable guerrilla warfare against a many-headed opponent.

After twenty years of fighting the Dutch managed to persuade Teuku Umar, a prominent Atjehnese chief, to come over to their side. For a while things went well. Teuku Umar was given men and equipment and fought successfully for the Dutch. After three years, however, he suddenly went over the side of the Atjehnese and put his newly acquired expertise to good use in the service of his fellow countrymen.

After Teuku Umar's death in action in 1899, the Dutch gradually gained the upper hand. They followed the strategy of supporting the traditional rulers against the Moslem leaders—a course which had proved successful in the war against the Paderis.* By 1903 Atjeh had been "pacified".

From the Dutch point of view the Atjeh War marked the beginning of a physical expansion which was to convert the Dutch East Indies from a largely Javanese affair into an empire which was to include Sumatra, Borneo and the Celebes. It also marked a turning point in Dutch colonial policy, a brief survey of which now follows.

Dutch Colonial Policy

For the sake of convenience one could divide the 350 years of Dutch influence in the East Indies into three periods. A "merchant" period from 1600-1800; a "planter" period from 1800-1870; and an "administrator" period from 1870-1941.

---

* The Paderis were a group of reforming Moslems who became involved in a struggle against the traditional leaders and the latter's allies, the Dutch. The war lasted from 1821 to 1837.

1600-1800

The history of the first period is the history of the Dutch East India Company, the Vereenigde Oost-Indische Compagnie or VOC.

During this period the Dutch strove to establish a monopoly of the trade, mainly in spices, of the area. Vast individual fortunes were made but contact with the Indonesians was minimal and was normally confined to making treaties with the appropriate rulers in Java, the Moluccas, Makasar, Palembang or wherever the desired crop grew.

The Dutch were of course forced into fighting local wars in order to safeguard their fortified ports but such expenditure, though catered for in the Company's charter, was heartily deplored by the directors in Holland, since it ate into the profit margins. At the same time as this additional military expenditure was being incurred, the home economy was declining. There was also increased competition from the English and French in the fields of trade, manufacture and shipping. These factors, combined with gross corruption on the part of its servants, all contributed to the decline of the VOC in the second half of the eighteenth century.

The end came on the last day of the eighteenth century when the Company was formally wound up.

1800-1870

As the VOC lay dying, new proposals were made as to the future conduct of affairs.

In 1800 a certain Dirk van Hogendorp put forward a plan whose main points were these: abolition of monopoly and a revenue "founded on the principles of freedom of trade, property in the soil and equality of imposts".[4]

Hogendorp had spent some years in voluntary exile in British India and became convinced that economic freedom was the key to salvation. He believed, as did Adam Smith and his British disciples, that the universal pursuit of individual interest would lead to the ultimate good of all.

These ideas found no favour with the Dutch investigation committee which reported in 1803 and in any case by this time Holland had become a vassal of France and had other, more pressing, considerations on her mind.

In 1806 Herman Willem Daendels, the "Iron Marshal", was sent to Batavia as Governor-General. Interested mainly in strengthening the defence of Java against a possible attack by the British he was equally ruthless in purging the administration of its corrupt elements as in employing forced labour to build roads and improve communications.

The most interesting feature of Daendel's régime was the down-grading of the "regents" of Javanese rulers. This was an effort to turn semi-independent rulers into salaried officials of the Dutch administration and was a radical departure from the normal practice of "indirect rule".

Daendels left in 1810 and was succeeded by Janssens who arrived just in time to surrender to Thomas Stamford Raffles, the Englishman who was sent to take over the Governorship of Java and its dependencies so that the French could not use the islands as a base from which to harass Britain's eastern trade.

Like Daendels, but from different motives, Raffles pursued the idea of replacing indirect by direct rule. His purpose, however, was to ensure that no-one should come between the Government and the individual rent-payer, both for humanitarian and practical fiscal reasons. Previously the peasants had been forced to pay tribute in kind either to the Dutch or to their own rulers through a series of intermediaries each of whom added their own "percentage" to the amount to be levied. Raffles aimed to cut out the intermediaries and deal directly with the peasant who was to pay land-rent, preferably in cash. In replacing forced deliveries of produce by cash Raffles wished to monetise the economy both because he believed it would bring more freedom to the individual and because he hoped the Javanese would soon have enough money to buy the cheap cottons of Lancashire.

After the defeat of Napoleon at Waterloo in 1815, the Dutch returned to Java. After an initial phase of economic "liberalism" in the style of Raffles during which further land was sold to private entrepreneurs the Governor-General, van der Capellen, decided to stop this process and intervene on behalf of the oppressed peasant. Unfortunately, as we have seen, his handling of the situation antagonised the Javanese princes and the five years' war against Dipo Negoro ensued.

By now there were already signs of a return to the old VOC monopoly policy. In 1824 the Nederlandsche Handelsmaatschappij (NHM) or Netherlands Trading Society was founded in order to provide competition against the other foreign merchants, particularly the British; the other new institution, the Java Bank, was founded to provide extra financial help for the NHM.

The Java War cost a great deal in men and money, and the colony was once more bankrupt; what is more significant, the motherland was bankrupt too. At this stage the Dutch only had two courses open to them: to abandon the Indies or to make them pay, and pay quickly.

The "Culture System"

To solve their financial problems the Dutch initiated the so-called "Culture System" by which the people could pay their rent in export crops instead of cash or rice. The Netherlands Trading Society was given the monopoly of the trade in these crops, the Java Bank supported it and the civil service saw to it that the crops were grown.

From the point of view of the twentieth century Indonesian nationalists, the grossest iniquity of the system was the notion of the *batig slot* or credit balance, which was the net profit made by the colonial administration out of the culture system. This sum was remitted direct to the Netherlands instead of being used for the benefit of the Indonesians.

From the Dutch point of view the system was a great success. Between 1831 and 1877 the *batig slot* amounted to 823,000,000 guilders.[5]

The culture system came in for severe criticism which was mostly directed against the sheer inhumanity of the system in practice and the powerlessness of the Dutch civil servant to help the victims.

Edward Douwes Dekker, the author of *Max Havelaar*, a semi-autobiographical novel about the culture system, is hardly an unbiased witness but his description of the effects of the system is worth quoting and must certainly have shocked his readers in Holland in 1860.

Writing of the *tani*, the peasant cultivator, he says: "The Government forces him to grow what it wants on *his* ground; it punishes him if he sells the produce to anyone else and furthermore fixes the price at which it is to be sold. The costs of shipping the produce via a monopolistic trading concern* are high. Then you have the commission paid to the native chiefs as an inducement; this also means a cut in the buying price . . . and yet a profit must be made. This profit can only be made by giving the Javanese just enough to prevent them dying of hunger and thus creating a labour shortage. Even the European official gets a special payment in proportion to the size of the harvest. So it is that the poor Javanese suffers under two masters and is often dragged off his own rice fields. Frequently the system causes famine. Famine? On the rich, fruitful, blessed ground of Java? Yes, reader."[6]

And what of the Dutch Assistant resident who had a solemn duty laid on him "to exercise a fatherly care" over the common people?

According to Dekker the Assistant Resident—and he had been one himself—was powerless to carry out his solemn duty. "Everyone knows that the European officer is liable to be transferred at any moment to another district, but the Regent, the mighty Regent, stays where he is."[7] In other words the common people were far more afraid of their rulers than of the transient European and it was almost impossible to get the cultivators to give formal evidence of the abuses.

The Dutch were in a dilemma. They knew that the success of the system depended on the co-operation of the rulers; they also knew that the latter would exploit the peasant. They had to choose whether to give real power to the Regent or to the Assistant Resident; they appear to have chosen the former.

In spite of all the profits it made, the Culture System was by no

---

* The Netherlands Trading Society.

means efficient. Its products were by all accounts of poor quality. Clive Day quotes Pierson as saying that: "the Government coffee culture gave not only a smaller product (three-fourths, according to one estimate) but of inferior quality, and the life of a coffee tree in Java was scarcely more than half of what it was in Ceylon, where the tree was properly cared for".[8] A British civil servant from Bengal was of the same opinion. "Here", he says, "little or no attention is bestowed on the cultivation of the plant. After the trees are planted they are left to take care of themselves and suffered to grow as they will. An interval of from six to eight feet only being allowed between the plants, the sun and air never reach them, and a Java coffee garden, therefore, has all the appearance of an unreclaimed jungle." Later on he says that "the Government seems quite indifferent about producing a superior description of coffee and is quite content so long as it continues to realise a certain amount of revenue from the cultivation of the product in question."[9]

One has to stress this element of inefficiency because it was the *tani* who suffered if there was any shortfall in the harvest. For another example of hardship we need to look no further than the other great money-maker of the time, the sugar-culture.

Here the peasant suffered in various ways. To begin with the sugar was planted on his *sawah* (rice ground) and thus threatened his food supply; second the Europeans—many of whom were administrators turned farmers—frequently knew much less than the Javanese about growing sugar; and finally, labour was so scarce that peasants were forced to travel many miles to do their stint of what amounted to forced labour on the plantations.

In the end it was a combination of economic necessity and common humanity that brought a gradual end to the culture system. The truth was that it was ceasing to be profitable. Falling profits, the uneasy public conscience and the intrusion for the first time of the Dutch Parliament into East Indian affairs ushered in the new "Liberal" policy and what we have termed the "Administrator period".

1870-1941

THE LIBERAL POLICY

The Liberal Policy was essentially a reversion to the policy of Raffles and van Hogendorp. The colonial Government was henceforth to leave the field of agriculture and commerce and concentrate on administration and the maintenance of a framework of security. Business was to be left to the businessmen.

Under the new dispensation land was again made freely available to individual buyers. This time, however, strict measures were taken to prevent abuse. Under the Agrarian Law of 1870 "native landowners were prohibited from alienating land to non-natives, and Europeans were not allowed to own other land than small urban tracts". Furthermore land was only available on a leasehold basis. The maximum life of a lease was seventy-five years—which explains why so many leases came to an end in the late 1940s and 1950s just in time for the Sukarno regime *not* to renew them.

This time there were more agricultural experts available and no doubt many of the new estates carved out of the wilderness were much more efficiently run than their predecessors. Some of the biggest fortunes were made in sugar. One Chinese owner of a plantation near Tjirebon built himself a replica, on a smaller scale, of the Governor-General's palace at Weltevreden (now the Indonesian Presidential palace, Istana Merdeka, in Djakarta) at a cost of 350,000 guilders.

Two other industries which flourished greatly were those of tin and oil. Both had royal connections. Prince Hendrik made a fortune out of the Billiton Tin Company, founded in 1852, and the Dutch royal family lent its support to the "Royal Dutch" oil company, more familiar to Indonesians under the initials BPM (Bataafse Petroleum Maatschappij). This was the company which later became associated with the Shell Transport and Trading Company. And yet for all this prosperity around him the peasant was not much better off; indeed many experts, including a Dutch official named van Deventer, reckoned that his standard of living had fallen.

In a famous article published in 1899 van Deventer drew attention to the plight of the peasant. He said that for too long Holland had been taking money out of the Indies; it was time some of the profits were ploughed back into the country for the benefit of its native inhabitants. Holland owed the East Indies a "debt of honour". In what a Frenchman maliciously described as "the best Dutch book-keeping manner" an exact figure was placed on the amount of the Dutch indebtedness to the "Inlander" namely 187,000,000 gold guilders. The suggestion was that if this sum could be spent on the Indonesians all would be well. This was the type of unimaginative thinking, labelled "thinking in guilders" by a Dutch Socialist,[10] which used so to enrage the anti-colonialists.

THE ETHICAL POLICY

Formation The following two paragraphs from Queen Wilhelmina's speech from the throne in 1901 are usually taken to mark the official opening of the so-called Ethical Era in the Dutch East Indies:

> As a Christian Power, Holland is duty bound . . . to support the Christian missions and to make the whole administration there realise that Holland has a moral vocation to follow in respect of the native population of that region.
> In this connection I am particularly struck by the diminished prosperity of the native population in Java; I wish an enquiry to be held into the reasons for this.

There was in fact no sudden change in policy, no sudden concern over the fate of "the native population". There was merely a converging of various economic and political forces. Among the more prominent forces were the Liberal policy, the Atjeh War, the Indies' budget deficits, the Civil Service and big business.

The Liberal policy had thrown the country open to private enterprise and this led to the remarkable increase in the number of Europeans living in the Indies—from 36,467 in 1872 to 58,806 in 1892. Employees of private firms now far outnumbered Government officials. This increase had at least two consequences: first, a demand for better amenities of all kinds, and second, a demand for an extension of the "Pax Neerlandica" to new, exploitable regions.

Whatever the reasons for the Atjeh War, it had several important consequences. It marked the beginning of the Dutch "forward movement" which did not end until the last soldier left Bali in 1914. It gave rise to strong public misgivings about the strength and direction of Islamic movements which surely coloured people's later reactions to the nationalist movement, the Serikat Islam. The discovery of the strength of Moslem feeling also resulted in a renewed emphasis on official support for the Christian missions.

The Atjeh war was also a main cause of our third item, the persistent budget deficits. The status of the Indies had changed. Previously it had been a *winstgebied*, an area where profits could be made for the motherland; now it was rapidly becoming a colony of settlement where more and more Dutchmen and other Europeans were making their lives and their homes. There was now a powerful demand from businessmen for the provision of law and order, public utilities and roads and railways. All this would cost the Government far more than it was then receiving in revenue under the existing tax system. The change from the Culture System to the Liberal Policy had meant *not* that no money was being made but that it was being made by businessmen rather than the Government. This new wealth was grossly under-taxed. In 1897, for example, seventy-five per cent of the Government's revenue came from the Indonesians themselves. Income tax, which would have made the Europeans contribute their just share to the revenue was not introduced until 1908, and even then was never a progressive tax; rich and poor alike paid the same percentage of their income.

A fourth pressure came from the colonial civil servants. With the fading away of the Culture System the civil servants were no longer directly concerned with production nor had they any financial interest in it. Unlike the British, the Dutch gave their district officers no financial or magisterial functions and the latter were, therefore, free to concentrate on putting their new liberal humanitarian ideas into practice by seeking to enhance the welfare of the villagers.

Finally, there was big business. Here there was a conflict of interest. Estate owners were interested in keeping wages and costs down and were therefore not particularly enthusiastic about the ethical policy. On the other hand the cotton manufacturers of the Twente in Holland and their agents in Indonesia were keen supporters of any move which might enhance the purchasing power of the Indonesian. Also on the side of the "ethicals" were the men engaged in the relatively new extractive such as tin and oil. They might not have been in favour of higher wages but appreciated that none of the ethical policy could be put into practice without the prior establishment of "peace and good order" (*rust en orde*), which was precisely what they needed if they were to carry on their profitable businesses.

Action Between 1898 and 1914 the Dutch "pacified" and brought under their control more territory than in the previous three hundred years of their presence in the East Indies. For the first time in history, or at any rate since the time of Madjapahit, the East Indies began to acquire some semblance of unity. Everywhere Indonesians began to be much more conscious of the Dutch presence.

The Dutch were certainly active. Having achieved peace and good order in Atjeh and elsewhere, General van Heutsz became Governor-General in 1904 and proceeded to put the economy on a sound footing, so that the Government could afford the increased expenditure on the welfare of the "Inlander".

Between 1905-16 forty-six million guilders were spent on public works which partly benefited the Indonesians. The main items were irrigation, roads and the extension of credit.

There were big advances on other fronts. Between 1905 and 1912 passenger and freight traffic doubled on the railways as did the tonnage of shipping visiting the twenty largest harbours.

There was great pressure for the spread of education. As in England at the time the question of education was beset by religious denominational pitfalls, and Ministers had to tread warily.

In the long run it was decided to support the mission schools (mainly in the Outer Islands) and to double the number of "2nd Class" schools (mainly in Java) which gave instruction in the three Rs in the vernacular. The number of these schools rose from 300 in 1907 to 650 in 1911.

Perhaps the most important innovation was the village or *desa* school, said to have been van Heutsz's brainchild. Under van Heutsz's scheme the village was to provide the school house and a contribution of ninety guilders a year while the Government was to provide two teachers per school and the necessary textbooks. By 1909 there were 723 *desa* schools; by 1912 there were 2,531 with 166,965 pupils. By 1940 there were 18,000 *desa* schools with about two million pupils.

On the political front a start was made with decentralisation and the setting up of municipal councils. Of itself this was not a move of vital importance since it mainly affected the Europeans, but it had an important by-product, namely the beginnings of legal political activity

which led in 1915 to the granting of the general right of political association and assembly.

Perhaps the most interesting and dramatic development was the
inauguration of the Volksraad or People's Council consisting of a
Chairman and forty-eight members half of whom were nominated and
the other half elected by members of urban councils. Although at first
the Volksraad had no legislative power it gave officials and certain
influential members of the Dutch and Indonesian public a chance to
air their views about the present and future conduct of the colony.
There was a flood of mostly adverse criticism which revealed the existence among the politically articulate of a strong desire for reform. As
a result of this and other pressures various committees and commissions
were formed to examine the need for constitutional changes.

By 1929 the Volksraad's powers had greatly increased. Its assent was
now necessary for Budget proposals and other domestic legislation and
it could petition the Government. The Governor-General and heads of
department were, however, not responsible to the Volksraad nor did
they pay much heed to its petitions if the latter did not accord with
official policy.

Although it may not have been very effective and although many
Indonesian politicians may have regarded as collaborators and traitors
those of their fellow-nationals who were nominated or elected to it, the
Volksraad not only gave many Indonesians a valuable insight into
administrative problems but by its very existence legitimised a certain
amount of political activity in the colony. It also gave, as Furnivall
pointed out, an unparalleled opportunity for Dutch officials to criticise
their own administration.

Reaction For every action, say the physicists, there is an equal and
opposite reaction: perhaps this rule also holds good in the political field.
The Dutch had taken action in the religious, economic, educational and
political fields: in every one of these fields there was an Indonesian
reaction.

In answer to the growing intrusion of Western culture the Javanese
upper class founded "Budi Utomo" whose stated aims were "the
harmonious development of the people of Java and Madura". In answer,
partly to the increased activity of the Christian missions but mainly
to the economic aggression of the Chinese trading community the
Serikat Dagang Islam (or Moslem Business Society) was born and was
given the official approval of the Governor-General in 1913 in the face
of widespread panic among estate owners who apparently feared that
the Moslems were about to wage a holy war against them.

But the Chinese did not merely act as stimulants to Moslem businessmen. With the overthrow of the Manchu dynasty and the victory of
the Republicans there was a burst of nationalism, which resulted in
concessions being made to the Chinese by the Dutch colonial government. At about the same time the Serikat Dagang Islam dropped the

Dagang ("business") out of its title and became the Serikat Islam, the first and only genuinely mass nationalist movement in Indonesian colonial history. It spread over Sumatra, Kalimantan (Borneo) and Sulawesi (Celebes) and by 1917 was said to have eight hundred thousand members.

The subsequent history of the Serikat Islam is typical of the many parties and movements of the time; Bousquet, the French observer of colonial Indonesia, said of them: "they are formed, then transformed, divided, merged or finally destroyed whether by the courts, or by some other factor".

The Serikat Islam was penetrated by Communists and eventually split into three main groups: a reformist Islam section, a sort of "Kaum Muda", which eventually linked up with an organisation known as Muhammadijah; a nationalist section which became in 1929 the Partai Serikat Islam Indonesia; and a Communist section which became first the "Red" Serikat Islam and then the Serikat Rakjat, or People's Union.

The other main contender in the field of Islam was the N.U. or Nahdatul Ulama. The N.U. was, in a sense, the complement of the Muhammadijah: its supporters came mainly from the ranks of the conservative rural Moslem leaders whose self-styled "orthodoxy" was strongly influenced by Moslem mysticism and Hindu-Javanese beliefs.

Out of the "Red" Serikat Islam branch in Semarang emerged the Indonesian Communist Party (PKI) under the leadership of Semaun, Darsono, Tan Malaka and the Dutchman Bergsma. After great success in the field of trade union activity and the infiltration of the Serikat Islam the PKI staged an uprising in Batavia (Djakarta) in November 1926 which was ruthlessly crushed by the Dutch; as was one two months later in Padang, Sumatra. Thirteen thousand suspects were arrested of whom four thousand five hundred were sent to prison. Several hundred were sent to a fever-ridden camp in New Guinea on the Digul river. By a curious coincidence the spot was already known as Tanah Merah or "Red Land".

Meanwhile in Holland Indonesian students had formed the Perhimpunan Indonesia or Indonesian Union. The PI in its time counted among its members some of the great men of Indonesian colonial and post-colonial politics: Mohammed Hatta, later Vice-President of Indonesia; Ali Sastroamidjojo, Prime Minister in 1956 and Mohammed Natsir, Prime Minister in 1950-51. Incidentally, all these three were arrested and imprisoned for their activities in Holland in 1927.

Members of the PI returning to Indonesia helped to start study clubs. Sukarno—later President—then a student at the Bandung College of Technology was a founder-member of the Bandung Study Club and it was also in Bandung that he founded in 1927 the PNI (Perserikatan Nasional Indonesia) described by a contemporary as "a projection of the PI in Indonesia". The main plank in the PNI's platform was the ending of Dutch rule. For three years the PNI flourished and achieved a membership of about ten thousand. In 1929 Sukarno and some of his fellow-members were arrested and in 1930 Sukarno was sent to prison.

After a brief period of freedom in 1932 and 1933 Sukarno was again arrested, tried and sent into exile: first to Flores and then to Bengkulu in Sumatra, where he remained until the Japanese invasion.

By the middle 1930s the Dutch had eliminated so many of the leading Indonesian politicians that the nationalist movement lost its sting, and by the time of the Japanese invasion had become a loose coalition of parties dedicated to achieving self-government by constitutional rather than revolutionary means.

The Time of the Japanese 1942-45

The Japanese invasion shattered the Dutch dream of staying in Indonesia for "another three hundred years".

In a few short weeks the Dutch were disgraced in front of their former subjects and removed from all their positions of power in administration, commerce and large-scale agriculture. While it is true that the Japanese had no intention, at first, of doing anything other than replacing the Dutch but otherwise preserving the *status quo*, their initial dethronement of the old colonial power was enough to set in motion an irreversible political process leading towards a future in which the Dutch could never again enjoy their former status. The first main Japanese objective was to win the co-operation of the Indonesians in the war effort against the western powers. Later, when they were in sight of defeat, their tactics changed somewhat and they appeared to be more concerned with putting as many obstacles as they could in the path of the returning colonial rulers.

The Japanese occupation was a seminal period in Indonesian history. It killed Dutch colonial rule; it gave hundreds of Indonesian civil servants their first experience of real power and responsibility; it set back the hopes of the old order, the major and minor aristocrats who had co-operated with the Dutch; it advanced the cause of the modernist Moslems; it gave the Communist party, which went "underground", a taste for guerilla warfare; it gave Sukarno, as the Japanese-sponsored nationalist leader, a unique opportunity to build up his prestige; it gave students a chance to organise themselves into Japanese-sponsored youth movements; it spread the use of Bahasa Indonesia as a common national language; and above all it gave hundreds of thousands of ordinary young Indonesians the chance to join military and para-military units and get invaluable experience in tactics and the handling of weapons. On the debit side the Japanese occupation gave many Indonesians a disrespect for civil authority and a taste for violence.

In August 1945 the Japanese faced certain and utter defeat. They made a firm offer of independence to Sukarno and Hatta and named August 22 as the appointed day. Meanwhile a group of younger men, ashamed that their country should have to wait for Japan to give them freedom, demanded that Sukarno and Hatta should declare independence at once. Sukarno hesitated but the younger men were adamant and the declaration was in fact made on August 17, 1945. Prominent among this younger group was Adam Malik, then a companion of men like the Moscow-trained Communist Tan Malaka but today Foreign Minister in a government which has set its face firmly against Communism, at any rate on the domestic front.

Revolution and Independence

The immediate post-war scene was dominated by two distinct but sometimes interacting struggles: a military one fought by Indonesia against the returning Dutch and their allies; and a political one for the positions of power and prestige in the new Republic.

Of the military struggle we will only record that it was long and bloody and only came to an end on December 27, 1949, when the Netherlands Government handed over to the Republic the whole of the former Netherlands East Indies except West Irian.

Formation of Political Parties

The political struggle might be said to have formally begun in October 1945 when a small committee headed by Sjahrir and Sjarifuddin decided to allow political parties to be formed in preparation for elections to a national representative council.

Of the many parties which sprang into life perhaps the most important were the Masjumi, the PNI, the Socialist Party and the PKI.

The Masjumi was a loose Moslem coalition which included such unlikely bedfellows as the Nahdatul Ulama, the Muhammmadijah and the Partai Serikat Islam Indonesia, all of whom in previous existences had found cause to differ with each other.

The PNI or Partai Nasional Indonesia was the most prestigious and popular party at this time, mainly because it bore the same initials as Sukarno's pre-war party and was believed to have the support not only of Sukarno but also of most of the civil servants to whom the rank and file Indonesian normally looked for leadership.

The Socialist Party (PSI) was a smaller party led by left-wing intellectuals like Sjahrir who had played a significant part in the wartime resistance movement and who had no great love for Sukarno. Also prominent in this party was Amir Sjarifuddin who later revealed himself as a lifelong member of the Communist Party.

The PKI (Indonesian Communist Party) was of no great moment at this time because many of its potential leaders were members of other parties and labour organisations and there was no coherent Communist "line".

In 1948, however, the new "hard" policy was laid down in a Communist conference in Calcutta and an enlarged "new" PKI was formed which contained many smaller "front" organisations. Under the new policy the PKI now regarded Indonesian non-communists as class enemies to be put in the same category as the Dutch colonial exploiters. This led to a premature attack, launched from Madiun in central Java, on their fellow countrymen at a time—1948—when the Republic was fighting for its existence against the Dutch. The rebellion was put down and the ringleaders shot or imprisoned. There was, however, no general slaughter of Communist sympathisers as it was recognised that the revolt was the responsibility of only a fraction of the PKI. This explains why many PKI leaders like Aidit, Lukman, Njoto and Sudisman —all members of the Politburo, the guiding committee of the PKI— lived to fight another day.

From 1950 onwards, after the official transfer of sovereignty from the Dutch to the Indonesians, the story is one of continuous move and counter move among the political *élite* with three main blocs, the Masjumi, the PNI and later the PKI—now recovered from Madiun— jockeying for power in the presence of a President far more powerful in practice than in theory.

The Army which was destined to play so decisive a role in years to come was at this time not a coherent force, particularly as a result of the "October 17 affair" in 1952 in which a group of officers organised a demonstration in favour of the dissolution of the provisional parliament and the holding of general elections. The group was led by the Chief of Staff, Colonel Nasution, who was subsequently removed from his post.

General Elections 1955-56

At the end of 1955 and the beginning of 1956 elections took place for seats in the new parliament. The results came as a shock to many people. They revealed the strength of the PKI and the remarkable way in which Aidit and his lieutenants had managed to shake off the legacy of Madiun; they showed that the PNI was the strongest party in the country but they also showed that Islam was still the most effective rallying cry. Unfortunately, the Moslem vote was split. The traditionalists of the Nahdatul Ulama, having abandoned their uneasy coalition with their modernist and "religious-socialist" brothers in the Masjumi, fought the elections as a separate party and met with great success.

To summarise the election results, the PNI polled over eight million votes, the Masjumi nearly eight million, the Nahdatul Ulama nearly seven million and the PKI over six million.

Just as significant as the number of votes won by each party was the area from which the votes were drawn. What one might loosely call a "Mataram-Sri Vijaya" pattern was revealed. Sri Vijaya was represented by the Masjumi which drew most of its votes from West Java,

Sumatra and the other islands; Mataram was represented by the PNI, NU, and PKI who drew their votes mainly from Central and East Java. One could press the analogy a bit further and say that *Sri Vijaya* was more outward looking and in favour of accommodation with the outside world while *Mataram* concentrated on internal unity and bristled with hostility against outsiders on matters such as West Irian and foreign enterprises in Indonesia.

But there was also another division between the PKI and the non-Communists. In this confrontation the Moslem parties tended to take the anti-PKI side for ideological reasons while the PNI played an equivocal role sometimes opposing and sometimes supporting the Communists but for reasons of *real-politik* rather than ideology.

The Breakdown of Constitutional Democracy

Three main factors shattered the uneasy post-electoral alliance of the PNI, the Masjumi and the Nahdatul Ulama. First the members of the coalition had very little in common except fear of the PKI; second the PKI had changed its policy to one of supporting "bourgeois nationalists" and had put its money on Sukarno, who now demanded that the Communists be represented in the Cabinet; and third, the Masjumi, whose votes as we have seen came mainly from outside Java, was increasingly embarrassed by the growing discontent, eventually turning to active revolt, in the Outer Islands.

In November 1956 Sukarno, ostensibly tired of the endless manoeuvres of the political parties and undoubtedly anxious to preserve Indonesia's unity, called for an end to alien Western institutions and their replacement by a system more suited to the temperament and circumstances of Indonesians.

Guided Democracy

Sukarno's "concept" (Konsepsi) involved a return to the Constitution of 1945, in which the President was given all the emergency powers which were very necessary at that time of crisis, and a system of consultation (Musjawarah) rather than competition in the Parliament. Western democracy with its divisive, individualistic "one man one vote" and the tyranny of the "50% plus one" majority was to be replaced by "Guided Democracy". The "guidance" would come from the leader in whom power was now to be formally concentrated and the "democracy" would be supplied by the Parliament whose deliberations would end not in a vote but in a unanimous "sense-of-the-meeting"-type of decision (mufakat).

The new era in Indonesian politics began in December 1956 with the resignation of Hatta from the Vice-Presidency. This was followed in quick succession in the next three months by the assumption of sole power in parts of Sulawesi and Kalimantan by local Army commanders;

the declaration of a State of War and Siege; the resignation of the Cabinet and its replacement by a body of reliable appointees hand-picked by Sukarno. Parliament continued to exist but was virtually ignored.

There was now a clear rift between the Javanese and non-Javanese. Not only had Hatta, a Sumatran, resigned but Masjumi had refused to take part in the new constitutional arrangements. Its leaders, and in particular Natsir and Sjafruddin, were not only out of sympathy with Sukarno's "concept" but with the whole management of the nation's affairs.

The climax came in November 1957 when a well-organised *coup* was carried out against Dutch firms. Dutch managers and employees were prevented from entering their business premises and their firms were taken over by junior Indonesian staff most of whom were members of SOBSI the Communist-led trade union.

For a time the whole economy came to a halt. The Army then moved in swiftly, took over the Dutch firms, ordered the trade unionists to return to their proper posts and then proceeded to "manage" the firms alongside their unwilling Dutch partners. Pressure was now put on the remaining Dutch to leave Indonesia.

The PRRI Rebellion

Faced with the prospect of losing at one blow most of his senior trained staff, Sjaffrudin, the Director of the Bank Indonesia—the central bank —went "on leave" to Central Sumatra where he was joined by Dr Sumitro, another economist, and Natsir of the Masjumi. There in the heartland of Hatta's Minangkabau territory, they declared a rival Revo-lutionary Government known by its initials PRRI.

The rebellion was fairly quickly suppressed and with surprisingly little bloodshed. On the political front Masjumi and the Socialist Party, of which Sumitro had been a member, were banned.

Return to the 1945 Constitution

With the decks thus cleared Sukarno proceeded to legitimise his position by proclaiming, on July 5, 1959, a return to the 1945 Con-stitution. The Constituent Assembly, whose task it was to formulate and approve just such a constitutional change, was dismissed for failing to fall in with the President's wishes.

The House of Representatives was put into a kind of limbo and its place taken by the *Madjelis Permusjawaratan Rakjat (Sementara)*— MPR(S)—or (Provisional) People's Consultative Assembly. This body was made up of representatives of the unbanned political parties—of which the main survivors were the PNI, NU and PKI—and various "functional groups" such as the armed forces, the police, the peasants, the religious denominations, youth and women's organisations and war-veterans.

During the next five years the economy went into a sharp decline. Prices of foodstuffs and clothing soared, the black market flourished and all kinds of drastic financial remedies were tried in vain.

This was the time of Sukarno's greatest political activity. The Indonesian air was thick with the slogans of "Guided Democracy" and on the international front there was "confrontation" with the Hague over West Irian and then with Kuala Lumpur over the formation of the Federation of Malaysia.

The confrontation with the Dutch was successful and Sukarno's greatest moment came when he landed at Kemajoran airport near Djakarta on May 6, 1963 to receive the plaudits of the people for having achieved his lifelong ambition to make the slogan "From Sabang to Merauke" a reality.

The confrontation of Malaysia on the other hand was disastrous. Although perhaps designed to take the people's mind off domestic economic troubles it merely added to them, by laying an increased burden on Indonesia's dwindling resources.

In the next eighteen months there were further dramatic events on the diplomatic front. Sukarno launched a vigorous anti-American campaign by attacking the United States in his annual Independence Day speech on August 17, 1964. This was the signal for the Djakarta mob to take to the streets and stone and burn American property. Again it was the Indonesians themselves who were the main sufferers. American aid was greatly reduced at a time when it was never more desperately needed.

Sukarno's next move was to leave the United Nations. He announced his attention of setting up a rival organisation which he would invite all the New Emerging Forces (NEFOs) to join. The complex which was supposed to house the NEFO conferences was never completed and stands today as a reminder of one of Sukarno's many unrealised ambitions.*

With few international allies left, Sukarno and Subandrio, his Foreign Minister, looked increasingly to China for support—a policy which met with the eager approval of the PKI, three of whose leaders —Aidit, Lukman and Njoto—held ministerial rank.

Adam Malik and the BPS

At this point the anti-PKI forces made a final attempt to stop Sukarno's drift to the extreme Left. Adam Malik and Burhanuddin Diah organised a movement known as the "Body for the Preservation of

---

* Part of it now houses the Legislature.

Sukarnoism" (BPS) whose main aim was to promote the non-Communist "Indonesian Socialism" which the President had propounded so often in days gone by.

Significantly the BPS was supported by the Army and over half the un-banned political parties with the main opposition coming from the PKI and the PNI. In the light of subsequent events one can see this moment as the most crucial in Sukarno's long political life. Faced with a choice between the Army, the "religious socialist" Moslems and Christian parties on the one hand and the PKI and PNI on the other, Sukarno for once did not come down between the two factions but quite definitely on the side of the Communists. On December 17, 1964 the President banned the BPS and on January 31, 1965 told interviewers that he could face a Communist take-over with equanimity "as long as they do not make trouble for the Indonesian state".[11]

The Gestapu *Coup*

On October 1, 1965 six of Indonesia's most senior Army generals were assassinated by members of a group later known as the "September 30 Movement" or "Gestapu" (Gerakan September Tiga Puluh). The leader of the group, Lt Col Untung, the commander of the Palace Guard, maintained that he had forestalled a plot by "The Council of Generals" to overthrow Sukarno.

Untung's reign was short-lived. He failed to receive the support from other Army units, and possibly the Communists, which he had anticipated and his men were soon forced to surrender by loyal forces commanded by Nasution and Suharto. By this time Sukarno had fled to Halim airport not far from Djakarta where his private aircraft was kept. By an unfortunate coincidence this was precisely the place to which the captured generals had been taken for execution and burial. Here too was Omar Dhani, the commander of the Air Force and a known Communist sympathiser.

On October 2, when the *coup* had already failed, "Harian Rakjat" the leading Communist daily paper came out in full support of the Gestapu *coup*. This was quite enough to confirm the already widespread suspicion that the PKI was the real power behind Gestapu.

Sukarno's first reaction was to try to cover up the whole affair. The Army by now was engaged in a massive anti-Communist drive but Sukarno still maintained his former relationship with the PKI. He also continued to cultivate the friendship of China in spite of a mounting popular campaign for the dismissal of Subandrio, "the lackey of Peking".

Suharto Takes Over

In February 1966 in a last gesture of defiance Sukarno reshuffled his Cabinet and removed General Nasution from the post of Defence

Minister. This was perhaps too much for the Army who struck back on March 11 by forcing the President to sign an order giving General Suharto all powers necessary to restore peace and stability.

Sukarno was now a mere figure-head. In the next six months he watched impotently as his foreign policy was completely reversed. Confrontation with Malaysia was called off and Indonesia rejoined the United Nations. Meanwhile as suspect after suspect was arrested for complicity in the Untung *coup* the clamour grew for Sukarno himself to be put on trial. Suharto was not to be drawn. Knowing that Sukarno still had many supporters he refused to risk a civil war by making a premature move against the President. Sukarno was not impeached but his power was even further eroded on March 12, 1967 when the People's Consultative Assembly appointed Suharto Acting President. The Assembly stopped short of dismissing Sukarno but decreed that his powers should be withdrawn until a new President was chosen in general elections to be held in 1968.

The New Order

On March 27, 1968 Suharto replaced Sukarno as President. The General was faced with grave political and economic problems. Correctly estimating that the economic problems should be given priority he nevertheless made some immediate concessions to the demand for more representative government. Just over two months after his installation as President he dissolved the Presidium of five ministers through which he had been governing and announced the formation of a new Cabinet of twenty-three, of whom only five were members of the armed forces. It was a "business" Cabinet in which ministers were chosen for their professional qualifications rather than their party affiliations. One of the most interesting features was the appointment to the Ministry of Commerce of Dr Sumitro, one of the ringleaders of the PRRI rebellion who had spent most of the years since 1958 in self-imposed exile abroad.

There was no sign of the elections which were to have been held in 1968 but changes were made in February 1968 in the composition of the MPR(S), the (Provisional) People's Consultative Assembly. Its numbers were enlarged; one hundred and twenty-three members, whose loyalty was suspect, were dismissed (if they had not already gone into retirement or hiding), and the large gap thus created was filled with supporters of the current regime.

If Suharto was in no hurry to advance on the political front he made astonishing progress in the economic field.

Burdened in 1965 with a legacy of international debts, hyperinflation, declining production, administrative chaos and widespread corruption, Suharto gave his small team of professional economists and financial advisers a free hand to try to get the country back on its feet.

The term was remarkably successful. By the middle of 1968 the inflation was under control and the currency, for the first time in at least twelve years, was beginning to look stable. Lending was cut back drastically and rates of interest soared.

The fiscal achievements of the Suharto regime not only made international loans more readily obtainable but attracted some of the foreign investors back to Indonesia. Even though they drove fairly hard bargains, Suharto's economists managed to persuade a good number of foreign companies to do business in Indonesia. The biggest investments were made in the extractive industries: concessions for exploration and development were sold for high prices to companies prospecting for minerals or seeking to exploit the country's considerable timber resources. There was also a fair amount of investment in hotels and other tourist amenities, but disappointingly little interest was shown in setting up manufacturing industries locally—a deficiency which Indonesian entrepreneurs could hardly be expected to make good at the high rates of interest then prevailing.

A Five-Year (1969-1973) Development Plan was announced in 1968 and was put into action the following year. Known familiarly by its acronym, "Repelita", the Plan's priorities lay in the areas of agriculture, industries supporting agriculture, light and small industries, mining industries, infrastructure and tourism. The government certainly made considerable progress in the fields of mining industries and tourism, but the all-important agricultural programme, into which eighty per cent of the resources were put, ran into difficulties and there was doubt as to whether Indonesia would be able to achieve self-sufficiency in rice production by 1974 as planned. Although inflation was cut spectacularly there was a steep increase in the price of petroleum products in early 1970 which caused a public outcry, mainly directed at the State oil company Pertamina whose managing director was an Army General named Ibnu Sutowo.*

Pertamina appeared to be making big profits and its military chief acquired a reputation as a conspicuous spender. Neither of these things endeared either Pertamina or the Army to the man in the street who, mistakenly no doubt, thought that the profits were being made at his expense.

With the economy on the mend Suharto allowed preparations to go forward for the much-delayed elections, the first to be held since 1955-1956. The President made it quite clear that the revival of politics did not herald a return to the "bitter experience of the 1950-1959 period of 'unlimited freedom' ". Indeed it could not be otherwise since Indonesia was to retain the Constitution of 1945 which gave considerable powers to the President but allotted Parliament a somewhat minor role. The

---

* Ibnu Sutowo relinquished his Army rank in 1970.

promise of elections brought the politicians to the forefront but it was soon apparent that their activities were going to be severely restricted.

In February 1968, for instance, permission was given for a new Moslem party to be formed in the place of the old Masjumi which Sukarno had banned in 1960. The new party, Partai Muslimin Indonesia (Parmusi), soon ran into trouble when, at its first official general meeting, it elected as Chairman Mohammed Roem, a former Foreign Minister and joint leader with Natsir and Sjaffrudin of the old Masjumi. The President immediately forbade any former Masjumi executive to occupy any high rank in Parmusi and Roem was subsequently replaced by Djarnawi Hadikusumo, the leader to whom Suharto had originally given his approval.

In February 1970 the President called leaders of the nine acceptable political parties together and suggested that they should form themselves into two main groups: the Nationalists and the Religious. The "religious" group was to comprise the NU, the PSII, the Parmusi and the Persatuan Tarbiah Islamijah (Perti), while the "nationalist" group would comprise the Murba, the PNI, the two Christian parties—Parkindo and Partai Katolik—and the IPKI.

The object of grouping parties in this way was to minimise the factionalism of the 'fifties. "People" said Suharto "become increasingly conscious that we must not waste a single second in fighting over sects and authority, in religious, tribal and regional conflicts and in the interests of narrow loyalties."[12]

It was of course clearly understood that the PKI would take no part in the elections, but in January 1970 a further regulation was announced forbidding any former member of the PKI or anyone involved in "Gestapu" from standing for election or even voting. At the same time it was announced that an embargo would be placed on any discussion of the validity of Pantja Sila or the Constitution of 1945.

In this way the only two issues over which there might have been serious ideological clashes were removed from the arena of public debate. There was to be no questioning of the secular foundation of the State and no more democratic control of the chief executive than was to be found in the Constitution of 1945. The veteran Mohammed Hatta remarked that even if elections were held it did not mean that democracy had returned to Indonesia; it would however mean that the young would have a chance to take over from the old.

As the restrictions and conditions affecting the elections multiplied there was a corresponding decline in the politicians' interest and by 1971 it looked as if Suharto had successfully defused the political time bomb.

If political troubles were going to come it seemed likely that they would come through illegal rather than legal channels. For all the sickening slaughter that had taken place (an estimated 500,000 had lost their lives) the PKI was not dead; or if its organisation was crippled the conditions which had given it so many supporters had not improved much, if at all.

Deprived of their legal channel of interest articulation—the PKI—and offered only a PNI shorn of its left-wing leaders such as Ali Sastroamidjojo and Surachman, the underfed and overcrowded peasants of Java had no organisation to stand between them and the bureaucrats and the Army.

Clashes between the Army and Communists or dissident peasants went on into the 'seventies and looked as if they would continue to do so unless and until the pressing social problems were solved by rapid economic development.

The Political Process

Such briefly is the historical background to the political scene in Indonesia in 1971. We turn now to a consideration of the Constitution upon which the political system is based and then to a discussion of some of the constants in Indonesian politics.

The Constitution

The Constitution at present in force in Indonesia is frequently referred to as the "Constitution of 1945" and is the same one to which Indonesia returned in 1959, after her unhappy experience of what Sukarno used to call "free-fight liberalism". The 1945 Constitution was drawn up at the beginning of the Revolution and gave the President the wide powers appropriate in the circumstances. In 1959 and in 1965 the country faced emergencies which were different in kind but equally serious and it was perhaps equally appropriate that her leaders should have chosen to make use of the almost dictatorial powers granted to them under the war-time constitution.

As depicted in official publications the foundation of the Constitution is Pantja Sila which has come to mean, under Suharto, both a repudiation of atheism in the shape of Communism and an affirmation of the principle of the secular state.

Beneath Pantja Sila is the People's Congress or MPR (Madjelis Permusjawaratan Rakjat). This Congress is composed of members of the House of Representatives or DPR (Dewan Perwakilan Rakjat) and "delegates of regional territories and other groups". In this context "other groups" refers to the so-called "functional" groups such as the armed services, religious bodies, youth, women's organisations, students, teachers, peasants and the like. In former times the PKI managed to be heavily represented by functional groups which it had infiltrated.

The MPR meets at least once every five years to elect a President and Vice-President and to lay down the broad lines of policy which it wishes the government to follow. The MPR had a membership of nine hundred and twenty, a third of whom were appointed.*

The DPR was a smaller body consisting of four hundred and sixty members, three hundred and sixty of whom were elected party politicians and one hundred were appointed to represent functional groups.* Meeting at least once a year, the DPR had to approve all proposed legislation whether it originated in the DPR or came from the President, who also had power to initiate legislation. It should be noted that in cases of emergency the President had the right to "enact ordinances taking the place of law" but the ordinances had to be ratified by the DPR in its next session.

Once elected to office by the MPR the President appoints Ministers to advise him and to act as heads of their respective departments. The Ministers need not be drawn from the MPR or DPR and are responsible only to the President. The President himself is vested with all the executive power and, in conjunction with the DPR, has legislative powers as well. He is the commander-in-chief of the armed services.

The elucidation of the Constitution of 1945 points out that although the President is not responsible to the DPR he is nevertheless not a dictator. The President is the "mandatory" of the MPR and if he exceeds his mandate or departs from it radically, the MPR can, in fact, meet in a special session to call him to account. The chairmanship of the MPR is a prestigious office and was, in 1971, filled by General Nasution, who might in certain circumstances act as somewhat more than just a figure-head.

Another institution which features in the Constitution and of which President Sukarno made use is the Supreme Advisory Council. Its composition is not specified and its relationship to the President and the Ministry is not clear but its role is to advise and make policy proposals.

"Judicial Power" says Article 24 "shall be vested in the Supreme Court and such subordinate courts as may be established by law." The "elucidation" affirms that the judiciary is independent and "free from the influence of the Government's authority". This separation of powers was certainly not a fact in the days of Sukarno, who spent much of his time denouncing this particular Western political concept. It remains to be seen whether the position of the judges will change under the "New Order".

The Sociological Background

Clifford Geertz in *The Religion of Java*[12] has drawn attention to the fact that Javanese society is divided into three main groups: *santri*,

---

* The election law of December 1969 decreed that seventy-five of the appointees in the DPR and one hundred and forty-four of the appointees in the MPR were to be selected by the armed forces.

abangan, prijaji. It would be more accurate to say that these are strands rather than groups because there are few clearly-defined boundaries and one person may have more than one strand woven into his character and background.

To the category *santri* belong those who are religious traditionalists, strict observers of the five basic duties of a good Moslem: the daily prayers, the weekly visit to the mosque, the almsgiving, the fast and the "hadj" or pilgrimage to Mecca. The *santri* receive all or most of their education at religious schools, *madrasahs*, where the accent is on religious rather than secular "modern" studies. The "modern" content of studies at religious schools is increasing but it does not approach the proportion offered in a secular school and it should be remembered that nearly half the schools in Indonesia are "religious". There are numbers of middle-class fairly well-to-do traders among the *santri* and it was these men who were the nucleus of the original Serikat Islam. *Santri* is a term often used to denote those who take religion seriously, and politically it refers to those who would normally vote for one of the Moslem parties. This is not, however, to say that there are no divisions among the faithful. On the contrary as is the case in all Moslem communities there are many sectarian rifts. The most important division is that between the "modernists" and the "traditionalists". The modernists, represented by a movement like Muhammadijah or a party like the old Masjumi or the more recent PMI, are the spiritual descendants of the Egyptian reformer Muhammad Abduh, who flourished towards the end of the nineteenth century, at a time when an increasing number of Indonesians were making the pilgrimage to Mecca and becoming thereby receptive to new currents of thought in Islam. The modernists tend to support a greater secular content in education and a greater involvement in modern secular politics. The traditionalists on the other hand oppose the increasing secularisation of life and put man's spiritual salvation before all other considerations. Left behind in the race for secular administrative authority and the top political posts—which require a technocratic education—the *santris* of Nahdatul Ulama and its sister organisations are content to have spiritual authority and a fair measure of economic power.

In contrast to the *santri* are the *abangan* and the *prijaji*. These two groups though differing greatly in wealth, authority and prestige share the same spiritual background and have the same symbiotic relationship between each other as exists in many countries between squire and peasant or landlord and tenant. The religion of the *abangan* in Java has a basic layer of animism which is common to most Southeast Asian peasants. Above this layer lies a fairly thick deposit of Hinduism which reveals itself not only in art, dance, drama and rite but also in a more than vestigial belief in hierarchy and the tradition of Hindu kingship. Permeating the animism and Hinduism is Islam, the nominal faith of the *abangan*, not clearly understood but a strong influence.

Not firmly attached to Islam, the *abangan* peasant has in the past been given two voting choices: the PNI which was also the party of his social superior the *prijaji*; and the PKI which appealed to him in his role as peasant and natural class enemy of the *prijaji*. The PKI also encouraged the *abangan's* natural dislike of the pious *santri*, who continually scolded him for his neglect of his religious duties. The *santris* in their turn were all too ready to hang the label "Communist" round every *abangan* neck.

We have used the squire-peasant analogy to illustrate the *prijaji-abangan* relationship but it should not be taken too literally. There are very few *prijaji* landlords; in fact there is not a great deal of land-lordism in Java. To be a *prijaji* is a matter, not so much of wealth or land-ownership but of one's birth, education, occupation and general way of life. It is a matter of social status rather than economic class. There are *santris* who are much wealthier than *prijajis* but the poorer *prijaji* will nevertheless be accorded a higher social rating. Geertz has described the *prijaji* as being essentially a bureaucratic "white-collar" nobility. The *prijaji* does work which is refined, *halus*, like teaching or being a civil servant; the *santri* and the *abangan* engage in rough, *kasar*, work, such as manual labour and trading. The same distinction may be found in many other parts of Southeast Asia and indeed Europe.

The political party of the *prijaji* is the PNI which, as one would expect, draws its main support from Java, the home of the *prijaji* culture. Sukarno himself was of *prijaji* stock and never lost sight of the fact that he was entitled to call himself "Raden", an appellation which denoted that he was marginally related to a noble family. In his autobiography he tells us that his father was descended from the Sultan of Kediri.[13] With his *prijaji* background and his instinctive "feel" for the peasants' way of thought Sukarno was not above building himself up as a mixture of the long-awaited "Ratu Adil" or Just Ruler of Javanese tradition and the Sultan Agung or Great Sultan at the top of the Hindu hierarchy. His successor, Suharto, although of *abangan* origin and therefore with less pretensions to innate superiority, is nevertheless much closer in style to Sukarno than to the *santri* generals and politicians who are currently among his supporters. In spite of all the verbal fireworks and dialectical excesses, Sukarno spent much of his life in pursuit of the Javanese ideal of harmony and order, called *toto tentrem* in the vernacular; one feels that Suharto in his characteristically un-flamboyant way was pursuing the same ideal when he became President. Certainly nothing could have been more *halus* than Suharto's treatment of his deposed predecessor.

Political Parties

The conditions in which the general elections were held in 1971 were quite different from those prevailing in 1955 when the previous elections took place.

The psychological atmosphere was quite different. These, the second general elections of independent Indonesia, represented a triumph for hope over experience. In 1955 people may have thought that the general election would not only prove that Indonesia had come of age, but would also provide the longed-for magic solution to her political problems. The deadlock that the elections produced and the instability which flowed from it shattered many illusions. In 1971, therefore, people approached the elections with caution and without great enthusiasm.

There had also been considerable changes in the political cast between 1955 and 1971. The main actors in the earlier elections had been PNI, PKI, Masjumi and NU. In 1971 all but one of these—the NU—were in considerable disarray.

The PNI bore the stigma of having been the party most closely associated with Sukarno and also of having leaders who had been ready to co-operate with the PKI. By 1971 the party had split and the so-called "PNI-Asu", the faction led by Ali Sastroamidjojo and Surachman, been forbidden by Suharto's government to take part in the elections either as voters or candidates. Some elements in the Army, notably in Sumatra, were for banning the PNI altogether, but Suharto realised the dangers of creating a vacuum on the Left and of allowing no political outlet to the many millions who were not attracted to the parties of Islam and Christianity. The anti-Communist faction of the PNI was led at the time of "Gestapu" by Osa Maliki and Usep Ranawidjaja, who subsequently received the aid of the Army in the latter's attempt to mobilise the support of the non-Communist Left. In September 1969 Osa Maliki died and by the middle of the following year there was already talk of a further split in the party between the Hardi and Hadisubeno factions. These two men represented two of the main sources of PNI's support. Hardi stood for the civil service and Hadisubeno, until his untimely death in April 1971, for the *abangan* peasants of Central Java from whom—in competition with the PKI—the PNI had drawn the bulk of its electoral strength in earlier days. The PKI had made great inroads into the PNI's *abangan* base after 1955 and now that the PKI was banned the PNI's obvious objective was to attract these votes without moving far enough to the Left to attract the displeasure of the government. Its success in this venture depended largely on how many former PNI supporters were prevented by the authorities from voting on the grounds that they had been directly or indirectly connected with "Gestapu".

The PNI was at least allowed to exist, although in reduced and confined circumstances. Two of the other giants of 1955, Masjumi and the PKI, were banned outright.

The banning of the Masjumi dated from 1960 and was the direct result of the association of some of the party's leaders in the PRRI rebellion of 1958. The fact that the party remained banned in 1971 throws an interesting light on the alignment of the political forces in

Indonesia at that time. The Indonesian scene has so often been depicted in terms of a straightforward struggle between the forces of Communism and anti-Communism that the other perennial tensions of Indonesian politics tend to be overlooked: the tensions between Java and the Outer Isles, between Modernist and Traditional Moslems, between *santri* and *abangan*, between Mataram and Sri Vijaya. The Masjumi remains banned not because it is pro-Communist but because it had aided and abetted an action which was in part mutinous, in part anti-Javanese and only in part anti-Communist.

The Masjumi remained banned but provision had to be made for some representation for the modernist, "religious-socialist", Moslems. Permission was therefore given for a new party, Partai Muslimin Indonesia (PMI), to be formed on condition that, to begin with at any rate, none of the old Masjumi leaders was to occupy any place on PMI's executive council.

The first leaders of the PMI or "Parmusi" were mainly from the Muhammadijah and included Djarnawi Hadikusumo and Lukman Harun—both acceptable to the Army. The first brush with the authorities came when a new executive was elected at the party's first general meeting later in 1968. Among those elected to top positions was Mohammed Roem, a former Foreign Minister and Masjumi leader. As a prominent participator in the PRRI/Permesta affair Roem was *persona non grata* with Suharto and he soon had to give way, at the President's request, to Djarnawi.

PMI's next set-back occurred in October 1970 when two prominent members John Naro and Ali Imran Kadir set up a rival "Parmusi". Both these men were promptly expelled from the PMI by Djarnawi and his executive who declared that the vast majority of members remained loyal to their original leaders.

At this point the President intervened and threw the party into even greater confusion. A new general Chairman, Minister of State Mintaredja, was appointed and Naro and Djarnawi were made first and second chairmen respectively. When members of the party protested strongly at the government's interference both Naro and Djarnawi were removed from office and the party was left to do as best it could under a leader imposed upon it from outside.

The only major Moslem party which had emerged almost unscathed from the upheavals of the 'sixties was the Nahdatul Ulama (NU) the party of traditionalist Moslems. Theologically opposed to the modernist Muhammadijah and politically opposed to the latter's political counterpart, the Masjumi, the NU had some assets and several handicaps. Among its assets was the fact that being basically more interested in religion than politics it had managed to survive the Sukarno regime as the representative of the "A"* in Nasakom. It had also had its

---

* *Agama*, meaning Religion.

moment of triumph in the post-1965 massacres of the Communists when its younger members helped to remove so many infidels permanently from the scene. One of the NU's leaders, Subchan Z.E., had indeed headed the KAP-Gestapu, the Action Front for the Crushing of "Gestapu", which was formed soon after the 1965 *coup*.

With the other Moslem parties in disarray the NU's prospects in 1971 seemed brighter than in 1955 but the party still suffered from some of its old handicaps. Its base was narrow, being confined not merely to Java but to Central and East Java. As a party which prided itself on not being "modern" it did not attract many of the rising young intellectuals and suffered from a general dearth of leaders with administrative experience. In the 1968 "development" cabinet the only representative of the NU was Muhammad Dahlan and he was allotted the one Ministry—Religious Affairs—which was customarily reserved for the NU.* In 1968 technocrats were in demand and the NU could not supply them.

Two other Moslem parties were allowed to participate in the 1971 elections: the PSII and "Perti".

The PSII (Partai Serikat Islam Indonesia) had once been a member of the post-War Masjumi but its leaders broke with Natsir some time before the latter became involved in the PRRI affair. Among its leaders in 1971 were Harsono Tjokroaminoto, Ibrahim, Bustaman and Lukman Siregar.

"Perti" (Pergerakan Tarbiah Islamijah) or the Islamic Education Movement was a mainly Sumatran party of no great consequence—it won four seats in the 1955 elections—which had been banned temporarily in 1968 during the so-called "redressing" of parliament. It was however allowed to renew its activities in January 1969 under the leadership of Rusli Abdul Wahid, a former Minister of State for Parliamentary Relations in Ali Sastroamidjojo's second cabinet.

In March 1970 the leaders of NU, PSII, PMI and Perti announced that they would form a "group" for the purposes of the elections. This move was in accordance with the President's suggestion of February 1970 that the political structure should be simplified, and that parties should form themselves into "religious" and "nationalist" groups. This was the first of the groups to be so formed but previous experience suggested that co-operation between such traditional antagonists as NU and the Muhammadijah, as represented by PMI, was unlikely to last long.

The remaining four parties require little explanation. For the Roman Catholics there was the Partai Katolik and for the Protestants Parkindo. For the Marxists who had not been associated with the PKI there was

---

* Idham Chalid (NU) was Minister of State for People's Welfare but not a member of the cabinet. On December 18, 1970 Idham Chalid became Minister for Social Affairs in the place of Mr Tambunan who died a week earlier.

Murba, a party which had been founded after the Madiun disaster by Tan Malaka as a "national" Communist alternative to the PKI. Led by men such as Sukarni, Maruto and Sugiarto, Murba filled a gap on the ideological Left and could boast that the influential Adam Malik had been a founder member and former Chairman. Unfortunately for Murba's chances of electoral success in 1971, Adam Malik left the party in order to become the leading light of Golkar, the party of the Establishment. Mr Malik evidently thought Indonesia's current plight demanded pragmatism rather than ideology.

Finally, there was IPKI (Ikatan Pendukung Kermedekaan Indonesia) the League for the Upholding of Indonesian Independence. Founded in the middle 'fifties by Army officers, including the then Colonel Nasution, IPKI was essentially an Army-backed party and its leaders included Dahlan Ibrahim who had served as Minister of State for Veterans' Affairs in 1956 and Professor Umar Seno Adji, who was appointed Minister of Justice in the 1968 Cabinet.

The biggest gap in the political field was that left by the banning of the PKI and there was much speculation among commentators as to where the PKI vote would go. It was, of course, the intention of the government that it should not go anywhere and this was the purpose of issuing the decree which disfranchised all former members both of the PKI itself and of its mass organisations such as the trade union SOBSI, and the peasants' organisation, Barisan Tani Indonesia. It seemed likely, however, that a fair proportion of the estimated fourteen million who had supported the PKI and its various front organisations in former times would slip through the security net. If this was so where would their votes go? One guess was that a number of Communist sympathisers would vote for one of the Christian parties. This guess was based on the undoubted fact that a large number of converts to Christianity had been made in Central and East Java in the wake of the PKI massacres. Since the converts were hardly likely to have been *santri* Moslems the presumption was that they were either former Communists or leftist members of the PNI.

The most likely recipient of ex-PKI votes would normally have been the PNI but now that the Ali Sastroamidjojo-Surachman wing of the PNI had been clipped the party offered few attractions for the "little man" who now saw it as the party of their traditional oppressors, the *prijaji* and the bureaucrats.

Functional Groups

Also competing with the political parties for a share of the 360 elective seats in the DPR were the functional groups or *golkar* (*golongan karya*). The golkar were loosely organised into seven groups or *kino* (*kolompok induk organisasi*) which were in turn co-ordinated to some extent by a joint secretariat known as Sekber Golkar. Sekber Golkar operated as a political party and was allotted an electoral symbol in just the same way as, say, the NU or the PNI.* Most—but not all—of the *kino* were headed by ex-Army officers and Sekber Golkar was heavily under the patronage of the military and of the Minister of the Interior, who was himself an Army officer.† It was clearly the hope of President Suharto that Sekbar Golkar should win a good number of Parliamentary seats in the 1971 elections. In this way two objects would be achieved: the popularity of the regime would be demonstrated and the President would also have a firm grip of the DPR, in which he was already assured the support of the majority of the appointed members.

In due course Sekber Golkar became by far the most comprehensive and heterogeneous party in Indonesian political history. Containing within its fold representatives of over two hundred different and disparate organisations it also attracted the support of branches of the regular political parties. Thus one of the PNI's biggest branches in West Java and eighteen branches of IPKI in North Sumatra decided to join Sekber Golkar and HMI, the largest Moslem student organisation, declared that it would support Sekber Golkar rather than Parmusi. Whatever the motives for these sudden switches of allegiance it was clear that the participation of the Functional Groups as a party in the 1971 elections was going to upset many of the other parties' calculations. This point was driven home when it was announced that two of the most prestigious men in the country, the Sultan of Jogjakarta and the Foreign Minister, Adam Malik, were going to head the list of candidates for Sekber Golkar.

The General Elections, July 1971

As the date for the general elections approached it became quite obvious that President Suharto was not disposed to leave anything to chance. Those who thought the 1971 elections would be a genuine opportunity for a free expression of public opinion were sadly disappointed. In the months before the polling day the government appeared to become increasingly nervous of the outcome and began to try to make it as difficult as possible for anyone not in total sympathy with its policies to make a good showing at the polls. Apart from censoring the news and banning public discussion of certain topics, the government made it obvious that all its considerable resources were going to be put behind its chosen political front, the allegedly "non-party" Sekber Golkar. Long before the election campaign was officially opened, and at a time when other political parties were prevented from disseminating propaganda, Adam Malik and other Sekber Golkar candidates were allowed to

---

* Electors in Indonesia vote for party symbols, not individual candidates.
† Amir Machmud. Previously commander of the Djakarta area. In 1971 he was also chairman of the election committee.

stump the countryside singing the praises of the Suharto regime, and recommending the electors to vote for the practical programmes of Sekber Golkar rather than the ideologies of its rivals.

This display of open partisanship by the government was counter-productive. It had the effect of discrediting the whole electoral process and thus minimising the latter's utility as an escape valve for the long-suppressed political emotions of the people; it also helped to create opposition where none or little had previously existed. President Suharto was in danger of making the same mistake President Marcos had made in the 1969 elections in the Philippines, namely of "fixing" an election which he was almost certain to win without resorting to any dubious methods. In 1971 there was fairly widespread approval and appreciation of achievements of President Suharto's government. The 1971 elections presented a good opportunity for the military regime to acquire greater legitimacy; it seemed a pity that instead of allowing what was after all a very limited kind of democracy to take its course, President Suharto should allow himself to try to predetermine the result by openly sup-porting one of the contestants and giving it financial support from public funds.

The President's wish was that Sekber Golkar candidates should win at least one hundred and thirty-one seats in the DPR so that they, with the hundred government appointees, would then form a majority in the four hundred and sixty man Parliament. In the event, Sekber Golkar did even better than was expected: by August 7, 1971 it had won 227 seats. With nine results to come in from West Irian the numbers of seats won by the various parties were as follows:

Party	No. of Seats
Sekber Golkar	227
Nahdatul Ulama	58
Parmusi	24
PNI	20
PSII	10
Parkindo	7
Partai Katolik	3
Perti	2

The other two parties, Murba and IPKI, won no seats.

The "non-party" Sekber Golkar's victory in the 1971 elections came as a grave blow to the other political parties and in particular to the Nahdatul Ulama and the PNI whose leaders protested strongly against the manner in which the victors had conducted their campaign. The fact remained that Suharto had won the electorate's approval of his style of government and it was now almost certain that he would be re-elected for a further five-year term as President by the MPR in 1972.

Constants in Indonesian Politics

We turn now to a brief consideration of some of the features of Indonesian politics which seem to remain constant beneath all the surface flux.

Java versus Non-Java

Throughout Indonesian history there has been a contrast, if not always a tension, between Java and non-Java. This may be symbolised in the difference between Mataram and Sri Vijaya; between a static bureaucratic, hierarchic culture and a freer, more mobile culture at once more democratic but also more narrowly Islamic.

This traditional difference has been reinforced in more recent times both by the concentration of the Dutch in Java and by the fact that most of Indonesia's foreign exchange earnings are derived from tin, oil and rubber, all of which are for the most part non-Javanese products. The non-Javanese complain that most of the proceeds are nevertheless spent in Java, which is the home not only of the central government but also of about sixty-six per cent of the population.

The Java-non-Java dichotomy is reflected to quite a large extent in the composition of the political parties as we have already seen in our discussion of the 1955/1956 elections.

It is also to be seen in the bureaucracy which at one time threatened to become the private preserve of the Javanese who virtually "colonised" the rest of Indonesia thus causing great resentment among the non-Javanese who frequently looked to their local military commander for support against their "foreign" rulers.

Islam versus Pantja Sila

Another constant in Indonesian politics is the struggle between Islam and Pantja Sila.

Sukarno realised that national unity could not be achieved on too narrow a base. He, therefore, proposed in a famous speech in 1945 that Indonesia should adopt five principles (Pantja Sila) one of which was belief in one, unspecified Deity. This he regarded as a suitable mean between the extremes of an Islamic State and a totally secular one.

There is no doubt that many Indonesians, particularly of the more fanatic Moslem variety, regarded Pantja Sila as a betrayal of Islam and a blank cheque for atheistic Communism.

For many years Moslem suspicions were allayed by Sukarno's constant public support for Moslem enterprises such as building mosques and financing the Hadj or pilgrimage to Mecca. The cracks began to appear at the time of the PRRI Rebellion which was widely seen both as Islam versus Communism and Java versus non-Java. The banning of the Masjumi in 1960 was the next step along the road to the holy war against the infidel, whose culmination was the slaughter of the Communists and the Chinese after the Untung *coup*.

In this connection it is interesting to note that President Suharto is an upholder of Pantja Sila. The Masjumi remained banned and although PMI arose in its place it was a PMI whose Masjumi elements were allotted discreet and minor roles. Moreover, Government Regulation No. 1/1970 made it an offence to raise questions about Pantja Sila and the 1945 Constitution, during the 1971 election campaign. Pantja Sila of course is capable of more than one interpretation. During the Nasakom period Pantja Sila was interpreted in favour of the PKI; in the New Order the first Sila, Belief in God, was interpreted rather more strictly.

The Bureaucracy

Finding the right man for the top job is not the main difficulty in Indonesia; if this were so the advent to office of men like the Sultan of Jogjakarta and Dr Sumitro would solve many problems. The hardest task confronting any Indonesian leader is that of getting his orders faithfully executed by the civil servants. For this he has to rely on the efficiency of a chain of command whose links are not only weak but in some cases not even joined to one another.

The civil service is centred on Djakarta and therefore tends to contain more than its fair share of Javanese who bring to it many of the ways of the traditional Javanese bureaucracies of the past. This reveals itself in the attitudes both of the civil servant to his job and of the general public to the civil servant.

Traditionally a place in the Javanese bureaucracy was the natural perquisite of men born into the ranks of the aristocracy. Today, achievement—that is to say academic success—has largely replaced ascription as a basis for recruitment but the notion still persists that a bureaucrat has rights rather than duties. This view is reinforced by the general public, who seem to expect a measure of arbitrariness in the behaviour of the bureaucrats and look for favours rather than their just dues. They also accept the fact such favours have on occasions to be bought.

The Indonesian civil service is not the apolitical machine of British tradition. It is true that in the early years many men flocked to join the service, in order to promote their country's and not just their own interests, but even then many political leaders regarded the bureaucracy as just another field for the operation of patronage. Perhaps if there had been one dominant political party no great harm would have been done but with four well-matched major political groups clamouring for a share of the spoils the chances of any kind of unified service emerging were very small. As a result the bureaucracy tended to exhibit vertical divisions with individual ministries becoming the private preserve not only of the main political parties but of functional groups like the armed forces, the trade unions and the Christian churches. If we add to this the existence of factions *within* ministries we may readily imagine why Indonesia has always found so many formidable obstacles in its path towards social and economic improvement.

To the Javanese bureaucratic tradition and the activities of political parties must be added three further factors which inhibit the implementation of political decisions.

The first is the avoidance of personal responsibility and the constant reference of decisions to the political head of the Department of Ministry.

The second is the break in the chain of command which makes it difficult for Djakarta to control the regions—the latter being frequently virtually autonomous.

Lastly there is the lack of personal financial incentive. Indonesian civil servants are grossly underpaid;* in the face, therefore, of the appalling inflation which has afflicted the country for so many years the honest bureaucrats have been compelled to take on other jobs to augment their salaries, while the dishonest have accepted bribes and commission.

The Army

In these circumstances it is not surprising that people should look to the Army for action in the belief that it has the cohesiveness and effectiveness which the civil service lacks. The belief is mistaken.

Though many officers are dedicated professionals, the Army, like the civil service, is not a dedicated apolitical body. It is in large part a "citizen" Army and has been heavily involved in politics ever since the Japanese first mobilised the Indonesian people.

The Army is not a monolith: as witness the PRRI rebellion and "Gestapu". The Army is a microcosm of the nation and therefore reflects all the latter's divisions. These differences are further reinforced by the territorial loyalties of some Army units. There are also units which have personal rather than territorial affiliations: thus in 1946 Sjahrir could count on support from the Siliwangi Division (whose commanders have included Nasution and Sarwo Edhie) and the Mobile Brigade.

Not being a monolith the Army, or rather that part of it which is temporarily dominant, has to have civilian allies. Thus the danger confronting any Army régime is that some civilian group, such as a combination of Moslem politicians and businessmen, may persuade some dissident Army divisional commanders—say from Sumatra—to stage a *coup*, bloodless or otherwise, on their behalf and with their financial and organisational backing. To forestall such a move the men in office have to please so many disparate elements and devolve so much power that it becomes very difficult to implement the economic plans drawn up by domestic and foreign experts.

---

* Indonesian civil servants have received considerable salary increases of late, but they still find it difficult to make ends meet.

In 1971 President Suharto appeared to have the armed forces well under control. He had brought the army, navy and air force together under one administrative roof and thus diminished the opportunities for independent empire-building by the operational commanders of any of these forces; he had also won a political and ideological victory over New Order "radicals" like Generals Kemal Idris, Sarwo Edhie and Dharsono who had advocated a clean and total break with the Old Order. This latter victory was significant in that it showed that Suharto, for all his avowed anti-Communism, was not willing to depart entirely from the Sukarnoesque—and Javanese—tradition of compromise and synthesis.

The Outlook for the 1970s

The Return of the Administrators

Professor Herbert Feith, in his book *The Decline of Constitutional Democracy in Indonesia*,[15] divided Indonesian leaders into two broad categories, the Administrators and the Solidarity-makers. The Administrators were pragmatic, practical, non-political men endowed with certain technical or professional skills and anxious above all to "get on with the job". The Solidarity-makers on the other hand were nation builders, visionaries, teachers, guerilla leaders, word spinners, men who relied less on achievement than on ascription or magnetic personal qualities for their power and influence.

The period between the declaration of Independence in 1945 and the implementation of "guided democracy" in 1958 witnessed a struggle between the Administrators and the Solidarity-makers from which the Solidarity-makers under Sukarno emerged the winners.

By 1968 it appeared that the Solidarity-makers had been replaced by Administrators. Certainly the "business" Cabinet of June 1968 contained many men who had been prominent Administrators in days gone by: men such as the Sultan of Jogjakarta (Economy, Finance and Industry), Dr Sumitro (Commerce), Harsono (Administrative Reorganisation) and Mr A. M. Tambunan (Social Affairs).*

Under the rule of the Administrators and the technocrats Indonesia's economy made a remarkable recovery. The rupiah became a hard currency, the inflation was virtually halted, foreign investment was vastly increased and prices became more or less stable. Outwardly all was well. Yet underneath the surface there were signs that Suharto had yet to solve the basic problems which had confronted Sukarno.

Sukarno, like his friend Nkrumah of Gana, had thought it more important to forge national unity and to "complete the revolution" than to solve economic and administrative problems. Suharto was following another course. His emphasis was on the suppression of

---

* Mr Tambunan died on December 12, 1970 and was replaced by Idham Chalid.

politics and ideology and the encouragement of stability and economic growth. In carrying out this programme the President encountered criticism from two very different quarters: the New Order radicals attacked him for allowing former supporters of Sukarno even the slightest scope; while many left-wing radicals, including Sukarnoist elements in the PNI accused Suharto of being afraid of nationalism, of betraying the revolution and of encouraging the very neo-colonial imperialists who should be the greatest enemies of all true nationalists. Inasmuch as criticism of the first kind came from senior Army officers Suharto dealt with it with surprising ease by merely posting the generals concerned to distant embassies or remote territorial commands. The "nationalists", however, posed a more difficult problem. Suharto no doubt hoped that the elections and the subsequent activities of the DPR would give his critics adequate opportunities for expressing their political views. Time alone would tell whether the neo-Sukarnoists were merely speaking for themselves or whether they were—to use Sukarno's words—the "mouthpiece of the message of the people's sufferings".

References

1. LESLIE H. PALMIER, *Indonesia and the Dutch*, Oxford University Press, London, 1962.
2. P. WHEATLEY, *Malay Peninsula In Ancient Times*, Eastern Universities Press, 1964, p. 87.
3. *Ibid.*, p. 99.
4. T. S. RAFFLES, *History of Java*, London, 1817, Vol. 1, p. xiii.
5. B. H. M. VLEKKE, *Nusantara, A History of Indonesia*, Van Hoeve, The Hague, 1959, p. 291.
6. "Multatuli" (E. Douwes Dekker), *Max Havelaar*, Donker, Rotterdam, n.d. p. 63.
7. *Ibid.*, p. 66.
8. CLIVE DAY, *The Dutch in Java*, Reprinted by Oxford University Press, London, 1966, p. 274 footnote.
9. A BENGAL CIVILIAN, *De Zieke Reisiger*, Simpkin Marshall, 1853.
10. D. M. G. KOCH, *Verantwoording*, Van Hoeve, The Hague, 1956, p. 64.
11. GUY J. PAUKER, "Indonesia: The PKI's 'Road to Power' " in R. Scalapino (Ed.), *The Communist Revolution in Asia*, Prentice-Hall, Englewood Cliffs, N.J., 1965, p. 284.
12. *Indonesian Current Affairs Translation Service*, January 1969.
13. CLIFFORD GEERTZ, *The Religion of Java*, Free Press of Glencoe, New York, 1960.
14. CINDY ADAMS, *Sukarno: An Autobiography as Told to Cindy Adams*, Bobbs Merrill, Indiana, 1965.
15. H. FEITH, *The Decline of Constitutional Democracy in Indonesia*, Cornell University Press, Ithaca, N.Y., 1962.

CHAPTER ELEVEN

The Philippines

The Filipino Background

In the world of Southeast Asia the Philippines stands out as an exception to almost every generalisation one can make about the area.

It has never known its own monarchy; it has not been noticeably affected by either Hindu or Confucian ideas; it was been colonised not once but twice by Western powers; it is the only country in the region which is largely Christian. It is, one might say, a basically Malay country and yet in its eagerness to assert its Malayness it has, at times, managed to make a diplomatic if not an actual enemy of Malaya, the very country for which it should have the greatest affinity.

In an earlier chapter we tried to show that a certain similarity underlies all the superficial differences between the various countries of Southeast Asia. To this particular generalisation the Philippines is no exception. The basic unit of Filipino society is the farmer, the tiller of land, the *tao*.

Today seventy-five per cent of the population lives in the rural areas where the mode of living has not altered greatly in the last three hundred years or more.

Of the Philippines before the arrival of the Spanish in the sixteenth century not a great deal is known. That there were no great kingdoms such as Madjapahit or Angkor is certain but there is very little in the way of inscription or monument to give us much guidance as to what there was instead. It is normally assumed that life among the Filipinos, during the centuries before the arrival of the Spanish was very much the same as it was when Magellan first set foot on Filipino soil in 1521.

If this is so the picture we get of pre-Spanish Filipino society is of fairly widely dispersed groups of people of Malay origin who had come originally by sea and occupied various coastal and riverine areas. The typical unit was a kinship-group called the *barangay* whose head was the *datu*. *Barangay* is the name of a type of boat and it is conjectured

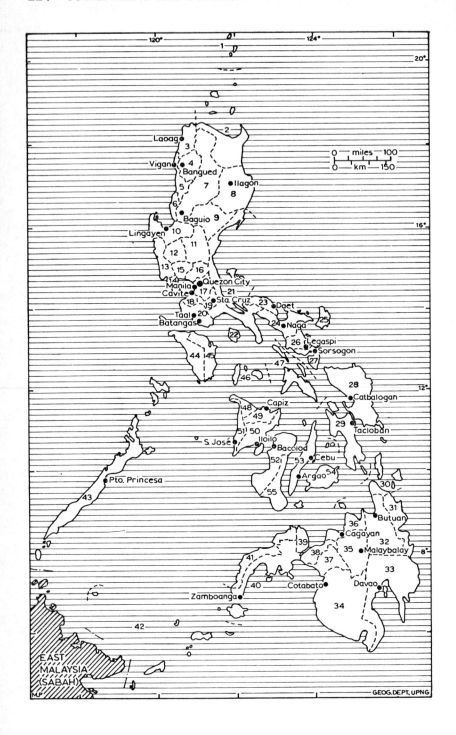

that the founder-members of these groups travelled together in these craft to the Philippines from Malaya and Indonesia.

Except in the Moslem areas of Sulu and Mindanao, there were no political units larger than the *barangay* and even the *datus* of the *barangay* were not so much rulers as elders. Nevertheless some of the *barangays* were large enough to contain, according to the Spanish, three grades of member: the *maharlicas* who were free men, warriors who fought in the service of the *datu* and were maintained by him; the *aliping namamahay* who were freehold farmers who gave half their crop to the datu and served as oarsmen in case of war or other emergency; and the *aliping saguigilir* who were not slaves, as the Spanish supposed but debt peons, men paying back a debt by labour. Peonage frequently arose out of debt, and debt is still the most common link between landlord and tenant in the rural Philippines today.

To what we have already said about "primitive" religion in Part I, Chapter 1, we will only add that early Spanish observers noted a propensity among some Filipinos to approach their chief god *Batula* through the medium of lesser spirits called *anitos*. The early missionaries found it comparatively easy to adapt such a system to fit the Catholic doctrine of the intercession of the saints.

In some areas considerable trade took place. Gold and silver was in use for currency. Local manufacturers were mainly of the "cottage industry" variety and included clothes and jewellery: indeed the chief who met Magellan was arrayed in great splendour and made a very favourable impression on the Spaniards.

Map 12. The Philippines

Key to Map 12 : Provinces of the Philippines

1. Batanes	18. Cavite	32. Agusan	44. Occidental
2. Cagayan	19. Laguna	33. Davao	Mindoro
3. Ilocos Norte	20. Batangas	34. Cotabato	45. Oriental
4. Abra	21. Quezon	35. Bukidnon	Mindoro
5. Ilocos Sur	22. Marinduque	36. Misamis	46. Romblon
6. La Union	23. Camarines	Oriental	47. Masbate
7. Mountain	Norte	37. Lanao del Sur	48. Aklan
8. Isabela	24. Camarines Sur	38. Lanao del	49. Capiz
9. Nueva Vizcaya	25. Catanduanes	Norte	50. Iloilo
10. Pangasinan	26. Albay	39. Misamis	51. Antique
11. Nueva Ecija	27. Sorsogon	Occidental	52. Negros
12. Tarelac	28. Samar	40. Zamboanga	Occidental
13. Zambales	29. Leyte	del Sur	53. Cebu
14. Bataan	30. Surigao del	41. Zamboanga	54. Bohol
15. Pampanga	Norte	del Norte	55. Negros
16. Bulacan	31. Surigao del	42. Sulu	Oriental
17. Rizal	Sur	43. Palawan	

Islam was already established in the southern islands in pre-Spanish times and in these areas sultans were to be found who commanded a much wider allegiance than the datus. The Spaniards called the Moslems "moros", or Moors after the traditional enemies of Catholic Spain in the Mediterranean. The Moros, like the Moslem Achinese of northern Sumatra, resisted colonial rule to the bitter end; they also resisted attempts at conversion to Christianity and are still, today, to some extent outsiders in a largely Catholic nation. Had the Spaniards arrived a century later the whole of the Philippines might have been Moslem and the course of history would have been quite different. As it was the Spaniards established themselves in Manila just in time to prevent Islam taking root in the island of Luzon.

Filipinos today look enviously at other countries of Southeast Asia and bemoan the lack of national monuments such as Angkor and Borobudur. They would like to point to some Golden Age of their own in the past, when a rich culture flourished and produced great works of art. In the absence of such a heritage and instead of taking legitimate pride in their unique record of post-colonial democratic government, Filipino writers tend to suggest that there was a flourishing indigenous culture all traces of which were systematically destroyed by the Spanish. "With the cross and the sword," writes one Filipino, "Spain stamped out the native culture, commerce and government. The people's codes and laws, their weights and measures, their literature and even their alphabet were destroyed."

There was a pre-Hispanic alphabet which did not survive and there was undoubtedly some literature, particularly in the Moslem areas, and no doubt some of this was destroyed by the Spanish* but to suggest that there was a wealth of literature is greatly overstating the case. A more sober view is taken by O. D. Corpuz, who suggests that there were very few early written records in the Philippines mainly because the Spaniards arrived before any but the simplest political organisations had evolved among the widely scattered and isolated *barangays*.

Whatever may be the truth about the Filipino past, most commentators agree that the Filipinos put their own stamp on all the Spanish and American customs and institutions which were imposed on them in colonial days.

The Spanish Heritage

Religion

The official statistics show that over ninety per cent of Filipinos are Christian and that of the Christians over seventy per cent belong to the

---

* J. L. Phelan in *The Hispanization of the Philippines*[1] says "there is little evidence that the Spaniards deliberately destroyed Philippine manuscripts".

Roman Catholic Church. Christianity is therefore the first and most obvious legacy of Spanish rule.

For British and Dutch colonisers the spreading of the gospel was not the foremost consideration. Indeed it was their usual practice to limit the activities of missionaries. Not so the Spanish and the Portuguese. The Portuguese came to the East, it was said: "in search of Christians and spices", and the winning of souls to the Church was likewise a prime consideration with His Most Catholic Majesty Philip II of Spain, from whom the Philippines takes its name. Having spread Christianity in their American colonies the Spaniards hoped to use the Philippines as a stepping-stone on the path to the greatest achievement of all—the Christianisation of Japan and China.

It is difficult for an outsider to assess in spiritual and theological terms the precise nature and depth of Filipino Christianity, but most observers seem to agree that the Filipinos over the centuries managed to adapt the teaching of the missionaries to fit their own spiritual and cultural experience. There were, however, other reasons why the Spanish priests were unable to transmit the pure milk of the Word undiluted to their flock. In the first place there were very few missionaries in the field. In the early period there were between two hundred and fifty-four and four hundred priests to minister to the entire population and no doubt a disproportionate number never left the neighbourhood of Manila. In such circumstances it is remarkable that the new religion spread at all, let alone that it spread comparatively quickly.

Second, it is said that the Church would have preserved the purity of its message much more successfully if she had encouraged the growth of a Filipino clergy. The Church's record in this respect was not good. For much of the Spanish period one of the main obstacles to the creation of a native clergy was the continual strife between the "regular" clergy and the "secular" clergy, the former being members of religious orders—for example Dominicans and Franciscans—the latter being ordinary parish clergy. In a new mission field such as the Philippines it would normally have been the practice for the regulars to carry out the initial evangelisation and for the seculars to take over as parish priests as soon as some sort of peace and order had been achieved. But when the time came for this transition to be made the regulars were so well entrenched in the countryside that they refused in most cases to make way for the seculars. They also refused as members of religious orders to allow the bishops to "visit" them even though they were carrying out the normal duties of a parish priest. The regulars were in a strong position. There was an acute shortage of clergy and the regulars for the most part strongly opposed the creation of a Filipino clergy.

An assault on the position of the regulars was made in the latter half of the eighteenth century when the Archbishop then in Manila took vigorous steps to train and ordain Filipinos. Unfortunately, the scheme was so hurriedly put together and the training so inadequate that the opinions of those who said that the Filipinos were unfit for the priest-hood turned out to be fully justified. By the time Filipinos were again admitted, in any large numbers, for the priesthood the whole affair had acquired a political flavour and it is not surprising that Filipino clergy were among the first and best-known martyrs in the cause of nationalism.

A third reason for the Filipinisation of Spanish Catholicism was the failure of the Spanish to spread their language. In forty years of occu-pation, the Americans probably produced four times as many English-speaking Filipinos as the Spanish had produced Spanish-speaking Filipinos in over three hundred years.

From time to time edicts went forth from Madrid by which Gover-nors were commanded to set up primary schools in which Spanish was to be the sole language of instruction. Half-hearted attempts were made to carry out the instructions but lack of teachers and funds caused most of the schemes to fail. Without a knowledge of Spanish it was very difficult for a Filipino to grasp the real meaning of many theolo-gical terms. As J. L. Phelan points out: "In conformity with the policy of deliberate rupture with the pagan past the key concepts of Chris-tianity were never translated into the Philippine languages. Lest the converts confuse or identify the Christian with the pagan such terms were ordinarily left in the Spanish form. Sometimes the Latin term was used."

Compadrazgo

One of the most important if unintentional by-products of the Chris-tianisation of the Philippines was the spread of *compadrazgo*, literally "co-parenthood".

In the Roman Catholic Church as indeed in some other Churches it is customary for a person to have godparents present and taking an active part on certain sacramental occasions, such as baptism and con-firmation. In Spain these sponsors were called *compadre* (godfather) and *madrina* (godmother) respectively.

From the very beginning the Spanish followed this particular Chris-tian custom: Magellan himself was the *compadre* of Humabon, the first Filipino chieftain whom he met and whom he immediately con-verted to Christianity.

With their strong sense of the ties of kinship—the old *barangays* were kinship groups—the Filipinos took readily to the idea of *compa-drazgo* and soon produced their own version of it, a version which permeates political life in the Philippines today. Although originally intended as a spiritual relationship *compadrazgo* soon acquired a much wider significance. The *compadre* found himself not only expected to be present on sacramental occasions but on all kinds of occasions regarded as significant in the life of the godson and his parents. The *compadre* was very often chosen from a higher social class, or from among the politically powerful, in the hope that protection and aid would be forthcoming in the hour of financial or legal need. Such favours were not obtained without cost and the parent would be obliged to work or fight, or perhaps vote, for the co-parent when required. In Filipino politics today influential men may be *compadre* to a host of people of whose political support he can then be assured.

Political Changes

The Spaniards made the *datu* official head of the *barangay, cabeza de barangay,* and gave him powers of tax collection. The position became hereditary and often remained so in practice even after the introduction of elections.

The Spaniards also created a new political unit, the township or *pueblo,* an administrative area whose centre was the *poblacion.* For ease of administration (and conversion) they tried to get the people of the countryside to cluster together round the *poblacion* under the eye of the *gobernadorcillo* (petty governor) and "under the bells" (as the saying went) of the parish church. The *gobernadorcillo* and the *cabeza* were Filipinos and together with one or two other officials formed the class of notables or *principalia.* The latter became increasingly powerful as time went by. They acquired large tracts of land and were often the sole recipients of any education offered by the Spaniards.

Above the *barangay* and the *pueblo* was the province. The head of the province, the *alcalde mayor,* was a Spaniard, and the quality of his rule was seldom improved by the fact of his being allowed to trade on his own account. It was not unusual for him to buy produce off the Filipinos at a very low fixed price and then re-sell it elsewhere at a vast profit.

We have spoken so far of the official institutions only. Unofficially —certainly at the level of the *pueblo*—the real power very often lay with the priest who was often the only Spaniard in the district and who took it upon himself to interpret the will of Spain to the local people.

At the apex of the political pyramid was the Governor-General, a man with very great powers who could safely ignore the orders of the King since an exchange of letters between Manila and Madrid might take as long as three years. In fact the formula "I obey but do not execute" was often used to indicate that the Governor-General acknowledged the good intentions of a particular order of the King but doubted that it was appropriate to the current situation in the Philippines.

There were two checks to the Governor-General's freedom to act as he pleased. The foremost was the Church which exercised great temporal as well as spiritual power; in large areas of the colony the Church *was* the temporal power and the Governor-General could not rule without it. Second there was the *residencia,* a kind of official audit of the outgoing Governor-General's behaviour during his term of office.

This was far from being a routine affair and in one or two cases proved disastrous to the persons concerned.

Economic Changes

Spanish colonisation began with the granting of *encomiendas* to deserving Spaniards as a reward for their services to the Crown. The *encomienda* was the right to collect tribute or taxes from the people of a certain area. The *encomendero* only had a right to these taxes: he was not given a grant of the land on which the Filipinos lived. The *encomenderos* seldom lived anywhere near the area from which the tribute came. The money was, in most cases, collected by the *cabeza de barangay* and sent on by him (minus some sort of "brokerage") to his master. The system was open to all kinds of extortion and abuse, but as in other countries the extortion was just as likely to be applied by the *cabeza* as the *encomendero*.

The bargain was not entirely one-sided. In return for the tribute the *encomendero* was expected to establish law and order in the area and to protect his wards from outside attack. His main duty, however, was to convert the Filipinos to Christianity. This last part of the bargain was often conveniently forgotten.

The *encomienda* system came under heavy fire both from the Filipinos and the Church. By the middle of the seventeenth century the private *encomiendas* had virtually disappeared.

Meanwhile the Spaniards imported the concept of private ownership of land and strengthened the position of the *datus* by allowing them to take over the ownership of the hitherto communally-owned *barangay* lands. Since the petty officials through whom the Spaniards, both lay and ecclesiastical, chose to rule also came from the ranks of the *datus*, the latter in due course formed a new economic class in Philippine society—the ancestors in fact of today's ruling class.

The Filipinos themselves remained the owners of by far the greater part of the available agricultural land. The next biggest landowners were the religious orders.

We have already remarked that the Spaniards came to convert the heathen and to this end a fair number of clergy both regular and secular, but mostly regular, came to the Philippines after braving a long and unpleasant sea voyage. When they got there they found the conditions primitive, the climate oppressive and funds sadly lacking. They also found that their main task was one of administration rather than conversion. In Philip II's Spain, Church and State were very closely linked and in the absence of lay administrators the Friar frequently found himself the temporal, as well as the spiritual, head of the community. Even when officials were appointed—whether Filipino or Spanish—it was often with the Church that real power resided.

The religious orders became landlords largely because this was the only way they could raise enough revenue to finance their missions. Some religious orders were good landlords—the Jesuits for instance— but the majority acquired such a reputation for meanness and avarice that it is small wonder that one of the main targets of Filipino nationalism in the nineteenth century was the Spanish clergy. The Filipinos became not so much anti-Christian as anti-clerical.

Education and Culture

One of the main vehicles of a nation's culture (in the narrower sense of the word) is its language. As we have seen the spread of their language was not greatly encouraged by the Spaniards and it is not surprising that very few Filipinos ever acquired any knowledge of Spanish literature or of Spanish philosophical or political thought. If they read anything in Spanish it was likely to be of a theological nature or else a harmless romantic tale with some kind of "improving" moral running through it.

The Spaniards feared that it would be dangerous to enable Filipinos to read the subversive antimonarchist and anticlerical literature current in Europe in the eighteenth and nineteenth centuries. They were right. The movements, first for reform and later for independence, were led mainly by men who had, by virtue of their wealth or influence, gained access to European thought by travelling to Europe or by reading some of the forbidden literature which circulated among the so-called "subversives".

Nationalism and Revolution

The roll of Filipino national heroes is a long one ranging from Lapu-Lapu, who struck a blow for freedom by slaying, or commanding the warriors who slew, Ferdinand Magellan in 1521, right down to Ramon Magsaysay, the President with the "Kennedy touch" who was killed in an air-crash in the middle of his term of office in 1957. Among the most famous heroes are three Filipino priests who were secretly tried, condemned to death and executed in 1872 on a charge of having been involved in planning a mutiny of Filipino troops at the garrison of Cavite, not far from Manila.

Of the three ill-fated priests—Burgos, Gomez and Zamora—Father Burgos was the best known. He was a man of considerable learning who held a responsible position in the archdiocese of Manila. He had already crossed swords with the Archbishop over the appointment of unsuitable "Peninsulars" (that is priests from Spain) to parishes in preference to well qualified Filipinos. By the mid-nineteenth century Filipino clergymen were well trained and well educated and it became quite clear that the Spanish discrimination against them was of a racist nature. Burgos was not afraid to publish his views in A *manifesto to the Noble Spanish People* (1864). He, thereby, automatically came under suspicion as a "subversive" and it is not therefore surprising that his enemies managed to implicate him in the Cavite mutiny.

Many of the Peninsulars against whose intrusion Burgos protested were refugees from anticlericalism in Spain. The same movement which made them leave their homeland and seek employment elsewhere also brought lay Spaniards with liberal political ideas to the Philippines. For a short time between 1868 and 1871 the barriers were down, the censorship relaxed and the growing number of educated Filipinos were briefly exposed to liberal European thought. Although as we have seen the controls were firmly back in place in 1872 a great impetus had been given to an irreversible process.

In 1887 Jose Rizal, a graduate of the Dominican College of Santo Tomas in Manila and of the General University of Madrid published a novel called *Noli Me Tangere*. The *Noli*, as it is now affectionately called, is by any standards a gripping novel and one which displays the author's gift for pathos as well as social satire. Even to the modern reader the anti-clerical vein which runs through the book is very obvious and comes across with great force. This was of course enough to make Rizal a notorious "subversive" in the eyes of the authorities, who were blind to the surprising charity which Rizal showed towards the Spaniards in general; and the restraint with which he personally conducted himself.

The *Noli* was followed by *El Filibusterismo*, a sequel in which the hero of the first book gradually realises that force is the only weapon which will bring the colonial rulers to their senses. The book is tragic and despite appearances it is clear that Rizal is not advocating the use of force.

Both these books and most of Rizal's other writings were published in Europe. In 1892 he returned to the Philippines and immediately became involved in nationalist politics, as a result of which he was arrested and deported to Dapitan in the island of Mindanao.

The aims of the "Liga Filipina" which Rizal founded just before he was arrested were entirely constitutional and peaceful. With Rizal's departure the "Liga" collapsed but was revived shortly afterwards by others, prominent among whom were Apolinario Mabini and Andres Bonifacio. Bonifacio, unlike his colleages, but like the hero of *El Fili-busterismo* believed that the time for moderation was over. He accordingly founded the *Katipunan ng mga Anak ng Bayan* (Society of the Sons of the People), an organisation with a harmless enough appearance which concealed the violent intentions beneath. It is interesting to note, however, that amid the otherwise harmless precepts of the "Teaching of the Society of the Sons of the People" one can find the subversive sentiment "All men are equal, whether the colour of their skins be white or black. One man may surpass another in wisdom, wealth or beauty, but not in that which makes him a man."

The Katipunan was founded during an economic recession in which the prices for local products had fallen disastrously. On top of this the rice fields of Luzon were attacked by locusts and the crop ruined. Moved mainly by impotent anger against their friar landlords many peasants joined the Katipunan.

In 1896 the revolt began at Balintawak* near Manila. It was violent but short-lived. After a quarrel over the leadership Bonifacio was replaced by Emilio Aguinaldo, who later had him executed for treason.

In 1897 the leaders of the revolt arranged a cease fire with the Spaniards and were exiled to Hong Kong with a sum of money on condition that they instructed their followers to surrender. In the event the exiles used the money to buy more arms for use at the next suitable opportunity.

They did not have to wait long. On May 1, 1898 Commodore Dewey entered Manila Bay and bombarded and sank the Spanish fleet. This became the signal for a renewal of the Philippine War of Independence but its outcome was quite different from that envisaged by Aguinaldo.

American Rule

America's acquisition of the Philippines was a by-product of her war with Spain over the latter's despotic rule in Cuba. As part of the war against Spain Commodore Dewey was given instructions to sink the Spanish fleet in Manila Bay. Exactly what further instructions Dewey had and what arrangements he made with Aguinaldo, and exactly what intentions President McKinley and Secretary of the Navy Theodore Roosevelt had towards the Philippines, are all questions that still await a definitive answer. The fact remains that after encouraging the Filipino nationalists to assist them to oust the Spaniards the Americans got the Spanish to cede the colony to them by the Treaty of Paris and then proceeded to wage a savage and eventually successful war against the very Filipinos who had so recently been their allies.

About his decision to take over the Philippines, President McKinley of the United States said "one night it all came to me this way—that there was nothing left for us to do but to take them all and to educate the Filipinos and uplift and civilize and Christianize them". He was as good as his word. Very soon the country was invaded by American grade school teachers, missionaries and civil servants, all eager to drag the Filipinos out of the long dark medieval Spanish monarchist night into the bright American republican day.

Constitutional Advance

It was in the constitutional field that the most spectacular advances were made. After a somewhat illiberal start under martial law the

---

* An episode commonly known as "the Cry of Balintawak" or simply "the Cry".

Americans changed as soon as the countryside was pacified to civilian rule under a Governor and a legislative body known as the Philippine Commission. Six years later, in 1907, the Filipinos became the sole members of the lower house of a two-chamber legislature, the first popularly-elected legislative body in Southeast Asia. By 1914 the Filipinos were in a majority in the upper house which in 1916 became the Senate and consisted entirely of Filipinos: two elected from each of eleven electoral districts and two appointed to represent the non-Christian areas.

Under Governor Harrison (1913-1921) great advances were made in the "Filipinisation" of the administration. By 1919 less than six per cent of the public servants were American. Harrison was bitterly criticised by his Republican opponents and by his successor Governor Wood, but he was deservedly popular with the Filipinos, whose feelings were voiced on a later occasion by Quezon in the famous words: "Better a government run like hell by Filipinos than a government run like heaven by Americans".

In 1916 in the Jones Act the Americans had promised the Filipinos "independence as soon as a stable government can be established". By this time, only eighteen years after the start of American rule there was, therefore, only one outstanding topic for discussion in Filipino political circles, namely the timing of the progress towards independence.

There was also only one effective political party. By 1907, the Nacionalistas under their leaders Osmena and Quezon had monopolised the cause of independence and by the end of Governor Harrison's term they had an overwhelming majority in both chambers of the legislature.

There was a temporary setback under Governor Wood (1921-1927) who employed his veto power frequently and so antagonised the Filipinos that all the Filipino political heads of departments resigned, but apart from this the path to self-government and then independence was, until the Japanese invasion, quite smooth.

In 1935 the Philippines achieved self government, the Governor-General became a High Commissioner and Quezon became the first President with Osmena as his Vice President.

Social Changes

The rapid constitutional advance achieved under American rule should not divert attention from the fact that the Philippine social structure altered very little.

We have seen how under the Spaniards the *principalia* became landowners, acquired political influence and emerged as a small fairly well-educated *élite*. For all their talk of democracy the Americans did little to alter the picture.

After initial resistance the Filipino *élite* co-operated whole-heartedly with the Americans and made sure that they and all their relatives and dependants got whatever jobs were going in the public service and in business. In a sense the very speed of the progress towards Filipinisation ensured that none except the existing educated *élite* would be eligible for the vacancies.

In Indonesia and Burma many of those who worked with the colonial authorities were regarded as "collaborators" and "traitors"; not so in the Philippines.

There, the very same families who had done well under the Spaniards continued to prosper under the Americans; and still run the country today. One may note here that one of the factors which helped the *élite* into office in the first instance and has tended to keep them in power ever since is the nature of the franchise in the Philippines. Literacy has always been required of the would-be voter and this has meant that the electorate was originally confined to a mere three per cent of the population in 1907 and has only widened very gradually since those days. Even now by no means all adults have the vote.

Economic Changes

On the domestic front the story is much the same. The peasants who had rallied to the "Katipunan" in the 1890's had done so mainly out of dissatisfaction with their lot under the friar landlords. When the Americans arrived and put an end to the collaboration between Church and State it was hoped that the friars would be parted from their extensive agricultural land holdings. So they were in due course. But the land passed to members of the existing Filipino *élite* and the tenants remained as badly off as before.

It may be remarked in passing that land ownership has always been one of the most contentious issues in the politics of the Philippines. It is a tribute to its political importance that land reform has figured so prominently among politicians' promises: it is a tribute to the unchanging structure of Filipino society that so little has come of these promises.

Then, as now, there were a number of ways in which the Filipino socio-economic *élite*, who formed the backbone of Congress and the Administration, could deal with unwelcome legislation. They could refuse to pass it, or water it down until it was quite harmless, or pass it but see that the funds needed to implement it were inadequate, or they could pass it in the sure knowledge that the bureaucrats would allow it to die of "red tape" and inertia.

The Americans, who were in case pledged to respect property rights, did little to solve the problem. President Quezon acknowledged the gravity of a situation which had led to riots and uprisings in Central Luzon, but his proposals for reform and for the protection of the *tao*, though accepted, were never properly implemented.

The Japanese Interlude

The Japanese landed in the Philippines in December 1941. By May 1942 the Americans had surrendered and General MacArthur had gone to Australia taking Quezon and Osmena with him.

The prominent Filipino politicians who were left behind had for the most part agreed as to their behaviour towards the Japanese: they would co-operate with them in order to get the Filipino people the best possible treatment.

In other parts of Southeast Asia the Japanese were able to acquire a certain amount of popularity by claiming to be the liberators of the countries from colonial rule. They encouraged nationalist sentiments both in order to get co-operation and also to make things more difficult for the colonial powers if they should return.

To the Filipinos, however, the Japanese had little to offer. The Americans had given them self-government and had promised them independence by 1946, a promise which they were to keep.

Nevertheless in 1943 the Philippines were declared independent and Jose P. Laurel, a member of the pre-war government, became President. Other prominent Filipinos "collaborated" and this could have led to ugly scenes after the war. In fact although General MacArthur denounced the collaborators no one was prepared to move against them (or at any rate the socially prominent ones) and in the long run their "collaboration" with the Japanese was seen to be no more or less blameworthy than their collaboration with the Spanish or the Americans.

One of the most important products of the Japanese occupation was the "Huk" movement. As in other countries the Communists were quick to organise a resistance movement against the Facist enemy and the Hukbo ng Bayan Laban sa Hapon (People's Army to fight the Japanese) was formed by Luis Taruc soon after the Japanese invasion. Although on the face of it the Huks were plain resistance fighters the Japanese were not their only target. The Huks attracted to their rank an army of discontented and impoverished peasants who were eager to get even with the landlords. The latter were liable to be "collaborators" in any case so the Huks could always maintain that they were being attacked for patriotic as much as economic motives.

Areas under Huk control experienced not only some genuine land reform but the first taste of democratic local self-government for many a year.

The people of the *barrio* (or village) elected a committee to run their affairs. The ballot was secret and everyone over eighteen had the vote: there were no tests or qualifications. Apart from aiding the Huk soldiers, the villagers founded and ran schools, law courts, transport, sanitation and all the other necessities of civilised life. They also terrorised the landlords and took over their property whenever they could.

There were of course many resistance fighters, among them the future President Magsaysay, who were not Huks or Communists but in the context of war all were comrades in arms.

Victory and Independence

The Americans returned in 1944. On July 4, 1946, exactly on schedule, the Philippines achieved independence.

The occasion was not an entirely happy one. It was marred not only by the bitter political in-fighting between "collaborators" and non-collaborators but also by the somewhat hard-headed and ungenerous spirit in which the Americans approached the questions of war-damage compensation and the future trade relations between the USA and an independent Philippines.

On the domestic political scene Osmena, the veteran Nacionalista leader, found himself opposed by a break-away group calling itself the Liberal Party and headed by Roxas, a former member of Laurel's collaborationist government, who had the powerful support of General MacArthur. Osmena was defeated and in the elections for Congress the Liberals also won handsomely. However, they caused a furore by refusing to admit three Nacionalista Senators and all seven Representatives belonging to the Democratic Alliance Party for whom the supporters of the Huks had voted in a block. Among those excluded was Luis Taruc the Huk leader.

The exclusion of these elected representatives made possible the passage of the controversial Trade and Rehabilitation Bills, subsequently known as the Bell Act and the Tydings Act, respectively.

The Bell Act had three main provisions. It guaranteed free trade between the Philippines and the USA until 1954 when tariffs would begin to be applied and then gradually increased year by year until they reached their full value in 1974. It tied the peso to the dollar. It also allowed American citizens equal rights with Filipinos in the exploitation of the natural resources of the islands—a provision which necessitated a much-begrudged alteration to the Constitution of the Philippines.

The Tydings Act was concerned with the rehabilitation of the Filipino economy. The damage to both life and property had been immense. It is estimated that some million Filipinos lost their lives as a direct result of the war and the economy was in ruins. In these circumstances the Filipinos looked to the Americans for full and generous compensation for the sacrifices they had made. The Tydings Act fell short of these expectations in several respects. It did not offer compensation for *all* claims. Furthermore, of those claims which were admitted only those for an amount under $500 were paid in full. Filipinos with claims in excess of $500 received about half the amount there and then, but had to wait twenty years for the balance and did not get the full amount even then if the claim was for more than twenty-five thousand dollars. The Act also allowed for back-pay to be given to resistance fighters, but not everyone who had fought the Japanese was eligible and this discrimination caused further bitterness.

The Americans made a bad situation worse, by insisting that the two Acts be linked together as one "package-deal"; they made it plain that unless the trade regulations were agreed to there would be no compensation. Roxas accepted these terms but was only able to get the bills through Congress by preventing the members mentioned earlier from taking their seats.

Roxas died in April 1948 and his place was taken by his Vice-President, Quirino, who subsequently won one of the most irregular presidential elections on record in 1949. It was commonly agreed that most of the allegations of foul play on the part of Quirino's men were probably true.

During the terms of office of both Roxas and Quirino the main problem on the domestic front was the pacification of the Huks. This problem could be looked at in two ways: as part of an Asia-wide Communist conspiracy or as a symptom of an age-old Filipino disease which could only be cured by drastic land reform. Ramon Magsaysay, a former guerilla leader, like Luis Taruc, could see both sides of the problem and gratefully accepted the aid of the Americans, who were perhaps more concerned with the fight against Communism. Magsaysay was appointed Defence Secretary in 1950. He waged a sharp and eventually successful campaign and won a reputation for both vigour and democratic camaraderie. His popularity was further enhanced when he arranged for soldiers to guard the ballot in the next congressional elections to prevent a repetition of the events of 1949.

With such a record behind him it was not surprising that Magsaysay won the 1953 presidential elections by an overwhelming majority. Magsaysay changed his political party allegiance at the eleventh hour and ran as a Nacionalista against his former Liberal chief Quirino—a fact which demonstrates the peculiarly fluid nature of Filipino politics.

As the first presidential candidate to go into the distant *barrios* and campaign among the villagers Magsaysay was well aware that land reform was urgently required. Unfortunately, his efforts met with no greater success than did those of his predecessors or successors. His main, if modest, achievement was the resettlement of some ten thousand families, including ex-Huks, in less densely populated areas of the Philippines.

Unable to give the tenant land, Magsaysay tried to give him protection against undue extortion by the landlord. In 1933 under Quezon the Rice Share Tenancy Act had been passed. Amongst other things the Act required contracts between landlord and tenant to be in writing and imposed an upper limit of ten per cent on interest on loans. It also laid down that the crop should be shared equally in cases where the tenant had borne half the expenses. The intention was good but the distance between Malacanang, the Presidential palace in Manila, and the barrio is great and the Act failed simply because its agents were usually the self-same *caciques* who owned most of the land.

In 1946 another Rice Share Tenancy Act was passed by Congress, this time guaranteeing the tenant thirty per cent even if the landlord paid all the expenses and seventy per cent if the tenant paid all the expenses. This Act was a failure. It is said that over seven per cent of the tenants of Central Luzon were paying over fifty per cent of their crop to the landlord.

Magsaysay now tried to give the tenant protection in law by setting up a Court of Agrarian Relations. He also encouraged the granting of credit facilities to tenants through rural banks and other institutions. Like so many others these schemes failed for lack of funds and by 1960 were said to be in a state of collapse.[3]

When Magsaysay died in an air-crash in 1957 his Vice-President Garcia became President and subsequently confirmed himself in office by winning the elections in November of that year. The contest was a close one and featured a third party, the Progressive Party, in addition to the Nacionalistas and the Liberals. The Progressives were headed by some of Magsaysay's younger supporters. These men later attached themselves to the Liberal Party and supported Macapagal in his successful bid for the presidency in 1961.

No great social advances had been made under Garcia's conservative rule and many hoped for better things when Macapagal's victory in 1961 brought into office men like Manahan, Manglapus and Pelaez, former Progressives, who had taken prominent parts in trying to implement Magsaysay's reforms.

Having already sponsored an ambitious five-year "Socio-Economic Plan" Macapagal managed with great difficulty to get Congress to pass the Agricultural Reform Bill in 1963. Power in Congress was and still is in the hands of the monied *élite* and these men saw to it that the provisions of the original bill were greatly watered down before they became law. The Act provided amongst other things for the conversion of share-tenancies into leaseholds but in the event very little was achieved because Congress would not vote the necessary extra funds needed to finance the operation.

No President of the Philippines had yet succeeded in getting re-elected and Macapagal was no exception. By the time the end of his term was in sight his Socio-Economic Plan had run aground and some of his chief supporters including the politically-mobile Pelaez had gone over to the Nacionalistas. Another defector was the Senate President Ferdinand Marcos, who was adopted as the Nacionalista candidate and was elected President of the Philippines by a good majority in November 1965.

In many ways Marcos's first term as President was highly successful. A record number of new school houses and new roads was built; there was a solid increase in the production of rice and the land reform pro-gramme was given a new and strong impetus. So successful indeed was Marcos that he became the first President in the history of the Philip-pines to be re-elected. On the debit side the main accusation against Marcos was that he achieved re-election only by spending so much on public works and patronage that the foreign exchange reserves were threatened, prices rocketed and the peso had to be devalued. In the process, it is said, Marcos also became one of the richest men in the country.

Marcos was perhaps too successful. By winning the 1969 elections in the way he did, Marcos succeeded in convincing the educated public that the constitution needed to be amended in such a way as to ensure that the performance could never be repeated. It was felt that if a President was not allowed to stand for re-election the temptation to spend the second half of his four-year term in spendthrift electioneering at the taxpayer's expense might be removed; it was, therefore, widely supposed that the Constitutional Convention to be held in 1971 would recommend that Presidents in future be allowed to serve for only one term—possibly of six, instead of four years' duration. The supporters of this constitutional amendment argued that non-reelective Presidents would be in a much stronger position effectively to carry out the political and economic reforms which they were always promising. If this argument was valid President Marcos in his second and last term should have been the most effective President in the history of the Philippines.

Unfortunately, it did not look as if this was going to be the case. Once the elections were over the nation was faced with paying the bill. The Philippines was forced to obtain a third "tranche" from the International Monetary Fund. As a condition of the loan the IMF insisted on a readjustment of the foreign exchange rate of the peso, tightening of credit, a cut-back on government expenditure and strict controls in imports and foreign exchange. Following so quickly upon the carefree expenditure of the election campaign these stern financial measures, involving as they did a sharp rise in prices and a clamp on industrial expansion, caused much economic distress and political un-rest. There were several angry demonstrations by students against Marcos and against the United States of America. These protests can have come as no great surprise to Marcos, many of whose pre-election predictions were being so falsified by events. In his "State of the Nation" address to a joint session of Congress in January 1969, the President had drawn special attention to the external stability of the currency, the internal stability of the general price level and the glowing prospects for industrial expansion; eighteen months later all these brave words had to be swallowed and it looked as if most of Marcos's second term would be devoted to regaining the ground lost in the second half of his first term.

The Constitution

The Philippines is a republic. It has a unitary form of government with executive power vested in the President; legislative power in a bi-cameral Congress and judicial power vested in "one Supreme Court and in such inferior courts as may be established by law".

Despite the great strength of the President the American-type system of checks and balances operates fairly effectively: the President frequently has his wings clipped by both Congress and the Supreme Court. It is also generally agreed that the judiciary, except at the lowest levels, enjoys relative freedom from political pressure. Unfortunately, it is often precisely at the lowest levels that justice is most needed and least easy to obtain.

The President

On paper the President of the Philippine Republic has great power. "The President shall have control of all the executive departments, bureaus, or offices" and "exercise general supervision over all local governments as may be provided by law, and take care that all laws be faithfully executed". He is commander-in-chief of all armed forces; he may "suspend the privileges of the writ of *habeas corpus* or place the Philippines or any part thereof under martial law".

The President has wide powers of patronage. In conjunction with the Commission of Appointments, which consists of twelve Senators and twelve members of the House of Representatives with the Senate President as chairman, the President nominates and appoints all heads of departments and bureaus; officers of the armed forces from the rank of colonel or its equivalent and above; Ambassadors, Consuls and a whole host of minor executives. Although Municipal Mayors, Mayors of Chartered Cities and Barrio Captains are now all popularly elected the President can still exert great influence over local government through his power to appoint local officials in the line departments of central government and through his right to scrutinise and approve the budgets of local governments. The President also has the power to decide which projects shall have prior claim on the limited funds to be disbursed through the many special agencies which are set up from time to time to deal with such tasks as rural reconstruction, agricultural extension, land reform and the like; such a power to determine priorities gives the President much political leverage.

Although the President is undoubtedly the most important individual in the entire political system his power is severely limited in several directions both by constitutional checks and by the very nature of the political process.

The constitutional checks are provided by the Supreme Court and Congress. In a land of lawyers the Supreme Court has great prestige and members, though originally political appointees, have the political independence which comes from security of tenure and pride in their legal heritage. This independence the judges have used from time to time to check extra-legal and unconstitutional acts of the executive.

Congress, too, has been able to put obstacles in the path of ambitious Presidents. Unfortunately, its powers have too often been used to block or water down progressive social legislation, especially in the field of land reform.

The other check on the power of the President is provided by the very nature of Filipino politics. Being the chief patron in a land where "patronage is for the most part the subject matter of politics", the President would seem to be in a very strong position: yet he is in a sense the system's chief victim. As many sociologists have observed the patron-client relationship, which is so prominent a feature of the Filipino scene is dyadic in nature: the giver and the receiver are bound together in a reciprocal bond which makes each indebted to the other. His supporters need the President, but the President also needs his supporters; and in the absence of strong party loyalties he has to be careful not to offend those who might help him to be re-elected.

The Congress

The Congress consists of two Houses: the Senate and the House of Representatives. There are twenty-four Senators elected on a nation-wide basis. Each Senator serves for six years and a third of the Senators resign every two years and are either re-elected or replaced. Representatives, of whom there are currently one hundred and four, are elected for a four-year term. Elections for the entire House take place every four years at the same time as the election for President and Vice-President. Representatives are elected from single-member constituencies each with—theoretically—the same number of inhabitants.

The powers of the two Houses are about equally balanced, although there is the usual provision that all Bills of a financial nature must originate in the House of Representatives.

An interesting feature of the Constitution is its provision that Representatives must be at least twenty-five years of age, Senators not less than thirty-five and Supreme Court Judges and Presidents not less than forty. The traditional respect for elders is thus institutionalised and the ascending importance of the four institutions symbolised by the ascending lower age-limit. In 1963 the average age of Representatives was 2 and that of Senators 55.6 years.

As a class members of Congress tend to be middle-aged, conservative and overwhelmingly of upper and upper-middle class origin. About two-thirds of all the legislators are lawyers and they have all enjoyed the sort of education which is only available to less than five per cent of the population. In these circumstances one neither looks for, nor finds, much legislation of a radical nature issuing from Congress. Not that there have never been any radical Congressmen. In 1946 six candidates of the "Democratic Alliance" were elected to Congress. The DA was organised by a group of men who had been prominent in the anti-Japanese resistance movement. Its members included men who had served with the Communist-infiltrated Huk movement as well as men of wealth and fame such as Judge Jesus Barrera and J. Antonio Araneta, the latter a member of one of the richest families in the Philippines. The DA candidates were backed by the peasants of Central Luzon and won their contests by handsome majorities.

One of the first issues before the 1946 Congress was the question of "parity" rights for American citizens. The Philippine government was under heavy pressure to attach an addendum to the Constitution stating that for the next twenty-eight years American citizens would have equal rights with citizens of the Philippines in the pursuit of trade, commerce and exploitation of natural resources. Such a provision required to be passed by a three-fourths majority of all members of both Houses. It became clear, however, that it would not be so passed in the face of the opposition of the Democratic Alliance. Excuses were then found to prevent the DA members as well as some of their Nacionalista allies from taking their seats in Congress on the grounds that their election had been procured by fraud and terrorism. After this the "parity" clause was passed and is now part of Article 18 of the Constitution.

This episode is not, of course, typical but it and other later incidents suggest that Congress is unlikely, for some time to come, to see an effective alternative, based on ideology or class, to the more or less homogeneous Liberal-Nacionalista "establishment".

The Judiciary

The Supreme Court of the Philippines has a deservedly high reputation both for the quality of its members and its ability to resist political pressures. If at times it seems to have come down on the side of conservatism and has prevented the Chief Executive from taking short cuts in order to achieve his objects this is because the Court's duty is to uphold the rule of law rather than to make value judgments. On the question of land reform, for instance, it was thought unlikely that the Supreme Court would consider a holding of only twenty-four hectares as falling in the category of lands which could be expropriated, upon just payment, by the State as provided for in the Constitution. As a result the smallest holding to which the Agricultural Land Reform Code could apply was put at seventy-five hectares, a higher figure than the "progressives" wanted. On the other hand the Code has been challenged on at least two occasions and its constitutionality has both times been upheld by the Supreme Court.

At a lower level the picture is not so bright. The little man—"Juan de la Cruz"—finds it difficult to obtain justice or even access to the courts. The Supreme Court may be on his side but, when he tries to obtain redress at the *barrio* level against the landlord, he is confronted by many obstacles both financial and legalistic. That this is so may be inferred from the fact that since serious attempts were made to implement land reform numerous voluntary agencies have come into being for the sole purpose of assisting the tenant to obtain his rights. It was evidently thought that the tenant was unlikely to be able to obtain justice unaided. As Senator Jose W. Diokno, himself a lawyer of distinction, put it: "To the tenant and the lessee—if I have read the Central Luzon experience correctly—the issue now is not whether the Land Reform Code is constitutional or unconstitutional or whether some of its provisions are bad or good, but whether law itself is law . . .". Bad as the situation may be it is reassuring to know that in the Philippines it is still possible to expose the ills of society without being put under house arrest or in jail—a fate suffered by many outspoken critics of the Sukarno regime in Indonesia.

Local Government

The Philippines is divided into sixty-six provinces which in turn contain cities and municipalities which are further subdvided (except for Manila) into barrios. Cities and municipalities are of the same rank but the latter are less densely populated. Some cities—about fifty in all—are "chartered" and thereby acquire provincial status. All chief executives—governors of provinces, mayors of cities and barrio captains—are elected in the normal way by all qualified voters for four-year terms.

The Philippines is a unitary state with a heavily centralised form of government and in spite of the Decentralisation Law, the New Barrio Charter, the Local Autonomy Act and other measures it is still the case that local governments do not enjoy much independence.

Four-fifths of the taxes paid by Filipinos go towards maintaining the departments of the central government; the remainder is available for spending by local governments. Since most of this money is used up in paying the admittedly meagre salaries of locally-employed officials, there is little left over for the provision of the roads, bridges, schools and artesian wells which alone impress the local electorate.

If more money is required the governors, mayors and barrio captains must turn to their Congressmen and even the President for help. Every year Congressmen are given allocations from the public works bill to spend in their constituencies. These are the so-called "pork-barrel" funds for which the local executives must fight and which will normally be allocated on a political basis in return for electoral support.

The President himself has a contingency fund which he also uses to good political effect, especially in a re-election year.

This dependence of the local governments upon Manila for funds goes far to nullify attempts to decentralise the administration. The situation will not improve until local governments have greater taxing powers and, which is more important, greater wealth in the countryside from which to draw the taxes.

The Political Process

Uniquely among Southeast Asian states the Philippines has held elections at regular intervals, accommodated two major and opposed political parties and allowed changes of governments to take place along strictly constitutional lines. The incidence of violent crime may be high but otherwise the Philippines exhibits an enviable political stability.

The secret of this stability is probably to be found in the historical continuity of Filipino society, paradoxical as this may sound in view of the fact that the Philippines is the only country in Southeast Asia to have been colonised twice—first by the Spanish and then by the Americans. It is nevertheless largely true that the *ilustrados*, who today command most of the political and economic heights, come from largely the same families which belonged to the class of *principalia* in Spanish times, and from which during American colonial rule came the politicians, administrators, businessmen and technicians.

In contrast to many other colonial subjects in the region, the Filipinos did not have to struggle to acquire independence from their masters: it was promised to them almost from the start and the path towards it was mapped out well in advance. The Filipinos enjoyed a great measure of self-government well before the Second World War and the final withdrawal of the overt American political presence did not give rise to any false millenarian expectations or leave a power vacuum behind. In Indonesia, for instance, the social structure was badly shaken by the struggle for independence: in the Philippines there was no such traumatic experience; some of the outward appearances may have changed but there were few changes in the social and political power structure.

Although political and economic power in the Philippines appears to be concentrated in relatively few hands it would be a mistake to think of the political process there in terms of, say, Cambodia where there is a similar unequal distribution of wealth and influence. Whereas in Cambodia there is, or was, an abrupt discontinuity between throne and peasant, a wide gap only to be bridged by magic and charisma, in the Philippines there is a much more visible nexus between the Presidential Palace and the barrio hut. There is a whole network of mutual obligations, of *compadrazgo* and of kinship ties which holds society together and makes the poor man in the barrio feel that he is not entirely alienated from "the business of the city". Yet if there is an ideology in the Philippines it resembles in many ways Sihanouk's "Our Buddhist Socialism"; one might call it "Our Catholic Socialism". Like Prince Sihanouk the Filipino *élite* tends to think that its station in life is part of the Divine Plan, and that it must not concern itself too much with trying to alter this state of affairs. The Filipino *élite* seeks to remedy the ills of society, not so much by increasing the earning power of the peasants as by relieving their misery by charity and hand-outs. In this way two objects are achieved: the lot of the poor is improved and the pious donors acquire grace just as their Buddhist counterparts acquire merit. There are other resemblances. Just as Prince Sihanouk liked to associate himself personally with the agricultural equipment which unexpectedly enriched the lives of remote villagers so the President of the Philippines likes to link his name with the tangible benefits of government aid. Prince Sihanouk was accustomed personally to hand over spades, shovels and waterpumps to the farmers; President Marcos went so far as to have his own name displayed prominently on the side of trucks belonging to the government's Rural Development Programme. The major difference between the two styles is that whereas the Cambodian Prince played the part of the god in friendly human form, the Filipino President likes to project the image of the local boy who made good.

Political Parties

Filipino party politics reflect the socio-economic power structure. On the face of it there are two major parties, the Nacionalista and the Liberal, which contend for power in much the same way as do the Republicans and Democrats of the United States of America. In fact, however, party labels mean even less in the Philippines than in the USA; there is no ideological or class difference between the two parties and politicians and their supporters cross and recross the party boundaries with regularity and indifference. A man's allegiance to his party ends where his allegiance to his patron begins. Filipino politics, from the elections of barrio captains to the elections of Presidents, are concerned with personalities and power and are conducted in these terms. The names "Nacionalista" and "Liberal" are like the differently coloured shirts worn by opposing football teams: they serve to distinguish the champions from the challengers, the "Ins" from the "Outs".

There is no single clear-cut explanation why there should be only two major political parties in the Philippines but there are several contributory factors which can be identified.

In the first place the main political contest is for one office, the

Presidency, and the current office-holder's party is in such a strong position that it can only be dislodged by an organisation which can match or nearly match the resources of the incumbents. In these circumstances the opposition cannot afford to be significantly divided; the majority must be ranged behind one particular candidate under one particular party banner.

Another reason for the existence of only two parties is the absence of ideology from the political scene. The parties have no rigid ideologies and are thus able to accommodate all shades of opinion within their folds. The "Huk" movement for example has long been branded "Communist" and "Maoist" yet it is a certainty that deals have been made between "Huk" leaders and both Nacionalista and Liberal politicians seeking electoral support in "Huklandia".

Then there is the Constitution itself. Unlike most others in the world it not only mentions political parties but allots important roles to members of the two—and only the two—leading ones. For instance Article 6 Section II sets up Electoral Tribunals for each House of Congress and states that each shall be composed of nine members, that is three Justices of the Supreme Court and six others: "three upon nomination of the party having the largest number of votes and three of the party having the second largest number of votes. . . ."

Finally, there is the provision in the 1953 Revised Election Code for the appointment of election inspectors for duty at the polling booths. Each precinct has just two inspectors, one from each of the two leading parties and these men are responsible for deciding the validity of the ballots. This is only the official side of the inspectors' work; unofficially they will act as the agents of the party they represent and will help to keep a check—by fair means or foul—on the way people vote. "Party figures are of course greatly interested in 'who is ours and who is theirs' since the dispensing of patronage after the election will be strongly conditioned by this knowledge."

The ability to have such agents on the spot—paid for out of public funds—gives the two leading parties a further advantage over possible rivals.

Summary

Although the political process is often presented as an endless series of intra-*élite* struggles for the sweets of office, this is by no means the whole truth. Politics is not merely the business of the *élite*; there is a kind of vertical integration in society which during a Presidential election for a time links everyone together from the street-urchin who receives a free T-shirt inscribed "Vote for Marcos and Lopez" to the Presidential and Vice-Presidential candidates themselves. For example not long before the 1969 elections President Marcos and his "First Lady" Imelda personally handed out 2,000 cheques to as many barrio captains for expenditure on minor public works in the village.

Unorthodox such behaviour may have been, but it was a highly effective political gesture in that it served to bind the barrio captain to Marcos in a very strong bond of obligation or *utang na loob*.

Even if political power is in the hands of a small *élite* there is no lack of criticism both in Congress and outside it. Nor are the violent attacks of one party on the other a mere formality: they and the frequent exposures of corruption by the newspapers are all part of the age-old tradition of "fiscalisation",* as the Filipinos call it, which began with the Spanish institution of the *residencia* and continues to be upheld by outspoken members of Congress, by academics and Jesuits and by the least inhibited journalists in Southeast Asia. In the words of Teodoro M. Locsin, the editor of "Philippines Free Press", "We have a two-party system all right; abuses are checked by regularly throwing the abusers out of power; at any rate, there could be more abuses than there are. We are free, or more or less free. This is a democracy, thanks to the two-party system."

References

1. J. L. PHELAN, *The Hispanization of the Philippines*, University of Wisconsin Press, Madison, 1959, p. 18.
2. *Ibid.*, p. 58.
3. DAVID WURFEL, "The Philippines" in G. M. Kahin (Ed.), *Governments and Politics of Southeast Asia*, Cornell University Press, Ithaca, N.Y., 1964, 2nd Edition, p. 750.
4. O. D. CORPUZ, *The Philippines*, Prentice-Hall, Englewood Cliffs, N.J., 1965, p. 46.

---

* The word "fiscalisation" derives from the Spanish *fiscal*, the name given to a Spanish priest's native assistant who, among other things, "pointed out" to the priest "those who were remiss in their religious obligations".[4]

PART III

Ideologies and the Military in Southeast Asia

CHAPTER TWELVE

Ideologies in Southeast Asia

Introduction

In discussing the ideologies to be found in Southeast Asia it may be helpful to make it clear from the start that we intend to use the word "ideology" in as broad a sense as possible. We do not, for instance, wish to commit ourselves beforehand to the view that all ideologies are by definition "false" in that their pictures of the world never correspond with reality. Such a view is taken by those who suggest that all ideologies are, to use Karl Mannheim's words, "more or less conscious disguises of the real nature of the situation".[1] There is clearly a good deal of truth in this statement. Lacking omniscience nobody can hope to give an explanation or even a description of any event or sequence of events without disguising the real nature of the situation: such a person may also be conscious that he is so distorting what he thinks to be the real situation. Knowing this, are we therefore justified in jumping to the conclusion that every ideology is a more or less deliberate attempt to mislead people?

Leaving this last question to be answered by the philosophers, we propose not to prejudge the issue but merely to assume for the moment that not all the prescriptions and descriptions which are commonly called ideologies fall into Mannheim's category.

For present purposes, then, the word "ideology" will be used to denote any body of ideas which offers answers to some or all of the moral and teleological questions posed by human beings or which proposes ends to be striven for and means appropriate to the achievement of those ends.

Within this wider band of ideologies-in-general will be found political ideologies. The line between political and non-political ideologies is not hard and fast: as Apter has pointed out, any ideology can become political; likewise ideologies which are not labelled "political" may well have political consequences.

National Loyalties

In Southeast Asia the first task of most nationalist leaders was that of nation-building. In Europe "language was the badge of nationality"[2] but in Southeast Asia the colonial powers had carved out their domains with such scant regard for linguistic, ethnic and geographic considerations that European ideas of what constituted a nation had little relevance. Since no nation's pride would allow a diminution of its sovereignty by any adjustment of its boundaries, national loyalty had to expand or contract to fill the space provided for it by the accidents of colonial history.

This was not the only difficulty facing the new leaders. They also had to contend with the apathy left by years of indifference or hostility on the part of the colonial powers towards nationalist aspirations.

In most cases the colonial powers did little or nothing to promote any feeling of common nationality: the exception was the Philippines where the relatively enlightened American administration allowed the Filipinos to build and operate their own political institutions, well before the Second World War; in addition to which the Filipinos had already to a great extent achieved nationhood and its attendant mythology in the brave days of the struggle for independence from Spain.

Such coherence as these ex-colonies possessed was largely a product of a common administration and a common enemy or "other" by whose very presence the colonial subject acquired at least a negative definition. But even this negative definition became extremely tenuous in, for instance, Burma and Laos where the colonial power had several different administrative arrangements and treaty relationships in various parts of the country. To confuse the issue further there was the conscious "divide and rule" policy of recruitment for the police and army from ethnic or religious minorities, a tactic which often had the effect of creating new sub-nationalisms.

With secession ruled out and national unity within the colonial boundaries automatically assumed to be a desirable goal, leaders proceeded to fashion a new set of symbols as a focus for the loyalties of all.

The first move of new governments was to make use of the aura of authority which had surrounded the departing colonial power. The first independent leaders frequently stressed by deed if not always by word that they were the legitimate inheritors of the throne vacated by the white man. They did this by leaving the administrative framework more or less intact and by legitimising their assumption of power by emphasising the role of such democratic institutions as Parliaments and Bills of Rights in the new regime. In countries where the mystique of

Hindu kingship was a part of the political culture the mere "capture" of the sacred capital city was itself strong evidence of the legitimacy of the new ruler; for this reason, amongst others, none of the "new" states moved the seat of government away from the established capital city although in all cases where the name was not an indigenous one it was "localized".*

But the mere taking over of power and authority from a regime which was now beginning to be seen as illegitimate was not enough. The need was felt to propagate a new ideological framework in which the new rulers would be seen as legitimate, not only as successors to the colonial powers but in the context of indigenous pre-colonial or non-colonial tradition. Thus Sihanouk projected himself not as the successor to the French *Résident Supérieur* nor yet as the man chosen by the French to succeed King Monivong, but as the lineal descendant of the oldest monarchy in Southeast Asia; whose legitimacy would be demonstrated by the performance of a great programme of public works and pious deeds in the tradition of Jayavarman VII. In like manner Sukarno reanimated the myths and legends of Madjapahit; the Laotians revived memories of ancient Lan Xang; while in Burma U Nu increasingly relied on the Buddhist tradition of meritorious acts to support his own legitimacy.

Unfortunately, many of these reanimations of past glories also served to revive memories of past rivalries and injustices. Except in the case of Madjapahit it was impossible to find an ancient kingdom the boundaries of which were co-terminous with those of the modern state, with the result that too great an emphasis on, say, the great days of Khmers merely served to alienate the Vietnamese living in Cambodia and to remind Cambodians that parts of South Vietnam were Cambodia *irredenta*. In Burma, too, an emphasis on good Buddhist deeds was not likely to appeal to animist or Christian hill-tribes. In the Philippines where there is a small but important Moslem minority in the South, it is safe to invoke memories of Rizal because although the latter was a Christian, his most famous books had a very strong anti-clerical bias.

National Identity

Partly to mobilise the creative powers of potentially hostile ethnic groups but mainly to give the new nation a sense of dignity and a pride in its own culture Southeast Asian political leaders have been required to redefine the nation.

There seem here to have been five main possibilities: to stress the main ethnic group; to stress the main cultural or religious element; to invent a new nationality; to stress the continuity of political institutions; to appeal to commonsense.

---

* Thus Djakarta for Batavia, Kota Kinabalu for Jesselton.

In Cambodia, where the population is all but homogeneous, the accent is on Khmer nationhood and the continuity of the political institution of the monarchy. In Burma various tactics have been tried: in U Nu's time the appeal was very often to Buddhism—"we are all Buddhists really, even the Communists"; on the other hand in the earlier hectic days of transition to independence Aung San realised the dangers of defining the national identity in terms of religion, race or language and made strenuous efforts to lay a more pragmatic base for the nation by suggesting that a new nationality could be created by acts of co-operation and a sense of common destiny. "A Nation," he said, "is a collective term applied to a people, irrespective of their ethnic origin, living in close contact with one another and having common interests and sharing joys and sorrows together for such historic periods as to have acquired a sense of oneness. Though race, religion and language are important it is only their traditional desire and will to live in unity through weal and woe that binds a people together and makes them a nation and their spirit a patriotism."[3]

In colonial Malaya the political institution of the Malay Sultanate was left intact but the reality of power lay with the British to whom both Chinese and Malays could defer without losing their ethnic identities. When the British left, sovereignty reverted to the Sultans and the answer to the question "Who am I?" was liable to be framed in terms which were almost exclusively Malay rather than Malayan. Tunku Abdul Rahman's method of dealing with this potentially dangerous situation was to temporise and to try to postpone for as long as possible the seemingly inevitable crisis in the hope perhaps that economic prosperity might kill ethnic rivalry and materialism triumph over ideology. Events have not proved him entirely wrong but if the crisis is averted it will be because the Chinese will have decided to acquiesce in the Malayisation of Malaysia.

Nationalism as an Ideology in Southeast Asia

Southeast Asian nationalism as expressed in identity- and loyalty-forming words and deeds is not normally based on any explicitly "global" ideology. There is, however, one exception. Sukarno's concepts of nationalism and internationalism as expounded in his "Pantja Sila" speech bear a strong resemblance to those of Mazzini whose works Sukarno had undoubtedly read. Mazzini's influence can be seen not only here but in the very nomenclature of the early nationalist movements: "Young Java" and Young Indonesia" were clearly based on the Mazzinian prototype "Young Italy".

Mazzini spoke of nationality as being an integral part of the Creator's plan: God "divided humanity into distinct groups upon the face of the globe, and thus planted the seeds of nations".[4] Mazzini also called upon geography to support his thesis: "God has stretched round you sublime and indisputable boundaries; on one side the highest mountains of Europe, the Alps; on the other the sea, the immeasurable sea."[5] Compare this with Sukarno's words in the "Pantja Sila" speech of June 1, 1945: ". . . the Indonesian people are all the human beings who according to geopolitics ordained by God Almighty live throughout the entire archipelago of Indonesia from the northern tip of Sumatra to Irian."[6]

Like Mazzini before him, Sukarno did not stop at nationalism: "We . . . should also aim at making one family of all nations. . . . Nationalism cannot flower if it does not grow within the garden of internationalism." In like vein Mazzini had asserted that "the unity of civilization could only be attained by first solving the question of nationalities . . . before associating ourselves with the Nations which comprise Humanity we must exist as a Nation".

Socialism in Southeast Asia

There were two phases in the history of the impact of Socialist thought on the politicians of Southeast Asia: the colonial and the post-colonial phases.

In the first phase those nationalist leaders who were looking for ideological support for their anti-colonial crusades sometimes found it in their traditions of the "holy war" or perhaps some millenarian belief such as the Ratu Adil; but more often their inspiration came from abroad, from the writings of Karl Marx or one of his numerous ideological descendants.* In this phase it was the anti-colonial content of the writings which was attractive particularly if it professed to give scientific proof that colonialism and imperialism were doomed. In an age when Europeans were seen to possess overwhelming technological superiority it was doubly satisfying to employ a "scientific" weapon against them.

In the colonial period the rest of the Marxist creed tended to be glossed over since it was capable of causing divisions in the nationalist ranks if it was propagated with too much zeal. In Indonesia the doctrinal inflexibility of the Moscow-inspired Socialists led to the break-up of the Serikat Islam and the beginnings of the formulation of an "Indonesian" Socialism in which, among other things, a distinction was made between "good" and "sinful" capitalists.

When independence had been won and the new leaders were occupying the seats of power, there was no great enthusiasm for an ideology based on the class struggle. Thus although leaders frequently subscribed to the notion of an international class struggle in which the rich nations were the bourgeoisie and the poor the proletariat, they were quick to deny that the analysis was relevant to their own countries.

---

* Particularly, in British colonies, Harold Laski of the London School of Economics.

Sukarno for example replaced the proletariat by the class of Marhaen which was so broad that it seemed to include most of the nation, including those "good" capitalists who were working to improve the lot of the Marhaen.

Prince Sihanouk, who for all that he had stepped down from the throne and become a Sahachivin* still needed the ascriptive authority of Hindu kingship, denied the validity of the Marxist analysis. While admitting the existence of classes he denied that it was necessary for the lower classes to overthrow and dispossess their masters in order to achieve social and economic justice. "Marxism," said Sihanouk, "teaches people that it is necessary to exterminate princes who, because they have 'blue blood', 'bleed the people white'. But a Prince who really respects Buddhist precepts must always—while fully aware of the implications—be ready to be exploited or 'bled white' by the underprivileged."[7]

One feature of Socialism which has received fairly widespread acceptance is the need for the State to play a major role in social and economic affairs. In this sense most Southeast Asians can say "We are all Socialists now". Such a ready acceptance of the State's role is hardly surprising since, in the absence of a strong indigenous capitalist class, the State is usually the only institution with enough funds or credit at its disposal to undertake the major educational, welfare, industrial and agricultural projects to which most governments have committed themselves.

It is of course possible to argue that this State Socialism is merely a continuation under another name of the benevolent despotism of the more enlightened colonial regimes. While there is truth in this it must also be admitted that there is also a strong ideological content present. Of this perhaps the best example is to be found in the field of education where in most cases egalitarianism has replaced elitism as the basic philosophy. One can also find much evidence to suggest that need has replaced the ability to pay as the accepted criterion for the distribution of other social benefits.

The Rise of "National" Socialisms

In the course of the last twenty-five years three countries of Southeast Asia have produced their own national brands of Socialism. There has been Sihanouk's "Buddhist Socialism", Sukarno's "Socialism à la Indonesia" and more than one version of Burmese Socialism.

These are several possible reasons why Southeast Asian leaders desired to establish an indigenous variety of Socialism. In the first place, though the Marxist class analysis was acceptable in colonial times it proved somewhat embarrassing in the days when non-European business-

---

* Loosely translated as Comrade.

men, whether Chinese or "sons of the soil", supplied much of the financial backing for independence movements and nationalist parties. Second, there was the natural desire to make it clear that the country's own ideology was not merely a carbon copy of some product of Moscow or Paris or Bloomsbury. Third, there was the desire to emphasise that one's own Socialism was a patriotic one. To stress the international aspects of Socialism was to risk attracting the same odium which attached to most Southeast Asian Communist parties whose links with foreign powers and traditional enemies cast strong doubt on the patriotism of their members.

Critics may say that none of these Socialisms is anything more than an attempt to sanctify the *status quo* in terms acceptable to the political public and the world at large.

Such a criticism would be hard to refute. Writing of the spirit of Burmese politics Pye remarks: "it is nearly impossible to demonstrate any connection between the manifestations of ideology and significant Burmese political behaviour." In Cambodia, as we have seen, Prince Sihanouk was quite ready to formulate Socialism in terms of *noblesse oblige* rather than the drastic reordering of society. In Indonesia Sukarno was in practice quite ready to accept financial help from men like Dasaad, the head of one of Indonesia's largest private concerns, whom he once described as "the richest capitalistic Socialist in the country".[8]

Yet one should not be too harsh in his judgements. The Socialist leaders of Southeast Asia had to have regard to the "realities of the situation" and their Socialism was liable to be of a pragmatic kind: patriotic, xenophobic, flexible but in most cases aimed at trying to establish the equivalent of Sukarno's *masjarakat jang adil dan makmur*, the just and prosperous society.

The most cerebral of Southeast Asia's Socialists, Lee Kuan Yew, posed the dilemma with great precision at the opening session of the 1965 Young Asia Socialist Conference held in Bombay.

> "I am," he said, "an unrepentant Socialist. But in my own state, I have to concede that because it takes a long time to inculcate the high values of public duty and sense of service to the community, performance has been best only when workers are offered high incentives for high performance. Our building programmes have progressed rapidly because we allowed the individual worker to earn as much as he can over his other workers by working as hard as he likes. Our lowest productivity level is in many sections of our own Government services such as our publicly-owned dockyards where managers are on a salary scale instead of the profit-sharing and bonus schemes of private industry. . . . We have had to recognize these faults. . . . But in order to get economic growth we have had to base our policies on the principle 'From each his economic best. To each his economic worth.' The ultimate ideal

'From each his best. To each his need' can only be relevant after we have moved away from ignorance, illiteracy, poverty and economic backwardness."[9]

Communism and Communists in Southeast Asia

Neither Communism as an ideology nor Communists as a political force have enjoyed much success in Southeast Asia. There is only one effective Communist government in the region, although Communists share power *de jure* in Laos (and until recently in Indonesia); and *de facto* in parts of South Vietnam and Cambodia. In general the history of Communist movements in Southeast Asia has been, from the Communist viewpoint, a sad one: a succession of abortive and ill-timed *coups*, unsuccessful civil wars, brutal suppression, ostracism and exile.

On the ideological plane Communism suffers from its strongly atheistic and anticlerical content. In the Moslem areas like Malaysia and Indonesia this has the effect of challenging both the established religion and the "establishment". In the Buddhist countries the challenge is not so great since Buddhism lays greater stress on works than faith, but there is still a real conflict.

In both Moslem and Buddhist contexts the Communists have tried to prove that the problem does not really exist and that it is quite possible to be a good Moslem or Buddhist *and* a Communist. For example, in Sumatra in the early 1920s Communist propaganda was designed to enlist the support of Moslems by stressing that none of the aims of the Communist Party was in conflict with Moslem aims and that it would be impious *not* to support an organisation whose programme would, if put into effect, strengthen Islam and undermine the rule of the infidel Dutch.[10]

In Burma great efforts were made, for differing reasons, by both Buddhists and Communists to prove that Buddhism and Communism were not incompatible with each other.

Ba Swe, a former Prime Minister and President of the Socialist Party, once said: "Marxist theory is not antagonistic to Buddhist philosophy. The two are, frankly speaking, not merely similar: in fact they are the same in concept."[11] In the same speech, however, as Tinker points out, Ba Swe made a distinction between Marxism and Communism. This was in 1952. Six years later, when consensus was no longer deemed to be a possibility, U Nu said there was no difference between Marxism and Communism; both were to be condemned as being incompatible with Buddhism.[12]

In Cambodia Sihanouk was quite happy to accept some of the ideals of Marxism while rejecting the doctrine of class warfare. On the theological plane he regarded Communism as "simply a different religion to ours".* He found in it "many merits" but recommended his people "to follow our Buddhist way". Unlike Ba Swe, Sihanouk made no effort to pretend that Marxism and Buddhism were "the same in concept" but he was prepared to tolerate its existence "as long as it does not attack us". Such a spirit of wary tolerance served also as the basis of Sihanouk's foreign policy.

Although Communists have been suppressed and outlawed in Indonesia, Malaysia, Burma and the Philippines, and are under severe pressure in Laos and in South Vietnam, the fact remains that Communism has won many supporters. What then are its attractions?

Ideologically Communism's appeal lies in its being regarded as scientific, modern and yet at the same time supplying a millenarian vision of the future. The theory of the "withering away of government", for instance, may not mean much to the peasants of Southeast Asia, but it must have its attractions to a class which regards government as one of the Five Great Evils.

In fact the great strength of the Communist parties lies in their practical programmes rather than their theories. That is why they have met with considerable success in the crowded paddy fields of Central and East Java, the Mekong delta and the plains of Central Luzon. The Communist Party stands for activity; while other political parties doze between elections and forget their promises, the Communist cadres are up and about seeking justice for the oppressed tenant and the landless and caring for the afflicted. In all aspects of life which most concern the lowest ranks of Southeast Asian society—corruption, injustice, high prices, the failure to implement schemes for land reform—the Communists generally project a more favourable image than the existing ruling parties.

The comparative lack of success of Communist parties in other parts of the region may be attributed partly to the antagonism between Communism and the established religions, partly to the absence of a serious land problem in much of the area, but also to two other important factors: their ambiguous stand in respect of the nationalist movements and their identification with certain minority ethnic groups.

In Indonesia the PKI is regarded as having betrayed the nationalist cause on at least two memorable occasions: at Madiun when they stabbed the nationalists in the back in the middle of the struggle for liberation and again in 1965 when it was thought that they were about to sell Indonesia to Peking. On the second occasion the PKI's known links with China enabled the Indonesian "sons of the soil" to work off part of their angry frustration on the ever-unpopular Chinese traders.

A similar but far more obvious identification of Communism with

---

* This, and the quotations following, is taken from *Our Buddhist Socialism* by Prince Sihanouk.[7]

the Chinese occurred in Malaya where most Communists were in fact Chinese and could also with justice be blamed for holding up the country's progress towards independence.

Where Chinese are not available or amenable the Communists frequently seek out the hill tribes and the men of the deep jungles, particularly in sensitive border areas. Such tribes invariably have feuds with the men of the plains and are ready to assist any enemy of their enemies. These tactics are usually successful for the establishment of a "Ho Chi Minh trail" or a "Sihanouk trail" but the identification of Communism with a particular ethnic group makes it very difficult for the Communists to expand into the rest of the country and to gain the support of the enemies of the minority group.

A Syncretist Ideology: the Case of Indonesia

Politics throughout most of Southeast Asia is to do with people rather than ideas: with leaders, followers and inter-personal relations rather than ideologies. In Burma, according to Pye ". . . politics revolve mainly around personalities".[13] The same can be said of Laos where the key factors in the political situation are familial, hierarchical and tribal loyalties. In the Philippines one thinks of the great *compadrazgo* networks and the fluidity of party lines. In Malaysia there is loyalty to Sultan and chief; in Cambodia and Thailand there is the instinctive awe of the institution of kingship and its attendant hierarchy. In all these cases consciously formulated ideologies seem to have little importance. Is ideology then nothing but a "fig-leaf to clothe the power struggle?" In most cases this is probably true but one could with plausibility argue that Indonesia has produced the one indigenous ideology which is more than a mere cloak for reality.

Pantja Sila

For all the scorn that has been directed at Sukarno's political ideologising the fact remains that two of his key concepts—Pantja Sila and Guided Democracy—are still part of the Indonesian scene and the time may well come when Indonesian leaders will regret the passing of "Nasakom" and seek to put something very like it in its place.

If the two main functions of an ideology are "to bind the community together" and to organise "the role personalities of the maturing individual" Pantja Sila certainly fulfils its functions. In its insistence on nationhood as part of a Mazzinian divine plan, it emphasises the unity of Indonesia; on the other hand in its overt avoidance of the Islamic state it seeks to provide a legitimate role for the Hindus, Christians and animists within the state. In its insistence that Indonesian democracy is not to be a slavish imitation of European models, Pantja

Sila asserts the separate identity of the Indonesian nation; while the inclusion of the principle of "internationalism" ensures that Indonesia for all its new and separate identity can still feel part of the wider brotherhood of nations. S. Takdir Alisjahbana, one of the late President Sukarno's most outspoken critics, admits that "as a means of uniting various political ideals and objectives in the early stages of creating an independent Indonesian state, the compromise represented by the Pantja Sila was one of first-rate importance".[14] It was thus, in his estimation, a highly successful ideology. He objects to it, however, on the grounds that it was neither a "logical construct" nor a "reflection of the internal realities of Indonesian government".

As to the first point there is admittedly no single thread running through the Pantja Sila but on the other hand no one principle is inconsistent with any other one. As to the second point, nobody knew better than Sukarno what the "realities" were and the whole aim of Pantja Sila was precisely to try to resolve the open conflicts of Indonesian politics. "I want you to understand," said Sukarno, "that this Pantja Sila is already a compromise, the making of which has involved blood and tears. Anyone who opens our history, especially for July 1945, a month before the proclamation of Indonesia resounded through the heavens, anyone who consults the records of our discussions, our debates, our quarrels with one another—for at that time we were close to hating each other—will understand that the Pantja Sila is a compromise."[15]

Sukarno did not pretend that there were no differences; he only desired that the problems should not be stated in such stark and exclusive terms. His approach, like that of Radhakrishnan, was "this *and* that" rather than "this *or* that". Such an approach was nothing new for Sukarno; it had been part and parcel of his attitude to the political and religious divisions of Indonesia ever since his earliest days. It was part of his genetic inheritance as the son of a Javanese Theosophist father and a Balinese Hindu mother. For Sukarno all Reality was One and all apparently conflicting creeds merely different aspects of the One Truth. For Sukarno, as indeed for millions of Javanese, there was no contradiction involved in being both a Moslem and a Marxist; one could accept the Marxist critique of society without abandoning one's duty to Allah.

The fact remains that Pantja Sila is still, even after Sukarno's downfall and death, the basic philosophy of the Republic; it is indeed strictly forbidden to question it publicly. Against heavy odds there has grown up a strong sense of national identity in Indonesia and, in spite of the fact that ninety per cent of it is nominally Moslem, every move to establish an Islamic state has been strongly resisted. These achievements are in great measure due to the power of Pantja Sila and its ceaseless propagation by Sukarno.

Guided Democracy

Political systems based on the Washington and Westminster models are unlikely to succeed unless there is considerable ethnic and cultural homogeneity and a high degree of consensus about the ends of political action. Where these conditions are present politics will consist of "contests within the framework of the political system" rather than a "contest *about* the political system".

Pantja Sila was Sukarno's attempt to create the national unity and consensus without which no form of government can achieve useful results. It must be accorded a measure of success since, in spite of rebellions and individual defections and the setting up of alternative governments, no part of Indonesia has ever seceded from the Republic. There has been a good deal of pressure for increased autonomy but very little for outright secession.

Consensus there may have been about the boundaries of the new nation but there was little agreement among the politicians about how the parliamentary and cabinet system should be operated. After a promising start the old divisions reappeared and the old enmities were revived and the Army and the new post-Madiun forces of the Communist Party loomed ever larger as the possible alternative authoritarian successors to constitutional democracy.

In 1956 Sukarno first asked the nation to consider whether there was a workable Indonesian alternative to the "free-fight liberalism" of the West. He said that Indonesia "could no longer afford this Western democracy with its majority voting, where fifty-one per cent wins and forty-nine per cent ends up with a grudge". He suggested that any new system should be built upon the traditional village system of "*musjawarah* and *mufakat*—deliberations and agreement".

It should be noted that Sukarno, unlike some prominent Indian political philosophers, did not pretend that the villagers always reached consensus unaided. The villagers had to be consulted but they did not make the final decision. The key man in the village was the leader, be he chief or *lurah*: it was he who decided what action was to be taken. "Only strong leadership is capable of synthesizing the final decision; otherwise the system will not work."[16]

Although in the event Sukarno cut down the number of political parties severely he was not an advocate of "partyless" politics in the manner of J. P. Narayan. His main suggestion was that the accent should now fall on *leadership* in a "democracy with leadership" as referred to in the 1945 Constitution to which the nation returned in 1959. Under this constitution the roles of the representative bodies, the People's Council and the Parliament were reduced to laying down guide-lines and acting as co-legislators respectively. The President provided the "strong leadership" and was given powers greater than those accorded to a United States President. To assist the President there was a cabinet appointed by him and responsible to him as well as a Supreme Advisory Council and a National Planning Council.

Sukarno's first innovation was the introduction of the "gotong rojong" principle by which every major political party was to be represented in the cabinet. In similar fashion the Supreme Advisory Council was to have representatives from all the "functional groups" which made up the nation: trade unionists, peasants, intellectuals, businessmen, Protestants, Catholics, Hindus, Moslems, women, youths as well as members of the armed forces and some Ministers. "I regard the Council as a reflection of our society", said Sukarno, "while the Cabinet would be a reflection of Parliament."[17]

The second innovation was the replacement of voting by consultation (*musjawara*). Mindful of the bitter struggle which had to be endured before the great compromise of Pantja Sila was reached, Sukarno did not want this hard-won unity to be sacrificed to the principle of majority rule. Sukarno made the point very clearly in a speech in 1953 to the students of the University of Indonesia. "Democracy, what we mean by democracy, is not just 'half plus one are always right'. . . . If it was just a matter of voting, then why hold *musjawarahs*, why hold debates. It would be better to just assemble. Assemble! Ready? And now an issue, for instance, the issue of Islam or not? Vote! Result: half plus one are always right. Now the issue of Communism, vote! No more discussion, just vote."[18]

The period of Sukarno's "Guided Democracy" was disastrous in so many ways that the concept itself is in danger of being treated as just another of Sukarno's empty slogans. Does it deserve this fate?

It is surely significant that more adverse criticism has been directed at Sukarno's misuse of "Guided Democracy" than at the concept itself. One of Hatta's main objections was that the members of Parliament were appointed, not elected. Alisjahbana objected, as did Hatta and others, to the banning of the main Moslem and Socialist parties and their newspapers. "It is clear," said Alisjahbana, "that the principles of *gotong-rojong* and familial solidarity or Indonesian democracy, which require deliberations and agreements, in the guided democracy of Sukarno were misused for the purpose of providing a basis for his dictatorship and his absolute power."[19] The criticism here is of the implementation of the idea rather than the idea itself. Some years earlier the same writer had said: "By 1957, when President Sukarno declared himself in favour of 'democracy with leadership', he was really putting into words something which had been generally felt in Indonesia. Democracy, as it had been experienced for the last twelve years, could be carried no further."[20]

Experience has shown that "free-fight" liberalism does not suit Indonesia. Investigation would probably also show that in Indonesia as in Malaysia and elsewhere the average peasant knows little and cares less about parliamentary democracy: he is interested in the two things which the percipient Sukarno was always promising: food and clothing (*sandang-pangan*). But if the masses are mainly interested in an efficient but not-too-interfering government there is always the problem of satisfying the small political public. A large proportion of the last-named have been exposed to liberal, social-democratic thought, whose values they have internalised; they now find it very difficult to convince themselves that anything short of "free-fight liberalism" is intellectually or morally defensible. The task of the ideologists has, therefore, been to make the political public realise that any successful political system must have its roots in the political culture of the country concerned and that there is nothing disreputable in having a model which departs from Western norms.

For too long the recently emancipated colonial territories were asking themselves the wrong questions and trying to solve the wrong problems. Perhaps overawed by the fact that they had successfully used Western ideologies to win independence from the West they automatically assumed that the political structures of the West would not only suit their own countries but were the best that could be devised. In Indonesia Sukarno was one of the comparatively few who objected to this kind of thinking and he, significantly, had been entirely educated in Java and had not been outside Indonesia until he was over forty years old. Sukarno made it his task to find a political format which would suit the real Indonesian Identity (*kepribadian Indonesia*). The format which he devised no doubt also suited his own lust for power but the fact that Pantja Sila is still the national philosophy and that Suharto himself practises what can only be described as "guided democracy" should make one wonder whether Sukarno's "konsepsi" was altogether invalid.

The Anglo-Saxon model of democracy has as its two most vital ingredients a strong two-party system and a high degree of cultural homogeneity. In Holland, where there are much sharper religious differences and many more parties the system only works because most people are prepared to think of themselves as Dutchmen first and Catholics or Protestants second. The average Indonesian on the other hand finds it difficult either to replace his primordial loyalties by loyalty to the State or to add loyalty to the State to his other loyalties to kin, region and religion. It is not surprising, therefore, that there should have been a great proliferation of political parties and that the coalitions by means of which alone government was possible should have been shifting and unstable.

The competitive Western political model failed in Indonesia precisely because it emphasised and indeed institutionalised the very divisions which are the bane of Indonesia's political life. The Guided Democracy which followed, received a bad press and harsh adverse criticism, not so much because of its inherent faults but rather because of the eccentricities of the Guide. Sukarno is dead, but the format of

Guided Democracy lives on; it is the writer's opinion that if the new regime can gradually be de-militarised, Guided Democracy may yet prove to be an attractive model to nations struggling with the twin problems of modernisation and national integration.

References

1. P. E. SIGMUND, *The Ideologies of the Developing Nations*, Frederick A. Praeger, New York, Revised edition 1967, p. 3.
2. R. EMERSON, *From Empire to Nation*, Harvard University Press, Boston, 1960, p. 132.
3. W. C. JOHNSTONE, *Burma's Foreign Policy*, Harvard University Press, Boston, 1963, p. 316.
4. J. MAZZINI, *The Duties of Man*, Everyman's Library Edition, London, 1966, p. 52.
5. *Ibid.*, p. 52.
6. H. FEITH and L. CASTLES (Eds) *Indonesian Political Thinking*, Cornell University Press, Ithaca, N.Y., 1970, p. 42.
7. NORODOM SIHANOUK, *Our Buddhist Socialism*, Ministry of Information, Phnom Penh, 1965, pp. 49-50.
8. CINDY ADAMS, *Sukarno: An Autobiography as told to Cindy Adams*, Bobbs Merrill, Indiana, 1965, p. 120.
9. *Socialist Solution for Asia*, Ministry of Culture, Singapore, n.d.
10. B. SCHRIEKE, *Indonesian Sociological Studies*, Van Hoeve, The Hague, 1959, Part 1, p. 155.
11. H. TINKER, *The Union of Burma*, Oxford University Press, London, 1967, 4th Edition, p. 177.
12. F. TRAGER, *Burma*, Pall Mall, London, 1966, p. 130.
13. L. W. PYE, *Politics, Personality and Nation Building*, Yale University Press, New Haven, Conn., 1962, p. 155.
14. S. TAKDIR ALISJAHBANA, *Indonesia*, Oxford University Press, London, 1966, p. 133.
15. H. FEITH and L. CASTLES, op. cit., p. 168.
16. CINDY ADAMS, op. cit., p. 279.
17. H. FEITH and L. CASTLES, op. cit., pp. 87-88.
18. H. FEITH and L. CASTLES, op. cit., p. 170.
19. S. T. ALISJAHBANA, op. cit., p. 154.
20. S. T. ALISJAHBANA, op. cit., p. 136.

CHAPTER THIRTEEN

The Military in Southeast Asia

At the beginning of 1971 the governments of five Southeast Asian countries were headed by Army Generals: Thanom in Thailand, Lon Nol in Cambodia, Ne Win in Burma, Thieu in South Vietnam and Suharto in Indonesia. This still leaves a fair number of governments in civilian hands: enough to make it difficult to justify sweeping generalisations about the "erosion of democracy" and the inevitability of military dictatorship. One may nevertheless legitimately ask whether there is a trend towards autocracy in general and military autocracy in particular. While we do not propose to answer this question directly in this chapter we hope to give some relevant data upon which an answer might be based.

The first point to be made is that, except in Thailand, the Army has come to power in each of these countries at a time of crisis, the sort of crisis that would in any case demand some kind of military solution.

To deal with the exception first. In Thailand the Army has for many years been an integral part of what Fred W. Riggs has called the bureaucratic policy. The present dynasty was after all founded on a military *coup d'etat*.* The 1932 coup as we have seen was the work of both civilians and officers of the armed services and every *coup* since that time has involved members of both groups. It is not, therefore, so much that the military have taken over in Thailand but rather that the current ruling clique has a military man at its head. Moreover, although Thailand is not facing an immediate crisis she has an internal insurgency problem both in the South and the north-east as well as the

---

* By General Chakri in 1782.

threat of a spill-over of the Indo-Chinese War across her borders with Laos and Cambodia. Again, whereas in the copy-book military dictatorship the generalissimo is at the top of a monolithic pyramidical structure, this is not the case in Thailand where General Thanom is more a chairman than a dictator and the men with whom he works are themselves heads of separate bureaucratic empires which are to some extent independent and self-supporting.

In South Vietnam the *coup* which overturned the Ngo Dinh Diem regime was led by an Army General, Duong Van Minh, but it was aimed not at a faltering experiment in democracy but at a dictatorship as absolute as any to be found in Southeast Asia. The Army has stayed in power ever since but this is as much a consequence of the military crisis and the enormous American presence and influence as of a desire, strong as it has since become, on the part of the military to cling to office.

The case of Indonesia would be close to an example of the "ideal type" of military take-over were it not for the fact that constitutional democracy had already died the death in 1957 at the hands of a civilian President and that the *coup* which brought the Army to power was directed *against* the Army. It is true that Colonel Untung maintained that the "Council of Generals" was preparing a *coup* against President Sukarno, but his claim is yet to be substantiated. In any case General Suharto's behaviour after the *coup* indicated not only that he was unwilling to move too quickly against Sukarno but that he also intended to include much more than a token number of prominent civilians in the government.

In Burma the situation was quite different. There General Ne Win and the armed forces were actually invited to take over the government while the civilians put their house in order. Given that Ne Win was himself a politician and had served as Deputy Prime Minister and Minister of Defence, it is not surprising that he tried with some success to build himself a political base while temporarily in charge of the administration of the country. The Army did not merely hold the ring in the absence of U Nu; on the contrary it made many changes and set up a variety of new commercial, educational and political institutions, some of which still survive. With what we can now see clearly as ulterior motives the Army was anxious to build a reputation for honesty and efficiency in order perhaps to legitimise in advance its next incursion into politics. A 576-page book called *Is Trust Vindicated?* was published for this purpose; it contained "A chronicle of the various accomplishments of the Government headed by General Ne Win during the period of tenure from November 1958 to February 6 1960" and was a detailed apologia for military rule. When Ne Win seized power in 1962 it was at a time of political and military crisis: there seemed to be no clear successor to U Nu, who apparently wished to retire from public life, and insurgency, civil war and subversion were rife in the provinces.

In Cambodia power passed from Prince Sihanouk into the hands of General Lon Nol and Prince Sirik Matak but one can hardly speak of a military take-over. Both men had served as Prime Ministers in previous governments and both had been asked by Prince Sihanouk a year before to take whatever measures might be necessary to improve the health and stability of the Cambodian economy. That Cambodia is now in a state of war and siege is not a consequence of Lon Nol's becoming Prime Minister but rather directly attributable to the incursion of the Americans and South Vietnamese forces into Cambodia in "hot pursuit" of the Viet Cong.

In summary, then, we may say that military regimes in Southeast Asia have been established, as a general rule, in circumstances of crisis and that such crises have usually been of such a kind as would have called for drastic measures in any country of the "third" or any other world; one has only to think in this connection of events in 1970 in Northern Ireland and Canada. If democracy has been eroded in these countries it is not because the people themselves are "unfit" for it but because the very special ethnic, social and cultural conditions in which alone "loyal oppositions" can flourish simply do not exist.

A Typology of Armies

For the purpose of this brief analysis of the role of armies in Southeast Asia it may be useful to distinguish five broad categories of army: the nationalist, the bureaucratic, the professional, the army of liberation and the people's army.

The Nationalist Army

For examples of the "nationalist" army one may turn to Burma and Indonesia. Both countries' armies had similar beginnings under colonial rule. In both countries the colonial powers attempted to create small highly professional bodies whose main role was conceived in terms of internal security rather than national defence. For these reasons the bulk of the soldiery was recruited disproportionately from minority religious and ethnic groups. In 1917, for example twenty-five per cent of the Royal Netherlands East Indies' Army was from Ambon, a small somewhat remote island whose inhabitants were largely Christian. The Javanese, rightly, were the largest ethnic group—forty-five per cent—in the army but one cannot help feeling that they were recruited mainly for their willingness to take part in possible actions against the unruly Achinese of North Sumatra.

In Burma the story is much the same. In 1938 the figures for the armed forces were as follows:

Officers		*Other Ranks*	
Burmans	4	Burmans	159
Other Indigenous	75	Other Indigenous	3040
Indians	36	Indians	1423
British	163	British	1587

The most populous ethnic group, the Burmans, who formed about sixty-four per cent of the population of Burma, contributed a mere 2·5 per cent share to the Burma Army. The British recruited mainly from the Chins, Kachins and Karens who were not only ethnic but religious minorities, being in the main non-Buddhists.

In both the Dutch East Indies and colonial Burma the army was recruited on a political basis. As soon as the political scene changed the composition of the army changed with it. During the Japanese occupation there was an enormous surge in the recruitment and mobilisation of the dominant ethnic groups in both countries.

In Burma thousands of young men rushed to join the Burma Independence Army, which became for the time being the physical expression of the Thakin movement. It was led by Aung San and included Ne Win among its other prominent members. The BIA was not only thoroughly political: it was also composed almost exclusively of ethnic Burmans, mostly from Lower Burma where the British colonial presence had been strongest. Its failure to recruit from among the hill tribes was not only indicative of its inability physically to penetrate to these areas but was a symptom of a radical reversal of the political order; in the new era to be a member of one of the previously favoured hill-tribes was to be tarred with the pro-colonial brush.

By the time the British returned to Burma former members of the BIA had become the backbone of the PVO or "People's Volunteer Organisation" a sort of "old comrades" association or "returned soldiers" league which in turn was Aung San's private army and part of the AFPFL. Had Aung San not been assassinated the first phase of Burma's life as an independent country would have been guided by an army general backed by a political coalition one of whose strongest elements was a "civilian" army. If one would nevertheless have hesitated to call the resultant regime a military one he should also perhaps review his attitude towards the seizure of power of General Ne Win, the former Rangoon University student and second in command to Aung San of the BIA. Ne Win may be seen as completing interrupted and unfinished business rather than intervening and innovating. In this context it is interesting to note that all but three members of the Revolutionary Council in 1962 were former fighters with the BIA.

The fact that the new regime chose to call its cabinet the Revolutionary Council is surely significant as is also the prominent reference to the founding father, Aung San, in the "Burmese Way to Socialism". These are indications that Ne Win saw himself as the inheritor of the mantle of Aung San: the man who would consummate the Revolution by uniting the nation and building a just, socialist state. In this sense he would not be breaking with tradition but rather getting the revolution back on the path marked out for it by Aung San.

Ne Win's methods were initially the same as those of his dead master. Aung San, when founding the AFPFL in 1945 invited "all patriots and patriotic political parties" to join it; in the same way Ne Win tried to get the three main existing legal parties to join the military to form one comprehensive political party. When this effort failed Ne Win eventually banned all parties and tried to build up his own, sole cadre party, the BSPP or "Lanzin". Unfortunately, Ne Win lacked the charisma of Aung San and his regime became more and more introverted and exclusive. The link-up with the peasants and workers never materialised and the Lanzin turned out to be a school for the political indoctrination of military officers; while of the just and socialist society nothing remained except "shared poverty".

In Indonesia the story is not quite the same but the pattern is similar. The modern Indonesian army was born during the Japanese occupation. Before 1942 the Army had been small, professional, with its lowest ranks recruited disproportionately from the "Outer Islands" and its commissioned and non-commissioned officers almost exclusively of Dutch or Eurasian origin. By 1945 several hundred thousand men— mostly Javanese—had been given military or para-military training and many Indonesians had received their first experience of commanding platoons, companies and even in a very few cases battalions. More importantly they had been indoctrinated with the spirit of nationalism and hostility to all things Western.

During the battle against the returning Dutch the Army was the spearhead of the Indonesian Revolution. It was a highly politicised and politically motivated force which worked hand in glove with many of the leading civilian politicians. Ruslan Abdulgani, then Secretary-General of the Ministry of Information, wrote in 1952 that "the Parliament, the party system and our army were clearly according to the history of their birth, three twin (sic) children, their father the Preparatory Commission for the Independence of Indonesia and their mother the Indonesian people".

From 1949 to 1957 men like Hatta tried to elevate parliament and the party system while relegating the army to a subordinate role. This period of what has been called "constitutional democracy" ended with the declaration of a state of war and siege in March 1957. From this moment the Army, the third child of the Revolution, was restored to the fold: its role was further legitimised when Indonesia returned to the 1945 Constitution which allowed for the representation of "functional groups" like the armed forces in the legislature.

General Nasution, then the Army Chief of Staff, said of the return to the 1945 Constitution: "Under the old liberal system military members were only State apparatus, who cannot take part in the State political leadership. In the past we saw a clear separation between politicians and military and between political and technical. A minister held political leadership because he assumed responsibility to Parliament while a Chief of Staff or Secretary-General or a government civil servant were only technical assistants giving advices and implementing political decisions. Now we have abolished this system of power separation à la Western Democracy's Trias Politica, because the most important thing is not the separation of power but the mobilization of all forces. . . ."[1] "The Armed Forces' functional group co-operates side by side with political groups and functional groups . . . to achieve our revolution's goals."[2]

"We have deviated from the revolution but now we rediscover it. . . ."[3]

General Nasution delivered this speech when Sukarno was still at the height of his political power but he was not merely paying lip-service to the President. Nasution, like many of his generation, looked back with nostalgia to the days of the Preparatory Commission in 1945 when it was envisaged that there should only be one party, one parliament and one army. The "rediscovery of the revolution" to Nasution, as to Sukarno, meant the rediscovery of unity, "the mobilisation of *all* forces".

Nasution is now (1971) chairman of the People's Consultative Assembly while his former subordinate General Suharto is the President of Indonesia. The Army has intervened, has taken over from the civilians but only because its hand was forced by the actions of Colonel Untung, with or without the assistance and complicity of the PKI. Yet though there have been fundamental changes in economic and foreign policy one cannot say that there has been any great discontinuity in domestic politics. There has been no suggestion of a change to a more liberal constitution and there is still the same rejection of the 1949-1957 experiment with parliamentary democracy and "free-fight liberalism". The PKI has been very badly mauled and declared illegal, yet Suharto, like his predecessor, is sensitive to the dangers of leaving a vacuum on the Left and if NASAKOM is dead NASASOS appears to have taken its place in the New Order. Pantja Sila, which like the Constitution is also a product of 1945, is still the foundation of the Republic. To those who think of armies in Western terms Indonesia is just another example of a developing country taken over by the military. To men who think like Nasution the picture is different: for them the "People's Army" is playing its proper part along with other functional groups in the development of the country. In the words of a pamphlet issued by the Army Information Services: "Participation of the Armed Forces in the Republic of Indonesia is no militarism."

It would, however, be misleading to suggest that there is no difference between Suharto's approach and that put forward in Nasution's speeches in the Sukarno era. In his capacity as President, Suharto has made it quite clear that charismatic leadership and the "cult of personality" is a thing of the past. Sukarno-worship and the propagation of Sukarno's ideology has been outlawed but many of the political institutions associated with the heyday of Sukarno remain. The main difference is that there is no longer to be a delicate balance between the Army, the Communists, the Nationalists and the Moslems; the Army undoubtedly intends to be the main force in government for many years to come. It will, however, seek to legitimise its position in three main ways: it will participate in the 1971 elections as the main force behind Golkar; it will try to ensure that General Suharto is subsequently elected by the People's Consultative Congress (MPR) as President; and above all it will claim legitimacy by directing public attention to the economic and social progress which has been made under its rule.

The Army as Part of the Bureaucracy

F. W. Rigg describes Thailand as a "bureaucratic polity" by which he means a polity in which there is no significant external force such as a Parliament or a political party, which can bring effective pressure to bear on the bureaucracy. In the absence of such a force the bureaucracy itself is the arena in which the political game is played.

Prominent among the branches of the bureaucracy is the Ministry of Defence headed currently by Field Marshal Thanom Kittikachorn who is also Prime Minister. Ever since the days of Sarit there has been a Supreme Command which has embraced three branches of the armed services; so far the Supreme Commander has also been the Minister of Defence.

The fact that the two Supreme Commanders to date, Sarit and Thanom, have also been Prime Ministers might lead one to suppose that the military had well and truly taken over the role of the civilian politicians. The truth, however, is less simple.

In the period from 1932 to 1958 seventy-seven per cent of all cabinet ministers were officials but of these one hundred were civil servants while eighty-four were military officers.[4] Further analysis has shown that although only Army officers can command the allegiance of the Army and although Army officers are an essential ingredient for a successful *coup*, nevertheless civilians have always played a prominent and indispensable part in Thai governments.

In the current cabinet, for instance, seven out of the thirteen members are civilians. It is true that some of the Secretary-Generals of Departments are military men, yet this does not mean that the military are free to choose the best positions in the civil bureaucracy: on the contrary, there seems in the words of one observer to be "a tacit understanding that civil posts will not be used for military patronage on any sizeable scale".[5] Military officers are an important part of the

Thai *élite* but there is just as much competition to enter the ranks of the civil bureaucracy as there is to get a place in the Royal Military Academy.

No account of the role of the military in Thai politics would be complete without mention of the Police. The Police Department is a division of the Ministry of the Interior and is, therefore, separate from the Army, yet it has important para-military functions, the chief of which is the guarding of Thailand's frontiers—a task entrusted to the Border Patrol Police. The fact that the Police General has under his command forces which are just as well equipped as much of the Royal Thai Army, means that he is able to play a key role in politics from time to time. Notable Police Generals include Field Marshal Sarit (while he was also Prime Minister), Phao Sriyanon and the present incumbent Prasert Ruchirawong, all of whom concurrently held seats in the Cabinet in one of their other roles as for instance Prime Minister or Minister or Deputy Minister of the Interior.

The apogee of the Police Department's political influence—and its nadir in the esteem of the public—was reached under Phao, whose use of the position to obtain a "cut" out of almost every nefarious racket that was being run in the country was probably only equalled by General Le Van Vien in Saigon in the early 1950s. After the struggle between Sarit and Phao had been settled in Sarit's favour subsequent Prime Ministers took good care to keep the police force under Army control to prevent its being used as a political power base. Since Sarit came to power the Minister of the Interior, the Police Chief's political superior, has been an Army officer. In 1970 the Minister of the Interior was General Prapass Charusathien, who was also First Deputy Premier.

The ordinary Thai's pragmatic attitude to the role of the military in politics has been well summed up by members of a Thai publishing house:

> Some say that if professional military people in Thailand would leave politics to the civilians then he would have true democracy. However, it is fallacious to equate military people with dictatorship. There have been both civilian and military dictators in the world. Some of the worst dictators in the world have been civilians. Some of the best administrators have been military men. Even in Thailand we have seen that civilian governments have not always been able to administer the country well enough to maintain true democracy and develop the country. What is needed is co-operation between all elements of our nation, including military and civilians, without trying to label one group as dictatorship prone.[6]

One cannot fail to recognise the similarity between these last words, and those of General Nasution, quoted earlier: "the most important thing is not the separation of powers but the mobilisation of all forces. . . ."

The Military in Laos

Internal Fragmentation and External Pressures

One cannot apply to Laos the same categories of thought that are suitable to Thailand and Cambodia. Nothing is simple in Laos; everything is complex. There is not one Army but many armies; there is not one ethnic group but many; there is not one seat of government but several, of which Vientiane is "first among equals".

Laos must be seen as an area circumscribed by an artificial manmade boundary in which live various ethnic groups whose actual habitats do not often conform to the boundaries. Of these groups the largest are the Lao who form about fifty per cent of the population of Laos. Yet there are more Lao in Thailand than in Laos and the Lao therefore tend to feel themselves attracted westwards. The Lao are plainsmen and just as they overflow to the West so the hill-tribes of Laos overflow to the north, south and east. The hill-tribes on the other hand do not form a solid bloc but are separated from each other by terrain, language and custom and have affinities with Burma, China, Vietnam and Thailand.

Within the ethnic groups and also connecting them to the macro-political world are the leading families, which owe their position either to ascription or to military or commercial achievement. Politics in Laos then is largely a matter of shifts in the balance of power between these groups and families.

Governmental institutions repeat this pattern. The Army is no exception. Laos is divided into five military regions and in each of these it appears that an agreement has been reached between the military commanders and the leading civilian families as to their respective spheres of influence and the "percentages" each will receive for services rendered. There are, of course, changes in the power structure and sometimes it is difficult to say who is the patron: the soldier or the civilian. In some cases the senior Army officers are related by blood or marriage to the leading local family and the distinction between military and civilian becomes blurred. In the South, for example, General Phasouk Somly, who married into the Champassak family, is now apparently able to dispense some of the political patronage which used to be the sole preserve of Prince Boun Oum.

The Royal Lao Army, then, is no monolith, and the tendency towards regional autonomy is reinforced by the nature of the terrain, the absence of railways, the scarcity of all-weather roads, and the poverty of the telecommunications network.

However, no army and no unit of an army can exist without supplies or the means to buy them and loyalties can wear thin where these necessities are absent. The United States government, as by far the major source of supplies and pay is in a strong position to ensure some degree of cohesion and loyalty to the centre in the Royal Laotian Army. Kong Le was helpless when the Russians ceased sending him supplies while many a military commander was won to the side of Phoumi by his promise to "pay the salaries of officials and soldiers who joined him".[7]

Military Coups in Laos

Many theories about the intervention of the military in "developing" countries are of the "Robinson Crusoe" type popular in elementary economics: they postulate a closed polity in which the army and the civilians operate in a tight vacuum, sealed off from the outside world. Explanations based on these restricted foundations are only partially valid and go very little of the way to accounting for military intervention in a country like Laos, where external factors are so important.

The *coup* of Kong Le, for example, might be depicted as the action of a middle ranking officer determined to step in to remedy the administrative deficiencies of the corrupt and incompetent civilians. Such a line of thought was undoubtedly an element in Kong Le's motivation but his was no textbook authoritarian antidemocratic *coup*: on the contrary his main aims were to effect a change of personnel, a change of spirit and above all a change in foreign policy. He had no wish to abolish the institutions of representative democracy: indeed he was most careful to observe all the correct procedures in this respect.[8] Kong Le's rage was directed against the intervention by the Viet Minh and the Americans which had brought corruption to the government in Vientiane and bloodshed to the countryside.

The counter-*coup* of Prince Boun Oum and Phoumi Nasavan in December 1960 does not fit into a neat category either: Kong Le was not acceptable to the United States government, which then proceeded to plot his and Souvanna Phouma's overthrow. Phoumi's rise to power with Boun Oum was made possible only by direct American financial and material subvention. In all this Phoumi was also greatly assisted by his relative Field Marshal Sarit of Thailand who had also recently staged a successful *coup*: Sarit allowed supplies to be taken by the CIA backed "Air America" to Phoumi's base at Savannakhet.[9]

The aim of both Phoumi and Kong Le was to take Vientiane and effect a change of government. The important point is that both were operating within a given constitutional framework which included the monarchy, Parliament and the bureaucracy as essential features. In each case the motive power came from outside: Kong Le reacted against external pressure while Phoumi allowed himself to be propelled and sustained by it.

The Professional Army and Civic Action *

Cambodia and the Philippines:

a) CAMBODIA

Until the late 1950s in the case of Cambodia and the late 1960s in the case of the Philippines the armed forces of the Philippines and Cambodia were of the conventional Western kind playing a conventional non-political role.

In Cambodia it was the Khmer tradition that the King himself should lead the Army into battle on important occasions and Sihanouk in the 1950s frequently played this role. Sihanouk often called the Army the most important "instrument for independence" but the enemies of Cambodia's independence at this time were the Viet Minh and the Thai-backed Khmer Issarak and not the French: a fact which should be borne in mind when one thinks of the developments of the post-Sihanouk era.

After the 1954 Geneva Conference, Prince Monireth, who founded the Royal Khmer Armed Forces (FARK) in 1945 returned to his post as Inspector General of the Armed Forces and made it clear that he wished the latter to develop on "purely traditional lines". His nephew Prince Sirik Matak who was Minister of Defence and Chief of Staff at the time agreed with his uncle and added that guerilla warfare "did not give senior officers the chance to operate above battalion level. . . . "

In less than four years' time the role of the armed forces was radically revised. The exact reasons are not entirely clear but it seems that the examples of Burma and China were influential. The Cambodians had been favourably impressed by the achievements of the first military regime in Burma (1958-1960) and in 1962, the year of Ne Win's *coup*, the head of a Cambodian goodwill mission to Burma suggested that officers would "benefit more by going to Burma than to the USA or France, because the scale of works and the means employed are more readily applicable to Cambodia".

The year 1955 also marked the beginning of a reorganisation of the Chinese Army. China started building up a hierarchical officer corps and reintroduced such undemocratic practices as saluting. At the same time the soldiers were kept under constant supervision by civilian political cadres and "all officers from generals downwards had to serve for one month as simple privates in order to correct rightist tendencies". All units of the Army were also expected to spend part of the year helping the peasants to plant crops and gather in the harvest.

These examples of the successful involvement of the Army in the

---

* A great deal of this section is based on *L'armée au Cambodge et dans les pays en voie de développement du Sud-Est asiatique* by Colonel Maurice Laurent,[10] and *Notes on the Role of the Military in Socio-Economic Development* by de Borja, Gatmaitan and de Castro.[11]

work of national development were among the more important factors which made the Cambodians decide to formulate a new role for their Army. Perhaps the most important factor was the renewal of activities in 1958 by the Vietnamese who invaded Stung Treng province and by the Khmer Serei who made an attack on Siem Reap, the capital of the province of that name, in whose vicinity the ruins of Angkor Wat are to be found. It became evident that the traditional methods advocated by Prince Monireth were not wholly relevant to the type of warfare conducted by the Viet Minh and Khmer Serei.

In 1958 Lon Nol, then Chief of the General Staff of the armed forces, became Sihanouk's right-hand man in the task of reshaping the role of the Army. Initially the Army was given the important task of creating new provinces in those areas where the writ of the central government ran most feebly, the border areas where tribal minorities owed little allegiance to Phnom Penh and allowed the men of the Viet Minh and its successors to roam unmolested. In 1959 Andaung Pich in the far East of Cambodia was divided into two new provinces: Ratanak Kiri in the North, bordering Laos and Vietnam, and Mondol Kiri in the South, bordering South Vietnam. Another province, Koh Kong, was also created on the Gulf of Thailand between the provinces of Kampot and Pursat. In all these new provinces the Army opened up roads, set up communication networks, interdicted the supply routes of the guerilla bands and above all made a serious attempt to bring sound administration and economic advancement to these hitherto neglected areas. The whole operation was directed by Lon Nol who, with his military experience combined with his administrative experience as a previous Governor of Battambang, was well suited to the task.

In 1961 the troublesome province of Stung Treng was given a military Governor and in 1963 the Army took over the new province of Preah Vihar on the borders of Thailand.* Thus by 1963 the Army controlled about a third of the total land area of Cambodia, containing about one-thirtieth of the population. This was not the limit of the Army's participation in civilian affairs. The Army trained the first generation of leaders of the Royal Khmer Socialist Youth (JSRK) and also monopolised the direction of the *mouvement sportif* which was begun in 1960 and was designed to improve the performance in international contests of Cambodia's athletes. General Lon Nol became Commissioner-General of Sports.

On the economic front special Army units were formed and were trained to carry out certain pioneering tasks such as the opening up and "colonising" of virgin land, the employment for civilian purposes

---

* The border town of Preah Vihar contained a Buddhist temple of considerable religious significance to the Khmers. The temple was the centre of several border disputes between Thailand and Cambodia; in 1962 the dispute was settled by the International Court in favour of Cambodia.

of engineering equipment and the provision of small units capable of co-ordinating developmental work.

In enlisting the aid of the Army in the development of Cambodia Prince Sihanouk had no intention of allowing the military to rule the country. On the contrary the Prince was of the opinion that the only way of ensuring that the Army did not take over was to allow it to participate legitimately in national development. An Army which was kept apart from the main stream of national life could become estranged and alienated and might be liable to formulate national goals different from those proposed by the civil authorities.

In forming the Sangkum in 1955, Prince Sihanouk hoped to create a mass movement which would bring together all the major streams of Khmer life, including the military, the Buddhist clergy and the peasants. Up till 1955 the Army had been a professional one playing the traditional role of protecting the nation and especially its King. After 1955 the Army was brought into the political life of the nation: it attended Sangkum Congresses, moved resolutions and participated in mass demonstrations of national solidarity.

In 1971 it was still too early to assess the success or failure of Prince Sihanouk's attempt to solve the problem of Army-State relations.

The Cambodians were at war and the Army's numerical strength had risen from thirty thousand to over one hundred and fifty thousand. Sihanouk had been deposed, the Kingdom was now a Republic and an Army General, Lon Nol, was Prime Minister. Nevertheless there was still a civilian Head of State and there were many powerful civilians in prominent positions in the new government.

b) THE PHILIPPINES

Brought up in the American tradition of strict separation from the civil power, the Philippine armed forces have not yet threatened to break into the normal political process. The Philippine army, like that of Cambodia, is a professional one, but it operates in a tradition which differs from that of Cambodia in some important respects. In Cambodia the military and political élites are to some extent interchangeable and it is not thought strange that a man, particularly from one of the leading families, should play important roles in both the political and the military spheres. Prince Sirik Matak and his uncle, the late Prince Monireth, are cases in point. Cambodia thus represents what M. Janowitz has called the "aristocratic" model of political-military élite structure in which "the low specialisation of the military profession makes it possible for the political élite to supply the bulk of the necessary leadership for the military establishment".[12] The usefulness of this model lies in its ability to explain why one can still speak of Cambodia's being a civilian regime in spite of its having two Generals, Lon Nol and Sirik Matak, at the head of its government. As Janowitz says, "political control is still civilian control because there is an identity of interest between aristocratic and military groups".[13] The Army, in other words, is still the King's Army and exists to defend the existing regime and not to subvert it or to follow separate interests of its own.

In the Philippines, however, the relationship between the political and military *élites* is more like that of Janowitz's "democratic" model in which "the civilian and military elites are sharply differentiated" and their roles are performed according to certain strict ground-rules. David Wurfel has called the Philippines Army "one of the least politically oriented armies in South-east Asia",[14] and it is true that until Marcos became President the army's only major incursion into civilian affairs was in Magsaysay's time when it performed certain civilian functions, such as assisting with the land reform programme, as part of the campaign against the "Huks". During Marcos's first term, however, the armed forces were given a wider role. It was decided to make use of their skills and equipment in the implementation of the four-year (1967-1970) economic plan. The reasons for this decision were sound and practical. The nation badly needed a great expansion of the infrastructure of schools, roads and bridges and could afford to leave no resources untapped. The armed forces had idle resources. The nation was therefore logically obliged to use them. From the military point of view it was argued that conventional warfare was irrelevant in the fight against the ideologically-motivated "army of liberation". Such an army flourished in conditions of economic under-development and social injustice and the best way of defeating it was to win the economic and social battle. The armed forces therefore supported Marcos's plan.

Both Marcos and Sihanouk had strong political motives for seeking the co-operation of the military in the task of national development, but whereas Sihanouk was trying to forestall a possible take-over by the army, Marcos enlisted the aid of the armed forces because he calculated that their contribution to the construction of new roads, bridges and schools might prove decisive in the electoral battle. Events proved him right. The success of the infrastructure programme was undoubtedly responsible in great part for Marcos's unprecedented victory in the 1969 Presidential elections. It was also generally agreed that the programme would not have been the success it was without the help of the armed forces, for not only did they lend their skills and their costly American equipment but also their unique and vital communications network whose headquarters in Camp Aguinaldo served as the "Infrastructure Operations Centre".

What of the future role of the military in the politics of the Philippines? Is there a danger that the tiger may devour its rider? Filipino observers say this is unlikely. They give two main reasons. One is that promotion in the armed forces has always depended on political patronage—the President himself, after all, appoints all officers of the rank of colonel and above; the other is that officers usually retire, or are retired, at a fairly early age—generally in their mid-forties. Most of them can then use their influence with the politicians to acquire suitably responsible positions in the public service or in business. The military thus have a vested interest in preserving the existing arrangements.

Vietnam: the Army of Liberation and the People's Army

The National Liberation Front of South Vietnam (NLF) is another of the "fronts" (Mat Tran) with which Vietnamese history abounds. The Vietnamese have a talent for secrecy and intrigue in politics and the technique of the "front" seems to suit their particular genius.

The NLF was officially born on December 20, 1960. It was the heir, in the South, to the Viet Minh, another front organisation, which had been founded in 1941 to fight for the independence of Vietnam. In the days of the first Indo-China war there was only one simple objective: to eject the French. This the Viet Minh achieved in 1954 when it was agreed in Geneva that the French would relinquish their former colony and protectorate and withdraw their troops. By 1954, however, another struggle was developing: a many-sided internecine struggle for control of the nationalist movement between the Communists and various non-Communist groups. In the new struggle the issues were no longer clear; it was not now a question of colonialist against nationalist, but Catholic against non-Catholic, of *Montagnard* against lowlander, of Vietnamese against Cham and Khmer, of North against South. The men in Hanoi expected the Diem regime to collapse. When, so far from collapsing, it actually appeared to be consolidating its grip on the countryside the Communists of the old Viet Minh had to devise a new strategy to achieve their long-term objective, which was to unify Vietnam under Communist rule and later to extend this rule to the whole of former Indo-China.

To meet changed conditions new techniques were devised. The NLF was established with its military arm, the Liberation Army. Its main objectives could no longer be described in terms of anti-colonialism, since Ngo Dinh Diem had an impeccable anti-colonial record. Efforts were, however, made to put the neo-colonialist Americans in the place of the French and to depict Diem as an American puppet. This particular line of propaganda met with little success in the earlier years and it became clear that the main issues from which advantages could be gained were economic and social ones. The decision therefore was made to put the main emphasis on matters such as land reform and the autonomy of the village. It is precisely this stress on the non-military that distinguishes the NLF's Liberation Army from the conventional army. The point is well made in a booklet entitled "The Glorious Experiences of the Liberation Army", from which the following extract is taken: "The army's political tasks are fundamental. There must be unity between cadres and men, between army and people. It is of prime importance that these three principles be fully understood. They ensure that military action is subordinated to political action, that the army is united and that the people are closely united with the army. They win over the members of the enemy, subvert enemy morale and organization, and ultimately annihilate enemy resistance."[15] The subordination of the military to the political is characteristic of this type of army. The "armed struggle", as D. Pike observes, is "only that part of the revolutionary ice-berg above water".[16] The armed struggle is only one of the army's activities. The NLF, for instance, divides its operations into three groups: *dich van* or "action among the enemy", that is to say actual combat; *dan van* or "action among the people", that is to say action in the "liberated areas"; and *binh van* or "action among the troops", which refers to the winning over of enemy troops and cadres, civil servants and politicians by means of propaganda and other kinds of pressure. Of all the activities of the NLF it is *binh van* which Pike considers to be the most deadly. The Liberation Army, then, is above all a political army; its objectives are not so much to acquire territory or to inflict casualties but rather to gain control over institutions and people and to re-order society. Such aims cannot be achieved by sheer terror; there must be support from the people and genuine grievances which the revolutionaries can exploit—and remedy. In South Vietnam the main grievances concerned the shortage of land, the inhumanity of landlords, and the carelessness, rapacity, inefficiency and occasional tyranny of the government. The NLF duly exploited these grievances and were so successful that the Diem government was forced to take strong repressive measures. The result was a "denunciation of Communism campaign" which, by its very lack of discrimination, made more enemies than it eliminated. This experience proved that too much force could be counter-productive; if the NLF was to be defeated it had to be defeated on its own ground and with its own weapons. Magsaysay, a former "underground" fighter against the Japanese, recognised this when he said: "It would be useless for me to continue as Secretary of National Defence with the specific duty of killing Huks as the administration continues to foster and tolerate conditions which offer fertile soil to Communism".[17] Magsaysay's method of dealing with surrendering Huks was to give them land rather than prison sentences.

The great intensification of the shooting war following the assassination of Diem compelled the NLF to concentrate more on the armed struggle and its army received wide recognition as an efficient fighting force. The army's structure is quite simple and follows fairly closely the pattern of the People's Army. The army's forces are of two kinds: "regular" and "irregular". The latter consist of village guerilla units—static, not very well-armed—and combat guerilla units whose members are younger, more mobile and better armed and trained. The "regulars" consist of "main force" units, which are more like conventional troops and may be employed anywhere where the need arises, and "regional" troops, who are at the disposal of the district and provisional NLF administration.[16] To guard against factionalism—which is the ARVN's main defect—the NLF has seen to it that the whole Army structure is permeated by trusted political cadres and is strictly controlled by them. There is "no such thing as NLF army autonomy" writes Pike, and explains later that " . . . within the military apparatus, the political officer or political commissar served as a further mechanism of Communist control over the officer corps'.[18] Pike refers here to a "further" mechanism; perhaps the most important mechanism is the careful and continuous indoctrination of the military officers themselves.

Once a country has been liberated, an Army of Liberation becomes a People's Army. The transition is not an easy one and partakes of many of the difficulties which beset any army as it moves from a wartime to a peacetime footing. The physical danger is largely absent, the sense of urgency not so great and rather different qualities are required of both officers and rank and file. In an army run on Communist principles the change is not so traumatic. Such an army has always been subject to strict political control and is accustomed to receiving orders from civilians. "Every Communist must understand this truth:" said Mao Tse-tung: "Political power grows out of the barrel of a gun. Our principle is that the Party commands the gun; the gun shall never be allowed to command the Party."[19] In North Vietnam there is no doubt that the Lao Dong "controls the gun". In South Vietnam the army and its generals have played and are still playing an outstanding political role: in the North the army, in spite of its great prestige, remains firmly in its appointed place. The People's Army began to achieve greater prominence when the Americans started to bomb North Vietnam in February 1965; and it became increasingly important as more and more pressure was brought to bear on its comrades in the south. North Vietnam was now on a war footing and the People's Army had the twofold task of preparing to defend the country against a possible invasion and of supplying the needs—in terms of men, materials and training—of the NLF's Liberation Army. These tasks made great demands of the peasant farmers of North Vietnam. There were fewer hands available on the farms but more food to be supplied to the troops; there were even fewer goods to buy in the stores. It is at times like these that the army's "closeness to the people" is tested. For the People's Army, whether in peace or war, never loses sight of the fact that it is a class army fighting a battle against a class enemy—the bourgeois and the landlord. The army is composed largely of members of the peasantry and working classes and it seeks at all times to enlist the willing co-operation of its fellow peasants and workers. This is its strength; this is the one characteristic which most distinguishes it and the Liberation Army from the Army of the Republic of Vietnam (ARVN). The difference in approach of the two opposing forces in South Vietnam is rather like the difference between the lives of policemen and soldiers: the policemen have to live with the results of their actions; the soldiers can be withdrawn to the safety and seclusion of their barracks. The men of the Pathet Lao and the Liberation Army live and work and fight with the people. The men of the ARVN have tended in the past to behave like a conventional Western army, functionally specific and aloof from the civilian population. In the words of D. J. Duncanson "the High Command was encouraged . . . to regard itself as an army of occupation in its own country. . . . The army owed little to the local people, since its pay, like everything else it had, came out of American aid, not out of taxation."[20] This is the sort of mistake which the People's Army and the Army of Liberation, for all their other shortcomings, very seldom make.

Military Governments in Southeast Asia

Many claims have been made on behalf of military rulers in the countries of the Third World. That the rulers themselves should seek to defend themselves is not surprising: what is surprising is that not a few Western political scientists have come out in favour of military regimes. In the 1950s the commitment to Western-style parliamentary democracy was so great that the very suggestion that Southeast Asian peoples might be better off under authoritarian military rule would have been regarded as indicative of a cynical and colonialist outlook. Attitudes changed at the end of the 1950s when one by one the countries of Asia and Africa acquired military rulers or undemocratic and authoritarian civilian ones. Though some deplored the decline of constitutional democracy, others attempted to reappraise the scene with less biased eyes. Various schools of thought emerged. There were those who argued that the army was the organisation best equipped to give a country stability —the one thing it most needed. Stability in this context was generally used in a somewhat negative sense, denoting the absence of public disturbances and the ability to resist a Communist *coup*. Others, who thought stability too static and colourless an objective, advanced the claim that the army, having produced stability, was the organisation best equipped to promote modernisation and innovation. Adherents of this school of thought might still have deplored the absence of truly representative institutions and regular elections but they would have argued that these things were luxuries which could be added at a later date when the country could afford them

A third school of thought condemned those who blindly supported Western-style "51% democracy" and thought it to be of universal application. They pointed out that political institutions must grow naturally out of the political culture of a country if they are to survive. This school was inclined to look for answers among such concepts as "guided democracy", basic democracies, *panchayati raj*, Buddhist Socialism, partyless politics, *musjawarah* and the like. Members of this school were still supporters of democracy but were anxious to find a variety of democracy which, while recognisable as such, would suit the particular genius of the nation concerned.

A fourth school of thought brought together the arguments of the other three schools to produce the—to some—unpalatable conclusion that authoritarian, undemocratic rule might not only be the most efficient, modernising form of government but also the one best suited to the political culture of most of the countries of Southeast Asia. Such a conclusion shocked the democrats, appealed to some of the anti-ethnocentrics and pleased those who were committed, for various practical and diplomatic purposes, to supporting military regimes.

Let us now examine some of the claims which have been made in favour of military rule and see what validity they possess.

That there is a strong authoritarian element in the political culture of Southeast Asian countries is undeniable. The resignation of the peasant in the face of the uncontrollable forces of Nature, the traditions of Hindu kingship, the long history of arbitrary and oppressive rule by warriors culminating in the, at best, benevolent despotism of the colonial powers; all these factors must have produced at least an expectation of authoritarian rule and a rather feeble ability to imagine any alternative. Against this must be set the genuine attempts which have been made over many years by educationalists, politicians, agricultural extension workers, clandestine organisations and many others to give the peasant a wider outlook and greater independence of spirit. The peasants' expectations may still be small but not small enough to be ignored.

More attractive at first sight is the argument that the Army is the one institution which can produce stability. In the short term this is obviously true. Having a near-monopoly of force the Army is clearly in a position to occupy all the strategic heights of the polity and to put all the disturbers of the peace out of action. Stability is thus quickly achieved; but unless a complete run-down of the economy is to follow the army soon finds itself engaged in the day-to-day business of governing the country. As soon as it does this it begins to lose the one quality which made its intervention so apparently appropriate in the first place: its cohesion and discipline. The army appeals to the theoretician mainly because of its sheer monolithicity, its straightforwardness, its efficiency: the very qualities which are lacking at the moment of crisis. What is apt to be overlooked is the fact that the army has these particular qualities precisely because its objectives are fairly precisely defined and comparatively narrow in scope. Once the army becomes involved in trying to make political decisions the targets become blurred and the objectives vague and ill-defined. Choices and compromises have to be made; *political* criteria and not straightforward criteria of efficiency have to be applied. Very soon the soldiers are seeking the advice of civilians and, what is more disastrous, looking for support among the very politicians whom they have disparaged and displaced. At this stage the army loses its unity and discipline and starts breaking up into the factions which were probably latent even before the *coup*. Disunity and indiscipline is almost certain to occur even in the best armies when criteria other than military ones are used for promotion to responsible and senior positions. A junior headquarters clerk may make a much more efficient bureaucrat than a senior regimental officer but the moment bureaucratic skills are preferred to soldierly qualities the morale of an army will quickly decay.

Stability in any regime cannot last indefinitely without a certain measure of support, not only from the population at large but from the main political and social groups in the country. Here the army runs into another major difficulty. By definition the army is an exclusive organisation; it is not the civil service, the political *élite*, the school and university teachers or the religious organisations. Therefore, unless it tries to reconcile all these groups—which by hypothesis is probably impossible—it must exclude and offend some or most of them. Sukarno tried to keep a balance between the Army, the Moslems, the "secular" Nationalists and the Communists: he failed. His successor, General Suharto, quickly excluded the Communists and alienated an important section of the Moslems soon afterwards.

The claim then that the Army can produce any lasting stability is almost certainly unsubstantiated by experience. The proposition that it can unite the nation is also of dubious validity since it is usually unable even to preserve its own internal unity for very long.

At the heart of all the problems which confront the military when it ventures into the business of government is that its repertoire is so limited. The Army, like the colonial power, is only really happy with the apolitical state. The Army thinks in terms of administration not government. It prefers giving orders to making compromises. It is basically anti-political; indeed this is probably the main reason for its initial intervention. All military rulers ban some or all political parties, suppress and censor news media, curtail discussion, dismiss or emasculate legislative bodies and replace to a greater or lesser extent civil bureaucratic structures. Such actions inevitably mean that a great many channels of interest articulation and aggregation are blocked. Unless the military manages to set something up in their place the political system will soon be in grave disequilibrium and some radical adjustments will have to be made. The adjustments will either be repressive or concessive: if repressive, the military will lose popular support; if concessive, the military will be compromised and its grip weakened.

The claim that the military can deal effectively with Communists is certainly well founded: the military after all is trained to destroy. What, however, is not proven is that the military can effectively deal with Communism as such. In fact, one would have thought that the whole history of the Vietnam war is proof that the military is not a reliable long-term bulwark against Communism. To remove the causes of Communist success requires much suppler skills than the military possesses.

Finally, there is the claim that the military can provide the conditions in which modernisation can take place. This again may be well-founded if we are thinking of the short term but its validity for the long term has yet to be proved. It is certainly true for instance that quite startling economic gains have been made in Indonesia during Suharto's rule but it may well prove that these gains have been made mainly in the export sector which is financed and partly controlled by foreigners and that they will not be of any immediate benefit to the man in the village. In any case economic progress cannot continue to be made indefinitely in a political vacuum; yet this or something like it is what General Suharto is hoping may be possible. All experience is against him. Economic and social development involves social mobilisation and social mobilisation demands political outlets which an "administrative state" cannot provide.

All in all, in the words of Hugh Tinker, "as an alternative to representative democracy, military modernism is a nullity".[21]

References

1. A. H. NASUTION, *Towards a People's Army*, c.v. Delegasi, Djakarta, 1964, p. 21.
2. *Ibid.*, p. 22.
3. *Ibid.*, p. 17.
4. F. W. RIGGS, *Thailand*, East-West Center Press, Hawaii, p. 314.
5. W. J. SIFFIN, *The Thai Bureaucracy*, East-West Center Press, Hawaii, 1966, p. 157.
6. THE STAFF OF PRAMUANSARN AND GORDON H. ALLISON, *All About Thailand*, Pramuansarn Publishing House, Bangkok, 1967, p. 80.
7. H. TOYE, *Laos*, Oxford University Press, London, 1968, p. 147.
8. A. J. DOMMEN, *Conflict in Laos*, Pall Mall, London, Rev. Ed., 1970, p. 310.
9. H. TOYE, op. cit., p. 153.
10. MAURICE LAURENT, *L'armée au Cambodge et dans les pays en voie de développement du Sud-Est asiatique*, Presses Universitaires de France, 1968.
11. DE BORJA, GATMAITAN and DE CASTRO, "Notes on the role of the Military in Socio-Economic Development", *Philippine J. Public. Administration*, July 1968, **XII**, No. 3.
12. M. JANOWITZ, *The Military in the Political Development of New Nations*, University of Chicago Press, Chicago, Ill., 1964, p. 111.
13. *Ibid.*
14. G. M. KAHIN (Ed.), *Government and Politics of Southeast Asia*, Cornell University Press, Ithaca, N.Y., Rev. Ed., 1964, p. 716.
15. D. PIKE, *Viet Cong*, Massachusetts Institute of Technology, Cambridge, Mass., 1966, p. 232.
16. *Ibid.*, p. 99.

17. G. M. KAHIN, op. cit., p. 702.
18. D. PIKE, op. cit., p. 233.
19. S. SCHRAM, *The Political Thought of Mao Tse-tung*, Frederick A. Praeger, New York, 1963, p. 209.
20. D. J. DUNCANSON, *Government and Revolution in Vietnam*, Oxford University Press, London, 1968, p. 292.
21. H. TINKER, *Ballot Box and Bayonet*, Oxford University Press, London, 1964, p. 119.

Further Reading

Geography

Buchanan, K., *The Southeast Asian World*, Bell, London, 1967; Fisher, C. A., *South-East Asia*, Methuen, London, 1966; Hall, D. G. E., *Atlas of Southeast Asia*, Macmillan, London, 1964; McGee, T. C., *The Southeast Asian City*, Bell, London, 1967; Spencer, J. E., *Asia, East by South*, John Wiley, New York, Revised Edition, 1969.

Social and Cultural

Introductory and General

Burling, R., *Hill Farms and Paddy Fields*, Prentice-Hall, Englewood Cliffs, N.J., 1965; DuBois, C., *Social Forces in Southeast Asia*, Harvard University Press, Boston, 1959; Heine-Geldern, R., *Conceptions of State and Kingship in Southeast Asia*, Cornell University Press, Ithaca, N.Y., 1956; Karnow, S., *Southeast Asia*, Time/Life, New York, 1967; Le Bar, Hickey and Musgrave, *Ethnic Groups of Mainland Southeast Asia*, Human Relations Area Files, New York, 1964; Lewis, N., *A Dragon Apparent*, Jonathan Cape, London, 1951; Rowley, C. D., *The Lotus and the Dynamo*, Angus & Robertson, Sydney, 1960; Tilman, R. O. (Ed.), *Man, State and Society in Southeast Asia*, Frederick A. Praeger, New York, 1969; Tinker, H., *Ballot Box and Bayonet*, Oxford University Press, London, 1964; Tinker, H., *Reorientations*, Pall Mall, London, 1965.

Burma

Donnison, F. S. V., *Burma*, Benn, London, 1970; Nash, N., *The Golden Road to Modernity*, John Wiley, New York, 1965; Tinker, H., *The Union of Burma*, Oxford University Press, London, 4th Edition, 1967.

Cambodia

Steinberg, D. J., *Cambodia*, Human Relation Area Files, New York, 1959; Williams, M., *The Land in Between*, William Morrow, New York, 1970.

Indonesia

Baum, V., *A Tale from Bali*, Geoffrey Bles, London, 1937; Covarrubias, M., *Island of Bali*, Knopf, New York, 1937; Geertz, C., *The Religion of Java*, Free Press of Glencoe, N.Y., 1960; Jay, R. R., *Javanese Villagers*, Massachusetts Institute of Technology, Cambridge, Mass., 1969; van der Kroef, J. M., *Indonesia in the Modern World* (2 Vols), Masa Baru, Bandung, 1954 and 1956; Lubis, M., *Twilight in Djakarta*, Hutchinson, London, 1963; Sjahrir, S., *Our Struggle*, Cornell University Press, Ithaca, N.Y., 1968; Sjahrir, S., *Out of Exile*, Greenwood Press, N.Y., 1969; Wagner, F. A., *Indonesia*, Methuen, London, 1962; Wertheim, W. F., *Indonesian Society in Transition*, Van Hoeve, The Hague, 1960.

Laos

Le Bar, F. and Suddard, A. *Laos*, Human Relation Area Files, New York, 1960.

Malaysia

Gullick, J. M., *Indigenous Political Systems of Western Malaya*, University of London, London, 1958; Macdonald, M., *Borneo People*, Donald Moore Press, Singapore, 1968; Ooi Jin-Bee and Chiang Hai Ding (Eds), *Modern Singapore*, University of Singapore, Singapore, 1969; Ryan, N.J., *The Cultural Background of the Peoples of Malaya*, Longmans of Malaya, Kuala Lumpur, 1962; Wang Gung-Wu (Ed.), *Malaysia*, Pall Mall, London, 1964; Winstedt, R., *The Malays: A Cultural History*, Routledge & Kegan Paul, London, 1947.

Philippines

Carroll, J. J., *The Traditional Philippine Social Structure*, Paper delivered on November 27, 1969 as part of a series sponsored by the Private Development Corporation of the Philippines; Guthrie, G. M. (Ed.), *Six Perspectives on the Philippines*, Bookmark, Manila, 1968; Landa Jocano, F., *Growing up in a Filipino Barrio*, Holt, Rinehart and Winston, New York, 1969; Rizal, Jose, *Noli Me Tangere* (Tr. L. M. Guerrero) and *El Filibusterismo*, Longmans Green, Harlow, 1965.

Thailand

Janlekka, K., *Saraphi*, Geographical Publications, Bude, Cornwall, 1968; *All About Thailand*, Pramuansarn Publishing House, Bangkok, 1967;

Blanchard, W., *Thailand*, Human Relation Area Files, New York, Reprinted 1966; de Young, J., *Village Life in Modern Thailand*, University of California, Berkeley, Calif., 1955.

Vietnam

Chaliand, G., *The Peasants of North Vietnam*, Penguin Books, Harmondsworth, 1969; Hickey, G. C., *Village in Vietnam*, Yale University Press, New Haven, Conn., Reprinted 1967; Hammer, E., *Vietnam: Yesterday and Today*, Holt Rinehart & Winston, New York, 1966.

History

General

Allen, R., *A Short Introduction to the History and Politics of Southeast Asia*, Oxford University Press, London, 1970; Bastin, J. and Benda, H., *A Short History of Southeast Asia*, Prentice-Hall, Englewood Cliffs, N.J., 1968; Coedes, G., *The Indianized States of Southeast Asia*, East-West Center, Hawaii, 1968; Coedes, G., *The Making of Southeast Asia*, Routledge & Kegan Paul, London, 1966; Hall, D. G. E., *The History of Southeast Asia*, Macmillan, London, 3rd Edition, 1963; Harrison, B., *Southeast Asia: A Short History*, Macmillian, London, 3rd Edition, 1966; Holland, W. L. (Ed.), *Asian Nationalism and the West*, Macmillan, London, 1953; Steinberg, D. J. (Ed.), *In Search of Southeast Asia*, Frederick A. Praeger, New York, 1971; Tarling, N., *A Concise History of Southeast Asia*, Frederick A. Praeger, New York, 1966.

Burma

Ba Maw, *Breakthrough in Burma*, Yale University Press, New Haven, Conn., 1968; Cady, J. F., *A History of Modern Burma*, Cornell University Press, Ithaca, N.Y., 1958; Donnison, F. S. V., *Public Administration in Burma*, Royal Institute of International Affairs, O.U.P., London, 1953; Furnivall, J. S., *Colonial Policy and Practice*, Cambridge University Press, London, 1948, Reprinted New York University, 1956; Hall, D. G. E., *Burma*, University of London, London, 1960; Harvey, G. E., *British Rule in Burma 1824-1942*, Faber & Faber, London, 1946; Maung Htin Aung, *A History of Burma*, Columbia University Press, New York, 1967; Thakin Nu, *Burma under the Japanese*, St. Martin's Press, London, 1954; Tinker, H., *South Asia: A Short History*, Pall Mall, London, 1966; Tinker, H., *The Union of Burma*, Oxford University Press, London, 4th Edition, 1967; Trager, F. N., Burma: *From Kingdom to Independence*, Frederick A. Praeger, New York, 1966.

Cambodia

Coedes, G., *Angkor: An Introduction*, Oxford University Press, London, 1963; Coedes, G., *The Indianized States of Southeast Asia*, East-West Center, Hawaii, 1968; Coedes, G., *The Making of Southeast Asia*, Routledge & Kegan Paul, London, 1966; Herz, M. F. A., *A Short History of Cambodia*, Frederick A. Praeger, New York, 1958; Lancaster, D., *The Emancipation of French Indochina*, Oxford University Press, London, 1961; Osborne, M. E., *The French Presence in Cochinchina and Cambodia*, Cornell University Press, Ithaca, N.Y., 1969.

Indonesia

Benda, H. J., *The Crescent and the Rising Sun*, Van Hoeve, The Hague, 1958; Bousquet, G. H., *A Frenchman's View of the Netherlands Indies*, Oxford University Press, London, 1940; Day, C., *The Dutch in Java*, Oxford University Press, London, 1966; Feith, H., *The Decline of Constitutional Democracy in Indonesia*, Cornell University Press, Ithaca, N.Y., 1962; Furnivall, J. S., *Netherlands India*, Cambridge University Press, London, Reprinted 1967; Kahin, G. M., *Nationalism and Revolution in Indonesia*, Cornell University Press, Ithaca, N.Y., 1952; Mossman, J., *Rebels in Paradise*, Jonathan Cape, London, 1961; Raffles, T. S., *History of Java*, London, 1817; Souter, G., *New Guinea: The Last Unknown*, Angus & Robertson, Sydney, 1965; Vlekke, B. H. M., *Nusantara*, Van Hoeve, The Hague, 1959; Zainuddin, A., *A Short History of Indonesia*, Cassell Australia, 1968.

Laos

Laos, British Information Services R5489/67, 1967; Sisouk na Champassak, *Storm over Laos*, Frederick A. Praeger, New York, 1961; Dommen, A. J., *Conflict in Laos*, Pall Mall, London, Revised Edition, 1970; Lancaster, D., *The Emancipation of French Indochina*, Oxford University Press, London, 1961; Toye, H., *Laos*, Oxford University Press, London, 1968.

Malaysia

Bastin, J. and Winks, R. W., *Malaysia*, Oxford University Press, Kuala Lumpur, 1966; Buckley, C. B., *An Anecdotal History of Old Times in Singapore 1819-1867*, University of Malaya, Kuala Lumpur, 1965; Collis, M., *Raffles*, Faber & Faber, London, 1966; Cowan, C. D., *Nineteenth Century Malaya*, University of London, London, 1961; Emerson, R., *Malaysia*, University of Malaysia, Kuala Lumpur, 1964; Kennedy, J., *A History of Malaya*, St. Martin's Press, New York, 1962; Means, G. P., *Malaysian Politics*, University of London, London, 1970; Mills, L. A.,

British Rule in Eastern Asia, Russell & Russell, New York, Reprinted 1970; Moore, D. and Moore, J., *The First 150 Years of Singapore,* Donald Moore Press, Singapore, 1969; Ongkili, J. P., *The Borneo Response to Malaysia,* Donald Moore Press, Singapore, 1967; Roff, W. R., *The Origins of Malay Nationalism,* Yale University Press, New Haven, Conn., 1967; Runciman, S., *The White Rajahs,* Cambridge University Press, London, 1960; Tregonning, K. G., *A History of Modern Sabah,* University of Malaya, Kuala Lumpur, 2nd Edition, 1965; Wheatley, P., *Impressions of the Malay Peninsula in Ancient Times,* Eastern Universities Press, Singapore, 1964; Winstedt, R. O., *Malaya and its History,* Hutchinson, London, 7th Edition, 1966; Winstedt, R. O., *History of Malaya,* Marican, Singapore, 1962.

The Philippines

Coates, A., *Rizal,* Oxford University Press, London, 1968; de la Costa, H., *Readings in Philippine History,* Bookmark, Manila, 1965; Phelan, J. L., *The Hispanization of the Philippines,* University of Wisconsin, Madison, 1959; Zaide, G. F., *Philippine Political and Cultural History,* Philippine Education Co., 1957.

Vietnam

Buttinger, J., *Vietnam: A Political History,* Frederick A. Praeger, New York, 1968; Hoang Van Chi, *From Colonialism to Communism,* Frederick A. Praeger, New York, 1964; Duncanson, D. J., *Government and Revolution in Vietnam,* Oxford University Press, London, 1968; Hammer, E., *The Struggle for Indochina,* Stanford University Press, Stanford, Calif., 1966; Honey, P. J., *Genesis of a Tragedy,* Benn, London, 1968; Lacouture, J., *Ho Chi Minh,* Allen Lane, London, 1968; Lancaster, D., *The Emancipation of French Indochina,* Oxford University Press, London, 1961; McAllister, J. T., *Viet Nam: The Origins of Revolution,* Allen Lane, London, 1969; Osborne, M. E., *The French Presence in Cochinchina and Cambodia (1859-1905),* Cornell University Press, Ithaca, N.Y., 1960; Shaplen, R., *The Lost Revolution,* Andre Deutsch, London, 1966.

Politics

General

Allen, R., *A Short Introduction to the History and Politics of Southeast Asia,* Oxford University Press, London, 1970; Barnett, A. D., *Communist Strategies in Asia,* Frederick A. Praeger, New York, 1963; Crozier, B., *South-East Asia in Turmoil,* Penguin Books, Harmondsworth, 1966; Emerson, R., *From Empire to Nation,* Harvard University

Press, Boston, 1960; Kahin, G. M. (Ed.), *Major Governments of Asia*, Cornell University Press, Ithaca, N.Y., 1963; Kahin, G. M. (Ed.), *Governments and Politics of Southeast Asia*, Cornell University Press, Ithaca, N.Y., 1964; Pye, L. W. (Ed.), *Cases in Comparative Politics: Asia*, Little, Brown, New York, 1970; Pye, L. W., *Southeast Asia's Political Systems*, Prentice-Hall, New York, 1967; Shaplen, R., *Time Out of Hand*, Andre Deutsch, London, 1969; Scalapino, R. (Ed.), *The Communist Revolution in Asia*, Prentice-Hall, New York, 1965; Tinker, H., *Ballot Box and Bayonet*, Oxford University Press, London, 1964; Wertheim, W. F., *East-West Parallels*, Van Hoeve, The Hague, 1964; Peaslee, A. J., *Constitutions of Nations*, Martinus Nijhoff, The Hague, 1966; Brimmell, J. H., *Communism in Southeast Asia*, Oxford University Press, London, 1959; Osborne, M. E., *Region of Revolt*, Pergamon Press, Oxford, 1970.

Burma

Buttwell, R., *U Nu of Burma*, Stanford University Press, Stanford, Calif., New Edition, 1969; Donnison, F. S. V., *Burma*, Benn, London, 1970; Johnstone, W. C., *Burma's Foreign Policy*, Harvard University Press, Boston, 1963; Maung Maung, *Burma and General Ne Win*, Asia Publishing House, London, 1969; Pye, L. W., *Politics, Personality and Nation-building*, Yale University Press, New Haven, Conn., 1962; Smith, D. E., *Religion and Politics in Burma*, Princeton University Press, Princeton, N.J., 1965; Tinker, H., *The Union of Burma*, Oxford University Press, London, 4th Edition, 1967.

Cambodia

Field, M., *The Prevailing Wind*, Methuen, London, 1965; Leifer, M., *Cambodia*, Frederick A. Praeger, New York, 1967; Steinberg, D. J., *Cambodia*, Human Relation Area Files, New York, 1959.

Indonesia

Adams, C., *Sukarno*, Bobbs-Merrill, Indianapolis, Ind., 1965; Bone, R. D., *The Dynamics of the West New Guinea Problem*, Cornell University Press, Ithaca, N.Y., 1962; Feith, H., *The Decline of Constitutional Democracy in Indonesia*, Cornell University Press, Ithaca, N.Y., 1962; Geertz, C., *The Religion of Java*, Free Press of Glencoe, N.Y., 1960; Grant, B., *Indonesia*, Penguin Books, Harmondsworth; Kahin, G. M., *Nationalism and Revolution in Indonesia*, Cornell University Press, Ithaca, N.Y., 1952; van der Kroef, J. M., *Indonesia in the Modern World, Parts 1 and 2*, Masa Baru, Bandung, 1954 and 1956; Lijphart, A., *The Trauma of Decolonization*, Yale University Press, New Haven, Conn., 1966; McVey, R. (Ed.), *Indonesia*, Cornell University Press,

Ithaca, N.Y., 1963; Mintz, J. S., *Mohammed, Marx and Marhaen*, Pall Mall, London, 1965; Roeder, O. G., *The Smiling General*, Gunung Agung, Djakarta, 1969; Scalapino, R. A. (Ed.), *The Communist Revolution in Asia*, Prentice-Hall, New York, 1965; Sjahrir, S., *Out of Exile*, Greenwood Press, New York, 1969; Tan, T. K. (Ed.), *Sukarno's Guided Indonesia*, Jacaranda, Queensland, 1967; Wertheim, W. F., *Indonesian Society in Transition*, Van Hoeve, The Hague, 1960; Woodman, D., *The Republic of Indonesia*, Cresset, London, 1955.

Laos

Fall, B. B., *Anatomy of a Crisis*, Doubleday, New York, 1969; Field, M., *The Prevailing Wind*, Methuen, London, 1965; Le Bar, F., and Suddard, A., *Laos*, Human Relation Area Files, New York, 1960; Toye, H., *Laos*, Oxford University Press, London, 1968.

Malaysia

Bellows, T. J., *The People's Action Party of Singapore*, Yale University Press, New Haven, Conn., 1970; "Cobbold Report", *Report of the Commission of Enquiry, North Borneo and Sarawak*, Government Press, Kuala Lumpur, 1962; Josey, Alex, *Lee Kuan Yew*, Donald Moore Press, Singapore, 1968; Means, G. P., *Malaysian Politics*, University of London, London, 1970; Mahathir bin Mohamad, *The Malay Dilemma*, Donald Moore Press, Singapore, 1970; Milne, R. S., *Government and Politics in Malaysia*, Houghton Miflin, New York, 1967; Ooi Jin-Bee and Chiang Hai Ding (Eds), *Modern Singapore*, University of Singapore, Singapore, 1969; Osborne, Milton E., *Singapore and Malaysia*, Cornell University Press, Ithaca, N.Y., 1964; Purcell, V., *The Chinese in Modern Malaya*, Eastern Universities Press, Singapore, 1960; Ratnam, K. J., and R. S. Milne, *The Malayan Parliamentary Election of 1964*, University of Malaya, Kuala Lumpur, 1967; Wang Gung Wu (Ed.), *Malaysia*; Frederick A. Praeger, New York, 1964.

Philippines

Abueva, J. V. and de Guzman, R. P., *Foundations and Dynamics of Filipino Government and Politics*, Bookmark, Manila, 1969; Corpuz, O. D., *The Bureaucracy in the Philippines*, Institute of Public Administration, University of the Philippines, Manila, 1957; Corpuz, O. D., *The Philippines*, Prentice-Hall, New York, 1965; Grossholtz, J., *The Philippines*, Little, Brown, New York, 1964; Hollnsteiner, M. R., *The Dynamics of Power in a Philippine Municipality*, University of the Philippines, Manila, 1956; Taruc, L., *Born of the People*, International Publishers, New York, 1953.

Thailand

All About Thailand, Pramuansarn Publishing House, Bangkok, 1967; Insor, D., Thailand, Allen & Unwin, London, 1963; Riggs, F. W., Thailand, East-West Center, Hawaii, 1966; Shaplen, R., Time out of Hand, Andre Deutsch, London, 1969; Blanchard, W., Thailand, Human Relation Area Files, New York, Reprinted 1966; Wilson, D. A., Politics in Thailand, Cornell University Press, Ithaca, N.Y., 1962; Wit, D., Thailand: Another Vietnam?, Charles Scribner, New York, 1968.

Vietnam

Barnett, A. D., Communist Strategies in Asia, Frederick A. Praeger, New York, 1963; Burchett, W. G., Vietnam North, International Publishers, New York, 1967; Duncanson, D. J., Government and Revolution in Vietnam, Oxford University Press, London, 1968; Fall, B. B., The Two Vietnams, Pall Mall, London, 1963; Fall, B. B., Vietnam Witness, Pall Mall, London, 1966; Honey, P. J., Communism in North Vietnam, Massachusetts Institute of Technology, Cambridge, Mass., 1963; Honey, P. J. (Ed.), Vietnam Today, Frederick A. Praeger, New York, 1962; McCarthy, M., Hanoi, Penguin Books, Harmondsworth, 1969; Pike, D., Viet Cong, Massachusetts Institute of Technology, Cambridge, Mass., 1966; Salisbury, Harrison, E., Behind the Lines—Hanoi, Secker & Warburg, London, 1967; Shaplen, R., Time Out of Hand, Andre Deutsch, London, 1969; Warner, D., The Last Confucian, Penguin Books, Harmondsworth, 1964.

The Military

de Borja et al., Notes on the Role of the Military in Socio-economic Development, Philippine Journal of Public Administration, July 1968, Vol. XII, No. 3; Finer, S. E., The Man on Horseback, Pall Mall, London, 1962; Vo Nguyen Giap, People's War People's Army, Frederick A. Praeger, New York, 1965; Huntington, S. P., Political Order in Changing Societies, Yale University Press, New Haven, Conn., 1968; Janowitz, M., The Military in the Political Development of New Nations, University of Chicago, Chicago, Ill., 1964; Johnson, J. J. (Ed.), The Role of the Military in Underdeveloped Countries, Princeton University Press, Princeton, N.J., 1962; Laurent, M., L'armée au Cambodge et dans les pays en voie de développement du Sud-Est Asiatique, Presses Universitaires de France, 1968; Nasution, A. H., Towards a People's Army, C. V. Delegasi, Djakarta, 1964; Pike, D., Viet Cong, Massachusetts Institute of Technology, Cambridge, Mass., 1966; Riggs, F. W., Thailand, East-West Center, Hawaii, 1966; Siffin, W. J., The Thai Bureaucracy, East-West Center, Hawaii, 1966; Silverstein, J. (Ed.), Southeast Asia in World War II, Yale University Press, New Haven, Conn., 1966.

Ideologies

Adams, C., *Sukarno*, Bobbs-Merrill, Indianapolis, Ind., 1965; Alisjah-bana, S. T., *Indonesia*, Oxford University Press, London, 1966; Apter, D. E., *Ideology and Discontent*, Free Press of Glencoe, New York, 1964; Dahm, B., *Sukarno and the Struggle for Indonesian Indepen-dence*, Cornell University Press, Ithaca, N.Y., 1969; Emerson, R., *From Empire to Nation*, Harvard University Press, Boston, 1960; Fall, B. B. (Ed.), *Ho Chi Minh on Revolution*, Frederick A. Praeger, New York, 1968; Feith, H. and Castles, L. (Eds), *Indonesian Political Thinking*, Cornell University Press, Ithaca, N.Y., 1970; Josey, Alex, *Lee Kuan Yew*, Donald Moore Press, Singapore, 1968; Johnstone, W. C., *Burma's Foreign Policy*, Harvard University Press, Boston, 1963; Mazzini, J., *The Duties of Man*, Everyman's Library, London, 1966; Pye, L. W., *Politics, Personality and Nation-building*, Yale University Press, New Haven, Conn., 1962; Rose, S., *Socialism in Southern Asia*, Oxford University Press, London, 1959; Schrieke, B., *Indonesian Sociological Studies*, Van Hoeve, The Hague, 1959; Sigmund, P. E., *The Ideologies of the Developing Nations*, Frederick A. Praeger, New York, Revised Edition, 1967; Norodom Sihanouk, *Our Buddhist Socialism*, Ministry of Information, Phnom Penh, 1969; Tinker, H., *Union of Burma*, Oxford University Press, London, 4th Edition, 1967; Trager, F., *Burma, From Kingdom to Independence*, Frederick A. Praeger, New York, 1966; Trager, F. (Ed.), *Marxism in Southeast Asia*, Stanford University Press, Stanford, Calif., 1960; Weatherbee, D. E., *Ideology in Indonesia*, Yale University Press, New Haven, Conn., 1966; Worsley, P., *The Third World*, Weidenfeld & Nicolson, London, 1964; Lee Kuan Yew, *Socialist Solution for Asia*, Ministry of Culture, Singapore, 1965.

Index

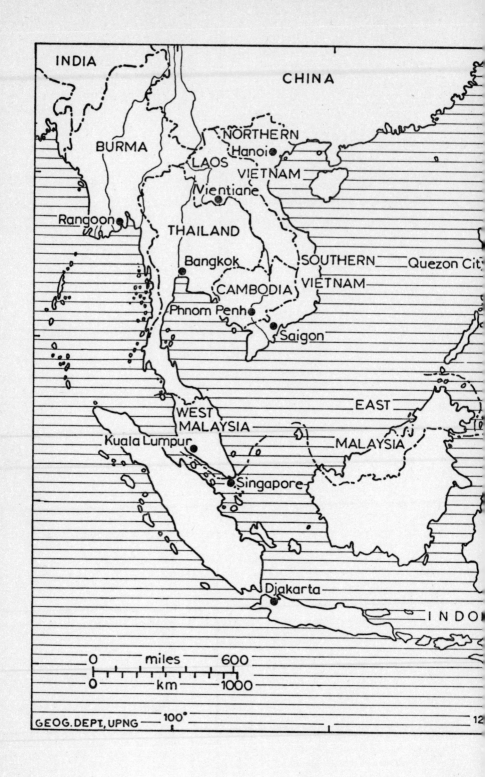